W9-BJR-846

People and Plans

BASIC BOOKS, INC., Publishers | New York | London

PEOPLE and PLANS

Essays on Urban Problems and Solutions

Herbert J. Gans

FOR LOUISE

PREFACE

Planning is a method of public decision-making which emphasizes explicit goal-choice and rational goals-means determination, so that decisions can be based on the goals people are seeking and on the most effective programs to achieve them. In theory, city planning should be an application of that method to cities, but in practice, it has been an art plied by a profession dedicated to a set of narrowly architectural goals and to land-use and design programs for realizing them. As a result, city planning has not paid much attention to people's goals, effective means, or to the urgent problems of the cities. This book is a critical examination both of city planning and of the problems of the city.

I entered the planning profession in 1950, a sociologist less interested in teaching his discipline to the next generation than in applying sociological thinking to social problems and policy. As a result, I became one of a handful of planners who were also sociologists and attempted to bring sociological concepts and data to bear on the policy issues of planning.

The essays collected here are some fruits of that attempt. The volume has all the disadvantages of a collection; a set of individual essays can never achieve the integration of a book. I have tried, however, to achieve as much integration as possible, both in the selection and ordering of essays and in their editing. Although the majority of the essays are reprinted as originally published (or mimeographed) with only slight revisions to improve clarity or to update them, many others have been partly rewritten or abridged to reduce repetition. (Whatever change an essay has undergone is indicated in a footnote at the start of each essay.)

Most of the essays were written for planners, although they deal with the social aspects of planning for which sociological analysis is most relevant. Others are sociological pieces that draw policy implications for planning, and yet others, particularly those in Parts IV and V of the book, were written for a wider audience to call attention to the urgent problems of the city and its people.

The introductions to the six parts of the book explain how the individual essays came to be written and for which audiences, but some general remarks on what the essays have in common are in order.

First, the collection reflects my research and professional activities. In 1949, while still a graduate student in sociology, I carried out two small studies in Park Forest, a new suburban town later made famous by William H. Whyte, Jr., in *The Organization Man.* As a result, I developed a long-term interest in suburbs, in new towns, and—because Park Forest was described as a planned community—in city planning. Subsequently, I spent three years working for a variety of planning agencies and became a professional city planner. (At that time, one could still do so without graduate training in the field.)

In 1953 I returned to academic life to obtain my Ph.D. in city planning at the University of Pennsylvania, and to undertake another new town study. Having come to Park Forest when it was already fourteen months old, I wanted to be in a new town from the moment of its birth, to discover how communities, institutions, and groups came into being *de novo;* and to study the characteristics and problems of contemporary suburban life.

While I was waiting for the establishment of a new town, Martin Meyerson asked me to participate in his research on methods of planning. I spent the next three years on a study which dealt specifically with public-recreation planning, but actually sought to formulate and apply a theory and method of rational planning which Meyerson had outlined.[1] About the time this study ended, Levitt and Sons announced the opening of a third Levittown, in New Jersey, but near Philadelphia, and in 1958 my old dream of studying the birth of a community was realized.[2] The ideas generated by these two studies appear in many of the essays, but my research on the planning process is reflected particularly in the essays of Parts I and II; that on Levittown, in Part III.

Just before I began my research in Levittown, I had the opportunity to carry out a short community study in the West End, a working-class neighborhood in Boston.[3] Since the area was about to be torn down under the federal slum-clearance program, I saw the inequities that urban renewal created for the poor at first hand and became a critic of urban renewal. This led naturally to an interest in urban poverty and later in the War on Poverty. These interests are expressed in the articles of Parts IV and V.

Second, the collection seeks to discuss the ideas about which I feel most urgent, and these number five. One, which struck me soon after I became a planner—and would have struck any sociologist in the same way—is that the outcomes of architectural and site planning, and of most policies which seek to change the "physical" environment, have little impact on the behavior patterns and values of people. Planning which aims to improve living conditions must address itself to the significant causal elements of these conditions, which are usually economic, social, and political.

A second idea, which I owe to Martin Meyerson, is that planning must be and can be *rational*—rationality being achieved when planners develop plans or programs which can be proved to implement the goals that are being sought.

A third idea, really an offshoot of the first, is that planning must also be *user-oriented*; the goals which planners work toward must relate to the behavior patterns and values of the people for whom they are planning, and not just their own values.

A fourth idea, a corollary of the third, and one about which I feel most strongly, is that planners and other professionals do not monopolize wisdom about goals and values, that diversity is valuable, and that people are entitled to live in any way they choose, unless that way can be proved to be destructive to them or to their fellow men. Goals and values arise out of the opportunities and restraints which are encountered in everyday life, and different age and class groups inevitably have different goals and values. The planner ought to respect these and give people the opportunity, resources, and freedom to choose what they want to do. I am for democracy in all spheres of life, cultural, economic, and social as well as political, for I do not believe anyone has the definitive conception of the purpose of life.

The fifth idea is that genuine democracy cannot be achieved in America without much greater economic, social, and political equality and that this requires initially a concerted attack on poverty and segregation. Poverty, I believe, is not only at the bottom of the segregation that marks so much of American life, but is also the prime cause of the urban crisis and the major problem to be solved if cities are going to provide the quality of life which planners are seeking.

Third, the essays reflect my position as a sociologist in a conservative profession, many members of which are dedicated to traditional solutions that sometimes date back to the nineteenth century. As a result, several of the essays, particularly in Parts I, II, and III, were written to question the conventional wisdom of the profession. Not all planners are traditionalists—many of the younger professionals have rejected the old goals and methods—and when I attack "the planners," I mean the older and architecturally-trained professionals. But they still dominate the field today.

Fourth, the collection reflects my occupational role, that of a researcher and academician who is interested in social action but does not participate in the day-to-day activities of social-action agencies. As a result, I have been able to look at agency programs from a broader perspective than is available to the professional in a public bureaucracy; but the perspective is also less responsive to bureaucracy's routine tasks, typical restraints, and constant crises. Consequently, my policy proposals sometimes appear to be impractical and naïve.

This impracticality is in part intentional. As a sociologist, I realize fully the limitations under which planners and other professional bureaucrats work, and more often than not, I understand why they act as they do when I disapprove of their actions. Sociological analysis does not justify these actions; it only explains why they occur and why they are so often hard to change. But as a planner, I have not hesitated to evaluate such actions, although as often as possible less from my own point of view than from that of the people being planned for. And as a policy-oriented sociologist, I realize that institutions, bureaucratic and otherwise, can best be changed when they are confronted with political pressure. Therefore, I have sought to maximize what political pressure I can generate on behalf of policies I consider desirable.

The academician has little political pressure to generate however; he does not have a power base or a constituency of voters who can influence their elected representatives. If he has political skills, he can organize his own constituency; if not, either he can become an adviser to groups whose demands he favors, or he can advise—and put pressure on—professionals and elected officials in the government. Even so, his principal leverage in all these roles comes from his academic position, his expertise, and, if he is a social scientist, his research findings. He must use these levers to their fullest advantage, offering advice or applying pressure in the only ways open to him, with data, analysis, criticism, and policy proposals. All are necessary, for without data and analysis, the researcher is only advocating his impressions; and without constructive proposals to back up his critiques, the academician eventually alienates his clients, be they government officials or community activists.

But perhaps most important, the academic outsider must have faith that change is possible, and this sometimes requires him to pretend to be more naïve than he really is. He must not hesitate to suggest policies that are currently impractical or politically unfeasible, even when he knows this is the case, for given his own political weakness, he can only hope that his readers will accept his ideas and then put their political strength behind them to make them acceptable in the future. This does not always happen; indeed, it happens rarely; but society changes constantly, and an idea that first seemed impractical may become practical. The writer must make sure that it survives until its time has come, when social and political arrangements are in the proper conjunction for it to be implemented. Since this happy turn of events cannot be predicted, the academician's best strategy is to fight for his idea in the hope that mere repetition will eventually make it respectable and finally politically acceptable. Moreover, if the academician has become known as an expert and a "responsible" critic, he can sometimes obtain attention for seemingly impractical ideas.

However impractical the ideas put forth by the academician and responsible critic, they are rarely either utopian or radical. I share the biases that go with my role and perspective. Although I am stimulated by utopian writings, they are usually peopled by superhuman characters; too many utopias depend on man's being either a noble savage or an equally noble intellectual.[4] I feel much the same about the ideas and methods of American radicals. I frequently share their impatience with the sparsity and slowness of change; I admire their fervor and their perseverance; and I welcome the moral and political pressure they put on various Establishments; but I cannot share their belief in the need to overturn "the system."

I do not believe that there is a cohesive system which can be overturned at one fell swoop. American society consists of a congeries of interest and ideological groups and aggregates, competing within a conservative set of political, economic, and social institutions in which power and resources generally accrue to those already affluent in both, unless a majority of the voters can be banded together to rule otherwise. The decisions made by these institutions usually reflect the kinds of people who are elected or appointed as decision-makers, their often narrow goals, their good if frequently misguided intentions, their limited political choices and, most important, their constituencies. There are some ties between institutions and decision-makers, and sometimes they are even interlocking, but usually they act separately although in a common direction—guided, I suppose, by the fact that the majority of Americans are not dissatisfied enough by that direction to demand or even support the changes that minority groupings want.

The institutions which make the crucial decisions in and for America are constantly undergoing slow change. Some of them change more rapidly and drastically than others. If the votes or other sources of power for change could be created, there is no reason why many or all of these institutions could not change more rapidly and drastically than they do now. Indeed, if this were to happen, the total transformation of the system that radicals look for could be achieved, albeit in a piecemeal fashion.

Such change is difficult to bring about in America and it is much easier to propose revolution. But if anything can create the very system which radicals believe to exist here, it is the threat of a revolution, violent or nonviolent. Moreover, most of the deprived and dissatisfied Americans are quite unrevolutionary; they want only to be admitted as equals into the affluent society. Although revolutions are made by small minorities, no revolution, even if initially successful, has ever been able to reshape a society toward the values of a minority over the long run. Even Soviet Russia was unable to convince its peasants and workers to accept Marxist-Leninist culture; actually its new managerial elite is fast adopting the life-style of middle-class managers everywhere, and other parts of the population are striving for the same bourgeois affluence and comfort that they see in "capitalist" and other socialist countries.[5]

I suppose I work on the basis of a faith, often uneasy, that fundamental change is possible without revolution, and that a more equalitarian, democratic, peaceful America can be created. I believe that such a society must be brought about by diverse methods and types of political pressure, including those favored by radicals, but I also believe that the most urgent priority of change is action. I want immediate change that improves the condition of the deprived immediately, except when such change eliminates the possibility of greater improvement in the foreseeable future. I am not ready to wait for the millennium when the system is overturned.

NOTES

1. Herbert J. Gans, "Recreation Planning for Leisure Behavior: A Goal-Oriented Approach," unpublished Ph.D. dissertation, Department of City and Regional Planning, University of Pennsylvania, 1957.
2. Herbert J. Gans, The Levittowners: Ways of Life and Politics in a New Suburban Community (New York: Pantheon, 1967).
3. Herbert J. Gans, The Urban Villagers: Group and Class in the Life of Italian-Americans (New York: Free Press of Glencoe, 1962).
4. See Herbert J. Gans, " 'Communitas': Its Impact on City Planning," Dissent, VIII (1961), 326–332.
5. For a more detailed critique of the radical perspective, see Herbert J. Gans, "The New Radicalism: Sect or Political Action Movement," and "A Rational Approach to Radicalism," in Studies on the Left, V (Summer 1965), 126–131, and VI (January–February 1966), 37–46.

New York   H. J. G.

ACKNOWLEDGMENTS

Assembling a collection of essays written over a period of years gives me a chance to express my gratitude to all the friends who have helped me, influenced me, and shaped my ideas. I cannot name them all, particularly the ones whose ideas I have appropriated without knowing it; but of the people to whom I am indebted, the most important is Martin Meyerson. I met him first when I was a graduate student at the University of Chicago, looking for a community in which I could study political participation, and he told me about Park Forest. Thereafter, he supervised my master's thesis, encouraged me to become a planner, helped me establish myself in that profession, and invited me to work with him on his studies of the planning process. Our association resulted from thinking alike about many things, but I sometimes wonder what topics I would have studied and written about in the last seventeen years had I not met him when I was looking for that community.

The other people to whom I am most indebted I shall name in alphabetical order. Some are sociologists, others planners; some influenced me through their work, others through their qualities as people, and some in both ways. Among them are Robert Dentler, Leonard Duhl, John Dyckman, Nathan Glazer, Everett Hughes, Iris MacLow, Karl Mannheim (posthumously, through his books), Robert Merton, David Riesman (to whom I am also grateful because he introduced me to Martin Meyerson and others in this list), John Seeley, Lloyd Warner, Melvin Webber, and William Wheaton. I have surely left out many others, but some of them appear in the footnotes to the various essays.

I must also acknowledge Messrs. Glazer, Webber, and Wheaton as the most insistent of the friends who suggested I assemble this collection and Nathan Glazer again for helping me with editorial advice.

Contents

Part I ENVIRONMENT AND BEHAVIOR

Introduction

When I first came into planning, its focus was almost entirely architectural or "physical"; planners devoted themselves to master plans which rearranged the physical environment of the community by separating "residential" land uses from "commercial" and "industrial" uses; by advocating a variety of quasi-educational public facilities, such as libraries, playgrounds, community centers, in larger numbers than already present; and by enveloping the array of ordered land uses and properly placed facilities with a network of transportation facilities. The result would be a well-planned community, efficient in moving people and goods and in attracting taxes to the city coffers, beautiful so that people would have pride in their cities, and emotionally satisfying so that they could enjoy the good life.

As a sociologist, I had been taught to study people in terms of the groups in which they lived, the social structures they erected, the behavior patterns to which they resorted on a recurring basis, and the values which supported or altered these patterns—and none of these concepts seemed to pay much attention to land uses, public facilities, or expressways. This could indicate the deficiencies of sociological concepts, of course; but when I studied people and communities, it turned out that their notion of the good life also had little to do with land uses, public facilities, and expressways: they were concerned about work, income, health, family, neighbors, friends, church, and, if they were homeowners, space, comfort, status, and property values.

Consequently, I found myself in constant disagreement with the planners' basic assumption that the physical environment, man-made or natural, played a major role in people's lives and that reshaping this environment was the most urgent priority for social action to achieve the good life. I was skeptical about the importance of such burning planning issues as whether strip-shopping (a series of stores on a street) was inferior to the shopping center with adequate off-street parking, what the optimal size of cities ought to be, and whether zoning ordinances should classify row houses with apartments or with single-family dwellings.

These questions were sometimes relevant to people, but they were usually less pressing than questions of job security, work satisfaction, adequate income, family life, the avoidance of social isolation, peace of mind, or upward and downward mobility. Moreover, even when the planners' concerns were relevant to people, they were too often framed in terms that met the planners' professional goals, but excluded the concerns of their clients. Planners tended to design town centers that gave people a fine view of historic landmarks or a plaza in which to rest, but they failed to provide for the kinds of store that serve the less affluent shopper; they drew blueprints in which houses were clustered around a public open space, but deprived homeowners of their own backyard; and they advocated single-family housing at low densities without doing anything for the many people who could afford only a tenement or for those who preferred high-density living even if they could afford something else.

In other words, the planners were enamored of two environmental or physical fallacies: first, that the physical environment was a major determinant of society and culture; and second, that only an environment based on professional planning principles could deliver the good life.

The first essay raises the basic issue of environment versus culture, suggesting that if the environment matters at all in ways of living, it is only as that environment is defined by the culture of the people who live in it. The second paper draws on my findings in Levittown to suggest that my basic thesis is accurate: a change of environment—in this case, the move from the city to suburb—does not lead to significant change in behavior. Both papers suggest that if the planner really wants to plan the good community for the good life, he must pay more attention to people's primary values and to the obstacles, in the community and in the larger society, that stand in the way of what they consider the good life. The same theme pervades Chapter 3, a review of Jane Jacobs' *Death and Life of Great American Cities*. In her often insightful book, Mrs. Jacobs had fallen prey to the same fallacies as the planners she was attacking. She, too, had a recipe for how people ought to live in their communities, and like the planners she felt that the good life could be achieved through environmental planning. She rejected only the vision of the community advocated by the professional planners and wanted to retain the eighteenth- and nineteenth-century land-use patterns, site plans, and house types of New York's Greenwich Village or Boston's North End.

Chapter 4 attempts to develop my point of view into a theory of the community—or more accurately, an antitheory—applying the ideas I had developed as a planner to sociological issues. In modern society, where man's relationship to the land is indirect, diffuse, and often irrelevant, his life is shaped by the economy, the culture, and the power structure of his society. Whether he lives in a city or a suburb is much less important for understanding his behavior than his socioeconomic level and his life-cycle position, his job, income, education, and age. The people who can choose where to live will select the community that fits their way of life, and the crucial question to ask about communities is who chooses which, what makes people choose as they do, and what happens to people who have, for reasons of income and race, no choice at all.

I do not mean here to be reductionist; obviously, ecological factors play a role in people's lives, if only because they affect the economy from which they earn their income. Nor is the man-made environment irrelevant; people in Levittown changed their lives somewhat, particularly if they moved from an apartment to a single-family house. But sociological theory and planning practice must address themselves to those aspects of the environment that really matter, and if the planner wants to affect people's lives through his effort, he must understand the processes by which the environment exerts an impact on their behavior and their values.

1

The Potential Environment and the Effective Environment

I

Many city planners argue that the physical environment directly affects human behavior. In response, social scientists tend to deny that the environment has significant causal influence, asserting that culture and social structure are the crucial variables. For example, planners believe that single-family houses are significantly better for healthy child-rearing than are apartments located over or behind retail stores. As a result, their plans usually call for the elimination of such apartments and for their replacement by single-family housing. The social scientist would reply that the quality of child-rearing is determined by the economic, social, and cultural conditions impinging on the family in which the children are being raised and by the way parents react to and transmit such conditions to their children. He would recommend economic and social changes in order to improve the quality of child-rearing.

These arguments establish polar positions, which interfere in the solution of a significant planning issue. The planner's role in the community and his ability to change the community revolve around the manipulation of house types and land uses; often he cannot suggest the kinds of change advocated by the social scientist. Instead, he must know to what extent house types and land uses can affect child-rearing and to what extent the physical environment can influence human behavior in general. This paper attempts to develop a frame of reference for asking this question and to formulate a compromise that combines aspects of both polar positions.

Previously unpublished. Prepared in 1958 for the Committee on Social and Physical Environment Variables as Determinants of Mental Health (a semiannual seminar, known informally as the Space Cadets, convened from 1955 to 1965 by the National Institute of Mental Health and headed by Leonard J. Duhl).

II

The basic conception to be argued here is: The physical environment is relevant to behavior insofar as this environment affects the social system and culture of the people involved or as it is taken up into their social system. Between the physical environment and empirically observable human behavior, there exist a social system and a set of cultural norms which define and evaluate portions of the physical environment relevant to the lives of people involved and structure the way people will use (and react to) this environment in their daily lives.

Physical environment is a poor concept, because it includes both non-manipulable variables, such as the natural environment, and the manipulable man-made environment. Needless to say, the natural environment may have a direct effect on human behavior, as in an earthquake. However, the behavior that follows such a crisis is determined not simply by the natural disaster but also by the social context in which this disaster occurs; even here, the social system mediates the natural environmental event. Other portions of the natural environment are less relevant to human behavior, such as occurrences within the depths of the earth or at the bottom of the ocean, and are thus not incorporated in the social system and culture.

Another type of nonmanipulable environment is the climate, or at least those portions of it which are beyond human influence. For example, man cannot seriously affect the amount of sunlight to be received by the earth. He can, however, make decisions about how much sunlight is desirable and can orient man-made artifacts to maximize or minimize exposure to the sun. The planner can thus incorporate features of the natural environment into his site plan on the basis of a combination of biological facts and culturally accepted beliefs about the value of sunlight.

Most of the planner's activity concerns the manipulation of the man-made environment, and he thinks of this environment when he does "physical" planning. Insofar as he manipulates material objects, his planning is physical, but the forms and contents that go into the physical environment are as much the product of cultural values and social decisions as they are material objects. A park is a physical environment, but the choice and arrangement of flora, fauna, walkways, and facilities are based on decisions about the way society or the planner defines a desirable park. Consequently, it is much more important to decide whose culture will be reflected in the planner's scheme than what kinds of material object will be incorporated into the park. The planner may make decisions which reflect his personal or professional preference, which may—and usually are—based on the values of his own culture, or he can make decisions which reflect the culture of the people who will use the park. If there is conflict between his values and those of the people who will eventually use the park, the plan may not be adopted; or if adopted, it may result in a park that will not be used as much as it could have been; or the plan may be altered informally by people as they make use of the park.

Planners rarely see the social aspects of the man-made environment; they argue that the man-made environment as they define it can directly influence human behavior. They believe that the creation of a park will provide pleasure, aesthetic satisfaction, and better health through the exposure to fresh air, sunlight, and grass. I would argue, however, that it is not the park alone but the functions and meanings which the park has for the people who are exposed to it that affect the achievement or nonachievement of the planner's aims. The park proposed by the planner is only a *potential environment;* the social system and culture of the people who will use it determine to what extent the park becomes an *effective environment.* Without the park, the emotional and aesthetic benefits predicated by the planner cannot be made available, but without use of the park by the people for whom it is planned, these benefits cannot be achieved either. Presumably the visual presence of the park and its addition to light and air benefit even the nonuser; then the planner must decide whether the park is the best functional alternative for increasing visual pleasure and the supply of light and air and whether the benefits to be gained are worth the costs involved.

With respect to its influence on behavior, therefore, a man-made artifact is a potential environment, and the conception of that man-made artifact in the culture is the effective environment. The effective environment may thus be defined as *that version of the potential environment that is manifestly or latently adopted by users.* In one way, I am only restating the truism that an objective environment must be perceived subjectively before it affects behavior. However, the planner's conception of the park is no more objective than that of the user; each focuses on the elements of the environment relevant to him. The planner sees what I call the potential environment; the user is manifestly or latently aware of the effective environment.

The planner sees especially those parts of the potential environment that are:

1. Amenable to his manipulation, that is, those over which he has political or architectural control.

2. Related to his training. If he is a physical planner, he goes into considerable detail in analyzing the technical aspects of this environment, whether or not these are relevant to its use.

3. Visible to his perception in view of his position. The planner's perspective is that of a surveyor or spectator. He sees an environment as it appears on the map or the blueprint; he looks it over in initial phases of construction and again when it is completed. But unless the environment is planned for the neighborhood in which he lives, he sees it only fleetingly and does not use it. While he may project his conception of how it ought to be used onto its intended users, he does not use it as do the people who live with it.

The planner's perspective can be illustrated by the different perspective of the West Enders I studied in Boston. Most of the planning reports described the area as a neighborhood of five-story tenement buildings in narrow streets, without sufficient sun and air, and characterized by insufficient parking, garbage-strewn alleys, and high delinquency statistics. The people who lived in it saw something entirely different: cheap, spacious apartments, a neighborhood full of friends and family, and freedom from attack by delinquents (who did their antisocial work primarily outside of the West End).

The tenements built in the West End at the beginning of the twentieth century were an ingenious example of that period's speculative builder architecture designed to fit the demands of the law, the housing market, and the profit motive, but they did deprive the first and second floors of light and air. Air can be supplied by fans; but sunlight cannot be substituted. Even so, it is not at all certain whether these apartments were the danger to health that planners have suggested. The people who inhabited them probably got sufficient sunlight because they spent much time in the open, at work, at play, and in street-corner socializing. (It would be interesting to discover whether they spent more time outside than do the middle-class people whose values with respect to light and air inside the house are reflected in housing standards.) This is not meant to attack housing standards; however, if such standards give people an effective choice between $30-a-month apartments without sunlight and $75-a-month apartments with sunlight, it can easily be understood why poor people would much prefer the former.

III

These observations suggest that it is time to stop asking whether or not "better" housing as such improves the living conditions of its tenants and to inquire instead: What aspects of such housing have what impact on these tenants, within the context of their lives and the choices open to them? For example, most planners and housers would agree that moving people from walk-up tenement apartments to single-family dwellings would be beneficial. If they are lower-class families, with a culture in which child–parent relationships are not sociometrically as close as in the middle class, the single-family house may not have the same meaning or virtue for them as for the planners. Moreover, the technologically "better" housing must be viewed within the context of choices available to these people. If the single-family house is located in the suburbs far from job opportunities, it will not be beneficial to people who suffer from job insecurity. They should be living near the center of the city where they are centrally located with respect to job opportunities and mass transit facilities. If such housing is more expensive than what people had before, the advantages of modernity may be offset by deprivations resulting from new budgetary pressures. Or if such housing isolates people from a friendly social environment, it is not "better" for those whose life style calls for that environment more than for modern housing. Similarly, if planners locate a park in an overcrowded neighborhood without solving the housing problem in that area, the park may be interpreted by the neighborhood not as an improvement, but as an indication of the city's lack of interest in what its residents perceive as their real problems.

This is not an argument against more modern housing or more parks, but a reminder that the facilities planned must be better in terms of the frames of reference of both the planner and the users. In the terminology used previously, the planner's main tool is not the potential environmental item—the raw facility—but the facility as it would be defined in its effective environment. There are, however, three important qualifications to the primacy of effective over potential environment.

First, there may be potential environmental conditions that will affect all aspects of the effective environment. For example, the biologist Jack Calhoun argues that among rats, a certain level of density will result in such overcrowding as to paralyze their social system and result in depression, conflict, and eventual destruction of the rat population. In this instance, high density may well be an absolute environmental factor that operates regardless of the nature of the effective environment.

Calhoun and others have taken the findings of animal research to suggest that such absolute factors do control human behavior. Before one can agree with this argument, however, it is necessary to determine whether the findings of research on animals are transferable to human beings; whether higher densities will also have destructive effects on people. My hunch is that such findings are not always transferable, because the relationship of rats to their environment is different from that of people to theirs. Rats and other animals make direct use of the natural environment; it provides them with food and shelter. Most human beings do not make such direct use of the natural environment; they transform it into a man-made environment, adding the functions and meanings which I have called the effective environment. When they crowd a given space, they can adapt that space by building high-rise buildings, in which they may live at low floor densities if they can afford to do so, as on Park Avenue; or they may develop cultural norms which reject privacy, allowing a large family to live together in a small space. Indeed, some cultures place such high value on sociability and on living in social proximity that they become anxious at low densities. For example, many of the West Enders I studied enjoyed living among their peers in five-story tenements and were frightened by the low densities they saw in "the country," by which they meant the suburbs and exurbs. They could live satisfactorily at densities which would have been anxiety-provoking to middle-class Protestants, whose cultural norms of individualism apply as much to residential densities as to economic arrangements.

Conversely, Calhoun's findings apply very much to people when they live in the same relationship to their environment as do animals; for example, farmers, hunters, fishermen—and city dwellers looking for a parking space. When a tribe of hunters or a group of farmers live in an area without sufficient fauna or flora to provide food, the members of such groups will starve, turn against each other, or unite to conquer the lands of another group so that they can obtain the needed food supply. Until they are able to obtain that food supply, they may show the same social and emotional pathological reactions that Calhoun noticed among the rats he studied. Similarly, when parking spaces are insufficient, automobile owners will fight for the limited supply, as did the very West Enders who found their high-density apartments satisfactory.

Until the findings of research among rats are tested systematically among people—and among people with direct and indirect relationships to their environment—it is futile to argue that high density is always undesirable. Even so, some types of density may be bad for people as universally as for animals. Room overcrowding which forces even people from sociable cultures to live so closely together that they cannot avoid each other when their cultural norms demand privacy—for example, during sexual intercourse—is likely to have detrimental consequences. Similarly, structural overcrowding that leads to a breakdown of basic utilities such as plumbing facilities is undesirable for all people, regardless of their cultural norms for privacy and sociability.

Second, aspects of the potential environment may remain hidden; they may not be perceived by people and thus cannot become a part of the effective environment. For example, if the gasoline fumes exhausted by vehicles are shown to breed lung cancer, people living on major traffic routes who see nothing wrong with where they live because they have become used to breathing these fumes should be told that they are in long-run danger of lung cancer. If longevity of life is a commonly accepted major goal, the expert's concern with long-run processes would take precedence over the short-run view of the people involved. This does not answer the ethical question of whether it is sufficient to tell people of the long-run danger, or whether it is necessary to remove them from it if they do not do so themselves; for example, by clearing residential settlements adjacent to major highways. The ideal answer is, of course, to find solutions which maximize both long-run and short-run goals.

Third, the availability of the potential man-made environmental artifact may by its very presence result in some change in the social system, so that the artifact is taken into the effective environment by virtue of its availability. Public-recreation officials often argue that if a park were provided for a neighborhood, residents would use it, even if they can be shown not to make much use of parks at the present time. Similarly, architects claim that people would accept high-rise housing if such housing were properly designed. Neither logic nor empirical inquiry enables us to determine the validity of this argument. The future cannot be predicted, and while one might argue that fundamental change, in housing type preferences, for example, occurs only rarely, such change does take place. Moreover, our present knowledge is never so complete that we can say with all assurance that a proposed innovation would not in fact fit needs, for there might be hidden needs which do not come into view in even the best research.

Since innovation is itself a value, especially among professionals, such proposals deserve testing. The problem arises only when the proposed innovation is so costly compared to the promised benefits that the community with limited resources cannot risk the luxury of failure. Under those conditions, it seems to me that the burden of proof falls on those who claim that the proposed potential environmental artifact will bring change. They must prove that the likelihood of the change and its benefits are great enough to justify the costs involved. Research can provide some aid in this situation, for innovations are constantly being introduced in our society. These can be studied experimentally to determine under what conditions what kinds of innovation create basic changes from the prior situation; or under what conditions these changes are responses to important, if previously hidden, needs or demands in the group reacting to the innovation; or under what conditions innovations are rejected, that is, create no change.

IV

This statement of the relationship of physical environment and human behavior does not deny the assumption that the former influences the latter. It only attempts to insert between these two concepts the idea of the effective environment, so that the useless argument of whether or not there is a causal influence from the former to the latter can be replaced by the more fruitful question of when, how, how much, and with what effects this causal influence does occur. Until data to answer my question are available, the planner is likely to continue to believe or hope that the effective environment will be exactly like the potential environment. If the planner recognizes that the two environments can never be alike, however, he may become aware of the fact that he is inserting his own values into the process of transforming a potential environment into an effective environment. At that point, he may be able to begin to plan for the people who are intended to use the results of his work.

2

The Effect of a Community on Its Residents: Some Considerations for Sociological Theory and Planning Practice

I

The city planner plans for the improvement of the physical features of the community as a means of providing opportunities for better ways of living on the part of its residents. He believes that under ideal conditions physical changes will help materially to achieve a concept of the good life which is built into the plan itself, usually implicitly. In short, then, the planner wants to encourage alterations in the physical community *in order to produce a deliberate effect on the lives of its residents.*

This approach grew out of architectural ideology, which assumes that buildings, site plans, and other man-made and natural aspects of the physical environment do have direct behavioral and emotional effects on their users. This ideology has been supported by some sociological research and by popular beliefs. Thus, the early ecologists believed that the environment could be shown to have a direct effect on behavior. For example, some of the sociological studies of the "Chicago School" suggested that the slum as an urban zone carried with it the causes of juvenile delinquency, crime, mental illness, violations of sexual mores, and the like. Today, this simple model is no longer accepted by social scientist, but it lingers in popular writing. At the present time, a considerable public folklore exists about the negative effects of suburban residence on family stability, sexual behavior, sociability patterns, religious activity, voting, and mental health.

Many contemporary sociologists question this analysis, and a few have offered empirical data to support their critique. But debunking is

Previously unpublished. Presented to the Urban Sociology Colloquium, Rutgers University, New Brunswick, May 5, 1961.

not enough; the sociologist has to develop a systematic theory which deals with the effects of the community on its residents, separating actual effects from spurious ones and indicating how the actual effects create their impact. Such a theory not only will contribute to the understanding of the community but can provide technical information to the planner who seeks to affect residents in a deliberate manner. This paper attempts to begin the discussion of this problem, drawing on a review of some recent studies, personal observations, and theoretical speculations.

II

The sociological study of effects has so far been carried furthest in the analysis of the mass media. Klapper's summary of the existing research points out that the initial theory of mass-media effects was a *hypodermic* one: the media and their content were thought to have direct effects on their audiences, changing behavior and attitudes in line with directives explicit or hidden in the content.[1] Mass-media research of the past two decades has shown convincingly that this model is not satisfactory, and must be replaced by one which Klapper labels as *phenomenistic*. He argues that many of the alleged effects of the media stem from predispositions which motivate the audience to select the content, because it caters to these predispositions, and that the media tend to reinforce beliefs and behavior patterns already existing in the audience. Content which contradicts such predispositions is either ignored or reinterpreted to fit them. The media have a direct effect only if the content is so new that no predispositions have yet been formed or if it is of so little relevance to audiences that they will accept whatever they hear or see.

This is an oversimplified version of Klapper's model, but it can serve as a guide to the analysis of community effects. It should be clear that the original conception of community effects was based on a hypodermic model, and I propose that the new theory should resemble Klapper's phenomenistic model. Unfortunately, effects studies are difficult to carry out in the media and in the community, and the community is a more complex phenomenon than a television series or a magazine article. It is both a physical entity and a social one; it is both a political unit and an ecological one. It consists of houses and blocks, of neighborhoods and subareas, and is itself a part of a larger metropolitan area or region. Also, the resident is a part of the community in a much more direct and complex fashion than the TV viewer is a part of the program he is watching. Consequently, it is much more difficult to attribute effects to the community than to the mass media. Methodological problems should not, however, discourage speculation and empirical research before anything is accomplished.

Effects studies can be conducted in many ways. To my mind, the best approach is to study people who move from one community to another and to observe the behavioral changes that take place after the move. If these people can be interviewed before and after the move, it is possible to determine whether the changes that take place are:

1. *Intended changes,* reflecting predispositions existing before the move and reasons for the move itself.

2. *Unintended changes* that have resulted because of the move and can perhaps be ascribed to the physical or social characteristics of the new community.

This analysis should also attempt to describe how the changes in attitude and behavior came about, in order to show how the community impinges on the residents, and, equally important, what aspect of the community is actually responsible for the changes.

Such an analysis would provide the sociologist and the planner with considerable data on the structure and functioning of the community. If changes can be attributed to the community, and especially its physical aspects, it would suggest that the planner can affect behavior through direct changes in the community plan; if changes are primarily the result of predispositions, policy aimed at behavior change would have to affect the formation of predispositions.

III

The existing studies of community effects suggest (1) that the amount of change that can be ascribed to the community has been exaggerated and (2) that much of the change taking place can be attributed instead to the existence of predispositions on the part of the people moving into the community. Bennett Berger's study of automobile workers who moved from the apartments of a small industrial city to a suburban tract of single-family homes showed that the move to the suburbs had not resulted in any significant change in amount or nature of sociability, organizational participation, church attendance, voting, and political-party affiliation.[2] Moreover, Berger found no indication of interest in social or cultural mobility. He concluded that despite the auto workers' great satisfaction with the new home and with being homeowners, they remained working-class people and had no interest in adopting middle-class ways usually associated with suburbia.

My own research in Levittown, New Jersey, a predominantly lower-middle-class suburban community outside Philadelphia, suggests much the same conclusion. A preliminary analysis of interviews conducted immediately after the move and two years later suggests also that the major changes were:

1. New satisfaction due to homeownership.
2. Increased family morale resulting from availability of space.
3. More social activity with neighbors and friends.
4. More organizational participation.

The first two changes were the most important reasons for the move itself. Renters wanted to be homeowners, and growing families wanted the additional space they could get only in a four-bedroom house. The modernity of the house lightened the housekeeping tasks of the wife, and the additional space, indoor and outdoor, gave family members more privacy and allowed women to let their children play outdoors without worry or too much supervision. These are nearly universal effects of the move to suburbia which reflect widely held predispositions for family life, both in the middle class and in the upper reaches of the working class. The majority of those who reported increased sociability also noted that they had wanted to do more socializing in their new community and had looked forward to living with neighbors and fellow residents who were more compatible in terms of age and class than those near whom they had lived in the city.

A somewhat similar pattern obtained with respect to organizational participation. Most of the people interviewed were not active in organizations, and among those who were, the majority had been active before the move or wanted to be more active. Some people were, however, drawn into organizational activity because of the need for organizations in a brand new community. For example, people who had not intended to become active found themselves organizing churches and social groups. This is clearly an unintended effect of the move, but it is an effect of the newness, rather than of the nature of the community. If organizations had already been functioning, these people might not have become active. Some of the unintentionally active found that they enjoyed their activity and discovered previously unrecognized talent for leadership and organizational activity; for them, the community did have direct unintended effects. They are few in number, however.

The move to the suburb led to other unintended changes, but in most instances, these had a variety of effects on people's lives, depending on their predispositions and general cultural background. For example, the fact that some children were exposed to a better-quality education pleased the parents with "positive" attitudes toward education, but led to remarks by some others that the children were being overworked. Similarly, the decrease in spare time was welcomed by those who enjoyed gardening and for whom it became a new form of leisure; it was not welcomed by those who thought it an unending chore.

Finally, some unintended changes were negative for almost everyone. The most important of these was the increased cost of living. Some people accepted this voluntarily as the price of living in the suburbs and of achieving major predispositions. But others, especially those who had to make significant cuts in the family budget, rebelled, blaming it on the provision of municipal services.

IV

These observations have implications for the analysis of community effects. Intended changes are a combination of predispositions on the part of residents and the opportunity provided by the community to achieve these. The fact that the community provides an opportunity for the achievement of these predispositions cannot be considered as an effect on the predispositions. The new postwar suburban communities are a result of the predispositions of people for single-family, low-density housing—made possible by the rising incomes of the skilled working-class and lower-middle-class population—which have in turn stimulated the federal government and builders to attempt to satisfy the new demand.

The previously cited data suggest that the behavior patterns associated with the new suburban communities are in large part a result of the predispositions of their occupants and that the community itself generates few unintended changes in behavior. Most of the behavior that has been attributed to suburbia is typical of the age and class background of the population, irrespective of residence. It existed before people moved to the suburbs, although it was less visible in the city.

It could, of course, be argued that the predispositions for suburban living are themselves an effect of suburbia. Thus, it is commonly thought that the desire for suburbia on the part of today's new suburbanites is a result of their seeing the upper-middle-class suburbias of the past generation or the depictions of suburban life by the mass media. No one has yet isolated, or found ways of isolating, the origins of predispositions that lead to suburbia. I doubt personally that these predispositions are a result either of past suburbias or of mass-media depictions. Klapper's data lead one to question the power of the mass media in this connection. Also, most of the media content dealing with suburban life has followed, rather than preceded, the recent move to the suburbs. My hypothesis is that the predispositions have existed for generations, both in working-class culture and lower-middle-class culture, and that they represent long-run cultural preferences that were temporarily set aside by the need—often without choice—to live in higher-density housing.

Unintended changes are not based on predispositions and can therefore be attributed either to the moving process, to the newness of the community, or to the community itself. *The changes that can be attributed to the community itself can therefore be described as effects of the community.* It should be noted, however, that unintended changes can have a variety of effects, positive, negative, or neutral, depending on the social and cultural background of the people involved. The critics of suburbia have mistakenly assumed that the effects which they themselves felt would be experienced by everyone else. However, the effects that upset an intellectual or an upper-middle-class professional, such as the length of the journey to work or the inaccessibility of the city's cultural facilities, may be of less importance—or none at all—to a lower-middle-class or working-class family.

The formulation sells short the possibility of unconscious or subconscious effects; for example, the nervous-energy toll of lengthy commuting. Such effects are even more difficult to study than conscious ones, but they cannot be ignored in empirical research. However, until such empirical research is available, claims to their existence put forth by a variety of critics must be taken with a grain of salt.

Finally, it should be noted that I have defined effects here to include only unintended changes. It might be argued that behavioral changes which result from achieved predispositions, and frustrations which result from unachieved ones, should also be considered as effects of the community. Generally speaking, this argument is justified, especially in view of the fact that students of mass-media effects have insisted that effects cannot be understood apart from predispositions. The main drawback of the hypodermic model was its artificial separation of effects from the social context.

My justification for the definition used here is based on planning considerations. The planner's function is limited to affecting the community; he cannot select residents or move them around to fit his plan. Consequently, it is important to attempt to isolate the effects that stem from the community as abstracted from the residents, even though one should remind oneself that this abstraction is artificial and, if carried too far, dangerous.

V

So far, my analysis has been based on a simple model consisting of residents, the community, and the impact or impingement of the former on the latter, and vice versa. The concept of community is an abstraction, however, and one that hides more than it uncovers, at least with respect to effects. Community refers to a variety of physical and social areas and institutions within which and with which people live. In order to isolate the most important effects and to understand their workings, it will be necessary to become more specific. If one looks more closely at the physical and social environment in which people actually live, one can distinguish a series of community *layers* and a set of community *facets*. Some of these layers and facets impinge on people's lives and may affect them; others do not and are therefore less relevant to an effects study.

Most people who move to the suburbs do not buy a community, but a house. Some are attracted by the facilities provided by the builder, but they are a very small minority. If one traced what the late John Dean called people's "Indian Paths," one would find that people live in and around their houses and on the block, going from there to the homes of friends, churches, schools, shops, and, for a minority, public meeting places. If the community is seen as a series of layers, beginning with the house, the block, the neighborhood, and the politically defined community, it is clear that most people come in contact mainly with the first two. Only a small minority of people have regular contact with the social, civic, and political organizations that delineate their area of influence by the boundaries of the political community. Occasionally, the political unit acts in such a way as to impinge directly on the daily routine of its residents, at which time they may participate in its activities, especially if their predispositions and behavior patterns are upset, as is the case when taxes are raised. Otherwise, they participate only at election time. Needless to say, the political community often impinges on people without their being directly or immediately aware of it; people are then described as apathetic. When any layer of the community impinges on the behavior patterns of its residents, it may create either an intended or an unintended effect. The school impinges on the lives of students; this is intended by the parents. Often it seeks to impinge on the parents, but this is for many of them unintended and may be rejected.

The major community facets are physical and social. Planners believe that the physical environment, natural and man-made, impinges directly on the residents. Rosow has examined a number of studies and has shown that the physical environment has much less effect than planners imagine.[3] Often it is thought to impinge, but people evade this effect through what Rosow calls "nonconforming use," that is, an evasion of this impingement in order to maintain or achieve behavior patterns that are in line with their predispositions. The social environment has considerably more effect. This is best illustrated by Festinger's finding in Westgate, where the social life was so rewarding that people paid little attention to the physical defects of the housing.[4] Similarly, while the arrangement of houses on the block affects the amount of visual contact people will have, any but the most polite social contact is a result, not of physical features, but of social factors, such as shared interests or values.[5]

Combining the observations about community layers and facets suggests that from the point of view of effects, the social environment within the house and the block is most significant. The physical characteristics of the house can hinder family life if there is not enough privacy, although they cannot create a positive family relationship if this is not already present. For the women, life on the block is next in importance. The remaining layers of the community affect mainly the predisposed: the people who want to participate in voluntary organizations and in government. Only when the actions of these institutions impinge directly on the life that takes place in the home and on the block are they likely to have a direct effect on all the residents. They may, of course, have indirect effects, but in order for these to be felt, these must impinge directly on the life that goes on within the house, the block, and the few other locations which people choose.

The importance of the house and the block is well illustrated by data on behavioral changes connected with the move from city to suburb. The data which I have collected show that the major behavioral changes are a function of the change, not of settlement type, but of dwelling-unit type. It is the move from apartment to home, from living with transient tenants to more permanent fellow homeowners, which causes the major behavioral changes. For example, the move from suburban apartment to suburban single-family house has caused a greater change in resident behavior than the move from an urban single-family house to a suburban one.

Thus, the most important intended changes result from being in a single-family house, that is, the satisfaction of homeownership and the availability of space in and around the house. The more important unintended changes can be traced to the effect of the house; for example, improvements in health and disposition and the strain on the family budget because of the unexpected costs of homeownership. Some of the unintended changes are effects to be traced to the community, however, such as the quality of schooling, the separation from relatives, the opportunity to meet neighbors of different religious and ethnic backgrounds, the length of commuting time, and the increase in taxes. As mentioned earlier, some are short-range effects which are due to the community's newness—for example, increased organizational activity—but some can be traced directly to the nature or location of the community. It should be clear, however, that these are relatively few in number.

VI

The planner has traditionally concerned himself with changes in community design. If the community itself has few effects on the residents, however, the planner's approach is unlikely to have many behavioral effects. If future research justifies my hypothesis that most effects are based on prior predispositions, the planner who wishes to affect behavior has two alternatives: to develop plans that will achieve these predispositions, or to change people's predispositions so that they will be amenable to his plans. He has two further avenues of action. First, he can work in spatial areas and facets of life where predispositions are lacking, and therefore he can produce unintended changes. Here he can affect behavior, as long as his plans do not conflict with other predispositions. Second, the planner can act in those areas and facets of life in which people have no choice and in which they must accept whatever solutions, physical or social, are offered them. This kind of planning is likely to be manipulative and undemocratic; it is rejected, and rightfully so, by both the planner and his clients. It need not concern us further.

Let me return to the first three possibilities. I suggested first that the planner can develop plans calculated to achieve predispositions. He has traditionally paid little attention to people's predispositions, however. Planning began as a reform movement, not a client-centered service, and when predispositions conflicted with the requirements of planning ideology, they were rejected. Consequently, plans that will achieve predispositions have usually been pre-empted by the private housing market, although even the builders have not been sufficiently concerned with the customer's wishes, except in periods of a buyer's market. When planners have come up with better ways of achieving predispositions than builders, their recommendations have usually been accepted. For example, the curving streets that are now commonplace in suburbia were first advocated by planners. They found ready acceptance because they slowed down auto traffic and thus made it somewhat safer for children to play on the street. Curved streets also had status functions, by distinguishing the suburb from the city. They were accepted by the builder because he could create more lots out of the same acreage than with the grid plan. Generally, however, the planner has advocated policies that fit the predispositions of the upper middle class, but not those of the rest of the population. For example, his advocacy of high-density urban housing has so far found favor only with the cosmopolitan upper-middle class. His proposal for increasing suburban density to cut down urban sprawl is rejected by people who feel that row housing lacks privacy and that it is less desirable for other reasons than the single-family house. The planner's advocacy of more open space has also received little support, partially because the kind of open space he favors is not very important to the people who are supposed to use it.

The planner has also attempted to change people's predispositions by lobbying for and preaching about the kinds of plan he favors. He has not had much success so far, partly because predispositions are hard to change, and speeches or planning reports have little impact on them. If the planner had more power, he might be able to implement his recommendations and, by showing people that his solutions were better than previous ones, change their predispositions.

Now the planner has often asked for the power to show people that his solutions are indeed better, not only for the community but for their own predispositions. Sometimes he has been justified in doing so, but at other times he has not proved his case. For example, the planner has often argued for higher-density single-family housing—that is, for row housing—and has claimed that people dislike it because they have not been able to try the kind of row housing the planner or the architect has in mind. There is some justification for this claim, but most of the row-house schemes which have been proposed so far tend to meet the values of the professionals more than the preferences of the people who are to occupy them. I suspect that it is possible to design row houses which would be acceptable to people who now purchase single-family homes, but before they can be designed, planners and architects must conduct fairly extensive and intensive consumer research to discover the reasons for the popular antipathy to the row house. This antipathy is based largely on the lack of privacy which is found in most row-house schemes that have been built or placed on the drawing boards. If the consumer research is done, and its conclusions are allowed to influence row-house design, some of the problems of urban sprawl will be closer to solution than they are at present.

Thus, the planner can change people's predispositions, and he can also find better ways of satisfying existing predispositions. However, he can do so only if he attempts to understand and respect the existing predispositions and tries to find solutions that will take them into account. Where a change of predisposition is in order, the planner must be able to prove that the change will be beneficial to the people for whom it is intended. This can probably be done only through carefully planned innovations, which must first be treated as experiments and studied systematically for advantages and disadvantages before they can be advocated as more general policies.

The planner's main area of effective action is probably with those aspects of life and of the community that are not touched by prior predispositions, that is, those layers and facets of the community in which people are willing to accept something different and to expose themselves to unintended changes. As mentioned earlier, the planner has considerable leeway here, so long as his recommendations do not conflict with other predispositions. For example, if the planner can find ways of cutting the journey to work, his recommendations are likely to be accepted, because almost everyone prefers a short journey to a long one. However, his solution must be careful not to interfere with predispositions that lengthened the journey in the first place, that is, the preference for single-family housing and for private transportation. The presently proposed solutions require higher-density forms of housing and more mass transportation, but unless these solutions can arrive at new forms of such housing and mass transportation that can overcome traditional objections to them, it is unlikely that the journey to work can be cut.

I noted earlier that the community is an abstraction and that people live mainly in the house, on the block, and in a social rather than a physical environment. The planner generally thinks in terms of the community, especially as it is defined by the governmental agencies which employ him. Often he fails to see that this community does not impinge on its residents as much as he assumes and that his plans do not do so either. This is best illustrated by a brief examination of neighborhood theory. Many planners view the 3,000- to 5,000-person neighborhood as the basic planning unit, on the assumption that this community layer impinges most directly and frequently on people. This is not the case, however. The neighborhood is too large for any but the most superficial face-to-face relationships; most people have significant social contact only on the block and with friends outside the block. Moreover, since the neighborhood is not a political unit, neighbors may have no reason for interaction with one another. Thus, the neighborhood cannot create activities which might impinge on people. The elementary school, which is the center of the planner's neighborhood, actually impinges on only a minority of the residents. Its activities affect only the compulsory clientele (the students), the parents of those students who take an interest in the school, and other adults who participate in the organizational activities that are centered in the school. Residents without school-age children, and those without interest in their children's schooling or in organizational participation, are little touched by the school. Thus, the neighborhood has relatively little meaning for many of its residents, since it does not impinge on those aspects of their lives they consider important.

The fact that the neighborhood plays a minor role in people's lives and in their predispositions gives the planner freedom to design neighborhoods as he wishes them to be. At the same time, however, he is less likely to affect the lives of his clients. The planner who seeks to affect resident behavior must therefore concern himself with those layers and facets of the community that actually impinge on the residents. He can do this in the ways noted earlier: by responding to predispositions, changing predispositions, or creating new physical forms and social institutions that have unintended effects.

Even when he concentrates on layers and facets of the community that impinge on the residents' lives, the planner is often faced with the fact that people do not feel this impingement, either because it is a long-range one or because its impact is not clear. For example, the planner can usually predict congestion or undue tax increases long before they actually take place, but he has a hard time persuading people of his foresight. Likewise, the planner who advocates small classrooms may not be listened to because parents do not see that the individual attention which their children receive will benefit them educationally. This is a problem that faces not only the planner but many other professionals, including those concerned with mental health, metropolitan government, social planning, and making society more democratic. The low degree of political participation in our society is due to the fact that the impingement of government is often indirect and is not felt by the citizenry. This is called apathy, but using a pejorative word does not solve the problem.

I do not want to argue that impingements which are not felt by people do not exist. I want to stress, however, that in an action framework, unfelt impingements differ significantly from felt ones, and in order to implement planning policies through democratic methods, such policies must be translated into programs that result in felt impingements.

This translation is an extremely difficult process, and at present no one knows how it can be accomplished. It is possible that plans based on unfelt impingements can be tied to issues which are felt directly, so that they can be implemented. For example, people can be impressed with the need for metropolitan planning and government when basic suburban services break down; and they will be more favorable to a broad-based tax program when the property tax becomes so oppressive that it forces radical adjustments in family budgets.

These are questions which need much further research than they have so far received. As planners become convinced that the solutions which they have traditionally favored cannot be implemented or do not achieve the intended goal, the need for a systematic study of effects may impinge on the planner. The current boom in urban research may help to hasten the process.

NOTES

1. Joseph T. Klapper, *The Effects of Mass Communication* (Glencoe, Ill.: The Free Press, 1960).
2. Bennett Berger, *Working Class Suburb: A Study of Auto Workers in Suburbia* (Berkeley: University of California Press, 1960).
3. Irving Rosow, "The Social Effects of the Physical Environment," *Journal of the American Institute of Planners,* XXVII (May 1961), 127–133.
4. L. Festinger, S. Schachter, and K. Back, *Social Pressures in Informal Groups* (New York: Harper, 1950).
5. These patterns are discussed in more detail in Chapter 12.

3

Urban Vitality and the Fallacy of Physical Determinism

I

American intellectuals have begun to rediscover the city. Not since the days of the muckrakers has there been so much interest in local politics and in the "physical" features of the city—the problems of slums and urban renewal, middle-income housing, the lack of open space, the plight of the downtown business district, and the ever-increasing traffic congestion. The new concern with questions usually relegated to architects and planners has been stimulated especially by two recent changes in city life. The rapid influx of Negro and Puerto Rican immigrants has created slums in some neighborhoods where intellectuals live, forcing them to choose between fighting for neighborhood improvement and joining the rest of the middle class in flight. At the same time, the postwar building boom—in office buildings as well as residential projects—is altering and destroying some favorite intellectual haunts like New York's Greenwich Village and Chicago's Near North Side.

This change has provided new material for one of the basic themes of the ongoing critique of American society: the destruction of tradition by mass-produced modernity. During the 1950's, the critique centered on the ravages produced by mass culture and by suburbia. In the 1960's it is likely to focus on the destruction of traditional urbanity by new forms of city building.

Many of the ideas behind the new urban critique have come from the writings of Jane Jacobs, an associate editor of *Architectural Forum*. Now she has put her ideas into a book which seems destined to spearhead the attack, just as another book by an editor of another Luce magazine—William H. Whyte's *Organization Man*—spearheaded the attack on sub-

A review of Jane Jacobs, *The Death and Life of Great American Cities*. Published originally as "City Planning and Urban Realities," *Commentary*, XXXIII (February 1962), 170–175. Reprinted from *Commentary* by permission. Copyright © 1962 by the American Jewish Committee.

urbia. *The Death and Life of Great American Cities* is a thoughtful and imaginative tract on behalf of the traditional city, an analysis of the principles that make it desirable, an attack on the city planner—whom Mrs. Jacobs takes to be the agent of its transformation—and a program of new planning principles that she believes will create vital cities and vital neighborhoods.

II

The vital neighborhood—and vitality is Jane Jacobs' central aim— should be diverse in its use of land and in the people who inhabit it. Every district should be a mixture of residences, business, and industry; of old buildings and new; of young people and old; of rich and poor. Mrs. Jacobs argues that people want diversity, and in neighborhoods where it exists, they strike roots and participate in community life, thus generating vitality. When diversity is lacking, when neighborhoods are scourged by what she calls the great blight of dullness, residents who are free to leave do so and are replaced by the poverty-stricken, who have no other choice, and the areas soon turn into slums.

According to Mrs. Jacobs, the most important component of vitality is an abundant street life. Neighborhoods that are designed to encourage people to use the streets, or to watch what goes on in them, make desirable quarters for residence, work, and play. Moreover, where there is street life, there is little crime, for the people on the street and in the buildings which overlook it watch and protect each other, thus discouraging criminal acts more efficiently than police patrols.

The abundance of street life, Mrs. Jacobs argues, is brought about by planning principles which are diametrically opposed to those practiced by orthodox city planners. First, a district must have several functions, so that its buildings and streets are used at all times of the day and do not (like Wall Street) stand empty in off hours. The area should be built up densely with structures close to the street and low enough in number of stories to encourage both street life and street watching. Blocks should be short, for corners invite stores, and these bring people out into the streets for shopping and socializing. Sidewalks should be wide enough for pavement socials and children's play; streets should be narrow enough to prevent intensive and high-speed automobile traffic, for the automobile frightens away pedestrians. Small parks and playgrounds are desirable, but large open spaces—especially those intended only for decoration and not for use—not only deaden a district by separating people from each other but also invite criminals. Buildings should be both old and new, expensive and cheap, for low rents invite diversity in the form of new industries, shops, and artists' studios.

Neighborhoods which are designed on the basis of these principles—and which provide Mrs. Jacobs with concrete evidence for her argument—are areas like New York's Greenwich Village and San Francisco's Telegraph Hill (where residences of all types, prices, and ages mix with small business, industry, and cultural facilities) and low-income ethnic quarters like Boston's North End and Chicago's Back-of-the-Yards district.

The new forms of city building, Mrs. Jacobs says, discourage street life and create only dullness. High-rise apartment buildings, whether in public housing or private luxury flats, are standardized, architecturally undistinguished, and institutional in appearance if not operation. They house homogeneous populations, segregating people by income, race, and often even age and isolating them in purely residential quarters. Elevators, and the separation of the building from the street by a moat of useless open space, frustrate maternal supervision of children, thus keeping children off the street. Often there are no real streets at all, because prime access is by car. Nor is there any reason for people to use the streets, for instead of large numbers of small stores fronting on a street, there are shopping centers containing a small number of large stores—usually chains—each of which has a monopoly in its line. The small merchant, who watches the street and provides a center for neighborhood communication and social life, is absent here. In such projects, the residents have no place to meet each other, and there is no spontaneous neighborhood life. As a result, people have no feeling for their neighbors and no identification with the area. In luxury buildings, doormen watch the empty streets and discourage the criminal visitor, but in public housing projects, there are no doormen, and the interior streets and elevators invite rape, theft, and vandalism. Areas like this are blighted by dullness from the start and are destined to become slums before their time.

The major responsibility for the new forms of city building Mrs. Jacobs places on the city planner and on two theories of city form: Ebenezer Howard's low-density Garden City and Le Corbusier's high-rise apartment complex, the Radiant City. The planner is an artist who wants to restructure life by principles applicable only to art. By putting these principles into action, he is methodically destroying the features that produce vitality. His planning theories have also influenced the policy-makers, and especially realtors, bankers, and other sources of mortgage funds. As a result, they refuse to lend money to older but still vital areas which are trying to rehabilitate themselves, thus encouraging further deterioration of the structures until they are ripe for slum clearance, redevelopment with projects—and inevitable dullness.

III

Anyone who has ever wandered through New York's Greenwich Village or Boston's North End is bound to respond to Mrs. Jacobs' conception of a vital city. Her analysis of the mechanics of street life, and of the ways in which people use buildings, streets, and vacant spaces in such areas, is eye-opening. The principles of neighborhood planning which derive from her observations—she is herself a resident of Greenwich Village—are far more closely attuned to how people actually live than are those of orthodox city planning. It would be easy to succumb to the charm of the neighborhoods she describes and to read her book only as a persuasive appeal for their retention. But since Mrs. Jacobs is out to reform all of city planning, it is necessary to examine her central ideas more closely.

Her argument is built on three fundamental assumptions: that people desire diversity; that diversity is ultimately what makes cities live and that the lack of it makes them die; and that buildings, streets, and the planning principles on which they are based shape human behavior. The first two of these assumptions are not entirely supported by the facts of the areas she describes. The last assumption, which she shares with the planners whom she attacks, might be called the physical fallacy, and it leads her to ignore the social, cultural, and economic factors that contribute to vitality or dullness. It also blinds her to less visible kinds of neighborhood vitality and to the true causes of the city's problems.

Ethnic neighborhoods like the North End, or the Italian and Irish sections of Greenwich Village, are not diverse, but quite homogeneous in population as well as in building type. The street life of these areas stems not so much from their physical character as from the working-class culture of their inhabitants. In this culture, the home is reserved for the family, so that much social life takes place outdoors. Also, children are not kept indoors as frequently as in the middle class, and since they are less closely supervised in their play, they too wind up in the streets.

If such districts are near the downtown area, they may attract intellectuals, artists, and Bohemian types, who also tend to spend a good deal of time outside their apartments, contributing further to the street life. The street life, the small stores that traditionally serve ethnic groups and other cultural minorities, and the area's exotic flavor then draw visitors and tourists, whose presence helps to make the district even livelier. The resulting blend of unusual cultures makes for a highly visible kind of vitality. It helps if the district is old and basically European in architecture, but traditional-looking frontages can be superimposed by today's clever builder.

In other working-class neighborhoods, especially those far away from the downtown area, street life is also abundant, but the people and the stores are neither ethnic nor esoteric. In middle-class neighborhoods, there is no street life, for all social activities take place inside the home, children play less often on the sidewalks, and the street is used only for transportation. Such neighborhoods look dull, notably to the visitor, and therefore they seem to be less vital than their ethnic and Bohemian counterparts. But visibility is not the only measure of vitality, and areas that are uninteresting to the visitor may be quite vital to the people who live in them.

This possibility must also be considered for the new luxury and middle-class housing projects. Since they are largely occupied by childless middle-class people, they look even duller than other areas, just as their newness makes them seem more standardized to the visitor than older areas in which the initial homogeneity of buildings has been altered by conversion or just covered by the accretions of dirt and age. It is clear that we need to learn how residents live in such projects before we can be sure of the validity of Mrs. Jacobs' charges.

In proposing that cities be planned to stimulate an abundant street life, Mrs. Jacobs not only overestimates the power of planning in shaping behavior but in effect demands that middle-class people adopt working-class styles of family life, child-rearing, and sociability. The truth is that the new forms of residential building—in suburb as well as city—are not products of orthodox planning theory, but expressions of the middle-class culture which guides the housing market and which planners also serve. Often the planners serve it too loyally, and they ignore the needs of a working-class population. Thus, Jane Jacobs' criticism is most relevant to the planning of public housing projects, for its middle-class designers have made no provision for the street life that these particular tenants probably want.

But middle-class people, especially those raising children, do not want working-class—or even Bohemian—neighborhoods. They do not want the visible vitality of a North End, but rather the quiet and the privacy obtainable in low-density neighborhoods and elevator apartment houses. Not all of their social life involves neighbors, and their friends may be scattered all over the metropolitan area, as are the commercial and recreational facilities which they frequent. For this, they want a car, expressways, and all the freedom of movement that expressways create when properly planned. Middle-class people tend to value status over convenience, and thus they reject neighborhoods in which residence and business are mixed—or in which there is any real diversity in population. Having no love for walking or for riding public transit, they have brought shopping centers into being. Nor does their life style leave much room for the small merchant. Since their tastes are no longer ethnic, but not yet esoteric, they prefer the supermarket to the small store, for it does provide more choice—if only among prosaic items—and its wider aisles facilitate gossip with neighbors.

One can quarrel with some of these tastes, but the fact is that the areas about which Mrs. Jacobs writes were built for a style of life which is going out of fashion with the large majority of Americans who are free to choose their place of residence. The North End and the Back-of-the-Yards district are not holding their young people, who tend to move to the suburbs as soon as they have children to raise. Even in Europe, the old working-class districts invariably empty out when prosperity reaches the blue-collar workers.

The middle-class visitor does not see these cultural changes. Nor does he see that the houses in these traditional districts are often hard to maintain, that parking is often impossible, that noise and dirt are ever present, that some of the neighbors watch too much, and that not all the shopkeepers are kind. Because the traditional districts are so different from his own neighborhood, and because he is a visitor, he sees only their charm and excitement. He therefore is most understandably reluctant to see them disappear.

But for the planning of cities, the visitor's wishes are less important than the inhabitant's. One cannot design all neighborhoods for a traditional style of life if only a few people want to live this way. Nevertheless, areas like the North End and the Village are worth saving. They provide low-rent housing for people with low incomes; they give pleasure to visitors and may even attract tourists; and they are appealing reminders of our European heritage and our pre-automobile past. The city would be a poorer place without them.

IV

Even so, the future of the American city is not going to be determined by the life or death of the North Ends and the Greenwich Villages. The real problems lie elsewhere. Mrs. Jacobs' concentration on these areas diverts her from properly analyzing the more fundamental problems, even while she makes some highly pertinent comments. This can be best illustrated by examining her discussion of slums and her proposals for urban renewal.

As noted earlier, she argues that slums are caused ultimately by lack of diversity. Homogeneous and dull areas are deserted by residents who have the resources to go elsewhere and are replaced by people who have no other choice and who, for reasons of poverty and racial discrimination, are forced to live in overcrowded conditions. She suggests that if these areas could be made more diverse, the initial occupants might not leave, and owners would then be able to rehabilitate the buildings.

This analysis is too simple. People leave such areas, not to seek diversity, but to practice new life styles, and additional diversity would not persuade them to stay. It is true that some areas occupied by non-mobile ethnic groups, notably the North End and Back-of-the-Yards, hold their residents longer than other areas. It is also true that these areas are not slums; they are low-rent districts, and Mrs. Jacobs is right in insisting on the distinction. Slums (she calls them perpetual slums) are areas in which housing and other facilities are physically and socially harmful to the inhabitants and to the larger community, primarily because of over-crowding. Low-rent areas (which she calls unslumming slums) may look equally dilapidated to the casual observer—and planners sometimes base their decisions only on casual observation—but they are not overcrowded and they are not harmful. Mrs. Jacobs criticizes urban renewal—and rightly so—for confusing such areas with real slums and clearing them needlessly with grievous hurt to their inhabitants. She proposes that they can be rehabilitated by providing home and tenement owners with easier access to mortgage funds and by planning for greater diversity. This proposal has merit, although landlords probably would not undertake as much rehabilitation as she envisages unless the area were attracting middle-class people with quasi-Bohemian tastes, as in the case of the Village and Philadelphia's West Rittenhouse Square district.

But such neighborhoods—and purely working-class ones like the North End—are numerically unimportant in most cities. It is also no coincidence that they are occupied almost exclusively by whites. Their improvement cannot solve the problem of the real slums. These slums are caused not by dullness—they are often similar in plan and architecture to low-rent areas—but by the overcrowding of already old buildings by poverty-stricken and otherwise deprived nonwhites, who have no other place to go. To be sure, such people usually move into areas being deserted by their previous residents, but even when the older residents are not leaving, the same thing can happen. Chicago's Hyde Park district was not being deserted by its middle-class residents, but portions of it became a slum because the Negro Black Belt to the north simply could not accommodate any more inmigrants.

Once an area becomes an overcrowded slum, rehabilitating the structures is no solution. The crucial step in rehabilitation is the uncrowding of the buildings. But slum structures are owned by absentee landlords who have no incentive to rehabilitate because they reap immense profits from overcrowding. Even if they were willing to convert rooming houses back to apartments, most of the slum dwellers who would then have to move would not be able to do so. They cannot afford to pay the rentals demanded for an apartment, and since they are nonwhite, other districts of the city are unwilling to accept them even if there are vacant apartments, which is rarely the case.

The slums cannot be emptied unless and until there is more low-cost housing elsewhere. Private enterprise cannot afford to build such housing. The traditional solution has been to rely on public housing, but thanks to the opposition of the real-estate men and the private builders, it has never been supplied in large enough amounts. Even then, it had to be located in the slums, because other city districts were unwilling to give over vacant or industrial land. In order to minimize clearance, public housing has had to resort to elevator buildings, and in order to protect itself from the surrounding slums, it has constructed fenced-in projects. In order to satisfy its powerful opponents that it was not wasting tax money on ne'er-do-wells, it has had to impose institutional restrictions on its hapless occupants, and in order to avoid competition with the private housing market, it has been forced to expel tenants whose income rises above a certain level.

Mrs. Jacobs suggests that the government stop building public housing and instead subsidize builders to make their units available to low-income tenants. This is a useful suggestion, and one that has been proposed by planners and public housing advocates before. But earlier attempts to scatter low-income housing in other ways have been rejected by the recipient neighborhoods. Mrs. Jacobs' scheme has more merit than some earlier ones, but I doubt whether middle-class areas in the city and suburbs will make room for the large number of nonwhite poor who need to be taken out of overcrowded slums.

The sad fact is that until we abolish poverty and discrimination—or until the middle class becomes tolerant of poor nonwhite neighbors—the government is probably going to have to build more low-income ghettos.

Unfortunately, Mrs. Jacobs' anger with the planners is so intense that she blames them for the sins of private enterprise and the middle class, and she is eager to return functions to private enterprise which it has shown itself unable and unwilling to perform. She also forgets that private enterprise—acting through the well-heeled builder and realtor lobby in Washington—is responsible for some of the more obnoxious features of the urban-renewal laws and for hamstringing public housing in the ways I have indicated. Her blanket indictment of planners detracts from the persuasiveness of her other proposals and antagonizes people who might agree with her on many points. More important, it is likely to win her the support of those who profit from the status quo, of the nostalgic who want to bring back the city and the society of the eighteenth and nine-teenth centuries, and of the ultra-right-wing groups who oppose planning —and all government action—whether good or bad.

V

Orthodox city planning deserves considerable criticism for its antiurban bias, for giving higher priority to buildings, plans, and design concepts than to the needs of people, and for trying to transform ways of living before even examining how people live or want to live. But not all the planners think this way—actually, much of the theory Mrs. Jacobs rejects was developed by architects and architecturally trained planners—and some of her ideas have in fact been set forth by planners themselves.

No one, it is true, has stated these ideas as forcefully as she or in-tegrated them into an over-all approach before. The neighborhoods with which she is most concerned cannot serve as models for future planning, but the way in which she has observed them, the insights she has derived, and the principles she has inferred from her observations can be and ought to be adapted for use in planning cities and suburbs in the future. Her book is a pathbreaking achievement, and because it is so often right, I am all the more disappointed by the fact that it is also so often wrong.

4

Urbanism and Suburbanism as Ways of Life: A Re-evaluation of Definitions

The contemporary sociological conception of cities and of urban life is based largely on the work of the Chicago School and its summary statement in Louis Wirth's essay "Urbanism as a Way of Life."[1] In that paper, Wirth developed a "minimum sociological definition of the city" as "a relatively large, dense and permanent settlement of socially heterogeneous individuals." From these prerequisites, he then deduced the major outlines of the urban way of life. As he saw it, number, density, and heterogeneity created a social structure in which primary-group relationships were inevitably replaced by secondary contacts that were impersonal, segmental, superficial, transitory, and often predatory in nature. As a result, the city dweller became anonymous, isolated, secular, relativistic, rational, and sophisticated. In order to function in the urban society, he was forced to combine with others to organize corporations, voluntary associations, representative forms of government, and the impersonal mass media of communications. These replaced the primary groups and the integrated way of life found in rural and other preindustrial settlements.

Wirth's paper has become a classic in urban sociology, and most texts have followed his definition and description faithfully.[2] In recent years, however, a considerable number of studies and essays have questioned his formulations.[3] In addition, a number of changes have taken place in cities since the article was published in 1938, notably the exodus of white residents to low- and medium-priced houses in the suburbs and the decentralization of industry. The evidence from these studies and the changes in American cities suggest that Wirth's statement must be revised.

There is yet another and more important reason for such a revision. Despite its title and intent, Wirth's paper deals with urban-industrial

Reprinted from Arnold M. Rose, ed., *Human Behavior and Social Processes* (Boston: Houghton Mifflin, 1962), pp. 625–648, by permission of the publishers. I am indebted to Richard Dewey, John Dyckman, David Riesman, Melvin Webber, and Harold L. Wilensky for helpful comments on earlier drafts of this essay.

society, rather than with the city. This is evident from his approach. Like other urban sociologists, Wirth based his analysis on a comparison of settlement types, but unlike his colleagues, who pursued urban-rural comparisons, Wirth contrasted the city to the folk society. Thus, he compared settlement types of preindustrial and industrial society. This allowed him to include in his theory of urbanism the entire range of modern institutions which are not found in the folk society, even though many such groups (for example, voluntary associations) are by no means exclusively urban. Moreover, Wirth's conception of the city dweller as depersonalized, atomized, and susceptible to mass movements suggests that his paper is based on, and contributes to, the theory of the mass society.

Many of Wirth's conclusions may be relevant to the understanding of ways of life in modern society. However, since the theory argues that all of society is now urban, his analysis does not distinguish ways of life in the city from those in other settlements within modern society. In Wirth's time, the comparison of urban and preurban settlement types was still fruitful, but today, the primary task for urban (or community) sociology seems to me to be the analysis of the similarities and differences between contemporary settlement types.

This paper is an attempt at such an analysis; it limits itself to distinguishing ways of life in the modern city and the modern suburb. A reanalysis of Wirth's conclusions from this perspective suggests that his characterization of the urban way of life applies only—and not too accurately—to the residents of the inner city. The remaining city dwellers, as well as most suburbanites, pursue a different way of life which I shall call "quasi-primary." This proposition raises some doubt about the mutual exclusiveness of the concepts of city and suburb and leads to a yet broader question: whether settlement concepts and other ecological concepts are useful for explaining ways of life.

The inner city

Wirth argued that number, density, and heterogeneity had two social consequences which explain the major features of urban life. On the one hand, the crowding of diverse types of people into a small area led to the segregation of homogeneous types of people into separate neighborhoods. On the other hand, the lack of physical distance between city dwellers resulted in social contact between them, which broke down existing social and cultural patterns and encouraged assimilation as well as acculturation —the melting-pot effect. Wirth implied that the melting-pot effect was far more powerful than the tendency toward segregation and concluded that, sooner or later, the pressures engendered by the dominant social, economic, and political institutions of the city would destroy the remaining pockets of primary-group relationships. Eventually, the social system of the city would resemble Tönnies' Gesellschaft—a way of life which Wirth considered undesirable.

Because Wirth had come to see the city as the prototype of mass society, and because he examined the city from the distant vantage point of the folk society—from the wrong end of the telescope, so to speak— his view of urban life is not surprising. In addition, Wirth found support for his theory in the empirical work of his Chicago colleagues. As Greer and Kube[4] and Wilensky[5] have pointed out, the Chicago sociologists conducted their most intensive studies in the inner city.[6] At that time, these were slums recently invaded by new waves of European immigrants and rooming-house and skid-row districts, as well as the habitat of Bohemians and well-to-do Gold Coast apartment dwellers. Wirth himself studied the Maxwell Street Ghetto, an inner-city Jewish neighborhood then being dispersed by the acculturation and mobility of its inhabitants.[7] Some of the characteristics of urbanism which Wirth stressed in his essay abounded in these areas.

Wirth's diagnosis of the city as Gesellschaft must be questioned on three counts. First, the conclusions derived from a study of the inner city cannot be generalized to the entire urban area. Second, there is as yet not enough evidence to prove—nor, admittedly, to deny—that number, density, and heterogeneity result in the social consequences which Wirth proposed. Finally, even if the causal relationship could be verified, it can be shown that a significant proportion of the city's inhabitants were, and are, isolated from these consequences by social structures and cultural patterns which they either brought to the city or developed by living in it. Wirth conceived the urban population as consisting of heterogeneous individuals, torn from past social systems, unable to develop new ones, and therefore prey to social anarchy in the city. While it is true that a not insignificant proportion of the inner-city population was, and still is, made up of unattached individuals,[8] Wirth's formulation ignores the fact that this population consists mainly of relatively homogeneous groups, with social and cultural moorings that shield it fairly effectively from the suggested consequences of number, density, and heterogeneity. This applies even more to the residents of the outer city, who constitute a majority of the total city population.

The social and cultural moorings of the inner-city population are best described by a brief analysis of the five types of inner-city residents. These are:

1. the "cosmopolites";

2. the unmarried or childless;
3. the "ethnic villagers";
4. the "deprived"; and
5. the "trapped" and downward-mobile.

The "cosmopolites" include students, artists, writers, musicians, and entertainers, as well as other intellectuals and professionals. They live in the city in order to be near the special "cultural" facilities that can be located only near the center of the city. Many cosmopolites are unmarried or childless. Others rear children in the city, especially if they have the income to afford the aid of servants and governesses. The less affluent ones may move to the suburbs to raise their children, continuing to live as cosmopolites under considerable handicaps, especially in the lower-middle-class suburbs. Many of the very rich and powerful are also cosmopolites, although they are likely to have at least two residences, one of which is suburban or exurban.

The unmarried or childless must be divided into two subtypes, depending on the permanence or transience of their status. The temporarily unmarried or childless live in the inner city for only a limited time. Young adults may team up to rent an apartment away from their parents and close to job or entertainment opportunities. When they marry, they may move first to an apartment in a transient neighborhood, but if they can afford to do so, they leave for the outer city or the suburbs with the arrival of the first or second child. The permanently unmarried may stay in the inner city for the remainder of their lives, their housing depending on their income.

The "ethnic villagers" are ethnic groups which are found in such inner-city neighborhoods as New York's Lower East Side, living in some ways as they did when they were peasants in European or Puerto Rican villages.[9] Although they reside in the city, they isolate themselves from significant contact with most city facilities, aside from workplaces. Their way of life differs sharply from Wirth's urbanism in its emphasis on kinship and the primary group, the lack of anonymity and secondary-group contacts, the weakness of formal organizations, and the suspicion of anything and anyone outside their neighborhood.

The first two types live in the inner city by choice; the third is there partly because of necessity, partly because of tradition. The final two types are in the inner city because they have no other choice. One is the "deprived" population: the very poor; the emotionally disturbed or otherwise handicapped; broken families; and, most important, the nonwhite population. These urban dwellers must take the dilapidated housing and blighted neighborhoods to which the housing market relegates them, although among them are some for whom the slum is a hiding place or a temporary stopover to save money for a house in the outer city or the suburbs.[10]

The "trapped" are the people who stay behind when a neighborhood is invaded by nonresidential land uses or lower-status immigrants, because they cannot afford to move or are otherwise bound to their present location.[11] The "downward-mobiles" are a related type; they may have started life in a higher class position, but have been forced down in the socio-economic hierarchy and in the quality of their accommodations. Many of them are old people, living out their existence on small pensions.

These five types all live in dense and heterogeneous surroundings; yet they have such diverse ways of life that it is hard to see how density and heterogeneity could exert a common influence. Moreover, all but the last two types are isolated or detached from their neighborhood and thus from the social consequences which Wirth described.

When people who live together have social ties based on criteria other than mere common occupancy, they can set up social barriers, regardless of the physical closeness or the heterogeneity of their neighbors. The ethnic villagers are the best illustration. While a number of ethnic groups are usually found living together in the same neighborhood, they are able to isolate themselves from one another through a variety of social devices. Wirth himself recognized this when he wrote that "two groups can occupy a given area without losing their separate identity because each side is permitted to live its own inner life and each somehow fears or idealizes the other."[12] Although it is true that the children in these areas were often oblivious to the social barriers set up by their parents, at least until adolescence, it is doubtful whether their acculturation can be traced to the melting-pot effect as much as to the pervasive influence of the American culture that flowed into these areas from the outside.[13]

The cosmopolites, the unmarried, and the childless are *detached* from neighborhood life. The cosmopolites possess a distinct subculture which causes them to be uninterested in all but the most superficial contacts with their neighbors, somewhat like the ethnic villagers. The unmarried and childless are detached from neighborhood because of their life-cycle stage, which frees them from the routine family responsibilities that entail some relationship to the local area. In their choice of residence, the two types are therefore not concerned about their neighbors or the availability and quality of local community facilities. Even the well-to-do can choose expensive apartments in or near poor neighborhoods, because if they have children, these are sent to special schools and summer camps which effectively isolate them from neighbors. In addition, both types, but especially the childless and unmarried, are transient. Therefore, they tend to live in areas marked by high population turnover, where their own mobility and that of their neighbors creates a universal detachment from the neighborhood.[14]

The deprived and the trapped do seem to be affected by some of the consequences of number, density, and heterogeneity. The deprived population suffers considerably from overcrowding, but this is a consequence of low income, racial discrimination, and other handicaps and cannot be considered an inevitable result of the ecological make-up of the city.[15] Because the deprived have no residential choice, they are also forced to live amid neighbors not of their own choosing, with ways of life different and even contradictory to their own. If familial defenses against the neighborhood climate are weak, as may happen among broken families and downward-mobile people, parents may lose their children to the culture of "the street." The trapped are the unhappy people who remain behind when their more advantaged neighbors move on; they must endure the heterogeneity which results from neighborhood change.

Wirth's description of the urban way of life fits best the transient areas of the inner city. Such areas are typically heterogeneous in population, partly because they are inhabited by transient types who do not require homogeneous neighbors or by deprived people who have no choice or may themselves be quite mobile. Under conditions of transience and heterogeneity, people interact only in terms of the segmental roles necessary for obtaining local services. Their social relationships thus display anonymity, impersonality, and superficiality.[16]

The social features of Wirth's concept of urbanism seem, therefore, to be a result of residential instability, rather than of number, density, or heterogeneity. In fact, heterogeneity is itself an effect of residential instability, resulting when the influx of transients causes landlords and realtors to stop acting as gatekeepers—that is, wardens of neighborhood homogeneity.[17] Residential instability is found in all types of settlements, and presumably its social consequences are everywhere similar. These consequences cannot, therefore, be identified with the ways of life of the city.

The outer city and the suburbs

The second effect which Wirth ascribed to number, density, and heterogeneity was the segregation of homogeneous people into distinct neighborhoods[18] on the basis of "place and nature of work, income, racial and ethnic characteristics, social status, custom, habit, taste, preference and prejudice."[19] This description fits the residential districts of the *outer city*.[20] Although these districts contain the majority of the city's inhabitants, Wirth went into little detail about them. He made it clear, however, that the sociopsychological aspects of urbanism were prevalent there as well.[21]

Because existing neighborhood studies deal primarily with the exotic sections of the inner city, very little is known about the more typical residential neighborhoods of the outer city. However, it is evident that the way of life in these areas bears little resemblance to Wirth's urbanism. Both the studies which question Wirth's formulation and my own observations suggest that the common element in the ways of life of these neighborhoods is best described as *quasi-primary*. I use this term to characterize relationships between neighbors. Whatever the intensity or frequency of these relationships, the interaction is more intimate than a secondary contact, but more guarded than a primary one.[22]

There are actually few secondary relationships, because of the isolation of residential neighborhoods from economic institutions and workplaces. Even shopkeepers, store managers, and other local functionaries who live in the area are treated as acquaintances or friends, unless they are of a vastly different social status or are forced by their corporate employers to treat their customers as economic units.[23] Voluntary associations attract only a minority of the population. Moreover, much of the organizational activity is of a sociable nature, and it is often difficult to accomplish the association's "business" because of the members' preference for sociability. Thus, it would appear that interactions in organizations, or between neighbors generally, do not fit the secondary-relationship model of urban life. As anyone who has lived in these neighborhoods knows, there is little anonymity, impersonality, or privacy.[24] In fact, American cities have sometimes been described as collections of small towns.[25] There is some truth to this description, especially if the city is compared to the actual small town, rather than to the romantic construct of antiurban critics.[26]

Postwar suburbia represents the most contemporary version of the quasi-primary way of life. Owing to increases in real income and the encouragement of homeownership provided by the F.H.A., families in the lower middle class and upper working class can now live in modern single-family homes in low-density subdivisions, an opportunity previously available only to the upper and upper-middle classes.[27]

The popular literature describes the new suburbs as communities in which conformity, homogeneity, and other-direction are unusually rampant.[28] The implication is that the move from city to suburb initiates a new way of life which causes considerable behavior and personality change in

previous urbanites. A preliminary analysis of data which I am now col-
lecting in Levittown, New Jersey, suggests, however, that the move from
the city to this predominantly lower-middle-class suburb does not result
in any major behavioral changes for most people. Moreover, the changes
which do occur reflect the move from the social isolation of a transient
city or suburban apartment building to the quasi-primary life of a neighborhood of single-family homes. Also, many of the people whose life has
changed report that the changes were intended. They existed as aspirations before the move or as reasons for it. In other words, the suburb
itself creates few changes in ways of life.[29]

A comparison of city and suburb

If urban and suburban areas are similar in that the way of life in both
is quasi-primary, and if urban residents who move out to the suburbs do
not undergo any significant changes in behavior, it is fair to argue that
the differences in ways of life between the two types of settlements have
been overestimated. Yet the fact remains that a variety of physical and
demographic differences exist between the city and the suburb. However,
upon closer examination, many of these differences turn out to be either
spurious or of little significance for the way of life of the inhabitants.[30]

The differences between the residential areas of cities and suburbs
which have been cited most frequently are:

1. Suburbs are more likely to be dormitories.
2. They are further away from the work and play facilities of the
central business districts.
3. They are newer and more modern than city residential areas and
are designed for the automobile rather than for pedestrian and mass-
transit forms of movement.
4. They are built up with single-family rather than multifamily structures and are therefore less dense.
5. Their populations are more homogeneous.
6. Their populations differ demographically: they are younger; more
of them are married; they have higher incomes; and they hold pro-
portionately more white collar jobs.[31]

Most urban neighborhoods are as much dormitories as the suburbs.
Only in a few older inner-city areas are factories and offices still located
in the middle of residential blocks, and even here many of the employees
do not live in the neighborhood.

The fact that the suburbs are farther from the central business district
is often true only in terms of distance, not travel time. Moreover, most
people make relatively little use of downtown facilities, other than work-

places.[32] The downtown stores seem to hold their greatest attraction for the upper-middle class;[33] the same is probably true of typically urban entertainment facilities. Teen-agers and young adults may take their dates to first-run movie theaters, but the museums, concert halls, and lecture rooms attract mainly upper-middle-class ticket-buyers, many of them suburban.[34]

The suburban reliance on the train and the automobile has given rise to an imaginative folklore about the consequences of commuting on alcohol consumption, sex life, and parental duties. Many of these conclusions are, however, drawn from selected high-income suburbs and exurbs and reflect job tensions in such hectic occupations as advertising and show business more than the effects of residence.[35] It is true that the upper-middle-class housewife must become a chauffeur in order to expose her children to the proper educational facilities, but such differences as walking to the corner drugstore and driving to its suburban equivalent seem to me of little emotional, social, or cultural import.[36] In addition, the continuing shrinkage in the number of mass transit users suggests that even in the city many younger people are now living a wholly auto-based way of life.

The fact that suburbs are smaller is primarily a function of political boundaries drawn long before the communities were suburban. This affects the kinds of political issue which develop and provides somewhat greater opportunity for citizen participation. Even so, in the suburbs as in the city, the minority who participate are the professional politicians, the economically concerned businessmen, lawyers, and salesmen, and the ideologically motivated middle- and upper-middle-class people with better than average education.

The social consequences of differences in density and house type also seem overrated. Single-family houses on quiet streets facilitate the supervision of children; this is one reason why middle-class women who want to keep an eye on their children move to the suburbs. House type also has some effects on relationships between neighbors, insofar as there are more opportunities for visual contact between adjacent homeowners than between people on different floors of an apartment house. However, if occupants' characteristics are also held constant, the differences in actual social contact are less marked. Homogeneity of residents turns out to be more important than proximity as a determinant of sociability. If the population is heterogeneous, there is little social contact between neighbors, either on apartment-house floors or in single-family-house blocks; if people are homogeneous, there is likely to be considerable social contact in both house types. One need only contrast the apartment house located in a transient, heterogeneous neighborhood and exactly the same structure in a neighborhood occupied by a single ethnic group. The former is a lonely, anonymous building; the latter, a bustling microsociety. I have observed similar patterns in suburban areas: on blocks where people are homogeneous, they socialize; where they are heterogeneous, they do little more than exchange polite greetings.[37]

Suburbs are usually described as being more homogeneous in house type than the city, but if they are compared to the outer city, the differences are small. Most inhabitants of the outer city, other than well-to-do homeowners, live on blocks of uniform structures as well; for example, the endless streets of row houses in Philadelphia and Baltimore or of two-story duplexes and six-flat apartment houses in Chicago. They differ from the new suburbs only in that they were erected through more primitive methods of mass production. Suburbs are, of course, more predominantly areas of owner-occupied single homes, though in the outer districts of most American cities homeownership is also extremely high.

Demographically, suburbs as a whole are clearly more homogeneous than cities as a whole, though probably not more so than outer cities. However, people do not live in cities or suburbs as a whole, but in specific neighborhoods. An analysis of ways of life would require a determination of the degree of population homogeneity within the boundaries of areas defined as neighborhoods by residents' social contacts. Such an analysis would no doubt indicate that many neighborhoods in the city as well as the suburbs are homogeneous. Neighborhood homogeneity is actually a result of factors having little or nothing to do with the house type, density, or location of the area relative to the city limits. Brand new neighborhoods are more homogeneous than older ones, because they have not yet experienced resident turnover, which frequently results in population heterogeneity. Neighborhoods of low- and medium-priced housing are usually less homogeneous than those with expensive dwellings because they attract families who have reached the peak of occupational and residential mobility, as well as young families who are just starting their climb and will eventually move to neighborhoods of higher status. The latter, being accessible only to high-income people, are therefore more homogeneous with respect to other resident characteristics as well. Moreover, such areas have the economic and political power to slow down or prevent invasion. Finally, neighborhoods located in the path of ethnic or religious group movement are likely to be extremely homogeneous.

The demographic differences between cities and suburbs cannot be questioned, especially since the suburbs have attracted a large number of middle-class child-rearing families. The differences are, however, much reduced if suburbs are compared only to the outer city. In addition, a detailed comparison of suburban and outer-city residential areas would show that neighborhoods with the same kinds of people can be found in the city as well as the suburbs. Once again, the age of the area and the cost of housing are more important determinants of demographic characteristics than the location of the area with respect to the city limits.

Characteristics, social organization, and ecology

The preceding sections of the paper may be summarized in three propositions:

1. As concerns ways of life, the inner city must be distinguished from the outer city and the suburbs; and the latter two exhibit a way of life bearing little resemblance to Wirth's urbanism.

2. Even in the inner city, ways of life resemble Wirth's description only to a limited extent. Moreover, economic condition, cultural characteristics, life-cycle stage, and residential instability explain ways of life more satisfactorily than number, density, or heterogeneity.

3. Physical and other differences between city and suburb are often spurious or without much meaning for ways of life.

These propositions suggest that the concepts "urban" and "suburban" are neither mutually exclusive nor especially relevant for understanding ways of life. They—and number, density, and heterogeneity as well—are ecological concepts which describe human adaptation to the environment. However, they are not sufficient to explain social phenomena, because these phenomena cannot be understood solely as the consequences of ecological processes. Therefore, other explanations must be considered.

Ecological explanations of social life are most applicable if the subjects under study lack the ability to *make choices,* be they plants, animals, or human beings. Thus, if there is a housing shortage, people will live almost anywhere, and under extreme conditions of no choice, as in a disaster, married and single, old and young, middle and working class, stable and transient will be found side by side in whatever accommodations are available. At that time, their ways of life represent an almost direct adaptation to the environment. If the supply of housing and of neighborhoods is such that alternatives are available, however, people will make choices, and if the housing market is responsive, they can even make and satisfy explicit *demands.*

Choices and demands do not develop independently or at random; they are functions of the roles people play in the social system. These can best be understood in terms of the *characteristics* of the people involved;

that is, characteristics can be used as indices to choices and demands made in the roles that constitute ways of life. Although many characteristics affect the choices and demands people make with respect to housing and neighborhoods, the most important ones seem to be *class*—in all its economic, social, and cultural ramifications—and *life-cycle stage*.[38] If people have an opportunity to choose, these two characteristics will go far in explaining the kinds of housing and neighborhood they will occupy and the ways of life they will try to establish within them.

Many of the previous assertions about ways of life in cities and suburbs can be analyzed in terms of class and life-cycle characteristics. Thus, in the inner city, the unmarried and childless live as they do, detached from neighborhood, because of their life-cycle stage; the cosmopolites, because of a combination of life-cycle stage and a distinctive but class-based subculture. The way of life of the deprived and trapped can be explained by low socioeconomic level and related handicaps. The quasi-primary way of life is associated with the family stage of the life cycle and the norms of child-rearing and parental role found in the upper working class, the lower-middle class, and the noncosmopolite portions of the upper-middle and upper classes.

The attributes of the so-called suburban way of life can also be understood largely in terms of these characteristics. The new suburbia is nothing more than a highly visible showcase for the ways of life of young, upper-working-class and lower-middle-class people. Ktsanes and Reissman have aptly described it as "new homes for old values."[39] Much of the descriptive and critical writing about suburbia assumes that as long as the new suburbanites lived in the city, they behaved like upper-middle-class cosmopolites and that suburban living has mysteriously transformed them.[40] The critics fail to see that the behavior and personality patterns ascribed to suburbia are in reality those of class and age.[41] These patterns could have been found among the new suburbanites when they still lived in the city and could now be observed among their peers who still reside there—if the latter were as visible to critics and researchers as are the suburbanites.

Needless to say, the concept of "characteristics" cannot explain all aspects of ways of life, among either urban or suburban residents. Some aspects must be explained by concepts of social organization that are independent of characteristics. For example, some features of the quasi-primary way of life are independent of class and age, because they evolve from the roles and situations created by joint and adjacent occupancy of land and dwellings. Likewise, residential instability is a universal process which has a number of invariate consequences. In each case, however, the way in which people react varies with their characteristics. So it is with ecological processes. Thus, there are undoubtedly differences between ways of life in urban and suburban settlements which remain after behavior patterns based on residents' characteristics have been analyzed and which must therefore be attributed to features of the settlement.[42]

Characteristics do not explain the causes of behavior; rather, they are clues to socially created and culturally defined roles, choices, and demands. A causal analysis must trace them to the larger social, economic, and political systems which determine the situations in which roles are played and the cultural content of choices and demands, as well as the opportunities for their achievement.[43] These systems determine income distributions, educational and occupational opportunities, and, in turn, fertility patterns and child-rearing methods, as well as the entire range of consumer behavior. Thus, a complete analysis of the way of life of the deprived residents of the inner city cannot stop at indicating the influence of low income, lack of education, or family instability. These must be related to such conditions as the urban economy's "need" for low-wage workers and the housing-market practices which restrict residential choice. The urban economy is in turn shaped by national economic and social systems, as well as by local and regional ecological processes. Some phenomena can be explained exclusively by reference to these ecological processes. However, it must also be recognized that as man has gained greater control over the natural environment, he has been able to free himself from many of the determining and limiting effects of that environment. Thus, changes in local transportation technology, the ability of industries to be foot-loose, and the relative affluence of American society have given ever larger numbers of people increasing amounts of residential choice. The greater the amount of choice available, the more important the concept of characteristics becomes in understanding behavior.

Consequently, the study of ways of life in communities must begin with an analysis of characteristics. If characteristics are dealt with first and held constant, we may be able to discover which behavior patterns can be attributed to features of the settlement and its natural environment.[44] Only then will it be possible to discover to what extent city and suburb are independent—rather than dependent or intervening—variables in the explanation of ways of life.

This kind of analysis might help to reconcile the ecological point of view with the behavioral and cultural one and possibly put an end to the conflict between conceptual positions which insist on one explanation or the other.[45] Both explanations have some relevance, and future research and theory must clarify the role of each in the analysis of ways of life in various types of settlement.[46] Another important rationale for this approach is its usefulness for applied sociology; for example, city planning. The planner can recommend changes in the spatial and physical arrangements of the city. Frequently, he seeks to achieve social goals or to change social conditions through physical solutions. He has been attracted to ecological explanations because these relate behavior to phenomena which he can affect. For example, most planners tend to agree with Wirth's formulations because they stress number and density, over which the planner has some control. If the undesirable social conditions of the inner city could be traced to these two factors, the planner could propose large-scale clearance projects which would reduce the size of the urban population and lower residential densities. Experience with public housing projects has, however, made it apparent that low densities, new buildings, or modern site plans do not eliminate antisocial or self-destructive behavior. The analysis of characteristics will call attention to the fact that this behavior is lodged in the deprivations of low socioeconomic status and racial discrimination and that it can be changed only through the removal of these deprivations. Conversely, if such an analysis suggests residues of behavior that can be attributed to ecological processes or physical aspects of housing and neighborhoods, the planner can recommend physical changes that can really affect behavior.

A re-evaluation of definitions

The argument presented here has implications for the sociological definition of the city. Such a definition relates ways of life to environmental features of the city qua settlement type. But if ways of life do not coincide with settlement types, and if these ways are functions of class and life-cycle stage rather than of the ecological attributes of the settlement, a sociological definition of the city cannot be formulated.[47] Concepts such as "city" and "suburb" allow us to distinguish settlement types from each other physically and demographically, but the ecological processes and conditions which they synthesize have no direct or invariate consequences for ways of life. The sociologist cannot, therefore, speak of an urban or suburban way of life.

Conclusion

Many of the descriptive statements made here are as time-bound as Wirth's.[48] In the 1940's Wirth concluded that some form of urbanism would eventually predominate in all settlement types. He was, however, writing during a time of immigrant acculturation and at the end of a serious depression, an era of minimal choice. Today, it is apparent that high-density, heterogeneous surroundings are for most people a temporary place of residence; other than for the Park Avenue or Greenwich Village cosmopolites, they are a result of necessity, rather than choice. As soon as they can afford to do so, most Americans head for the single-family house and the quasi-primary way of life of the low-density neighborhood, in the outer city or the suburbs.[49]

Changes in the national economy and in government housing policy can affect many of the variables that make up housing supply and demand. For example, urban sprawl may eventually outdistance the ability of present and proposed transportation systems to move workers into the city; further industrial decentralization can forestall it and alter the entire relationship between work and residence. The expansion of present urban-renewal activities can perhaps lure a significant number of cosmopolites back from the suburbs, while a drastic change in renewal policy might begin to ameliorate the housing conditions of the deprived population. A serious depression could once again make America a nation of doubled-up tenants.

These events will affect housing supply and residential choice; they will frustrate, but not suppress, demands for the quasi-primary way of life. However, changes in the national economy, society, and culture can affect people's characteristics—family size, educational level, and various other concomitants of life-cycle stage and class. These in turn will stimulate changes in demands and choices. The rising number of college graduates, for example, is likely to increase the cosmopolite ranks. This might in turn create a new set of city dwellers, although it will probably do no more than encourage the development of cosmopolite facilities in some suburban areas.

The current revival of interest in urban sociology and in community studies, as well as the sociologist's increasing curiosity about city planning, suggests that data may soon be available to formulate a more adequate theory of the relationship between settlements and the ways of life within them. The speculations presented in this essay are intended to raise questions; they can be answered only by more systematic data collection and theorizing.

NOTES

1. Louis Wirth, "Urbanism as a Way of Life," *American Journal of Sociology,* XLIV (July 1938), 1-24. Reprinted in Paul Hatt and Albert J. Reiss, Jr., eds., *Cities and Society* (Glencoe, Ill.: The Free Press, 1957), pp. 46-64.

2. Richard Dewey, "The Rural–Urban Continuum: Real but Relatively Unimportant," *American Journal of Sociology,* LXVI (July 1960), 60–66.

3. I shall not attempt to summarize these studies, for this task has already been performed by Dewey, Reiss, Wilensky, and others. The studies include:

Morris Axelrod, "Urban Structure and Social Participation," *American Sociological Review,* XXI (February 1956), 13–18.

Dewey, *op. cit.*

William H. Form *et al.,* "The Compatibility of Alternative Approaches to the Delimitation of Urban Sub-areas," *American Sociological Review,* XIX (August 1954), 434–440.

Herbert J. Gans, *The Urban Villagers* (New York: Free Press of Glencoe, 1962).

Scott Greer, "Urbanism Reconsidered: A Comparative Study of Local Areas in a Metropolis," *American Sociological Review,* XXI (February 1956), 19–25.

Scott Greer and Ella Kube, "Urbanism and Social Structure: A Los Angeles Study," in Marvin B. Sussman, ed., *Community Structure and Analysis* (New York: Crowell, 1959), pp. 93–112.

Morris Janowitz, *The Community Press in an Urban Setting* (Glencoe, Ill.: The Free Press, 1952).

Albert J. Reiss, Jr., "An Analysis of Urban Phenomena," in Robert M. Fisher, ed., *The Metropolis in Modern Life* (Garden City, N.Y.: Doubleday, 1955), pp. 41–49.

Albert J. Reiss, Jr., "Rural-Urban and Status Differences in Interpersonal Contacts," *American Journal of Sociology,* LXV (September 1959), 182–195.

John R. Seeley, "The Slum: Its Nature, Use, and Users," *Journal of the American Institute of Planners,* XXV (February 1959), 7–14.

Joel Smith, William Form, and Gregory Stone, "Local Intimacy in a Middle-Sized City," *American Journal of Sociology,* LX (November 1954), 276–284.

Gregory P. Stone, "City Shoppers and Urban Identification: Observations on the Social Psychology of City Life," *American Journal of Sociology,* LX (July 1954), 36–45.

William F. Whyte, *Street Corner Society* (Chicago: University of Chicago Press, 1955).

Harold L. Wilensky and Charles Lebeaux, *Industrial Society and Social Welfare* (New York: Russell Sage Foundation, 1958).

Michael Young and Peter Willmott, *Family and Kinship in East London* (London: Routledge and Kegan Paul, 1957).

4. Greer and Kube, *op. cit.,* p. 112.

5. Wilensky, *op. cit.,* p. 121.

6. By the *inner city* I mean the transient residential areas, the Gold Coasts and the slums that generally surround the central business district, although in some communities they may continue for miles beyond that district. The *outer city* includes the stable residential areas that house the working- and middle-class tenant and owner. The *suburbs* I conceive as the latest and most modern ring of the outer city, distinguished from it only by yet lower densities and by the often irrelevant fact of the ring's location outside the city limits.

7. Louis Wirth, *The Ghetto* (Chicago: University of Chicago Press, 1928).

8. Arnold M. Rose, "Living Arrangements of Unattached Persons," *American Sociological Review,* XII (August 1947), 429–435.

9. Gans, *op. cit.*

10. Seeley, *op. cit.*

11. *Ibid.* The trapped are not very visible, but I suspect that they are a significant

element in what Raymond Vernon has described as the "gray areas" of the city in his *Changing Economic Function of the Central City* (New York: Committee on Economic Development, Supplementary Paper No. 1, January 1959).

12. Wirth, *The Ghetto*, p. 283.

13. If the melting pot had resulted from propinquity and high density, one would have expected second-generation Italians, Irish, Jews, Greeks, and Slavs, to have developed a single "pan-ethnic culture," consisting of a synthesis of the cultural patterns of the propinquitous national groups.

14. The corporation transients, who provide a new source of residential instability to the suburb, differ from city transients. Since they are raising families, they want to integrate themselves into neighborhood life and are usually able to do so, mainly because they tend to move into similar types of communities wherever they go. See William H. Whyte, Jr., *The Organization Man* (New York: Simon and Schuster, 1956), and Wilensky and Lebeaux, *op. cit.*

15. The negative social consequences of overcrowding are a result of high room and floor density, not of the land coverage of population density which Wirth discussed. Park Avenue residents live under conditions of high land density, but do not seem to suffer visibly from overcrowding.

16. Whether or not these social phenomena have the psychological consequences Wirth suggested depends on the people who live in the area. Those who are detached from the neighborhood by choice are probably immune, but those who depend on the neighborhood for their social relationships—the unattached individuals, for example—may suffer greatly from loneliness.

17. Needless to say, residential instability must ultimately be traced to the fact that, as Wirth pointed out, the city and its economy attract transient—and, depending on the sources of outmigration, heterogeneous—people. However, this is a characteristic of urban-industrial society, not of the city specifically.

18. By neighborhoods or residential districts I mean areas demarcated from others by distinctive physical boundaries or by social characteristics, some of which may be perceived only by the residents. However, these areas are not necessarily socially self-sufficient or culturally distinctive.

19. Wirth, "Urbanism as a Way of Life," p. 56.

20. For the definition of *outer city,* see note 6.

21. Wirth, "Urbanism as a Way of Life," p. 56.

22. Because neighborly relations are not quite primary and not quite secondary, they can also become *pseudo-primary,* that is, secondary ones disguised with false affect to make them appear primary. Critics have often described suburban life in this fashion, although the actual prevalence of pseudo-primary relationships has not been studied systematically in cities or suburbs.

23. Stone, *op. cit.*

24. These neighborhoods cannot, however, be considered as urban folk societies. People go out of the area for many of their friendships, and their allegiance to the neighborhood is neither intense nor all-encompassing. Janowitz has aptly described the relationship between residents and neighborhoods as one of "limited liability." *Op. cit.,* Chapter 7.

25. Were I not arguing that ecological concepts cannot double as sociological ones, this way of life might best be described as small-townish.

26. Arthur J. Vidich and Joseph Bensman, *Small Town in Mass Society: Class, Power and Religion in a Rural Community* (Princeton, N.J.: Princeton University Press, 1958).

27. Harold Wattel, "Levittown: A Suburban Community," in William M. Dobriner, ed., *The Suburban Community* (New York: Putnam, 1958), pp. 287–313.

28. Bennett Berger, *Working Class Suburb: A Study of Auto Workers in Suburbia* (Berkeley: University of California Press, 1960). Also Vernon, *op. cit.*

29. Berger, *op. cit.*

30. Wattel, *op. cit.* They may, of course, be significant for the welfare of the total metropolitan area.

31. Otis Dudley Duncan and Albert J. Reiss, Jr., *Social Characteristics of Rural and Urban Communities, 1950* (New York: Wiley, 1956), p. 131.

32. Donald L. Foley, "The Use of Local Facilities in a Metropolis," in Hatt and Reiss, *op. cit.*, pp. 237–247. Also see Christen T. Jonassen, *The Shopping Center versus Downtown* (Columbus: Bureau of Business Research, Ohio State University, 1955).

33. Jonassen, *op. cit.*, pp. 91–92.

34. A 1958 study of New York theatergoers showed a median income of close to $10,000, and 35 per cent were reported as living in the suburbs. John Enders, *Profile of the Theater Market* (New York: Playbill, undated and unpaged).

35. A. C. Spectorsky, *The Exurbanites* (Philadelphia: Lippincott, 1955).

36. I am thinking here of adults; teen-agers do suffer from the lack of informal meeting places within walking or bicycling distance.

37. Herbert J. Gans, "Planning and Social Life: Friendship and Neighbor Relations in Suburban Communities," *Journal of the American Institute of Planners,* XXVII (May 1961), 134–140.

38. These must be defined in dynamic terms. Thus, class includes also the process of social mobility, the stage in the life cycle, and the processes of socialization and aging.

39. Thomas Ktsanes and Leonard Reissman, "Suburbia: New Homes for Old Values," *Social Problems,* VII (Winter 1959–1960), 187–194.

40. Leonard J. Duhl, "Mental Health and Community Planning," in *Planning 1955* (Chicago: American Society of Planning Officials, 1956), pp. 31–39. Erich Fromm, *The Sane Society* (New York: Rinehart, 1955), pp. 154–162. David Riesman, "The Suburban Sadness," in Dobriner, *op. cit.*, pp. 375–408. W. Whyte, *The Organization Man, op. cit.*

41. William M. Dobriner, "Introduction: Theory and Research in the Sociology of the Suburbs," in Dobriner, *op. cit.*, pp. xiii–xxviii.

42. Sylvia Fleis Fava, "Contrasts in Neighboring: New York City and a Suburban Community," in Dobriner, *op. cit.*, pp. 122–131.

43. This formulation may answer some of Duncan and Schnore's objections to sociopsychological and cultural explanations of community ways of life. Otis Dudley Duncan and Leo F. Schnore, "Cultural, Behavioral and Ecological Perspectives in the Study of Social Organization," *American Journal of Sociology,* LXV (September 1959), 132–155.

44. The ecologically oriented researchers who developed the Shevsky-Bell social-area analysis scale have worked on the assumption that "social differences between the populations of urban neighborhoods can conveniently be summarized into differences of economic level, family characteristics and ethnicity." Wendell Bell and Maryanne T. Force, "Urban Neighborhood Types and Participation in Formal Associations," *American Sociological Review,* XXI (February 1956), 25–34. However, they have equated "urbanization" with a concept of life-cycle stage by using family characteristics to define the index of urbanization. *Ibid.* Also see Scott Greer, "The Social Structure and Political Process of Suburbia," *American Sociological Review,* XXV (August 1960), 514–526, and Greer and Kube, *op. cit.* In fact, Bell has identified suburbanism with familism: Wendell Bell, "Social Choice, Life Styles and Suburban Residence," in Dobriner, *op. cit.*, pp. 225–247.

45. Duncan and Schnore, *op. cit.*
46. Dobriner, "Introduction," in Dobriner, *op. cit.,* p. xxii.
47. Because of the distinctiveness of the ways of life found in the inner city, some writers propose definitions that refer only to these ways, ignoring those found in the outer city. For example, popular writers sometimes identify "urban" with "urbanity," that is, "cosmopolitanism." However, such a definition ignores the other ways of life found in the inner city. Moreover, I have tried to show that these ways have few common elements and that the ecological features of the inner city have little or no influence in shaping them.
48. Even more than Wirth's they are based on data and impressions gathered in the large eastern and midwestern cities of the United States.
49. Personal discussions with European planners and sociologists suggest that many European apartment dwellers have similar preferences, although economic conditions, high building costs, and the scarcity of land make it impossible for them to achieve their desires.

Part II CITY PLANNING AND GOAL-ORIENTED PLANNING

Introduction

If the physical environment plays only a minor role in people's lives and the community is not the most important social group in which these lives take place, traditional planning comes close to being irrelevant. The essays in Part II explore this thesis and propose an alternative, which I call goal-oriented planning.

The basic idea behind goal-oriented planning is simple; that planners must begin with the goals of the community—and of its people—and then develop those programs which constitute the best means for achieving the community's goals, taking care that the consequences of these programs do not result in undesirable behavioral or cost consequences.

This conception of planning I owe to Martin Meyerson and to a study that he, John Dyckman, and I undertook with a grant from the Russell Sage Foundation testing, his conception by an analysis of planning for health, education, and recreation facilities. Our first step was to identify the goals and behavior patterns of various actors connected with these facilities. These actors we thought of as the *suppliers* (for example, recreation officials), the *users* (of parks and playgrounds), and the *community,* by which we meant the decision-makers and the residents qua citizens (and members of interest groups), but also the public interest. Once goals had been determined, largely through sociological analyses, we hoped to use empirical behavioral data to determine what programs would best achieve the various goals of these actors and with what consequences, the eventual aim being a handbook which would tell the planner what programs and consequences were related to a specific goal. Beyond that, we sought to evaluate the goals of the various actors, determine which ought to be pursued by the community in planning for the three kinds of facilities, and suggest the order of priority for this pursuit. For example, in recreation planning, we wanted to tell the planner not only what programs would achieve the recreation goals of the suppliers and the users of public recreation but also what kind of goals the community ought to be pursuing to provide its residents with an opportunity for satisfying leisure behavior, which might well ignore the traditional facilities offered by the suppliers and might even preclude formal facilities. We hoped eventually to carry out such analysis not just for the individual facilities we were studying but for all community functions in relation to each other, so that the planner had some criteria for deciding whether to invest the community's incremental dollar or acre in housing, or education, or industry, or sewage disposal, or a tax cut.

The study was generated by two ideas held by Meyerson. First, he argued that city planning was irrational; that the programs it was proposing often did not achieve the goals it was advocating and led to undesirable consequences for the community as well. Second, he pointed out that the so-called planning "standards" by which planners determined what facilities ought to be provided by the community—for example, that one acre of playground should be allotted for every thousand people, or that three dollars per capita should be spent annually for public library operations —were only implementing the goals of the suppliers of recreation and library facilities. As a result, the suppliers obtained larger shares of the municipal budget, political power, and community prestige, but often neglected the demands of users, resulting in facilities that were underutilized or that appealed only to a narrow proportion of the total population. Moreover, applying these standards for capital investments meant commitments to operating expenditures and the provision of services without considering the consequences of such commitments. For example, the conventional standards for hospital construction also committed the community to existing hospitals so that public funds were being devoted to a medical practice which emphasized prolonging the life of the old and chronically ill. The planner, Meyerson suggested, should not accept such implicit choices; he should ask the basic planning question: For what health goals for what members of the community should public resources be allocated and in what order of priority?

Partly because of the ambitious scope of the study, it has not yet been published, but thinking through the various problems we tackled—I took on planning for recreation facilities—left me with several basic principles which I have since tried to apply as a planner and a writer about planning: that unless there are good reasons to the contrary, planning ought to be user-oriented and that public priority determinations ought to be compensatory wherever possible, so that the members of the community who obtained the least resources from the private sectors of society ought to obtain the most from the public sector.

Few of our basic ideas were original, and today, they have become almost commonplace in planning, at least in its lip service. Planners talk freely and loosely about the goals they are seeking to implement, although their actual plans usually still feature the traditional solutions of physical planning. Meanwhile, other professionals have developed approaches similar to the one we were advocating, and as I predicted in 1958 (in the second essay reprinted in Part II), they have now begun to replace the city planners in some city-planning functions. Initially, the cities turned to practitioners of linear programing and operations analysis, but these methods usually avoid the most difficult question of what goals are to be pursued. Today, they are themselves being superseded by Social Accounting and Program-Planning-Budgeting (P.P.B.), which try not only to relate programs to goals and resources but also to ask questions about the choice of goals.

Whether or not these questions can ever be answered systematically or operationally remains to be seen; the methodological problems of quantifying so-called social goals are serious, and even if they can be solved, the planner's recommendations on goal choice must still be reconciled with the goals chosen by elected officials and with those of the citizens, which are, after all, the goals the planners and elected officials ought to be pursuing. In a heterogeneous community however—and few communities are not heterogeneous—citizen goals are always diverse and often in conflict with one another, and which goals of which citizens ought to be ranked in what order in the community's public allocations is hard to determine. Such questions are political, of course, but they ought to be answered systematically as well as democratically, and no one has yet invented a viable method to complement the politicians' *ad hoc* solutions.

The essays reprinted here grapple with only some of these issues. The first is a sociological analysis of the planning profession, written as much for social scientists and the general public as for planners, which tries to explain why planning has been predominantly physical so far, and why it is turning more to people and their goals, and to the rational determination of means.

The other essays, written much earlier, discuss and apply the goal-oriented approach. Chapters 6 and 7 describe the approach. They were written in Puerto Rico, where economic planning had blossomed, and had even been given priority over physical planning. Then, in the late 1950's, Governor Muñoz Marín, concerned that the Central Planning

Board's emphasis on economic and physical planning was wreaking havoc with the quality of life on the island, asked the Board to plan for the preservation of Puerto Rican culture. Although his purpose seemed to have been to save a dying traditional, agrarian—and quite aristocratic— culture, the local planners, Puerto Rican and mainland in origin, and the many consultants invited to work with them interpreted his request more broadly. They tried to figure out what goals ought to be pursued by the Puerto Rican government for its society, and in the process, they rein-vented the now popular term *social planning,* although what they meant by it had little to do with the current definition, which is a euphemism for planning activities that benefit the poor.

The memorandum on social planning which summarized two weeks of consultation with the Puerto Rican planners was intended to help establish a work program for the Social Planning Division, including an annual Social Report to the Governor. Now, ten years later, Washington is con-sidering the creation of a Federal Council of Social Advisors, the prep-aration of an annual Social Report, and the application of "Social Accounting" by federal agencies to build "social" goals into their decision-making procedures.

Chapters 8 and 9 apply the goal-oriented approach to the two public facilities I studied while working with Meyerson and Dyckman: the library and recreation. The essay on the library is actually an amalgam of two papers; parts I and II were written to explain our approach to a conference of sociologists; Part III, prepared for a conference of librarians and planners, and of later vintage, sought to define the role of the public library vis-à-vis the urban poor. The essay on public recreation deals ostensibly with whether parks, playgrounds, and other "open spaces" are good for mental health, a question which the Outdoor Recreation Re-sources Review Commission was under political pressure to answer positively. Since I was skeptical about there being a simple one-to-one relationship between recreation and mental health, and since there were no empirical findings which demonstrated that recreation is important in preventing or curing mental illness, I argued that the Commission ought to adopt a user-oriented approach to recreation, feeling that if people en-joyed their leisure activities, their mental health could not possibly be impaired as a result.

5

City Planning in America: A Sociological Analysis

I

In its generic sense, planning is a method of decision-making which proposes or identifies goals or ends, determines the means or programs which achieve or are thought to achieve these ends, and does so by the application of analytical techniques to discover the fit between ends and means and the consequences of implementing alternative ends and means. Planning can be used to shape an individual's decisions, but most often it is carried out by large social systems to determine long-range ends and means. City planning applies this method to determine public investment and other policies regarding future growth and change by municipalities and metropolitan areas.

Although the city-planning profession and the city-planning agency are inventions of the twentieth century, city planning has existed ever since men began to build towns and to make decisions about their future. In most societies, but particularly in America, there has been little consensus about these decisions. The diverse classes, ethnic groups, and interest groups who live in the city have different conceptions of how the city ought to grow and change, what aspects of city development ought to be encouraged or discouraged by public policies, and who should benefit from policy and allocation decisions. Consequently, these groups have attempted, directly or indirectly, to influence the ends, means, and techniques of planning and even the role of the planners. A sociological analysis of American city planning must therefore ask: Who plans with what ends and means for which interest groups? Since the variables in this paradigm are affected by changes in the population and power structure of the American city, the analysis is best carried out historically.

Adapted with the permission of the publisher from "Planning, Social: II. Regional and Urban Planning," in David Sills, ed., *International Encyclopedia of the Social Sciences* (New York: The Macmillan Co. and The Free Press, 1968) XII, 129–137. Copyright © 1968 by Crowell Collier and Macmillan, Inc. The present version has a longer text and a shorter list of references than the Encyclopedia entry.

II

American city planning can be said to have begun with the laying out of the infant country's first cities, usually by engineers who mapped grid schemes of rectangular blocks and lots, largely for the benefit of land sellers and builders.[1] Most American cities came into being without prior planning, however, and with only sporadic attempts to regulate their growth. By the middle of the nineteenth century, therefore, the major cities were marked by ugliness, inefficiency, and disorder. The provision of utilities and other municipal services could not keep up with the rapid increase in population, and the cities became overcrowded and congested, with vast slums in which epidemics, unchecked crime, and political corruption were commonplace. Shortly before the Civil War, these conditions stimulated the formation of a number of civic reform movements[2] which were the forebears of contemporary city planning and of the ends and means it still emphasizes today.

The reform groups were made up of predominantly Protestant and upper-middle-class civic and religious leaders, whose major end was the restoration of order. They sought physical order through slum clearance and the construction of model tenements to improve housing conditions[3] and through the park and playground movement which tried to preserve the supposedly health-giving features of the countryside by building parks and other recreational facilities in the crowded areas. They sought social order through the erection of educational and character-building facilities such as schools, libraries, and settlement houses, hoping that these would Americanize the immigrants and make them middle-class in order to eradicate crime, vice, and even the harmless forms of lower-class hedonism. They promoted political order through the "good government" movement, which advocated nonpolitical methods of urban decision-making to eliminate the new political machines and the fledgling socialist movement. On a less manifest level, they were attempting to maintain the cultural and political power they had held before the arrival of the immigrants by imposing on the city the physical and social structure of the Protestant middle class, particularly as it then existed in rural areas and small, preindustrial market towns.

The means by which they proposed to achieve these ends included new legislation to regulate and control city growth; the use of public administration and later scientific management procedures to run the city; and the establishment of "facilities" such as parks and settlement houses, which would improve living conditions and alter the behavior of their users. After the reformers had built a few model facilities with private funds in the slums of several eastern cities, they realized that they lacked the resources to alter the entire city by this approach and so began to use their considerable social status and what remained of their political influence to propose that the cities take over their programs as municipal functions. In this process, they developed principles and "standards" to make sure that the facilities would be provided in the proper quantity and quality. For example, as early as 1890, the "playground movement" had begun to formulate standards specifying the number, size, and equipping of playgrounds, and in 1910, it proposed that there be one playground of two to three acres within a half-mile of every child and at least thirty square feet of playground space for every child in that service area.[4] Groups promoting other facilities developed similar standards, revised versions of which are still in use today.

The reformers' efforts were supported by other interest groups in the city who were threatened by the expanding slums and their immigrant population and who proposed two additional ends: beauty and efficiency. Architects who had set up a City Beautiful movement during the 1890's developed park and civic-center schemes to enhance the downtown districts of the city; for example, the Burnham plan for Chicago.[5] These plans were supported by downtown business and property interests, who wanted to promote land values in these areas and also advocated efficiency in government to keep taxes low. They were joined by property owners in high-income residential areas who were concerned about the invasion of commercial and industrial establishments and slums into these areas as the city continued to grow. They called on the cities to pass zoning legislation which would prohibit such influx and regulate what kinds of buildings and land uses were permissible by setting up zones for different land uses. Most of these proposals were also backed by the upper- and middle-class voters, who were similarly threatened by the growth of the city. They particularly favored zoning, for while pursuing order and efficiency, it also segregated land uses by class and effectively kept lower-class housing and industry out of their residential areas.

By the end of World War I, planning and zoning had become municipal responsibilities. Since their advocates usually opposed the political machines, these functions were incorporated in quasi-independent city-planning and zoning commissions, headed by lay boards of civic leaders and businessmen. Because of the emphasis on land use and the provision of facilities, the commissions were staffed principally by civil engineers and architects, who were called city planners. Soon thereafter, universities began to set up departments of city planning, almost always in architectural and engineering schools, to train people for the new municipal function and profession.

The new agencies and professionals codified and operationalized further the ends and means they had inherited from the reformers, principally through the comprehensive or "master plan," which programed desired alterations in the land-use pattern and the facilities system and proposed legislation and administrative tools to achieve the alteration. The first of these plans appeared in 1914. Since the preparation of the master plan is still a principal function of city-planning agencies today, and since the elements of the plan have changed relatively little over the past four decades, it is worth spelling out what goes into a master plan and, more important, what is left out.

The typical master plan is a portrait of the future condition of the city. It begins with a demographic and economic analysis of the city, including a projection of future growth and the size of population to be planned for. Then there are chapters and maps which describe the present deficiencies: slums; mixed land uses; shortages of open space and of recreational and other facilities; traffic congestion; air pollution; and the lack of adequate legislation and administrative machinery to control growth. The planning chapters outline the future ideal, a city without slums, divided into zones for each major land use, commercial, industrial, and residential; efficient highway and mass transit systems; and properly distributed open space and public facilities provided on the basis of facility standards. In the final section, the proposals for individual municipal functions and land uses are synthesized into a master-plan map, with recommendations for its implementation. These include a zoning ordinance to order land use as prescribed in the master plan; building codes to discourage slums; subdivision ordinances to regulate the building of new areas; a list of the needed facilities; proposals for governmental reorganization to co-ordinate development activities; and a rhetorical appeal to citizens and politicians to participate in and support the realization of the plan so as to achieve an orderly, efficient, and attractive community.[6]

In addition, the master plan also proposes ends and means to improve the quality of urban life, which are embodied in its basic building block, the so-called neighborhood unit. This unit is a residential area whose size is determined by the enrollment of the public elementary school located at its center. It is purely residential, although some shopping facilities for everyday needs and a playground are provided; it is free from through traffic and is bounded by and thus separated from other neighborhoods by the major traffic arteries.[7] The typical master plan divides the city into neighborhood units; groupings of such units called a community or district, served by district shopping centers, parks, libraries, and other facilities; and the downtown area, with its stores, offices, and central educational, cultural, and administrative facilities, sometimes combined into a civic center. The neighborhood is usually planned to be of low density, with single-family or row houses; apartment buildings are envisaged in or near the downtown area, and industrial districts are separated from residential and commercial areas as much as possible.

The master plan is essentially a technique for achieving the nineteenth-century ends of beauty, efficiency, and order and the small-town, middle-class neighborhood life favored by the reformers. It differs from their proposals by a greater emphasis on the ordering of land use and by the introduction of the concept of comprehensiveness, that is, the co-ordinated regulation of all phases of city development, public as well as private, so as to bring about an ideal city.

Many hundreds of master plans have been completed since 1920, some quite detailed and based on sophisticated analyses, and most of them developed on an assembly-line basis by public agencies and private consultants, especially for the smaller cities. Despite the diversity of urban life, most of the plans have been so similar that texts could be written about their preparation.[8] In terms of its impact, however, the master plan has been a failure. Although individual recommendations have often been implemented, no master plan has ever become a blueprint for the development of the city.

The failure of the master plan can be traced to the ends and means emphasized by the planners and to their view of the city, its growth processes, and the politics of planned change. Perhaps the crucial fault of the master plan was its environmental or physical determinism. Like the nineteenth-century reformers, the master planners assumed that people's lives are shaped by their physical surroundings and that the ideal city could be realized by the provision of an ideal physical environment. As architects and engineers, the planners believed that the city was a system of buildings and land uses which could be arranged and rearranged through planning, without taking account of the social, economic, and political structures and processes that determine people's behavior, including their use of land. This belief was supported by architectural ideology generally and also by plans for utopian and ideal cities which were constantly being proposed by architects and architecturally trained planners.[9] It was reinforced by an oversimplified interpretation of the findings of the urban ecologists, who seemed to correlate social pathology with the physical characteristics of residential areas, and by the thinking of real-estate economists, who saw planning as the achievement of high land values and found these in the residential districts of the homeowning upper and middle classes.[10] The maximization of land values was also favored by the city officials who employed the planners, because it increased tax revenues, and by the property owners who supported the planners, because it meant higher profits for them.

The ends underlying the planners' physical approach reflected their Protestant middle-class view of city life. As a result, the master plan tried to eliminate as "blighting influences" many of the facilities, land uses, and institutions of working-class, lower-class, and ethnic groups. Most of the plans either made no provision for tenements, rooming houses, secondhand stores, and marginal industry or located them in catchall zones of "nuisance uses" in which all land uses are permitted. Popular facilities considered culturally or morally undesirable were also excluded. The plans called for many parks and playgrounds, but left out the movie house, the neighborhood tavern, and the local clubroom; they proposed museums and churches, but no hot-dog stands and night clubs; they planned for industrial parks, but not loft industry; for parking garages, but not automobile repair stations.

The units into which the plan divided the city were determined by transportation routes and other physical boundaries and did not reflect the natural areas of established social groups or the ecological processes of neighborhood change, invasion, and succession. Neighborhood boundaries ignored class divisions in the population, except as these were manifested by differences in house types. The planners made a conscious effort to break up ethnic enclaves in order to achieve nineteenth-century goals of Americanizing the immigrants.

The planners' certainty about how people ought to live and how the city ought to look resulted in a nearly static plan, a Platonic vision of the city as an orderly and finished work of art. Favoring low density and small-town living, the planners sought to achieve the cessation of residential mobility and the control and minimization of future growth. The only land uses programed for future growth were those favored by affluent residents, high-status industrial and commercial establishments, the real-estate interests catering to these, and the tax collector.

The planners' inability to recognize diverse values also prevented them from seeing the role of politics in implementing the plan. Believing that their solution was the best blueprint for the future, they thought that they needed only to publish their report, obtain support from the civic leaders and businessmen who sat on the boards of the planning commission, and then impress elected officials that the plan expressed the public interest. The planners' opposition to partisan political methods of decision-making convinced them that the plan was "above politics" and that anyone who rejected it was acting from selfish and therefore evil motives.

Although the implementation of the plan would have required huge outlays of public funds and drastic political and economic as well as physical rearrangements, the master planners did not seriously consider that the ends they sought were opposed by many of the voters. The planners did not realize that most city residents place less value on open space than they do; that they do not live their life around the elementary school; and that they are not interested in rearranging the land-use pattern at great expense to achieve an order that is most visible on a map or from an airplane and to produce an efficient city that tends to benefit the businessman rather than the ordinary resident. Worse yet, the plan called for a middle-class life style for all, but it did not recommend economic programs to enable low-income people to move out of tenements and buy single-family houses. As a result, master plans have rarely generated any widespread enthusiasm among the voters, but have always aroused considerable political opposition from the groups who would have to pay economically, socially, and politically for the proposed changes without reaping any benefit from them.

The master planners were also hampered by conditions not of their making. For one thing, their authority to plan stopped at the city limits, although the growth processes which they sought to control cover a much wider area, and the people and facilities for whom they planned were beginning to move to the suburbs before master planning was even invented. Also, the planners were poorly funded, so that their conclusions were often based on whatever data, however inadequate, were already available. Yet their methodology was ultimately also a function of their own ends, means, and techniques. Their belief in physical determinism limited their analysis to the determination of the land-use implications of their demographic and economic projections; and their faith in the ends and means they proposed discouraged their concern with alternative ends, with the fit between ends and means, and with the consequences of their recommendations. For example, in planning for recreation, they applied the facility standards of the recreation movement without computing the cost in land, and capital, and operating costs and without even realizing that the professional associations who formulated these standards had a vested interest in maximizing the facilities they advocated. Case studies of the planning process show that the planners often made their recommendations on arbitrary grounds, without understanding their consequences[11] and without using the research they had undertaken.[12]

Yet if master plans had little impact on city development, some of the planners' ideas were adopted. Zoning was supported so enthusiastically by realtors and homeowners that many planning agencies spent all their time administering the zoning ordinance and could not work on master plans. The planners' neighborhood concept was adopted, in somewhat altered form, by the builders—and the purchasers—of the post-World War II suburbs, as was their idea that streets in which small children played ought to be free from through traffic. The planners' argument that excessive land coverage inevitably produced traffic congestion, that off-street parking was necessary, and that zoning too much land for commercial use in the hope of increasing tax income would also leave much land lying needlessly fallow were eventually accepted by city officials in principle, although often subverted by politically powerful private interests in practice. Also accepted was the basic master-planning concept that there ought to be a comprehensive development plan for the city which co-ordinated the construction of housing with the construction of the needed public facilities, enabling the city fathers to evaluate private individual development proposals and choose the best sites for public improvements. Being politically weak, however, the planners could not stand up to the powerful economic interests which opposed the implementation of these principles, and being apolitical, they frequently could not develop compromise solutions which would have salvaged at least some of their proposals.

Master-planning activity reached a new high after World War II, when towns near the central cities began to be enveloped by the new suburbia and called on planners to control the growth, often to prevent the influx of newcomers who would lower the status level of the community and require higher tax rates to build new schools and other facilities for them.

At the same time, however, planners working in the cities began to lose confidence in the master plan. Isaacs had questioned the very basis of the neighborhood unit by pointing out that it favored racial segregation,[13] and Bauer had argued that master planning, zoning, and subdivision regulations were contributing to the class and racial stratification of the new suburbs.[14] Yet the most persuasive skepticism about the master plan was produced by difficulties in its implementation and the static quality of the end product. As cities began to grow and to rebuild after the long hiatus of the Depression and World War II, many of the development proposals which came before the plan commission either conflicted with the plan or could not be evaluated by the standards and other criteria built into it. Since the proposals were made by politically influential groups or promised new tax revenues, the conflict between them and the plan was usually resolved in their favor. Some planners argued that in order to be useful, the master plan had to be constantly revised and updated, but others began to suggest that planning was not a method of describing the ideal city but a process of decision-making and that master planning was only one tool among many to be employed in this process.

The new conception of planning only foreshadowed a radical transformation in planning theory and practice which is now beginning to overturn many of the traditional ends, means, and techniques which the planners took over from their reformer ancestors. This transformation has come about because of changes in the condition and problems of the city, in the employers and clients of planning, and in the planners themselves.

III

In the last fifteen years, the growth of the American city has ended. As prosperity and the subsidies of the Federal Housing Administration have enabled the white lower-middle-class and working-class population to become homeowners in suburbia, the city has increasingly become the residence of a small number of rich people and a rapidly rising number of poor nonwhite residents. The latter are forced to live in ghetto slums, and these as well as the pathologies associated with poverty are reducing the livability of the city for the middle class and creating new problems for city officials. Low-income neighborhoods and residents cannot pay the taxes needed to provide them with municipal services, and the exodus of middle-class residents, stores, and industries to the suburbs is also depriving the city of its most profitable sources of tax income. Thus the city is forced to find new ways of maintaining itself even while it tries to cope with the exodus and the problems of the new low-income population. Some help has come from the federal government, which is increasingly participating in municipal activities through the financial support of new city programs.

City planning has also benefited from federal subsidy, and the federal government is rapidly becoming its major source of financing. Washington began to involve itself in planning activities during the Depression, when a National Resource Planning Board was established temporarily to undertake national and regional resources planning,[15] the National Resettlement Administration built four new so-called greenbelt towns, and the Public Housing Administration was established to clear slums and build housing on the cleared sites. After the war, the federal government began to fund local city-planning activities themselves, most extensively for transportation planning and urban renewal.

Master planners had concerned themselves with transportation ever since car ownership had begun to increase urban congestion and suburbanization. After the war, however, the new spurt in car-buying and the growth of suburbia resulted in the building of expressways, subsidized by federal grants, in every American city. They were intended not only to reduce congestion on local city streets but also to bring the suburbanite back to the city to shop, especially when suburban shopping centers began to make inroads on downtown retail trade and on the municipal tax revenue from that area. The new expressways made it more convenient to use cars and further encouraged the exodus to suburbia. As a result, they not only failed to reduce congestion but took more customers away from the already declining mass transit system and central business districts.

Consequently, by the late 1950's, a number of large cities began to formulate massive transportation planning studies which aimed to determine the location of future expressways and the revitalization of mass transit as part of a metropolitan area transportation system to serve the city and its suburbs. Since new transportation facilities stimulate other urban development and thus affect land-use patterns and the economic base of the cities,[16] the transportation planners were in effect formulating a new kind of master plan.[17]

In this process, they introduced several innovations into planning. Well financed and able to measure the amount and flow of traffic with relative ease, the planners obtained large masses of data and brought the newly available computer into planning to analyze them. Moreover, since the aim of their plan was limited to serving the transportation needs of the area and the achievement of the economically most productive and most efficient land-use patterns, they were working with a smaller number of ends than the master planners. This enabled them to formulate a number of alternative schemes, rather than a single one, using the computer and later the simulation model to choose among the alternatives for a final plan.[18] Because the studies were staffed by transportation experts, economists, and operations researchers, rather than by architects and master planners, the ends and means of traditional city planning were of lesser importance.

Finally, their plans were metropolitan. Because so much of the traffic flow was generated in the suburbs, transportation planning could not end at the city limits, and regional planning bodies were set up to do the studies. Metropolitan planning had been advocated by city planners and public administrators for a long time, for even the control of growth and the achievement of order and efficiency required a metropolitan government to co-ordinate municipal services and planning for the city and its suburbs in a single supergovernment, which would do away with the duplication and conflict among the many hundreds of local bodies.

Although private regional planning associations were set up in many cities and the Rockefeller Foundation financed a seven-volume New York Regional Plan in the 1920's, the appeals for both metropolitan government and planning fell on deaf ears. First, it was—and still is—difficult to define a metropolitan region, or any other region, for that matter, for the boundaries shift with the function whose ecological pattern is being studied. Thus, the region within which the urban economy affects its hinterland differs from that best suited to the creation of an effective police network or sanitation system. More important, however, the suburbs rejected any plan which would force them to share their power with or give up their local authority to the city. Since the cities are predominantly Democratic, working-class, and Catholic and the suburbs are predominantly Republican, middle-class, and Protestant, political, class, and religious conflicts were endemic and were magnified when cities became increasingly nonwhite.[19] Moreover, the suburbs had no great interest in metropolitan planning or co-ordination. Affluent homeowners can well afford the duplication of municipal services and are unwilling to accept any infringement on their local autonomy, not to mention the possible arrival of lower-status and nonwhite city residents in exchange for a slight saving in taxes.[20] These considerations may even prevent the implementation of the regional transportation systems now being planned.

The second, and in some ways more significant, stimulus for change in city-planning theory and practice has come out of urban renewal. In 1949, the federal government set up the urban-renewal program which funneled considerable amounts of money to the cities to make possible the elimination of slums. Intense political opposition to public housing prevented it from making any significant inroads on the slums, and the federal government therefore turned to private enterprise, hoping that it would rebuild on land that had been cleared and written down in price by federal grants. The program received strong local support from cities which expected that new building programs would increase their tax revenues and from downtown businessmen who saw urban renewal as a way of replacing the slum dwellers of the inner city with more affluent customers and later as a way of modernizing downtown districts with federal aid.

The theory behind urban renewal was the traditional nineteenth-century one that if slum dwellers were relocated in decent housing, they would give up their lower-class ways and the social pathologies thought to "breed" in the slums. Since inexpensive housing was in short supply, however, and the private redevelopers of cleared sites were building only luxury housing, the displaced were often forced to move into other slums, and they usually had to pay higher rents. In clearing entire neighborhoods, urban renewal also destroyed viable social communities, thus saddling the displaced with emotional costs as well. Nor did the first rebuilding projects contribute significantly to the housing stock and the economic and financial condition of the cities.[21] In the large cities, the unanticipated consequences of slum clearance created so much political opposition that by the start of the 1960's, when the market for luxury housing had been sated, the promiscuous use of the bulldozer was halted. Instead, renewal agencies began to experiment with rehabilitation, so as to minimize relocation, and the federal government began to provide new subsidies to builders and residents—albeit on a minuscule scale—for example, 221 (d) (3) below-market loans for the former and rent supplements for the latter —in order to increase the supply of low- and moderate-cost housing.

Initially, renewal had been carried out on a project-by-project basis, but once the choice sites desired by private builders had been used up, city planners were asked to develop a more comprehensive urban-renewal program. The selection of future renewal sites required the determination of the best reuse of the sites on the basis of city-wide considerations, and the federal government provided planning grants to the cities to create "workable programs" which had to demonstrate how individual projects fitted into a larger, more comprehensive renewal plan before federal renewal funds were made available. Subsequently, the federal government broadened its requirements—for example, by including social considerations in the choice of sites—and set up the Community Renewal Program. In 1966, the federal government made the integration of social and physical considerations in urban renewal complete by setting up the Demonstration Cities Program. Later retitled Model Cities, the new program will provide yet further subsidies to enable sixty to seventy American cities to rebuild and rehabilitate the physical and social structures of their major slum ghetto neighborhoods. In addition, private enterprise is being encouraged to participate more actively in the rebuilding of the slums, particularly through community-development corporations. In 1967, all these programs were still in the planning phase, although it was already evident that they would not be successful until the federal government was able to grant subsidies on a billion-dollar scale to provide housing for poor people.

In many cities, the community-renewal programs resembled the traditional master plan; but in others, the failure of urban renewal to help the slum dwellers, the federal encouragment of more socially oriented planning, and the new ideas and grants developed in connection with the War on Poverty have awakened planners to the need to solve the more basic problems of the low-income population.

The principal innovations are in the choice of ends and means and in the techniques of planning. Urban renewal is no longer conceived solely as a process of eliminating slums but as a means of dealing with the problems which force poor and nonwhite people into them. Many Model-City schemes are exploring various programs of job creation, opening up housing, educational, and other opportunities to nonwhites and improving social services in the hope that these, together with housing programs, will eliminate the deprivation of the slum dwellers as well as the slums. New ends, such as equality of opportunity and greater distribution of public resources to the poor, are being suggested to complement the ends of order and efficiency, particularly since the ever-increasing ghetto protests are leading to the realization that social order can be maintained only through greater economic and political equality. The planners' means are new as well, for programs intended to help people are added to those for changing the physical environment.

The extension of economic and other opportunities, even on a small scale, bears little resemblance to traditional planning solutions, and the outcome of the planning process is no longer envisaged as a master plan, but as a set of incremental or developmental programs that will improve present conditions, formulated so that they can be co-ordinated with the ongoing decision-making processes of city officials.[22]

Physical determinism is thus being replaced by a broader systems approach which seeks to deal with the causes of the problem. In this conception of the planning process, land-use studies are less relevant, and the renewal planners are turning to surveys of the present behavior and future wants of the populations for whom they are planning, analyses of the quality of opportunities and social services now available to them, and economic as well as political studies to determine the feasibility and the consequences of the programs and policies they recommend. Like the transportation planners, they are turning also to the computer, the simulation model, and systems analysis to handle their data.

This conception of planning also presages a change in the role of the planner. The city planner is no longer a nonpolitical formulator of long-range ideals, but is becoming an adviser to elected and appointed officials, providing them with recommendations and technical information on current decisions. This new role is an outcome of conditions and forces that preceded innovations in the planning method. Shortly after the war, a number of cities assigned city planners the task of preparing five-year capital budgets, although the annual capital budget was still drawn up at city hall. This assignment not only shortened the time span in which planners were working but took them out of their nonpolitical ivory tower and made them aware of the political considerations in the allocation of public funds. It also brought the planner much closer to the elected official, and many planning commissions are being reorganized into planning departments which take their place in the mayor's cabinet. This has also decreased the planners' traditional antipathy to politics. Urban-renewal activity quickened this change, for the funds which became available to cities as a result of the federal program encouraged mayors to give more power to urban-renewal agencies and sometimes to appoint re-development co-ordinators who supervised all housing, planning, and development activities.

The planner's rising influence must also be traced to other changes in the city and in city hall. The new problems of the city, and the gradual replacement of the working-class machine politician by middle-class, college-educated politician-administrators, supported by professionally trained bureaucrats, have made city governments much more responsive to expert advice, while the reduction of class differences between the planners and the new politicians has improved communication between them. In addition, downtown business and property interests have become partial to the new planning, partly because they, too, face new problems they cannot solve themselves and partly because the planners share their concern with the revitalization of the central business district. Moreover, planners are becoming more sympathetic to the city and are giving up their traditional antiurban ideology. As the suburbs threaten to engulf the city and to endanger the survival of the upper-middle-class cultural and civic institutions which have traditionally been located in the city, the planner has become an advocate of urbanism. He supports schemes to bring the middle class back into the city, and in the suburbs he has been proposing apartment and town-house development to provide real or symbolic expressions of "urbanity."

Finally, with federal funds rapidly becoming a major source of support for local planning, and with state planning agencies and metropolitan ones also participating in local planning activities, the planner is no longer as closely tied to the small group of local businessmen and civic leaders who have traditionally supported him against his political opponents. This has encouraged him to pay more attention to the needs of other and less vocal interest groups in the city and, since the advent of the War on Poverty, particularly the low-income population. This is part of a more general re-evaluation of the relationship between the planner and the citizens, which began with the realization that the traditional appeal for citizen participation in planning was often only a demand for citizen ratification of the planner's decision and is now leading to proposals and experiments for direct citizens' participation in planning for their own neighborhood.[23]

The changes in the conditions under which planners work have been complemented, and even preceded, by changes within the planning profession and in the recruitment of planners, especially the entrance of social scientists into city planning.

The entry of social scientists into city planning began in the 1930's, when social scientists helped to conduct national and regional planning studies in various federal agencies. After World War II, the University of Chicago drew on some of these men to establish a planning school which taught national as well as city planning and was the first to stress social-science rather than architectural techniques. Subsequently parts of this curriculum spread, albeit slowly, to other planning schools and attracted students with social-science backgrounds, so that today, architects and engineers are fast becoming a minority in the student body.

The Chicagoans approached planning as a method of *rational programing*. Briefly, they argued that the essence of planning was the deliberate choice of ends and the analytic determination of the most effective means to achieve these ends—means which make optimal use of scarce resources and, when implemented, are not accompanied by undesirable consequences. Ends, the Chicagoans argued, are imposed not, by planning ideology or by a priori determinations of the public interest, but by political and market processes and by other forms of feedback from those affected by planning. Means and consequences are determined through predominantly empirical analyses and by other studies which test the fit of means to ends and predict the consequences of these means.[24]

Rational programing has much in common with concepts of planning and methods of rational decision-making being developed in political science, public administration, and management and is reducing the differences between city planning and planning for other clients and ends. In turn, this has enabled city planning to use the personnel and approaches of other disciplines, including operations research, decision theory, cost-benefit analysis, input-output studies, information theory, and simulation models as well as sociological and manpower analyses for understanding the behavior, attitudes, and ends of the clients of planning.

The social scientists and the rational programers owe no allegiance either to the master plan or to physical determinism. Aided by research findings which indicate that the portions of the physical environment with which city planners have traditionally dealt do not have a significant impact on people's behavior and by studies of social organization and social change which demonstrate that economic and social structures are much more important than spatial ones, the rational programers devote their attention to institutions and institutional change, rather than to environmental change.

The new conception of planning has also affected general land-use planning, creating a greater concern with the social and economic functions of land use and leading to incremental policy formulations for rearranging it. Even urban design, traditionally based primarily on aesthetic considerations, is now paying attention to the social processes that shape what city planners call the urban form.[25]

Nevertheless, traditional master and land-use planning has recently received new support through the revival of another nineteenth-century concept: the new town. Originally conceived as a way of moving urban slum dwellers into the countryside and halting the growth of cities, the new town is a relatively self-sufficient and independent community located beyond the city limits which would provide local employment opportunities for many of its residents, thus reducing their journey to work, the city's traffic congestion, and the alleged defects of the suburbs as so-called bedroom communities.[26] The current development of new towns by private builders is giving master planners new hope that if the master plan and related traditional schemes cannot work in established cities, they might be applied on the *tabula rasa* of a new town. It seems likely, however, that the same political and market forces that prevented the implementation of the master plan will also frustrate portions of the new-town schemes, particularly if they do not meet the wishes of the people who will have to be attracted as home buyers.[27]

IV

At present, rational programing is rapidly achieving dominance at the level of planning theory and is being advocated and used by professors and researchers in the profession. It has, however, not yet been accepted by most city-planning commissions and departments and is thus far from being incorporated at the level of day-to-day planning practice. Instead, the city-planning practitioners have typically reacted to the new theory— and the new urban problems—by adding programs of "social planning" to the traditional land-use approach, now often called "physical planning." In its American usage the term social planning comes from social welfare, where it refers to interagency co-ordination of social-work programs. In city planning, the term is used to describe planning for people, and espe-

cially for low-income ones, probably because physical planning has ca-
tered so largely to building programs for more affluent city residents. The
dichotomy between physical and social planning is theoretically unjustifiable, because physical plans affect people, rich and poor, as much as do
social plans. Even so, planning agencies are now adding social-planning
divisions to their staffs, and a professional literature on social planning is
coming into being.[28]

The first social-planning activities were intended to meet the requirements of the community-renewal program and to correct the inequities of
slum clearance for the slum dwellers, but increasingly they are being
carried out to co-ordinate city planning and renewal with the community-
action activities and other programs of the War on Poverty. Frequently,
however, social planning is only a modernized version of previous attempts
to impose middle-class ways on the low-income population, with "human
renewal" educational and social-work schemes to "rehabilitate" the slum
dwellers while—or even in lieu of—improving their living conditions, thus
subverting the antipoverty efforts into yet another device for maintaining
the present inequality of the low-income population. This possibility has
led to proposals for bringing planners into closer contact with the low-
income population. Davidoff[29] has suggested that because most planners
are employed as technicians to pursue the interests of the so-called Establishment—that is, city hall, the political party, and the business community—other planners ought to become "advocate planners"—that is,
technical consultants and even spokesmen for the low-income population
—paralleling a similar proposal in the legal profession.[30] In addition, a
number of planners have pointed out that because of the profession's ties
to the Establishment, it has evaded its responsibility to take action on
racial discrimination and economic inequality.[31] In several cities, planners have begun to work with local civil rights groups and community
organizations in poor neighborhoods; they have formed a national professional association, Planners for Equal Opportunity, to complement the
more conservative American Institute of Planners, and they are rejecting
orthodox beliefs about how to plan for the slum ghetto; for example, by
questioning the profession's advocacy of integrated housing as a means
of improving the living conditions of the mass of poor Negroes.[32]

These activities are leading to the politicization of the city-planning
profession. It appears that the profession is being split into progressive
and conservative wings, the former calling for social planning to reduce
economic and racial inequality, the latter defending traditional physical
planning and the legitimacy of middle-class values. The rational programers are a third wing, seeking to develop an approach that makes it pos-

sible to plan for all interest groups, but they, too, are split over the issue of working with or against the Establishment.

In their day-to-day practice, city-planning agencies tend to favor the conservative wing and the traditional land-use approach to planning, although they are both threatened and influenced by the progressives and the rational programers. Not only are the agencies in existence to conduct land-use planning, but most of the directors and senior staff members are trained in this approach, and some of the leading practitioners in the profession still come from architectural and civil-engineering backgrounds. Rational programers and progressives are more often found among the junior staff and have less influence on agency activities. Moreover, since planners are employees of municipal bureaucracies, they are expected to conform to agency policy on the job, and in some cities they are even restrained from off-hours participation in activities and groups that question or oppose agency policy. This naturally reduces the impact of progressive ideas on local planning activities.

The future direction of city planning is at present uncertain. As architecturally trained planners become a minority in the profession, city planning will undoubtedly make more use of the concepts and methods of rational programing and will pay more attention to the social and economic problems of the city. It is also possible, however, that established city-planning agencies will continue to maintain the physical planning tradition and that new agencies, staffed by professionals from other disciplines, will be assigned to deal with the social and economic aspects of urban growth and change.

V

I should note that the preceding analysis is inevitably influenced by my personal involvement in the progressive and rational-programing wings of the planning profession. Many traditional city planners, pointing to their new influence and constantly rising agency budgets, would argue not only that the ends of creating efficient and attractive cities through physical planning are still valid but that they speak to the needs and wants of the majority of the metropolitan area population, which is now affluent enough to want both these ends. Others argue that physical planning to attract the upper-middle class back to the city is crucial if the city is to continue to play a significant role in American civilization.

Although research on residential aspirations and the results of present renewal activities suggest that it is probably impossible to reverse the middle-class exodus from the city,[33] there can be no question that physical planning is needed in every city, if only to modernize it, raise its efficiency in housing and moving workers and residents, and prevent further deterioration of its financial and physical condition. The ends of physical planning may be most relevant to the suburbs and to the newer communities of the western United States, although even they do not always favor the particular kinds of order, efficiency, and attractiveness which physical planners seek. In the older American cities, however, poverty, unemployment, and racial and class discrimination, and their pathological consequences are not only the most crucial problem but also a major cause of the low quality of city living, the middle-class exodus, and the city's financial difficulties. The inequalities and pathologies of the urban low-income population must therefore be eliminated before the attractive, efficient, and slumless city for which physical planners are striving is to be realized. When the latter can be persuaded of the validity of this concept, it may be possible to achieve a synthesis of the so-called social and physical planning approaches to create a city-planning profession which uses rational programing to bring about real improvements, not only in the lives of city residents but also in the condition of the cities themselves.

NOTES

1. Hans Blumenfeld, "Theory of City Form, Past and Present," *Journal of the Society of Architectural Historians,* VII (1949), 7–16.
2. Arthur Mann, *Yankee Reformers in an Urban Age* (Cambridge: Belknap, 1954).
3. Roy Lubove, *The Progressives and the Slums: Tenement House Reform in New York City, 1890–1917* (Pittsburgh: Unviersity of Pittsburgh Press, 1962).
4. Joseph Lee, *How to Start a Playground* (New York: Playground and Recreation Association, 1910).
5. Daniel H. Burnham and E. H. Bennett, *Plan of Chicago* (Chicago: The Commercial Club, 1909).
6. Charles M. Haar, "The Content of the General Plan: A Glance at History," *Journal of the American Institute of Planners,* XXI (1955), 66–75; and "The Master Plan: An Impermanent Constitution," *Law and Contemporary Problems,* XX (1955), 353–377. Allison Dunham, "City Planning: An Analysis of the Content of the Master Plan," *Journal of Law and Economics,* I (1958), 170–186. David Farbman, *A Description, Analysis and Critique of the Master Plan* (Philadelphia: Institute for Urban Studies, University of Pennsylvania, 1960–mimeographed).
7. Clarence A. Perry, "The Neighborhood Unit," in *Regional Survey of New York and Its Environs* (New York: Committee on Regional Plan of New York and Its Environs, 1929), VII, 22–140. James Dahir, *The Neighborhood Unit Plan* (New York: Russell Sage Foundation, 1947).

8. Edward M. Bassett, *The Master Plan* (New York: Russell Sage Foundation, 1938). T. J. Kent, *The Urban General Plan* (San Francisco: Chandler, 1964). F. Stuart Chapin, Jr., *Urban Land Use Planning* (2d ed.; Urbana: University of Illinois Press, 1964).
9. Thomas A. Reiner, *The Place of the Ideal Community in Urban Planning* (Philadelphia: University of Pennsylvania Press, 1963).
10. Homer Hoyt, *The Structure and Growth of Residential Neighborhoods in American Cities* (Washington: Government Printing Office, 1939).
11. Martin Meyerson and Edward C. Banfield, *Politics, Planning and the Public Interest* (New York: Free Press of Glencoe, 1955). Alan Altshuler, *The City Planning Process* (Ithaca: Cornell University Press, 1965).
12. Frances F. Piven, "The Function of Research in the Formation of City Planning Policy," unpublished Ph.D. dissertation, University of Chicago Department of City Planning, 1962.
13. Reginald Isaacs, "The Neighborhood Theory: An Analysis of Its Inadequacy," *Journal of the American Institute of Planners,* XIV (1948), 15–23.
14. Catherine Bauer, "Social Questions in Housing and Community Planning," *Journal of Social Issues,* VII (1951), 1–34.
15. Norman Beckman, "Federal Long-Range Planning: The Heritage of the National Resources Planning Board," *Journal of the American Institute of Planners,* XXVI (1960), 89–97.
16. Robert B. Mitchell and Chester Rapkin, *Urban Traffic: A Function of Land Use* (New York: Columbia University Press, 1954).
17. Henry Fagin, "The Penn Jersey Transportation Study: The Launching of a Permanent Regional Planning Process," *Journal of the American Institute of Planners,* XXIX (1963), 9–18.
18. Alan M. Vorhees, ed., "Land Use and Traffic Models," *Journal of the American Institute of Planners,* XXV (special issue—1959), 59–103. Britton Harris, "Plan or Projection: An Examination of the Use of Models in Planning," *ibid.,* XXVI (1960), 265–272.
19. Edward C. Banfield and Morton Grodzins, *Government and Housing in Metropolitan Areas* (New York: McGraw-Hill, 1958).
20. Scott Greer, *Metropolitics: A Study of Political Culture* (New York: Wiley, 1963).
21. John W. Dyckman, "National Planning for Urban Renewal: The Paper Moon in the Cardboard Sky," *Journal of the American Institute of Planners,* XXVI (1960), 49–59. Bernard J. Frieden, *The Future of Old Neighborhoods* (Cambridge: Massachusetts Institute of Technology Press, 1964). Martin Anderson, *The Federal Bulldozer: A Critical Analysis of Urban Renewal 1949–1962* (Cambridge: Massachusetts Institute of Technology Press, 1964).
22. Melvin M. Webber, "The Prospects for Policies Planning," in Leonard J. Duhl, ed., *The Urban Condition* (New York: Basic Books, 1963), pp. 319–330.
23. Peter H. Rossi and Robert A. Dentler, *The Politics of Urban Renewal* (New York: Free Press of Glencoe, 1961). James Q. Wilson, "Planning and Politics: Citizen Participation in Urban Renewal," *Journal of the American Institute of Planners,* XXIX (1963), 242–249.
24. Meyerson and Banfield, *op. cit.* Martin Meyerson, "Building the Middle-Range Bridge for Comprehensive Planning," *Journal of the American Institute of Planners,* XXII (1956), 58–64. Paul Davidoff and Thomas A. Reiner, "A Choice Theory of Planning," *ibid.,* XXVIII (1962), 103–115. Webber, *op. cit.*
25. Kevin Lynch, *The Image of the City* (Cambridge: Massachusetts Institute of Technology Press and Harvard University Press, 1960).

26. Clarence S. Stein, *Toward New Towns for America* (New York: Reinhold, 1957).
27. Edward P. Eichler and Marshall Kaplan, *The Community Builders* (Berkeley: University of California Press, 1967).
28. Harvey S. Perloff, "New Directions in Social Planning," *Journal of the American Institute of Planners,* XXXI (1965), 297–303.
29. Paul Davidoff, "Advocacy and Social Concern in Planning," *Journal of the American Institute of Planners,* XXXI (1965), 331–337.
30. Edgar S. Cahn and Jean C. Cahn, "The War on Poverty: A Civilian Perspective," *Yale Law Journal,* LXXIII (1964), 1317–1352.
31. Melvin M. Webber, "Comprehensive Planning and Social Responsibility," *Journal of the American Institute of Planners,* XXIX (1963), 232–241.
32. Frances F. Piven and Richard A. Cloward, "Desegregated Housing: Who Pays for the Reformers' Ideal," *New Republic,* CLV, No. 25 (December 17, 1966), 17–22.
33. Nelson Foote *et al., Housing Choices and Housing Constraints* (New York: McGraw-Hill, 1961). John Lansing, Eva Mueller, and N. Barth, *Residential Location and Urban Mobility* (Ann Arbor: Survey Research Center, 1964— mimeographed).

6

The Goal-Oriented Approach to Planning

I

City planning grew up as a movement of upper-middle-class-eastern reformers who were upset by the arrival of the European immigrants and the squalor of their existence in urban slums and the threat which these immigrants, and urban-industrial society generally, represented to the social, cultural, and political dominance the reformers had enjoyed in small-town agrarian America. These early planners did not concern themselves much with explicit goals; they were a movement with missionary fervor which had no need to question its goals. Instead, they devoted themselves to developing programs calling for a change in the physical environment, for they believed that physical change would bring about social change.

As reform groups and businessmen gave city planning increasing support, it became a profession. Its physical emphasis naturally attracted architects, landscape architects, and engineers; these developed planning tools that were based to a considerable extent on the beliefs which the movement had accepted. Thus, they made master plans which assumed that once land-use arrangements had been ordered "comprehensively," the social and economic structure of the community would also change.

They also made up standards which provided a formula by which the amount of land needed for a specific use could be determined in relation to the numbers of people involved. These standards were assumed to be means to the planners' goals. However, no one ever asked what these goals were and whether or not the standards would achieve them. For example, planners advocated one acre of playground per thousand people because they were in favor of "wholesome recreation" and believed the playground provided it. But the planners did not consider whether they

Previously unpublished. Revised version of a paper read to a joint meeting of the Puerto Rico Planning Society and the Puerto Rico Economic Association, San Juan, Puerto Rico, February 1958.

had a right to attempt to regulate leisure behavior, whether wholesome recreation was a desirable goal, whether the playground had anything to do with providing recreation, or whether enough children actually used the playground (for wholesome or other pursuits) to justify the costs of the playground in land and public funds. Actually, the public recreation standards, like most of the others, were made up by a single-purpose organization, itself descended from the reformist recreation movement, whose goal was to maximize the amount of land and public funds to be allocated to its services. Since city planners were ideologically and sociologically close to these movements, they accepted the standards without question. If they had applied all the community facility standards which they usually favored all at once, they would have discovered that there would not have been enough land left in the community for housing and industry nor enough money in the public till to run the rest of the community's operations.

During the first half of the twentieth century, few planners seem to have been bothered by these inconsistencies. Nor did they notice that the standards and their other techniques and solutions offered little help with the most important problem which the politician had to resolve: how to allocate limited public resources among a variety of pressing demands for land and funds, not all of which could be satisfied.

In recent years, urban problems have increased to such an extent that politicians are beginning to call on planners for help. At the moment, city planning seems to be extremely successful, if judged by such criteria as the number of planners being hired, the increase in salaries paid, and the amount of newspaper space devoted to appeals for better planning. At the same time, however, city planning may be in an extremely critical phase, for unless it can provide real aid to the solution of the city's problems, its momentary success will suddenly turn to failure, and planners will be replaced by other professions that will help to solve those problems.

II

I shall try now to describe the kind of planning that I think is necessary for our day and age, which I label *goal*-oriented planning. I would define goal-oriented planning as developing programs or means to allocate limited resources in order to achieve the goals of the community (and its members) ranked in order or priority. The crucial elements in this definition are *goals,* the *programs* to achieve them, the *consequences* of achieving these, especially cost in relation to resources, and the criteria of ordering goals and programs in the *priority* of those to be achieved first, or later, and those to be given up. I cannot describe the whole approach here, but shall focus on two major aspects of this approach: the determination of goals and the determination of programs to achieve goals.

The most difficult problem is to determine *whose* goals and *which* goals are to be achieved. I noted before that in the past the planner had his own goals for how people should behave, but that he was never explicitly concerned with goals. The goal-oriented approach calls for exactly the opposite; it stresses the need to make all goals explicit, and suggests that the goals to be achieved are those which the members of the community consider desirable.

However, the members of the community are not always agreed on goals. Renters want services; owners want tax reduction. Store owners in the central business district want high-income residential areas to surround this district; low-income residents without job security want to live near the district so that they can be close to the centers of transportation and a variety of jobs. People also have different goals depending on whether they are suppliers or users of public services. For example, public-recreation officials want people to seek their leisure in parks, playgrounds, and recreation centers; children seem to prefer the streets; teen-agers, commercial recreation; and adults, the facilities in their own homes. The community as a whole also has goals for recreation; it wants to eliminate individually or socially destructive forms of leisure behavior. Thus, it is necessary to decide whose goals are to be implemented, whose are to be set aside, and, where possible, whether conflicting goals can be combined in some way so that as many as possible are achieved. More often, however, conflicting goals force the community and its decision-makers to choices which will aid one interest at the expense of another.

The planner does not determine goals; this is the job of the community and its elected representatives. Even so, the planner should try to help these representatives in the process of goal determination by analyzing their present activities to show them what implicit goals they are pursuing—and with what consequences—and by making studies of the behavior patterns and attitudes of the citizenry that would provide data on the goals of the various sectors of the community's population.

In his goal-determining function, the planner is thus a technician-aide to the elected decision-maker. This assumes, however, that the decision-maker is a truly representative leader. Planners used to assume that the politician was inherently evil; only recently have they begun to see that he represented sectors of the population with goals which differed from the professional-upper-middle-class goals of the planner. However, it may happen that the politician is elected without being representative and is thus able to pursue the goals of only the most powerful or most affluent portion of his entire constituency or his own personal goals without being responsive to any constituency. Once the planner is convinced that the goals of the community itself are not served by such a decision-maker—and this is not an easy judgment to make—his other roles as citizen and professional give him the right, and even the duty, of fighting for what he thinks is right and of using all means at his command, including political ones, for this purpose. In this fight, he should continue to remain the servant of the community and especially of the politically neglected members of the community.

The most important role of the planner is, however, to tell the community and its leaders that if they want to achieve Goal X, they must institute Program Y, requiring certain costs and resulting in certain consequences, and if they want to achieve Goal A, they must implement Program B.

The second aspect of the goal-oriented approach is the determination of programs to achieve goals. For example, when the community's goal is to eliminate the economic, social, psychological, and residential problems of slum dwellers, the programs usually suggested by planners have involved slum clearance and the relocation of the residents into standard housing. We are beginning to learn, however, that conventional programs do not always achieve their goals. There is some indication that the economic and other problems of slum dwellers do not disappear when they are displaced from slum housing and relocated into standard housing, or when they are moved into brand new public housing. If we really want to improve the condition of slum dwellers, some of the money used for slum clearance should be diverted to programs which would result in higher wages for slum dwellers, provide them with education for the social and economic skills needed in the city, and develop other programs that will alleviate social and psychological problems associated with poverty.

Similarly, if the community wants to maximize public health, planners must do more than plan for hospitals, health centers, and sanitation devices. First, the goal itself must be defined more clearly. Is the community concerned with prolonging the life of the old or chronically ill? Is it interested in maximizing the health of those who cause epidemics? Is it concerned with saving those who would otherwise die during infancy? Once goals have been spelled out, programs must be defined in relation to them. Municipally provided hospitals and health centers cure people, but often fail to reach those who are most in need of them. If the latter are the greatest menace to public health and to themselves, however, it is necessary to develop the kind of facilities and programs that they will use.

The point I want to emphasize is that goals must be defined operationally, and programs must be created which will actually achieve these goals. In this connection, the planners' job is to bring together data from all kinds of disciplines which can be used to develop such programs. If we want to build a bridge that will not collapse, we have sufficient engineering data to develop a program almost guaranteed to achieve that goal. Now, planners must collect or stimulate the collection of data to develop programs for the achievement of more complex goals. Puerto Rico seems to have been successful in developing programs for raising incomes and productivity. For other goals, planners will have to call on sociologists, anthropologists, psychologists, students of consumer behavior, and others, as well as on the architects, engineers, municipal finance experts, and public administrators whom they have traditionally used as resource persons. Many of the data needed for such program planning are not yet available, and in such cases, the planner must develop the best assumptions and estimates about phenomena for which he has no data. Then, when the planning has been implemented, he should follow up the results, to see whether or not his assumptions were right. Thus, data are created for similar goal-program relationships in the future. Better still, if the planner can experiment, he should try two different programs to achieve the same goal and then do follow-up research to discover which one worked better.

This discussion of the goal-oriented approach to planning has been too brief to consider how to determine benefits and costs for each program. Nor has it touched on the most difficult problem of all: how to help the political decision-maker in the final phase of the process, when he has to allocate resources among competing goals and in what proportion, and when he must determine which goals are most deserving of high priority and implementation and which must be postponed or given up.

In its brief history, planning has developed from a missionary movement to a profession based on the beliefs of that movement, but with a strongly architectural and engineering emphasis. In terms of the approach I have outlined, planning in its next phase would be a profession resembling in many ways the discipline of an applied social science. While it would depend on the social sciences for many of the data relating goals and programs, it would be an art in formulating its special synthesis of these data. Obviously it would continue to require traditional physical planning, with architectural and design techniques, in the implementation of space-oriented programs.

However, planning as I have defined it is, or should be, only one species of a larger genus of community decision-making, for the process proposed here is applicable to all phases of goal-seeking decisions. Ideally, all community decisions should aim toward achieving the goals that the community deems important and should be arrived at in the ways outlined above. I do not favor the planners' taking over the community's decision-making functions; rather, I suggest that the planning approach described here can be used for all kinds and levels of community decision-making and by all types of decision-makers, political as well as professional.

Two important qualifications must be appended. First, the presentation of an approach is relatively simple; its application is not; but an approach does not really exist until it can be used in actual decision-making, and many obstacles stand between my statement of the approach and its application. Second, I suspect that political decision-makers may already use an approach similar to the one I am suggesting. What one might call their "political benefit-cost accounting" is not altogether different from goal-oriented planning, even though politicians make their decisions without explicitly formulating goals, determining what programs will best achieve their goals, or measuring the benefits and costs of alternative programs. Still, before planners reject political decision-making processes, they should analyze them to determine how close the results are to the results that would stem from goal-oriented planning methods.

Nevertheless, whatever the problems of the goal-oriented approach, it is clear that planning and community—or societal—decision-making blend into each other and that every community decision is in some way related to the goals which planners are concerned with, just as planning must end up with a community or societal decision. In the long run, then, planning should become an applied social science and an art of community or societal decision-making.

7

Memorandum on Social Planning

I. The nature and functions of social planning: a redefinition of terms

The development of a Social Planning Division in the Puerto Rico Planning Board may be viewed sociologically as a reaction to the processes of urbanization-industrialization and rapid social change. Some of the consequences of that change, such as the disappearance of traditional patterns of living, and increases in so-called "indices of social disorganization," such as delinquency and suicide, have created a demand for a planning process which would determine whether certain social, cultural, and psychological goals should now have priority over the goals of economic development. Indeed, it has been suggested that Puerto Rico's income level is now sufficiently high so that more attention can be paid to social goals. As a sociologist, I feel, however, that the concern with social planning is based on the belief in government circles that social change and the urbanization-industrialization process in Puerto Rico ought to be slowed down.

An examination of the literature on underdeveloped areas would probably show that demands to re-evaluate the pace of economic transformation develop in every rapidly changing society, especially among those sectors of the population who have emotional and political involvements in the old order. Since many of the leaders who spark "development" are usually drawn from the elites of the preindustrial order, this response is to be expected.

An understanding of the context in which the Social Planning Division originated is important in considering its nature and function. From the beginning, I found it impossible to work with an assumption that placed

Previously unpublished. An abridged and revised version of a memorandum originally prepared for the President of the Planning Board, Commonwealth of Puerto Rico, in March 1958. Many of the ideas in this paper were developed in discussions with the staff of the Social Planning Division of the Board, particularly Janet Reiner and Everett Reimer.

social goals over or against economic goals; since there were situations in which social goals might well be less important than economic goals, this assumption would predetermine and bias the future work of the Social Planning Division from the start. Moreover, in the discussions toward a methodology to evaluate social goals, it became clear that the concept of a social goal was operationally impossible. First, since all goals affect at least a portion of the society and the social system, all goals are social. Second, economic goals are, at another level of analysis, not only economic. For example, the economic goal of income and productivity increase is also a means to a "higher" goal—raising standards of living— and that goal in turn is instrumental for the goal of providing the opportunity for a fuller, richer life to members of Puerto Rican society.

Goals cannot be described by adjectives such as *economic* or *social.* When any kind of goal is adopted by the government for the society, it becomes a *societal* goal. At the level of programs (defined as means or conditions known or assumed to achieve a goal) it is then possible to consider economic, social, physical, engineering, and other *programs* that can achieve the societal goal. *Social* may be used as an over-all administrative category to include all noneconomic, nonphysical programs.

This discussion implies a distinction between two kinds of social planning. *Societal planning* is concerned with evaluating social goals and developing in broad outline the kinds of program to achieve the goals chosen. *Social programing* may be defined as the development of noneconomic, nonphysical programs for goals "adopted" by societal planning.

Despite its totalitarian-sounding label, societal planning would not be concerned with planning people's lives. Quite the opposite: it would attempt to develop a framework for planning the allocation of resources of the society for the goals which the members of the society themselves want and for developing long-range extensions of the short-range goals that most people are concerned with personally. Undoubtedly, in some situations decision-makers could restrict the choices people can make. This step should be taken only if the collective benefit of the society is clearly involved or if the decision-makers can determine that such restriction would benefit people's long-range goals on the basis of superior knowledge about the consequences of present short-range goals.

The fundamental value underlying all goals to be considered by the Social Planning Division is that Puerto Rican society should maximize the choices its people can make in all spheres of life and should give them the opportunities—socioeconomic, educational, and political—to make such choices. This is a general statement; societal planning would have to determine how existing resources can be used to maximize which choices for what people and which choices and people have first priority. The maximal-choice criterion is appropriate as the basis for all other values because it leaves members of the society free to make their own choices and to live as they wish, once they have the opportunities for choice. This prevents the possibility that goals for living set by a majority must deprive minorities with other ways of life and vice versa.

II. The methodology for societal planning

Any methodology for societal planning must fulfill three criteria: First, it must help to provide answers to planning decisions which are eventually embodied in budget and legislation decisions. The answers necessary can be summarized in the following list of questions:

(a) How much—i.e., quantity of resources?

(b) Of what—i.e., programs?

(c) For whom—i.e., for what clients?

(d) Why—i.e., to achieve what goals?

(e) For how much—i.e., what social and economic costs?

(f) Under what conditions—i.e., with what other consequences, especially demands made on the people for whom the Division is planning?

Second, the methodology must provide techniques for goal choice, for the selection of programs to achieve these goals, and for determining the consequences of these programs on costs and the functioning of the society.

Third, the methodology dealing with goal choice must be flexible to allow for the multiplicity of goals and interests in society and for the changes these are undergoing over time. Concurrently, however, the methodology must provide criteria or values which are absolute in the heuristic sense, so that goals and alternative programs can be evaluated against them.

A. *Over-all methodology*

The over-all methodology may be described as *goal-oriented planning*. There are essentially two approaches to this kind of planning. One approach begins with a goal choice and proceeds thence to programs and consequences. The other begins with various alternative programs, analyzes their implicit goals, and then revises the programs to achieve explicitly stated goals. The first approach may be outlined as follows:

1. Statement of goal in operational terms.

2. Development of program alternatives to achieve the goal.
3. Analysis of three types of consequences of implementing these program alternatives:
   (*a*) Goal achievement: do the programs achieve the goals?
   (*b*) Costs: what are the costs, in various kinds of resources, for effectuating the programs?
   (*c*) Other consequences: what effects do these programs have on other aspects of the social system and on the achievement of other goals?
4. Comparison of programs: which of the alternative programs functions best and most efficiently with respect to:
   (*a*) Achievement of goals.
   (*b*) Maximization of benefits over costs.
   (*c*) Minimization of undesirable consequences.
5. Comparison of goal in relation to other goals:
   (*a*) Comparison at the level of costs: is the goal worth the costs and the shifting of resources from other goals?
   (*b*) Comparison at the level of goals: is the goal worth the detrimental consequences, if any, on the achievement of other goals?
   (*c*) Development of goal priority: how does the goal rank with others in a priority system?
6. Final planning decision:
   (*a*) Acceptance or rejection of goal and program, with given consequences.
   (*b*) Alteration of goal and program to minimize undesirable consequences.

This approach has some limitations; it assumes that the planners can rank the society's goals in order of priority and then develop programs for these goals. Moreover, this approach tends to neglect existing programs. Conversely, starting with goals allows the planner to think about goals without the restraint of existing programs and is therefore useful for the development of new ideas. For example, if the planner's goal is to accelerate the acculturation of poor rural migrants to urban life, new programs can be developed to attempt to achieve this goal, rather than to assume without proof that tearing down the rural houses of such people and rehousing them in the city will help achieve the desired acculturation.

The alternative and more feasible approach to goal-oriented planning begins with present program alternatives and evaluates the goals implicit in them. These alternatives may be existing or proposed programs contained in a legislative proposal, a budget draft, or a master plan. The methodology can be outlined as follows:

1. Statement of all proposed alternatives, if possible in operational terms.
2. Analysis of the consequences of each alternative if it were implemented:
   (a) Goals: what goals would be achieved for different sectors and client groups in the society?
   (b) Goals: what goals would not be achieved if the alternative were not implemented?
   (c) Costs: what are the costs, in social and economic resources? If possible, these should be stated as estimates of cost per unit of achievement, or per client, or per unit of scarce resources.
   (d) Other consequences: what effects would each program have on other aspects of the social and economic system and goals involved in each? Which are desirable and undesirable?
3. Analysis of goals.
   (a) Are the goals implicit in the programs the proper goals, i.e., those being sought?
   (b) If not: revise program alternatives until they are in line with the goals actually sought.
   (c) If yes:
      (1) Which of the alternatives achieves more important goals at least cost of the scarcer resources and with least undesirable consequences?
      (2) Which alternative, if not provided, would result in more undesirable consequences for the society?
      (3) What alterations can be made in one or the other alternative to achieve the goals of both at least cost?
      (4) What innovations can be suggested to achieve the important goals of both at least cost?
4. Presentation of alternatives to decision-maker.
   (a) Analysis of each alternative, with reference to goals, costs, and other consequences.
   (b) Recommendation for choice to be made on a *technical* basis: if decision-maker wants to achieve goal A, then he should choose program A, etc.
   (c) Recommendation for choice on an *evaluative* basis, indicating which programs will contribute most to the achievement of overall societal values.
   (d) Recommendations for choice on *other* bases. Here the planner is no longer technician, but governmental-political adviser, and might suggest his choice of alternatives, giving reasons for this choice, especially where it differs from the choice suggested by analysis under 4(c) above.

Which of the two appro ıches is more useful will depend on the kinds of problem that require solution. As already indicated, the first approach is probably more useful for innovation, while the second is more useful for evaluation of proposed alternative programs.

The heart of the planning process is to encourage the development of programs that will achieve the goals desired. Too much of current planning revolves around programs which are legitimated by tradition, rather than by any knowledge of whether they achieve the desired goal. Thus, it is important to develop a new tradition of asking, for any goal: What are the programs that would really achieve this goal, irrespective of existing programs? Likewise, for any program: What goals does this program actually achieve; what clients does it attract, and does it provide them with services they want or need? Or is it simply a program which satisfies the values of those who supply it, but does not appeal to any need or demand among intended users? Continued raising of such questions by planners who have no prior emotional or ideological commitment to any specific answer will produce visible benefits at the level of planning analysis.

It would be unrealistic to pretend that data for these analyses are now available or will be available in sufficient amounts in the future. Nevertheless, if the analyses themselves are valid, the lack of data should not be a deterrent to asking the right questions.

B. *The development of goals and criteria for evaluating goals*

Much of the work of the Division will hinge on the problem of what goals and whose goals are to be pursued and in what order of priority. These are crucial value questions, to be answered in the last analysis by the society and its elected decision-makers. However, the Social Planning Division can and should give aid, not only by providing answers for the technical formula "if this is the goal, then these are the programs, their costs, and consequences" but by providing advisory analyses on what the goals of the society are and should be.

As already noted, this requires a scheme that is flexible enough to take account of the multiplicity of goals and absolute enough to be used for evaluation. Everett Reimer and Janet Reiner have taken the work of Harold Lasswell to develop a matrix system of nine values, the maximization of which they assume is desired both by Puerto Rican society and by its individual members. The values are:

I. *The Welfare Values*
   1. Well-being
   2. Wealth

3. Skill
4. Enlightenment
II. *Deference Values*
5. Respect
6. Rectitude
7. Power
8. Love
III. *Aesthetic Values*
9. Beauty

Although this list has considerable merit, I have some questions about the values and the way they are stated. First, the values are not equal at the level of causality or priority. For example, without prior achievement of the welfare values, the deference values (or what I would call social values) cannot be realized. People who lack basic economic resources, so that their subsistence level is marginal and insecure and their fundamental aspirations are frustrated, cannot treat each other or themselves with the human dignity implied in the social values. This criticism implies that the values must be arranged in some order of causal as well as policy priority.

Moreover, the values are presently stated as psychological concepts applicable to individuals. In order for them to be useful in societal planning, they must be developed further. First, they must be specified to refer to the individual in various social roles, that is, as family member worker, user of leisure time, member of the community, and so on. A given value will have different meanings and different priority for the roles people play.

Second, the values must be restated also to refer to collectivities, such as specific Puerto Rican institutions, interest groups, and subcultures, and to the society as a whole. When the value under discussion affects an industry or service institution, I would subdivide the individual referent, so as to distinguish between the *supplier* and the *user* of the service. For example, if the program alternative is to channel economic growth into San Juan, the value is well-being, and the institution under analysis is the educational system, one would want to know not only whether the program would benefit the users of the service (the students) but also the suppliers (the teachers, principals, and administrators). In general, the user should have higher priority than the supplier.

Third, the values must be translated into operational goal statements about what kinds of goal Puerto Rico should seek. For example, skill is a general value, but the planners must know what kinds of skill are valued by different parts of the population and what skills are needed by the society in order to achieve the other values.

Also, as stated, the values do not allow for differences among people in defining them. For example, if beauty is considered a major value, it must be recognized that different subcultures in the society have different concepts of beauty and that what is ugly for one group may be beautiful for another. There are sharp differences between the aesthetics of the professional upper-middle class, which emphasizes function, simplicity, and subtlety, and that of the working class, which appreciates ornateness and prefers liveliness to subtlety. Whatever the values of the planner, both aesthetics have the right to exist and must be considered in societal planning.

Finally, and perhaps most important, the list must include what I would call priority values, that is, values which allow the planners and decision-makers to determine which values—and the goals that result from them—have priority, so that they can decide which goals must be sought first and which can be postponed and how scarce resources are to be allocated. I would propose three such values:

1. Universal benefits: the most desirable goals are those producing the greatest benefits for the largest number of people.

2. Incremental benefits: those people who now have the least of any value should have highest priority in benefiting from government programs.

3. Economizing: Resources should be allocated to maximize universal and incremental benefits at least cost, especially of the scarcest resources, and with the fewest undesirable consequences for other values and goals.

When values that refer to individuals are translated into planning goals and programs, it will become apparent that few goals and programs will have universal benefits, for almost all social change requires some individuals and groups to pay economic and other costs if others are to receive benefits. Consequently the incremental-benefit value is of crucial importance.

C. *A note on values, goals, and social processes*

The methodology has proceeded almost exclusively in terms of values, goals, and programs, ignoring the fact that society never has total control over its activities and is often controlled by broad and powerful social and economic processes. This is especially true for Puerto Rico, which is tied economically to the mainland and socially and culturally to a variety of traditions—mainland, Latin American, and Spanish.

However, the methodology can be adapted to the analysis of societal *processes* as well. Processes can be analyzed as reversible and irreversible, as amenable to action and not amenable to action, and as desirable or undesirable. A process that is reversible or otherwise amenable to action can be treated as a program alternative. An irreversible process is, of course, a fixed alternative and must be treated as such. However, an irreversible process can be amenable to action. Thus, urbanization is probably an irreversible process in Puerto Rico, but it can be affected by a variety of program alternatives, that is, by decisions about whether growth should be deliberately deflected into San Juan, or into other existing cities, or into newly built cities. Each of these alternatives has certain costs and benefits: For example, the present urbanization process, which brings people mostly to San Juan, may have economic benefits (such as the economics of scale of a large city) and economic and social costs (like the problems of acculturation to big-city life). Finally, all processes can be evaluated as desirable or undesirable because even the most irreversible process usually allows for the realization of some values and goals among many members of society. If a social process did not contribute to the implementation of such goals, it would be reflected in data on asocial and antisocial behavior. Thus, not only is the growth of San Juan an example of the urbanization process but it can also be interpreted as representing an opportunity for people to maximize as best they know how their wealth and well-being and to satisfy the new aspirations of the Puerto Rican standard of living better than they could in rural areas. There are probably few major social processes that violate the values of the majority participating in them.

Processes can thus be treated as program alternatives; and conversely, program alternatives can be treated as examples or portions of existing social processes. The planner who seeks to affect social processes should have some idea of the functions of existing processes before he attempts to develop substitutes. Social-science research has shown that even the most undesirable social processes always have some positive functions for some people that cannot be ignored. As Robert K. Merton has written:

> Any attempt to eliminate an existing social structure without providing adequate alternative structures for fulfilling the functions previously fulfilled by the abolished organization is doomed to failure. . . . When political reform [or planning, H.G.] confines itself to the manifest task of "turning the rascals out" it is engaging in little more than sociological magic. . . . To seek social change without due recognition of the manifest and latent functions performed by the social organization undergoing change is to indulge in social ritual rather than social engineering.[1]

III. Social programing

Societal planning is concerned with broad goal determination for the society and with evaluation of programs on a broad level for budgetary decisions. It asks, for example, what proportion of the budget should go for education, what proportion for health. Social programing would be concerned with the following:

1. Providing information to the societal-planning function on non-economic, nonphysical programs relevant to the goals with which societal planning is concerned. For example, the Societal Planning Unit would call on economic planners for economic programing and on the Social Programing Unit for data and planning analysis to frame programs in the social sphere. Conversely, the Social Programing Unit would provide information to the Societal Planning Unit on the social consequences of the programs the latter would develop. It would function as a resource office to societal planning, working out specific goal-program cost-and-consequence relationships in the noneconomic, nonphysical sphere for societal planning.

2. Developing a system of social data that would provide the Planning Board with a continual overview of social trends in the country, in much the same way as the Bureau of Economics and Statistics surveys annually the state of the economy. The problems of developing a system of social data are more complex than those of a system of economic data, and such a system should not attempt to copy directly that set up by economics. First, annual changes in "social" trends may not be as relevant for the society as economic trends. Second, social data are often more difficult to gather and interpret than economic material. Data on school enrollment tell only about the physical presence of children in school and provide no information about the more important question of how many children are learning what they ought to be learning.

3. Co-ordinating the planning and action programs of all government departments concerned with social programing. It is assumed that eventually every major government department will have its own planning staff and that much of the day-to-day programing function can be borne by these departments. The Social Programing Unit would then translate the over-all framework of the societal-planning approach into general programing assignments and work with other government agencies to bring such programing to fruition.

4. The term *social* in social programing should be defined loosely, and the scope of the Social Programing Unit should be broad in scope, so

that the Unit can develop programs for those societal goals which are not handled by economists, land-use planners, or architect-designers. Moreover, the Division should place major stress on programing in those spheres of social life in which formal agencies, particularly welfare agencies, are not active. In line with some of the tendencies that led to its formation, the Division should provide programing in the area of social change, both to ameliorate problems resulting from such change and to maximize opportunities for the members of the society involved in it. For example, the changing role of the teen-ager in the society means that his leisure-time activities will soon become a "problem" in urban areas. The Social Programing Unit should consider programing other than the stereotypical suggestions of playgrounds, parks, and recreation centers proposed by professional advocates of these facilities.

Similarly, the Unit should emphasize what I would call a *client-oriented* perspective on existing social service and welfare agencies. For example, some of the agencies find that actual clients are fewer in number and different in characteristics than intended clients. Health centers find that those who need its services the most are hardest to reach, and recreation departments sometimes discover their facilities are underused, even in the densest residential areas. The agencies responsible for these programs are often not in the best position ideologically or administratively to change the services so that they attract the non-attending among the intended clients or are made more suitable for the actual clients. The research and programing for such changes might be an important function for the Social Programing Unit.

NOTE

1. *Social Theory and Social Structure,* (2d ed.; Glencoe, Ill.: Free Press, 1957), p. 81.

8

Supplier-Oriented and User-Oriented Planning for the Public Library

I

This essay attempts to apply an approach to city planning that can be used to make plans not only for the future growth of the city but also for individual public institutions. City planning is a body of techniques and theories for co-ordinative decision-making which tries to distribute the community's resources in a manner which will best achieve the community's goals, whatever they may be. Consequently, when planning for a specific institution, the planner must ask to what extent that institution can achieve the community's goals, and on the basis of such goals, the planner would recommend how much of the community's resources should be spent on the institution and for what kinds of facilities and services.

Determining the community's goals requires attention to three interacting groups or entities: the *suppliers* of a service by an institution, such as the public library; the clients or *users,* or the readers; and the *community* itself. The community is an entity hard to define; it includes the citizens, their interest groups, decision-makers—and the public interest. In studying these three entities, one must discover how they operate as institutions and groups, their objectives, the programs or means they use to achieve them, and the consequences of these programs on the community.

The first two parts of this chapter are taken from an unpublished paper, "Planning, Institutional Policy and User Behavior: The Public Library—A Case Study," read at the Institute for Social Research, University of Chicago, May 1956. Part III is adapted from a paper prepared for the Symposium on Library Functions in the Changing Metropolis, sponsored by the National Book Committee and the Joint Center for Urban Studies, Massachusetts Institute of Technology and Harvard University, and published as "The Public Library in Perspective," in Ralph Conant ed., *The Public Library and the City* (Cambridge: Massachusetts Institute of Technology Press, 1965), pp. 67–73. The entire chapter draws on my "A Comprehensive Planning Study of the Public Library," an unpublished monograph prepared at the Institute for Urban Studies, University of Pennsylvania.

The study of the suppliers draws on current sociological research in the professions and occupations and requires an analysis of the relationship between institutional characteristics and the objectives and programs. A close knowledge of the institution is also needed to distinguish between *professed* objectives, the official and manifest ones which appear in organizational preambles, and the *practiced* ones which are often latent in the operating program.

When dealing with users, the terminology changes somewhat, for on the basis of current knowledge it seems fallacious to describe people's consumer behavior as having clear-cut objectives. Rather, people in these roles are making choices, conscious or unconscious, deliberate or impulsive, among various items offered by different suppliers. From a study of these choices, it may be possible to infer practiced objectives.

The synthetic or planning phase of the study rests on the assumption that it is possible for a community to develop a set of community objectives ranked in order of priority. At this point, it is not certain whether such a set can be developed or whether a heterogeneous aggregate like an urban community can even agree on one set. Assuming this is feasible, however, even in a primitive fashion, it would be possible, among public institutions at least, to decide who shall be able to implement what goals by what programs. Prior analysis will have determined what programs are likely to achieve what goals and which programs have consequences that are undesirable for goals of higher priority.

The frame of reference can be restated at least partially in terms of functional sociological and social-science theory. Like the functionalist, the planner sees the community as a system and attempts to plan for the achievement of objectives, some of them common to all members of the system and others not. The program and consequences with which he is concerned must be functional for the reference groups with which he is concerned, without being seriously dysfunctional for any other. (In actual practice in a political world, this often means dysfunctional for no group.) In one sense, the planner is trying to develop programs for a set of community objectives which will maximize functionality and minimize dysfunctionality for all reference groups. In this process, he analyzes social structures in terms of their manifest and latent functions. He is especially concerned with the latter, for he must isolate the unanticipated consequences of his programs, determine or estimate their influence on his set of objectives, and try to plan for the elimination of dysfunctional consequences. In planning for such situations, he will try to develop functional alternatives which will achieve the objectives without dysfunctional consequences for other parts of the system. The functional analysis is, therefore, particularly useful in programing the process of implementation, for the planner must understand the functional and dysfunctional consequences of any social pattern before he recommends the replacement of an existing pattern with an innovation.

The theory also places major emphasis on the analysis of the reference groups for whom various institutions and patterns may or may not be functional or dysfunctional. This analysis allows the planner to calculate his ranked objectives and community programs in terms of the publics which they will affect either functionally or dysfunctionally. It will also permit him to judge the political feasibility of any program and the compromises necessary if the objective of implementation is ranked high in his set of objectives. (Of course, in estimating political consequences, the planner cannot always know or predict when more energetic political action might achieve the total objective and when compromise is inevitably necessary; thus some contingency factor must be built into the evaluation of political consequences.)

II

This is the frame of reference; the remainder of the paper will apply it to planning for the public library. In defining its goals, the public library has struggled, like all service-giving agencies, between two conceptions of itself. One, which derives from the people who supply library services and which I call *supplier-oriented,* argues that the library is an institution which ought to achieve the educational and cultural goals of the librarian and his profession; the other, which I call *user-oriented,* argues that the library ought to cater to the needs and demands of its users. These are polar opposites, and in the library's actual goal choices both positions are included; the usual solution has been to uphold the supplier-oriented conception in its professional conferences and publications, but to adopt more of a user-oriented conception in actual practice, if only in order to get the library budget approved by the city fathers.

The suppliers of public library service are not only librarians but members of the public library movement, one of the several reform and "cultural uplift" movements of the middle and late nineteenth century. The contemporary objectives of the library must be understood within the historical context of this movement. The founders of the public library were allied with the public education movement and considered the library to be an outgrowth of this movement and an agency for postgraduate public education. This tradition goes back even further to Benjamin Franklin's discussion-club library and the mercantile and mechanics library of the Colonial period. These institutions were intended to stimulate the mobility strivings of young clerks, merchants, and mechanics and keep them out of lower-class leisure haunts.

The current objectives of the American Library Association continue these traditions through two somewhat contradictory themes. On the one hand, the library is conceived as an agency of cultural stimulation serving to persuade the public to seek five ends: self-education, gathering of information for occupational and citizenship duties, research, aesthetic appreciation and production, and the pursuit of socially and individually useful leisure-time activities. On the other hand, the library is envisaged as a storehouse for cultural materials of high quality through which users already motivated toward self-improvement can achieve the five ends. These two themes are professed objectives. They have been described as the librarian's faith, and an important though latent function is their symbolic and cohesive role in the profession.

In addition, the library has a set of practiced objectives which are built into the published standards by which it evaluates and plans itself. The main objectives are institutional growth and maximization of use. The need for library growth is based on the unproved assumption that the larger the library, the better its service to the users. Maximization of use is expressed through standards relating to user behavior, such as the number of books taken out or the number of reference questions asked annually. These are like sales quotas and are based on another unproved assumption: that reader-use patterns are determined solely by the adequacy, as defined by the library, of its book stock and reference desk. In fact, however, reader behavior is based as much on user goals as on the library's definition of adequate service.

What little is known about library-user behavior is based on a number of studies made over two decades, which were synthesized and evaluated by Berelson and Asheim in 1949.[1] Their data precede the era of television and the paperback book, but they indicate that in those days about 25 to 30 per cent of the American people read a book a month, and of these 25 to 40 per cent found their reading primarily in the public library. In an average community, the regular clientele consisted of not quite 10 per cent of the adults and a third of the young people. The data suggest that this clientele can perhaps be divided into four major publics, although no study isolating these publics has yet been made.

The largest group of users are elementary- and high-school students who use the library primarily for homework purposes. They take between 50 and 60 per cent of the books circulated in the average library. The next largest group is adults who read the best sellers and other fiction.

Although this public takes most of the adult books, it seems to consist of a small number of voracious readers. According to one study noted by Berelson, 20 per cent of the library users borrow three-quarters of the books. (Another study sets this figure as high as 10 per cent of the borrowers reading 98 per cent of the books.) These readers come mainly from middle- and lower-middle income groups and white-collar occupations. They have high-school diplomas or some education beyond grade school. A majority are under thirty-five, and many are women. This is by far the largest adult public.

The third public is very much smaller. It consists of opinion-leaders who use the library's contemporary fiction and nonfiction in playing their special community roles. A fourth group, also very small, includes the commercial, professional, and amateur researchers, who make heavy use of the reference room and the nonfiction collection.

One of the library's main policy dilemmas is the difference between the image of the adult user contained in the professed objectives and the behavior and characteristics of actual users. The picture of the self-improvement-oriented readers seeking the five ends of a quasi-intellectual culture contrasts sharply with the typical adult user who borrows popular light fiction for nonpurposive leisure and asks quite nonintellectual questions at the reference desk. We can only infer objectives here, but for this reader the books borrowed from the library probably serve many of the same functions as television and radio fare do for others.

The library's policy dilemma is most clearly seen in book-selection practices, but it manifests itself in other parts of library service. The official book-selection standards reflect the professed objectives, but in practice, the books acquired first are the best sellers and others for which there is strong local demand. The books more in accord with professed objectives have lower priority, and only the larger libraries can afford to buy them.

On the level of objectives, the conflict is between supplier-oriented and user-oriented goals. The former goals seek to direct user behavior to accord with institutional ideology. The latter goals, on the other hand, permit the users to shape, or at least to influence, the goals and programs of the institution, although not so much as in a commercial agency. On another level, the conflict is between the products of a popular culture and a modern version of the pre-mass-media-era high culture from which the library's ideology developed.

For the library, the choice between the two positions is a difficult one. If it rejects user-oriented objectives and popular culture, it loses many of its regular users. The desire for institutional self-preservation rules out this alternative. If it rejects high culture and supplier-oriented objectives, it denies the faith of its founders and its traditional ideology. Moreover, it surrenders the cultural and intellectual superiority it considers itself to have over bookstores or rental libraries. Nor is the librarian able to take a midway position. For one thing, the supplier-oriented librarian cannot really understand why his clients read "trash" or books of ephemeral value; the cultural and status gap is too wide to be crossed by anything except moral scorn. Furthermore, the library ideology developed in an era of self-reliance and assumes a self-motivated clientele, professed objective of reader stimulation notwithstanding. Moreover, Berelson's study indicates that very few readers voluntarily seek the librarian's guidance.

As I noted before, the solution developed by the library is a pragmatic one taken by other institutions in the same dilemma. On the whole, user-oriented objectives guide the everyday operations, while supplier-oriented objectives are reserved for journal articles, convention shop talk, and other in-group communication.

This is a short-range, *ad hoc* adjustment, with some functions and dysfunctions for suppliers, users, and community alike. The planner makes the assumption that there ought to be an optimal balance between the professed and practiced goals of suppliers, users, and community. On that basis, I should like to suggest a possible solution to the conflict.

This solution is based on the hypothesis that out of the multiplicity of leisure choices available to Americans, the ones they make tend on the whole to cluster in patterns which we might call leisure cultures or sub-cultures. These can be classified in many ways, but I shall use Van Wyck Brooks's trilogy of high-brow, middle-brow, and low-brow, as revived by Russell Lynes,[2] except that I shall use the three types as empirical categories, without the value judgments usually attached to them. If librarians were inclined toward discovering what their readers want—which they are not—they would make studies to determine in each of these cultural or taste levels what people read, how they read, what they get out of reading and out of what they read. What little research exists, however, shows only that people with a grade-school education, most of whose reading choices are in the low-brow category, cannot and do not easily read material written for the high-brow or even the increasingly college-trained middle-brow.

If research on book readers were available, we might well discover that some of the objectives the library wants its readers to seek are actually achieved, although by different books for people of different cultural levels. For example, perhaps the facts and insights a low-brow reader derives from a "light" novel are just as enlightening and relevant to his social and cultural situation as those the high-brow reader gets from a novel chosen by the literary critics. The beauty the low-brow reader finds in an apropos use of a familiar expression may be as satisfying to him as the high-brow's appreciation of Proustian style. The satisfactions which a low-brow may derive from an interpersonal activity may be achieved vicariously through reading by the high- or middle-brow, while in another sphere of life these patterns may be exactly reversed. Consequently, reading and reading choices may be related to social, cultural, and personality situations, rather than simply to taste and reading skill. We may even discover that nonpurposive leisure reading by the middle- and low-brow may be socially and individually as useful as the purposive reading which library ideology associates with high-brow fiction.

The above hypotheses imply a cultural pluralism or relationism based on instrumental criteria. These do not answer the question of whether high culture may not be intrinsically better than middle or low culture. However, unless such intrinsic judgments can deal with the question "better for whom and for what," they can apply only to individual choice, where the whom and the what are given. For a public institution which serves a number of publics, however, instrumental criteria seem to be more relevant.

The empirical evidence may or may not justify these relationist notions. If it does, the consequences for library policy may be significant. If low-brow or middle-brow books have the same functions as high-brow ones for readers of "lower" cultural levels, then the conflict between supplier-oriented and user-oriented goals can be eliminated, with the former being achieved through the latter. The library could maintain its self-improvement and educational objectives, and still set up programs by which readers would be attracted and satisfied, by developing new distinctions between good and bad books for each of the cultural levels, rather than deciding a priori that all low-brow books are intrinsically bad. Similarly, the library might develop user-oriented criteria for other programs, such as book-reviewing and reader guidance, which do not assume or demand high-brow loyalties from the reader. While such a policy might reduce the library's not always deserved status as an institution of high culture, it would increase rapport between the library and its users and might lead to some real reader stimulation by the library and its personnel.

This kind of question is typical of those which the community must ask in order to rank the library in its set of community objectives and its allocation of resources. In their most general form, these community questions are three: what is the value of reading to the community; what is the function of the book with relation to reading; and finally, what is the function of the library in both?

The value of reading has only been recently questioned in our book-oriented culture, and most effectively perhaps by several experiments and studies which suggest that television and film may be more effective than the book in communicating certain kinds of factual materials; for example, in teaching science to youngsters. Similarly, if communication effectiveness is the goal, abridgments, magazines, comic books, and the electronic media may be superior to the book, even if they lack its prestige. In other words, if the community goal of the library is to communicate information to the citizenry, other media may be more effective than the book, and the library as we know it ought to be replaced.

In order to limit the range of alternatives, I shall assume that the library should continue to be primarily an agency for distributing book and related reading materials. The function of the library, and the planning of its facilities, ought to be determined by whatever goal or goals the community considers important vis-à-vis books and the value of reading. If the community's goal is to maximize reading by the largest number of readers, for example, then the relationist policy of choosing books to cater to the community's distribution of taste levels would be the best alternative. Conversely, in the era of paperbacks, the community might decide that the main goal ought to be the provision of books and other materials not available on the drugstore rack. This was suggested by the Public Library Inquiry sponsored by the Carnegie Foundation; it proposed that the library ought to perform functions not handled by the mass media and serve as a reservoir for books and other materials of high culture and academic and experimental value. On the other hand, one could also argue that because poor people are not well served by the mass media—there are few magazines or TV programs for poor people—the library ought to cater more to the increasing number of the poor, particularly in the city. Yet other alternatives are possible; a community could set up a library based on the librarian's professed objectives alone. In that case, however, it would have to develop substitute facilities for the present users.

The questions I have posed do not have to be asked every time the community builds a new branch library; rather they are questions to be considered in setting up long-range comprehensive plans. Even then, they ought to be asked primarily by community decision-makers and library planners and answered with the help of the social sciences. The city planner's real task is to co-ordinate the answers of all the community's institutions, relate them to community objectives, and then implement them in relation to the available resources.

III

Although it is impossible to make community-goal choices for the library in the abstract, for that depends on the distinctive conditions in individual communities, it is possible to make some general choices among the alternatives most often proposed. The remainder of the paper discusses six alternatives, including my own, which I believe will best meet the needs of the library in today's metropolis. The first two alternatives are supplier-oriented; the remainder are user-oriented.

The first alternative views the library as a storehouse for cultural materials, a reservoir of significant books. One of the previously mentioned supplier-oriented goals of the library profession, it has recently been revived by the American Library Association's proposal for regional libraries that would mediate between the central and the branch library. The regional library emphasizes the quality of its collection; it is less concerned with the needs and demands of actual users.

The second alternative sees the library as an agency of cultural stimulation, as an educational institution. It will motivate people to read—convert some from nonreaders to readers, so to speak—and help others, already reading, to shift from "ephemeral" to quality books. As I noted earlier, this conception of the library has not received much support from its users; only the children seek education deliberately when they use the library to do their homework, and many of the other borrowers are looking for recreational fare. Moreover, the library has not been effective as an educational institution; few librarians are trained as educators or have the time to educate their clients even if they are so trained.

These supplier-oriented conceptions of the library are highly regarded by the profession, but they are less desirable from the point of view of community planning. If a library is not attractive to many users, it is difficult to demand for it a large share of scarce public resources. A library that is not used sufficiently is a waste of resources, even if its goals are noble and the size and quality of the collection are outstanding. Consequently, the library must be user-oriented; it must be planned to attract enough users to justify public expenditures. It is doubtful whether a library system designed to attract primarily high-brow users would be in the public interest; these users generally have access to a university library or can afford their own books. The question is, which users should be planned for?

One user-oriented alternative is to plan the library for all users, which Ennis describes as the cafeteria.[3] This was the practice before the age of the paperback, when libraries supplied recreational reading to the middle-class population, in addition to serving children and students. The paperback has cut sharply into fiction circulation, and Ennis is right in questioning this type of library.

A second user-oriented approach is to plan for people who are not being served adequately by bookstores, book clubs, paperbacks, or university libraries. This is the practice of many libraries today that are catering to the sharply rising numbers of children and students and also to a more slowly rising number of readers of nonfiction of the best-seller variety as the old adult audience for fiction is disappearing. This is a desirable solution. The library need not compete with the paperback book, especially the low-priced one. Not only is a drugstore more accessible than the public library but it allows the average reader to indulge freely his taste for entertainment and fantasy without feeling guilty about his choice of leisure reading. Best sellers are available in paperback almost as quickly as they are in most public libraries. Moreover, paperbacks are cheap and need not be returned. For those who can afford them, they represent a reasonable source of leisure reading. Conversely, children and students either cannot afford books, do not wish to buy them, or simply cannot get them as cheaply and efficiently as adults can get their books at the corner drugstore. They and people who want nonfiction reading of the nonbest-seller sort will be dependent on library service until paperback publishers meet their demands.

A third user-oriented alternative is for libraries to identify a distinct clientele and to serve it as efficiently as possible. Whether the clients are the opinion-leaders suggested by Berelson or the low-income population, such an alternative is too limiting for a public institution; it transforms the library into a highly specialized agency, and it ceases being a public library.

The final user-oriented alternative, which I favor, is based on two assumptions. First, the library should serve a specific *set* of clienteles, mainly the people now not served adequately by other methods of distributing printed materials. Second, the library should serve the people who live near it, for the studies compiled by Berelson have shown that most libraries serve people living within one-half to one mile away, or to put it another way, that most people will just not go much farther to borrow a book. This is probably still true in today's cities and, with corrections for car and bicycle use, in the suburbs as well. It is even valid for the main library, as studies show that a large proportion of its users come from areas closest to it. Furthermore, this datum is a major reason for the success of the drugstore paperback rack.

The fact that the library can only attract people within a relatively small radius means that it has no alternative but to serve whoever lives— or works—in that radius. Since most people get their books where they live, rather than where they work, the library is basically a neighborhood institution, and the most important part of the system is the branch library, that modest, unassuming structure that often gets so little recognition or status from librarians. The main library may be the flagship of the system, and its large collection and monumental architecture the pride and joy of the community boosters, but it is the branch library where people come to get their reading materials.

If the concept of the library as serving those within its service area is combined with the principle that it ought to cater principally to those people not served by other methods of book distribution, some more detailed comments can be made about library planning.

First, libraries will have to be planned for the kinds of people who live in its service area. In middle-class neighborhoods the contemporary library is desirable, with its emphasis on child, student, and nonfiction readers. These people can afford hardbacks or paperbacks for recreational reading and can accept the middle-class aura that surrounds the public library.

In low-income areas, which are increasingly important in the changing metropolis, this middle-class library is unsatisfactory. Here a library is needed that invites rather than rejects the poorly educated person, with book stock, staff, and catalogue system that are designed to help him read. It should be geared to two types of readers: the small number who are already motivated and may even have the middle-class values and skills that are prerequisite to using the library, and, more important, the much larger number of people who cannot afford paperbacks and would like to read, but are afraid or scornful of the ethos of the middle-class library. There is a third group of potential users here: adults who cannot read well, but would like to learn. The library should teach these people or work with adult-education agencies that can teach reading. The publishing industry might give paperback and hard-cover overstock to libraries in low-income neighborhoods. These books would be freely distributed in order to encourage reading and develop potential buyers. Most important, as Frank Riessman has pointed out, the library must be a permissive, inviting place to the low-income population that is now so numerous in the American city.

In areas populated largely by older people, the library might provide more reading rooms, stocked with newspapers and magazines as well as books. Here lonely people could come to read and to converse in a kind of informal community center, perhaps in a storefront that would provide companionship as well as reading.

In suburban areas, the library is predominantly a children's library and should be geared to the needs, the noise level, and the attention span of the youthful population.

Conversely, in business districts the library serves people with special informational needs, and there the branch would be, as in many cities, stocked with nonfiction and reference material for those who work there. In suburban industrial areas, such a public library might have to be on wheels.

The diversity of plans required to meet the needs of a small service area might overwhelm a library planner. But this fear is groundless, as ecological research has shown; neighborhoods are much the same the nation over and fall into recognizable types. From these, several corresponding library plans could be developed, patterned for the urban middle-class residents, older people, suburban middle-class areas, low-income areas, and business districts. Using consumer research in the specified neighborhood, the appropriate type of branch library could then be adapted.

If the branch is the major component of the library system, what is the role of the main library? It ought to be the reservoir of the high-quality collection and of infrequently used materials. A central staff of highly trained reference librarians could serve the entire metropolitan area through closed-circuit television. This main library should ideally be modeled on a metropolitan main library like that of New York City, although in most cities such a facility is out of the question. There, local university or college libraries can be connected administratively to the public library to serve the specialized research and scholarly users and functions. Although the reference staff and some of the book stock of the main library must be located centrally, both to the city and the suburbs, less demanded books could be stored in a low-rent district from where they could be shipped easily, and quickly, to either the main or a branch library.

This conception of the public library is only one among several possibilities. It is biased toward a user-oriented conception of the public library; yet it is also traditional in viewing the library as a book-centered institution, rather than as a communication-centered one. My traditionalism is in turn based on two assumptions: first, that the public library ought to serve readers, rather than data-retrievers; and second, that it is difficult to divert institutions from their traditional ways, which makes it more desirable to develop new institutions for new needs. This approach to library planning is based on the idea that existing institutions not only should perform effectively their original functions but also should be adapted to the changing needs of their communities.

NOTES

1. Bernard Berelson, *The Library's Public* (New York: Columbia University Press, 1949).
2. Russell Lynes, *The Tastemakers* (New York: Harper, 1954), Chapter 13.
3. Philip Ennis, "The Library Consumer," in Ralph W. Conant, ed., *The Public Library and the City* (Cambridge: Massachusetts Institute of Technology Press, 1965), pp. 13–32.

9

Outdoor Recreation and Mental Health

The problem—a historical survey

The over-all topic of this essay is the relationship between outdoor recreation and mental health. Whether or not such a relationship exists is a question that has been discussed in America for many years, and some light can be shed on the answer by a brief consideration of the conditions under which the question was first raised.

The deliberate planning and development of outdoor recreation in America, at least in its cities, date back to the middle of the last century, when Frederick Law Olmsted began to call for the establishment of urban parks. Olmsted was the sickly son of a well-to-do Connecticut merchant, who was advised for health reasons to spend as much time outdoors as possible. After some years of farming, a trip to Europe stimulated his interest in landscape architecture, and for the rest of his life he designed and supervised the construction of city parks, beginning with New York's Central Park in 1857. His interest in parks developed at a time when cities of the eastern United States were growing by leaps and bounds, pushing back the rural areas beyond the reach of the city dwellers, especially the large majority who lived in tenements.

Olmsted was raised in a small New England town, and like a number of other reformers of the period he was horrified by the rapid expansion of urban slums. He was upset not only by the overcrowding and the poor quality of housing but also by the social and cultural patterns which he observed in the slums. Olmsted felt that these conditions were inevitable

Reprinted from *Trends in American Living and Outdoor Recreation*, Outdoor Recreation Resources Review Commission Study Report 22 (Washington: Government Printing Office, 1962), pp. 233–242. The essay was written as a keynote paper for a conference on Leisure, Outdoor Recreation, and Mental Health held by the National Institute of Mental Health and the Outdoor Recreation Resources Review Commission at Williamsburg, Virginia, June 1, 1961. Some of the material is based on research reported in "Recreation Planning for Leisure Behavior: A Goal-Oriented Approach," unpublished Ph.D. dissertation, Department of City and Regional Planning, University of Pennsylvania, 1957.

consequences of city living and argued that if city dwellers could only spend some of their leisure time outdoors, their existence would be more bearable. He conceived of parks as urban facsimiles of rural landscapes, which would provide "tranquility and rest to the mind."[1] Less sensitive and temperate observers than Olmsted described parks—and later, playgrounds as well as other forms of recreation—as veritable cure-alls which would isolate young people from and immunize them against the delinquency, alcoholism, prostitution, and crime that abounded in the slums. Many of the other phenomena which they described as evils we today would consider as fairly typical aspects of working-class and lower-class family and neighborhood life. However, these advocates of recreation had grown up in middle-class, small-town surroundings and could not accept alternative ways of living. Consequently, they tried to use outdoor recreation to convert the lower-class city dweller to the patterns of their culture.

Olmsted and the other advocates of outdoor recreation did not use the term "mental health," but their statements imply that the provision of outdoor recreation would lead directly to mental health. In later years, when the term mental health became popular, the virtues of outdoor recreation were reformulated in mental-health terms. The implied relationship between outdoor recreation and mental health was never seriously questioned, because the people who advocated outdoor recreation were so firmly convinced of the health-giving virtues of rural life and the desirability of defending rural and small-town America against the surge of immigrants that there was no need for evidence. The skeptic needed only to look at the slums of New York, Boston, or Philadelphia, in which trees, grass, and fresh air were rare indeed, while crime and mental illness flourished.

In our day, however, the answer to the old question is no longer self-evident, for the development of various forms of outdoor recreation has not done away with the traditional urban evils. This brief historical survey is not intended to suggest that the nineteenth-century answer to the question is necessarily wrong or that it was once correct but is now wrong, or that it was all a result of Olmsted's poor health. What I am saying is that the traditional answer was developed by a culturally narrow reform group which was reacting to a deplorable physical and social environment and rejected the coming of the urban-industrial society. As a result, it glorified the simple rural life and hoped to use outdoor recreation as a means of maintaining at least some vestiges of a traditional society and culture. Given these conditions and motivations, no one saw fit to investigate the relationship between outdoor recreation and mental health empirically.

The nature of leisure and recreation

Before it is possible to discuss the relationship of outdoor recreation and mental health, it is necessary to define some terms. Leisure and recreation can be defined in many ways; leisure is usually thought of as a temporal concept, denoting the time not given to work, maintenance, and sleep; recreation, as the behavior patterns which fill this time. I want to define the terms somewhat differently, relating them in a way that I think is useful not only for understanding the phenomena involved but also for policy-making purposes. By leisure or leisure behavior I mean the activity, or inactivity, which people pursue during their spare time. By recreation I mean the artifacts, facilities, and institutions which people employ for leisure behavior. Outdoor recreation is one such facility; the television set, arts and crafts, and the vacation resort are others. Some recreation facilities are provided by governmental agencies; these are usually thought of as public recreation. Others are provided by semipublic, private, or commercial agencies, and many if not most are purchased commercially, but used privately in or near the home.

Recreation is thus considered a means to leisure behavior. Leisure behavior is subjective, and leisure cannot be planned, or planned for. All that government and commercial agencies can do is to plan recreation facilities, with the intent, and hope, that they will be attractive enough for people to use them in leisure behavior.

This distinction is important for two reasons. First, it emphasizes the fact that the mere provision of outdoor recreation is not enough, for if recreation is not used, it does not provide the satisfactions of leisure. Second, it stresses a particular value judgment that one should not plan any person's leisure behavior. Leisure is satisfying and desirable only when it is chosen freely and spontaneously; for if it is not, it cannot be leisure. Conversely, recreation should be planned for deliberately.

The nature of mental health and mental illness

The concepts of mental health and mental illness are much more difficult to define than recreation or leisure. Mental health, or positive mental health, as it is sometimes called, is especially difficult to define, because any definition must include some vision of the good life and the good society, and there are many differences of opinion about the nature of both.

One of the thorniest problems is the evaluation of class differences.

Many definitions of mental health employ a middle-class concept of the good life and the good society, implying therefore that the divergent ways of other classes, especially of the working class and the lower class, are pathological, rather than simply different. One way of resolving this dilemma, at least for me, is this definition: mental health is the ability of an individual as an occupier of social roles and as a personality to move toward the achievement of his vision of the good life and the good society.[2] Such a definition leaves room for cultural differences in the determination of the good life.[3] It also suggests that mental health is a social rather than an individual concept, because if society frustrates the movement toward the good life, the mental health of those involved may be affected.[4]

Leisure and mental health

It seems to me that the opportunity to obtain and the ability to indulge in satisfying leisure behavior are part of the good life, however that is defined by various American subcultures.

By satisfying leisure behavior I mean here the kind of activity that provides the individual with physical and emotional relaxation, reduction of fatigue, restoration of energy lost elsewhere, and general recreation without ill effects. I add this last phrase—without ill effects—to suggest two qualifications. First, I would not consider the destructive acts of a person bent on self-destruction as satisfying leisure behavior. Pathological gambling, heavy alcohol use, or high-speed auto racing under conditions of extreme risk may satisfy the seeker of self-destruction, but I would not consider his leisure behavior satisfying. I do not consider gambling, drinking, or even auto-racing as pathological recreation facilities, however, since they can also be used for satisfying leisure behavior. Second, socially destructive leisure behavior is also excluded from the definition of satisfying leisure behavior. Teen-agers may enjoy racing jalopies at high speed, even without much danger to themselves; but if they create driving hazards to others, their leisure behavior is antisocial. The determination of what is antisocial is not easy to make, and one must be careful not to surrender to the temptation of describing leisure behavior one does not like as antisocial, or for that matter, as bad for mental health. For example, use of the mass media and most forms of commercial entertainment has traditionally been considered undesirable by the advocates of outdoor recreation, but the available evidence does not indicate that normal use of these facilities is in any way antisocial or pathological.[5]

If satisfying leisure behavior as I have defined it is part of the good life, it would follow that it is also a constituent part of mental health.

Therefore, the recreation facilities which help to make leisure satisfying are necessary for the achievement of mental health.

I am saying that leisure and recreation are a constituent part of mental health, but they cannot by themselves bring about mental health, cure mental illness—or prevent it. The advocates of outdoor recreation have often argued the opposite; that satisfying leisure behavior is a causal factor in mental health and that the leisure behavior which is most satisfying is that available in outdoor recreation. There is at present no evidence to support this argument. I have suggested that leisure is a subjective concept and that what makes leisure satisfying depends as much on the individual who chooses it as on the facility involved. What is leisure for one person is work for another; what is extremely satisfying for one may be quite dull for another. Likewise, any given recreation facility, indoor or outdoor, can offer satisfying leisure behavior to one person and boredom to another.

As far as I know, there have been no reliable empirical studies of the relationship between outdoor recreation, mental health, and mental illness. There have been some studies of the impact of playgrounds and community centers on antisocial behavior, such as delinquency, which raise serious doubt about the existence of any impact beyond the reduction of minor vandalism due to boredom. It is true that playground programs or community-center activities sometimes convert a delinquent into a pillar of the community. When this happens, however, I suspect that it is due, not to the facility itself, but to the therapeutic talents of a leader who provides the delinquent with a surrogate father or brother, or to the existence of a group that offers him enough support to convince him that society is not always his enemy. This explains to me the success of the gang workers who have transformed fighting gangs into baseball teams. Although the surroundings in which this transformation often takes place may be recreational, this does not mean that recreation is a causal factor. Studies of recreation and delinquency tell us nothing about mental health, but they, and other studies of the users and use patterns in public recreation, lead me to believe that access to parks, playgrounds, and other forms of outdoor recreation does not by itself cure or prevent mental illness or bring about mental health.

My assumption here is that leisure and recreation are, comparatively speaking, relatively unimportant causal factors in achieving either mental health or the good life. They are essential and desirable, but they are not so important as economic opportunity and security, positive family life, education, the availability of a variety of primary and secondary group supports, and the like. Once again, I am in disagreement with the general climate of opinion on outdoor recreation. Its advocates have put forth three propositions which require consideration: that leisure time and the improvement of leisure behavior are one of the central issues of our society; that the improvement of leisure through outdoor recreation and other forms of public recreation can be used to solve deprivations in the nature of work, family life, and other basic institutions; and that leisure behavior can be used as a form of societal therapy.

It is true that there is more leisure time today than ever before, but I am not yet convinced that this is likely to be a serious problem, now or in the immediate future. Although the work week is shrinking, that shrinkage is presently slower than sometimes imagined. The average factory work week in 1960 was still 39.7 hours, down from 40.3 in 1959.[6] The wholesale and retail trade work week was 40.1 hours in January 1961, as it was in 1959 and most of 1960.[7] (Work hours in white-collar occupations are probably closer to 36 or 37 hours per week, however.) Current work-week figures differ little from those of earlier years. Thus, Dewhurst reports that the average work week in 1920 was 47 hours. By 1940 it had dropped to 41 hours, partly because of the Depression, but between 1940 and 1952 it decreased only to 39 hours, a change of 2 hours over 12 years.[8] Undoubtedly the development of automation will see sharper reductions in the work week, but the 30-hour work week is still not around the corner. Personally, I am not concerned about the leisure implications of shorter work weeks, but I am worried about the possibility of underemployment and mass unemployment.

While the hours available for leisure activities are thus increasing slowly, I suspect that the aspirations and expectations for that period are rising much more sharply. Not only are opportunities for various kinds of leisure behavior and recreation facilities broadening, but as incomes increase, more people than ever are able to participate in them. For example, a generation ago, boating and golf were upper-income-group sports; today, almost everyone of middle income who is not afraid of the water or too lazy to walk the fairways can participate in both.

Likewise, rising educational levels reveal new recreation facilities to people: summer theater, art movies, foreign travel, do-it-yourself activities, photography, and painting are some examples. It is true that television viewing is today the most important leisure activity as measured by number of hours, and a number of critics have used this datum and others like it to argue that people will be unable to cope with further increases in leisure time. They believe that people do not know how to spend the leisure time they have now and fear that further increases will lead to mass boredom, mental illness, and social unrest.

I think these fears stem from a lack of understanding of how people now spend their leisure hours. Moreover, the fears are founded on a rather rigid ideal of how these hours should be spent; namely, in the kind of leisure behavior favored by the recreation movement. Any time not spent in this kind of leisure behavior is thought to be wasted, and since so little time is now spent on it, the advocates of the preferred leisure behavior believe that people are wasting their leisure hours. From this value judgment it is easy to go one step further: to assume that the people themselves are unhappy and bored with the way they spend their spare time and would go berserk if there were further increases in spare time.

There is also a false historical assumption. The rise of the mass media has often been interpreted as a sign of the gradual deterioration of leisure behavior in our society. In this argument, statistics on media use are compared against a nostalgic version of history in which leisure time was given over to folk dancing, singing, and a variety of other simple, home-made forms of recreation. In actual fact, however, the major leisure-time activity before radio, movies, and television was total inactivity; sitting around, not doing anything—not even talking—but simply resting from an exhausting day's work.[9] Whatever may be wrong with the mass media, surely television viewing is better than passivity.

If the people of Levittown, New Jersey, a suburban community which I have been studying, are at all typical—and I believe they are—the problem is not one of too much leisure time or too much television, but of not enough extra hours, especially in the evening, and not enough vacation time, and not enough money to do all the things they want to do. Although the number of hours not devoted to work, meals, and sleep is large, actual time available for leisure behavior is still fairly limited. By the time the children are put to bed, household maintenance tasks are completed, and the grass is cut, people rarely have more than two to two and a half evening hours for leisure behavior, and only those blessed with a high cylinder metabolism have much energy for activities other than television, informal reading, socializing, or just resting. Week ends are cut up by a variety of nonleisure tasks which rarely get into the statistics on spare time, but do frustrate many daylong expeditions, not to mention week-end trips. Vacations are devoted to painting the house, and in our age of mobility to going "home" to visit relatives, and to dreaming about long trips for which there is neither enough time nor money. Finally, anyone who has ever taken an automobile ride with three children in the back seat knows well some of the other problems—admittedly prosaic—that complicate the use of leisure time.

I suspect that the "week-end neurosis" which Dr. Alexander Martin has described[10] exists mostly among professional people and others for whom work is so pressing or exciting that all other forms of activity pall; for such people, the week ends may be real problems, especially if they live in small communities where the cosmopolitan types of recreation and companionship are scarce. I am sure that there are many lonely people in our society whose leisure time is a period of boredom and frustration, but what they need is not only new forms of recreation but a method of reducing their loneliness, and this is not as simple as providing community centers or meeting places. There is also some evidence of boredom with the daily routine, especially by housewives, but this is a problem of work and family life that I do not think can be solved in leisure or with recreation. For example, I think boredom and dissatisfaction among young mothers are sometimes caused by their inability to get away from their children for a few hours. This is a failing of current child-rearing arrangements in our society; it is not a leisure problem.

I would not want to argue that this is the best of all possible worlds and that there are no emotional problems in American society. However, at present we do not know much about the nature or the prevalence of these problems—especially those that are resolved through neurosis and psychosis, the use of tranquilizers, or religious cults and other forms of escape. This is an important topic that deserves much more research and much less Sunday supplement speculation than it now receives. I am fearful that conclusions drawn by churchmen, social scientists, and psychiatrists based on insufficient evidence—and often on journalistic reports—have the unhappy effect of dulling the need for research.[11] Whatever the nature of these problems, I do not think they are primarily caused by poor leisure activity or by a lack of inner resources for leisure. Rather, I believe that pathological people tend to make their leisure hours pathological, too, and that pathological leisure is a symptom, rather than a cause. Incidentally, I suspect that the quality of leisure behavior among professional people and intellectuals is often poorer than among the rest of the population, because the occupational pressures which confront them are inevitably translated into the leisure hours. For example, I sometimes suspect the criticism that Americans are unable to relax applies most to the professional and intellectual subculture, but is projected by this subculture to the rest of the population.

This raises another important topic: that of productive versus unproductive leisure. The criticism of contemporary leisure behavior and the advocacy of outdoor recreation rests on the concept of productive leisure, that is, leisure which is a means to achieve such ends as individual self-development, the learning of new skills and ideas, the broadening of social contacts, and the development of emotional maturity in addition to enjoyment and relaxation. Unproductive leisure is that which merely fills up time or is dedicated only to enjoyment, entertainment, and the alleviation of boredom without contributing to more constructive individual and social goals.

Although I share several of the goals of productive leisure, I have some serious qualms about the concept, for three reasons. First, there is an assumption that only certain goals are productive, while others are not. Quite often, leisure which is considered to be unproductive is actually productive, but for other goals. For example, "hanging out" on street corners by working-class teen-agers, which is often described as useless killing of time, is much more than that: it contributes to such goals as individual self-realization, group cohesion, and reality-testing.

Second, the goals considered to be productive are those of the middle class, and especially those of an inner-directed sector of that class. Thus, hanging on the corner is unproductive because it does not lead to the achievement of middle-class goals. In a sense, the concept assumes that the leisure of well-educated people is productive; that of poorly educated ones is unproductive.

I believe this to be an unjustified assumption. It is clear that well-educated people pursue different kinds of leisure activities than poorly educated ones, but there is no evidence that the activities of the well-educated are more productive or improving or self-developing for them than the activities of the poorly educated are for them. Nor is there any evidence that the latter are more interested in entertainment and less in self-improvement than the former. In fact, I suspect that at each educational level, a few people use their leisure time for self-improvement, but the majority do not. The unperceptive critic assumes that all people are capable of enjoying or understanding the same kinds of activity regardless of educational level, and he thus judges the activities chosen by the poorly educated from the perspective of the well educated and finds them unproductive.[12]

I do not mean to say that the leisure activities of the poorly educated person are as good as those of the well-educated one. The latter's leisure behavior is more diversified, for he is trained to make more and broader choices, as well as more interesting ones. He can do this precisely because he is well educated. If the leisure behavior of the poorly educated person is to change, it can be done only by increasing educational opportunities and raising educational aspirations. It cannot be done by presenting him with the recreation facilities of the well educated and urging him to use them. It cannot be done either by providing recreation facilities and programs based on the concept of productive leisure, because being voluntary, they will not be used for the intended purpose, or they may not be used at all. I suspect this to be true of most playgrounds and community centers; their clients come to use the facilities, but pay little or no attention to the productive leisure goals of the staff or the program.

Third, the concept of productive leisure views leisure as a means, not as an end in itself. Leisure is being used to achieve nonleisure goals, to accomplish cultural and social changes that cannot be implemented in other institutions. As I noted at the beginning of the paper, this was one of the original purposes of the recreation movement, and it remains an important one today. However much I identify with many of the ends being sought, I also feel that leisure is the major, and perhaps the only, sphere of life in which people are free to make whatever choices they wish, to be nonutilitarian and spontaneous. This is an important value, which cannot be ignored. Ideally, leisure should be both free and productive (as defined by the recreation movement), but I do not believe this is possible. Since I do not think it is feasible to expect people to seek nonleisure goals during their leisure time, the goals of productive leisure must be sought in the institutions where they can best be achieved, in the economy, in the political sphere, and in education and family life particularly.

The attempt to use leisure for nonleisure goals is one aspect of a larger concept of the recreation movement: that the leisure behavior it favors and the kind of recreation it supplies can be used to counteract or solve the real, and some imagined, evils of urban-industrial society; for example, the dissatisfactions of assembly-line or office work, or to help to reconstitute a family which is being pulled apart by cultural differences among its members. I think that this notion is naïve, because leisure behavior is simply not that important either in causing or solving problems. Whatever evils exist in our society must be attacked directly. If work is unsatisfying, changes must be made in industrial organization and work methods. During the Depression, there were some well-intentioned experiments to teach the unemployed new leisure skills to while away the hours. However, these experiments failed. People who are made to feel useless by their society and its economy are so depressed that they cannot be motivated to participate in new kinds of activities, especially those which require learning. I suspect the same reaction prevails among old people and teen-agers;[13] those who feel socially useless cannot be "saved" through leisure. One of the satisfactions of leisure is its lack of utility, and someone who feels himself to be useless is not likely to be cheered up by additional dosages of nonutilitarian activity.

I am similarly skeptical about the role of leisure and recreation in altering family life. Forms of recreation that involve the entire family may be enjoyed by families that are already cohesive, and they may draw together uncohesive families temporarily. However, in families in which individual members are pulled apart by hostility or by the existence of basic cultural differences, joint activities are not likely to be a cure. For example, families whose children are culturally mobile and have little in common with their parents, or families with teen-agers who reject adult ways, and that includes many families with teen-agers, are unlikely to find activities that will appeal to all of them and can override the rather basic cultural differences I have mentioned.

This leads me directly to the last of the three propositions: that leisure and recreation can be used as forms of societal therapy. I use the term societal therapy to distinguish it from therapy in the individual or group treatment of mental illness.

I believe that education for leisure is desirable and that it is an important part of a liberal education, not only in college but also in elementary and high school. Indeed, I think we already provide it more than we recognize, although in an unconscious and unplanned manner. My evidence is the existence of differences in taste and leisure behavior preferences by educational background. I am skeptical, however, about the feasibility of using leisure, recreation, and leisure education as a more general form of societal therapy. Once again, this is an attempt to achieve nonleisure goals through leisure.

My remarks classify me with that group of people whom Dr. Martin describes as saying: "We do not need help, so stop bedevilling us . . . telling us what to do with our spare time, trying to organize our leisure for us. Just give us the facilities, the libraries, museums and playgrounds . . . our motor boats, the open sea, just give us the national parks. We'll make good use of them all. We'll enjoy our leisure."[14] I think that most Americans do not need leisure therapy and that leisure behavior, if it is to remain leisure, should not be planned. Dr. Martin is right, of course, in suggesting that there are people who cannot relax, and who cannot enjoy their leisure hours, but their disabilities appear to me to be symptoms of other problems, perhaps in the family and occupational spheres, and they must be attacked at the root. I cannot propose any solutions, but I suspect what is needed is both individual therapy and social reorganization.

Outdoor recreation and mental health

My basic assumption, which I mentioned earlier, is that satisfying leisure behavior is a part of the good life and therefore a constituent part of mental health. Consequently, the recreation facilities which help to make leisure satisfying are necessary for mental health. However, I do not believe that recreation generally, or outdoor recreation specifically, can by itself bring about or materially aid in the bringing about of mental health, that it can cure or prevent mental illness, or that there are significant relations between outdoor recreation, physical fitness, and mental health.

The assumption behind these questions is that the mere act of being outdoors and participating in outdoor recreation can have a fundamental therapeutic effect on people and can resolve emotional and social problems that have developed at work or indoors. I have not seen any data that would lead me to suspect that this fundamental therapeutic effect exists. Strenuous outdoor activity will engender physical fitness, but so will indoor activity in a gymnasium or a dance class. Moreover, whatever muscular or endocrinal effects physical exercise may have, and however much it may provide relaxation and a change from a sedentary routine, I doubt whether it can ever do more than bring about what the TV commercials call temporary relief of other problems. At best, it is a form of escape and, as such, good leisure behavior. Likewise, I do not think that being outdoors is responsible for whatever differences in stability and mental health exist between urban and rural people. If rural people are indeed mentally healthier, and I doubt this, I would imagine it to be due to other factors, such as the farmer's freedom and lack of occupational pressure. However, that would apply only to the family farmer, and if so, probably not to today's farmer, because changes in agriculture have made his existence problematic. It certainly would not be true of the migrant farm laborer.

The assumption which underlies these negative answers is that the outdoors and outdoor recreation cannot have any fundamental independent effect on people and that in order for outdoor recreation, or any other form of recreation, to have positive effects, there must be predispositions within the individual or the family toward these effects. In other words, outdoor recreation can provide satisfying leisure behavior if people are predisposed to enjoy such recreation.

The advocates of outdoor recreation have written voluminously and passionately about the joys of being outdoors, the gratifications that come with camping, hiking, the enjoyment of greenery, fresh air, and the communion with nature. They suggest that such activities produce something close to a religious experience, and presumably this leads to the belief that outdoor recreation can directly affect mental health.

I am sure that there are people for whom being outdoors provides very deeply felt emotional satisfactions, but I suspect that their outlook on life predisposes them to such intense feelings. I have known other people who derive similar benefits from walking through the streets of Manhattan, Paris, or Florence, and I have also known some people—residents of a densely populated urban tenement area in Boston—who, when taken out to Cape Cod by a settlement houseworker, were utterly bored and wanted to get back as quickly as possible to the physically and socially dense surroundings of their own neighborhood. They come from a culture which does not prepare them for being alone and for becoming immersed in nature, just as people who like to commune with nature come from a culture which rejects the hustle and bustle of urban-industrial society.

Those who cannot endure the physical beauties of the Cape Cod landscape and those who are really happy only out of doors are representatives of minority subcultures. For the large majority of Americans, participating in outdoor recreation is an enjoyable form of leisure behavior which provides a change of scenery, both physical and social, and offers an opportunity to relax, forget the daily routine, and explore new environments. This is due partly to the satisfactions that come from being outdoors and partly to the fact that most people get outdoors only during their leisure hours, whether evenings, week ends, or vacations. My studies in a suburban community suggest that the pleasures of being outdoors are as satisfying in a small backyard as they are in the majestic environment of a national-park landscape, although only systematic research would show if they are of equal intensity or duration. In any case, since being outdoors is identified with leisure time in American society, it is difficult to say to what extent the outdoors and to what extent predispositions toward leisure are responsible for the satisfactions to be derived from outdoor recreation. This topic, too, deserves systematic study.[15]

Some planning and policy implications

I have argued that satisfying leisure behavior is necessary, but not sufficient, for mental health and that satisfying leisure behavior is best produced by making available those recreation facilities which will appeal to people's leisure predispositions, that is, their leisure preferences, anticipated and unanticipated, present and future. Insofar as recreation can aid in the maximization of mental health, this is best done by providing those recreation facilities that are in demand and that are likely to be in demand in the future. This means that recreation planning must adopt a user-oriented approach, to find out what its consumers want now and what they are likely to accept in the way of as yet untried facilities. The first is easily done, but the latter requires experiments with innovations in order to see whether or not they will be accepted. Also, like other reform-oriented agencies, recreation planners must restrain themselves from giving people what they clearly do not want, even though the planner may feel strongly that they should want what he wishes to provide.

Unfortunately, little is known about leisure behavior and leisure preferences, partly because the reform orientation discouraged any interest in studies of these subjects. The data gathered by the Outdoor Recreation Resources Review Commission in its "National Recreation Survey,"[16] and the study "Participation in Outdoor Recreation"[17] are therefore of immense importance for future recreation planning—local, state, and regional as well as national—all over the country.

Let me conclude with a little speculation about contemporary leisure behavior trends and their implications for the planning of outdoor recreation. The speculation is based on a fairly exhaustive survey of user behavior and preference studies concerning public recreation.[18] From the little evidence that is available, it is clear that considerable changes have been taking place in leisure behavior in the post-World War II era. Not only have rising incomes and educational levels reduced total inactivity, but there has also been a reduction, if not in amount of time, then in the relative importance of indoor spectator activity. People still watch TV and go to the movies, but when time and money permit it, they make much greater use of outdoor facilities of all kinds.

Perhaps the most important such change has come as a result of the ability of the white working and lower-middle class to move to suburbia. This has stimulated an interest in gardening on a large scale, and for many people this is an extremely important form of leisure behavior. Car ownership and the changes in working conditions that make it possible for almost everyone to take vacations also have important consequences for leisure behavior. Many people still spend their vacations at home, but an increasing number take to the road and participate in sightseeing, picnicking, swimming, boating, camping, and a variety of other activities that can be conducted by a family with a car. In the future these trends are likely to increase, creating further demand for open space and outdoor recreation facilities.

Proper recreation planning must concern itself not only with the amount but also with the kinds of open space and facilities that will be needed. Here again there is some conflict between the traditional prescriptions of the recreation movement and the demands of the users. Because open space was and still is considered as a substitute for the departed rural idyl, the advocates of open space and outdoor recreation have stressed the need for more urban, suburban, and regional parks and for wilderness areas suitable for hiking, camping, nature study, and the like. As I read the available studies of the use of open space, the demand for these facilities and activities is quite small. What most people seem to want most urgently is not communion with nature, but the opportunity for individual and family activity of a not too strenuous or too primitive nature which can be conducted outdoors. Close to home, they want beaches and swimming pools, picnic areas, zoos, and areas suitable for a Sunday afternoon drive. Almost every study which has interviewed people about leisure-activity preferences has shown that the most frequent demand, and the first mentioned, is for swimming facilities. As the work week is reduced and the opportunity for week-end trips increases, they will want even more of these facilities, as well as places where they can spend a couple of days outdoors. They will want resorts or large park areas where the majority can stay in comfortable motels or cabins and where the minority who want to rough it can camp out. Incidentally, more people will also want summer homes or cottages in mountain areas, or near bodies of water, thus putting heavy pressure on the use of such land for private development.

If my hunches about trends in user behavior are correct, the metropolitan areas of our country will need a much larger number of parks that provide for the kinds of activity I have mentioned. These parks must be located near man-made or natural bodies of water, and they should offer nature's beauty as well as some of the conveniences usually associated with resorts or vacation areas. Ideally, they should offer a variety of outdoor recreation, commercial entertainment, restaurants, cafés, museum and zoo facilities, as well as the features usually found in a park. In urban areas, small parks, playgrounds, and swimming pools are badly needed in the dense residential sections of our cities, especially in neighborhoods where low-income people live in apartments, without cars, and without either the time or money for trips and vacations. Conversely, there will be less need for the traditional kind of park in suburban areas, where gardens as well as private and public pools are available. Lewis Mumford and Leonard Duhl have also insisted on the need for more lover's lanes, and I concur with their recommendation. More areas for Sunday drives will be needed, either in or near the cities, but easily accessible, and without the traffic congestion that characterizes most such areas now.

The demand for national and state park acreage is already much greater than the supply, and more parks are obviously needed. If the use of such space follows present patterns, people will visit these areas for day trips and week-end outings, and if they are on vacation, they may stop over for a few days, perhaps as part of a longer trip to visit relatives or friends. Traffic studies show that the main attractions in these parks are famous landmarks, scenic drives, areas for swimming, picnicking, and fishing, and sites where families can camp out or stay at motels and cabins. We need to know much more than we do about how many people are likely to use such parks, how far they will drive to get to them for week-end trips and for longer vacations, and exactly what parts of the parks they will want to use most frequently and intensely.

The increase in vacation trips and reductions in the cost of travel will also create greater demands for commercial resort areas, such as Cape Cod, Atlantic City, or Miami Beach. These have traditionally been too costly except for the very rich, but this pattern is changing, and the very rich are escaping to various Caribbean islands and other areas outside the American continent. Commercial resort areas are popular because they combine the enjoyment of the outdoors with the glamour and excitement of the more urban entertainment facilities—and with comfort. Public recreation planning has traditionally scorned such resort areas, but as the demand for them increases significantly, they must be considered as open space to be planned for in conjunction with more public—and more pastoral—acreage. Incidentally, I suspect that in the future, outdoor recreation planning will also have to consider vacations that have a distinctively urban destination, that is, visits to such metropolises as New York, Chicago, San Francisco, and New Orleans. These offer historic and architectural attractions as well as entertainment facilities and a cosmopolitan atmosphere. They are likely to draw people who seek a temporary respite from the quiet life of the suburbs.

The use patterns I have speculated about differ considerably from emotionally quiet, physically active, and solitary use of parks, reservations, and wilderness areas that is recommended by the recreation movement. There will also be an increasing demand for the use of wilderness areas, but even so, it will be numerically modest in comparison to the demand for other kinds of outdoor recreation. This creates a real planning problem, which gets right at the heart of the difference between the reform-oriented and the user-oriented approaches. The advocates of wilderness areas have traditionally valued these areas because they are not overrun by people; they have placed higher priority on the land than on people. They have done so partly because they love such areas—and they are worth loving; partly because they feel there is a desire to save such areas from what they feel to be the negative influences of man-made forms, be they urban settlements or private and public resort areas; partly because these areas are symbols of a pioneer era in American life with which they identify strongly; and partly because there is a need to conserve large land areas for future, and as yet unanticipated, recreation and agricultural requirements.

The planning problem is whether the value of conserving the wilderness for future generations is equal to the value to be gained by opening it up to higher-density recreation use now. Such a decision requires cost-benefit studies which measure the benefits of opening these areas for high-density use against the costs of giving up the wilderness.[19] These benefits and costs are not easy to measure or even to estimate, but without a systematic consideration, it is easy to make a wrong decision. One of the temptations is to fall back on the mystique that is associated with such areas and to argue that the "pure" pleasure of a few nature lovers is more desirable—and possibly more intense—than the irreverent, sometimes gaudy and seemingly less intense satisfactions of a large number of sightseers and campers. Intensity of pleasure is hard to measure, and often the reaction against higher-density use is simply a way of maintaining the areas for enjoyment by the reverent and more statusful few. Conversely, while decisions about use should be made on a democratic basis, planning only for present use commits scarce and irreplaceable resources for all time and deprives future generations of freedom of choice. Even so, I think planning for clearly established needs of today is more important than concern over needs unknown or needs hypothecated for the distant future. After all, we cannot know how future generations will spend their leisure hours, but we can know, and solve, the pressing problems of our own time.

Whether the planning concerns city parks or wilderness areas, the most desirable planning approach, both from a mental-health and a general welfare perspective, is one which seeks first to provide the various types of users with the facilities they now use and prefer. Afterward, there is also a challenge to develop new kinds of facilities and activities, to anticipate future wants, and to encourage people to develop new kinds of leisure behavior in years to come—including perhaps that quasi-religious communion with nature and the productiveness which the advocates of outdoor recreation have recommended for so long.

NOTES

1. F. L. Olmsted, *Public Parks and the Enlargement of Towns* (Cambridge: Riverside Press, 1870), p. 23.
2. This definition owes much to Marie Jahoda, *Current Concepts of Positive Mental Health* (New York: Basic Books, 1958).
3. The definition would have to be qualified to leave out self-destructive or socially destructive visions of the good life.
4. It is true, however, that some people can adapt to such frustrations without overt ill effects, although this may be due as much to the availability of group supports as to individual personality configuration and strength.
5. See for example, Joseph Klapper, *The Effects of Mass Communication* (Glencoe, Ill.: Free Press, 1960).
6. R. Stein and H. Travis, "Labor Force and Employment in 1960," *Monthly Labor Review*, LXXXIV (April 1961), 343.
7. *Monthly Labor Review*, LXXXIV (April 1961), Table C-1, p. 448.
8. Frederick Dewhurst *et al., America's Needs and Resources* (New York: Twentieth Century Fund, 1954), p. 1073.
9. For evidence that the leisure behavior of the "good old days" was also much more brutal and unwholesome than that of today, see Edward Shils, "Daydreams and Nightmares: Reflections on the Criticism of Mass Culture," *Sewanee Review*, LXV (1957), 587–608.
10. Alexander R. Martin, "Are You a Weekend Neurotic," *This Week*, June 10, 1956.
11. Some of these are quoted in Alexander R. Martin, "The Fear of Relaxation and Leisure," *American Journal of Psychoanalysis*, XI (1951), 42–50.
12. This point of view is explored more fully in Herbert J. Gans, "Pluralist Esthetics and Subcultural Programming: A Proposal for Cultural Democracy in the Mass Media," *Studies in Public Communication*, No. 3 (1961), pp. 27–35.
13. Paul Goodman has argued this point in his book about teen-agers, *Growing Up Absurd* (New York: Random House, 1960).
14. Alexander R. Martin, *Mental Health and the Rediscovery of Leisure* (Edinburgh: World Federation for Mental Health, August 1960—mimeographed), p. 2
15. This might be investigated by a study of the outdoor leisure behavior of people whose work is outdoors and requires considerable physical activity. Such a study might show that the leisure predisposition, rather than the environment, has the primary beneficial effects.
16. "National Recreation Survey," prepared by the O.R.R.R.C. staff on the basis of data collected by the Bureau of the Census, U.S. Department of Commerce, O.R.R.R.C. Study Report 19.
17. Eva Mueller and Gerald Gurin, assisted by Margaret Wood, Survey Research Center, The University of Michigan, "Participation in Outdoor Recreation," O.R.R.R.C. Study Report 20.
18. See Herbert J. Gans, "Recreation Planning for Leisure Behavior," Chapter 3.
19. For an attempt to develop such an approach, see *A User-Resource Recreation Planning Method* (Loomis, Calif.: National Advisory Council on Regional Recreation Planning, 1959).

Part III

Part III PLANNING FOR THE SUBURBS AND NEW TOWNS

Introduction

Although city planning originated as a movement to preserve the American small town, its conception of the ideal community has been influenced strongly by the suburb of the nineteenth and early twentieth centuries, then a residential district occupied largely by upper-middle-class people. The planner's advocacy of low density, the single-family house, a plethora of open space, of residential areas without industry or commerce, and of small neighborhoods built around the elementary school was best realized, if imperfectly, in the suburbs which sprang up around the American city about the turn of the century.

Since World War II, however, planners have sharply altered their view of the suburbs. As suburban living became available to lower-middle- and working-class populations, and as the suburban exodus seemed to drain taxes and prestige from the city, the profession has turned against the suburb. Borrowing the mythical picture of suburbia that had been developed by critics and journalists, they now accused the areas beyond the city limits of lacking urbanity and vitality, decried their architectural and demographic homogeneity, and sought to introduce high-density housing, industry, more population diversity, and other symbols of "urbanity." In the process, they revived a goal of the nineteenth-century reform movements: that people of all classes, ethnic groups, and races should live together in what they called a balanced community. The original formulators of this idea saw maximum heterogeneity as a means to the Americanization and bourgeoisification of the new lower-class immigrants—they expected middle-class people to civilize the newcomers

—but the planners of the mid-twentieth century valued heterogeneity as a means of reproducing urban vitality and, in all too few instances, of enabling poor and nonwhite city dwellers to leave the ghetto.

Behind this turn in planning thought was a pessimistic thesis; that the affluence of the post-World War II era was leading to the cultural homogenization of the society which would result in the decline of individualism and the creation of rootless mass men who lacked pride in their neighborhoods and communities. This thesis had been developed by the theorists of mass culture, but the planners adopted it, viewing the suburbs as a deterioration in American society that could be halted only by introducing urbanity and heterogeneity beyond the city limits.

The planners' hopes were soon dashed; the suburban planning agencies for which they worked were out to preserve homogeneity and to protect the communities from an influx of yet more city dwellers. Thereafter, the planners revived the idea of the new town, a quasi-urban community with its own industry, in which they thought they could introduce the ideal community that was not acceptable either in the cities or in the suburbs.

The essays reprinted in this part of the book were stimulated, in one way or the other, by these changes in planning ideology. My work in Park Forest, which was done before the rise of the suburban mythology, convinced me that this myth was basically inaccurate. I did not share the pessimism of the critics who were predicting the cultural decline of American society; indeed, I felt then as I do now, that the postwar affluence was a tremendously liberating force for most people—at least for white people above the poverty line—enabling them to achieve a measure of comfort, freedom of choice, and opportunity for individualism that their parents and grandparents never knew. The proliferation of consumer goods, popular culture, and suburban communities struck me as an expression of these new opportunities, allowing people to develop new kinds of diversity of taste and experience that had not been available to their ancestors in urban slums or in stagnant small towns.

For upper-middle-class people, however, these changes had negative implications. The expanding popular culture sometimes borrowed from high culture and upper-middle culture, forcing them to invent new kinds of literature, art, and music; it often pushed upper-middle-class people into a corner of the cultural market place they had previously dominated, and it reduced their cultural and political power in the society.[1] Similarly, the new suburbia that developed on the edge of older suburbs downgraded the prestige of these communities, or took up open land which the upper-middle class had used for recreation, for the preservation of its privacy, and for the maintenance of a pseudo-rural environment. In addition, the new suburbs drained tax monies from the cities in which the upper-middle class worked or to which it returned for cultural activities.

The planners, themselves members of the upper-middle class in spirit if not in income, reacted similarly, and like all groups who are losing some power and influence, they overestimated the power of the newly rising populations, exaggerated the dangers to their privileges and influence, and issued warnings about the imminent decline of American society.

As a cultural relativist in these matters, I could not see that the new cultural and residential forms were any better or worse than the old, and unless someone could prove that popular culture and suburbia of the 1950's were harmful to anyone, other than in reducing an individual's or group's power, their right to flourish ought to be defended, particularly since they were enriching the lives of so many people.

The first essay, on the ways of life of people in suburbia, expands on the analysis of Chapter 4, presenting some data on the satisfactions which people found in Levittown and the kind of community they established there. The second article, written to lead off a *New Republic* series (which never materialized) about diversity and homogeneity in American life, tries to describe the diversity of age and class that is replacing the traditional sources of diversity, ethnicity, and regional origin. I wrote the essay while I was still doing field work in Levittown, and my observations about America are based largely on what I had seen there and in the West End.

Chapters 12 and 13 were originally written as a research memorandum, proposing a large study to test whether or not site planning had any effect on neighbor relations and friendship choice, the so-called propinquity theory which had been developed by behavioral scientists who had studied war workers' and university students' housing projects. The theory and the early findings which supported it gave site planners a vision of being able, by their professional efforts, to influence people's social relations, and William Wheaton (for whom I wrote the memorandum) and I wanted to test its validity for more typical residential developments. The study was not carried out, but when I was in Levittown, I began to be dubious about the extent to which site planning did affect social relationships. Living amidst a group of fairly heterogeneous people, I also observed the satisfactions they obtained from having neighbors of similar backgrounds and interests, and I began to question the planners' belief that population homogeneity was always undesirable.

Although the idea of the balanced community, of different people living peaceably together, is very attractive, I found that among the Levittowners, heterogeneity was a mixed blessing; neighbors of vastly different backgrounds were as likely to fight as to enrich each other's lives. I tried to resolve my own conflict about the desirability of heterogeneity, which I valued mainly to justify the opening of suburbia to poorer and nonwhite people, and the success of homogeneity which I saw around me by proposing that planners design for homogeneity on the block and for heterogeneity in the larger community.

Chapter 14, written after I had completed my field work in Levittown, translates my sociological findings about the problems of suburban new town life into a series of planning proposals to solve these problems. It was prepared as a memorandum for James Rouse, a nationally known community developer, and for a Work Group of planners and social scientists he had recruited to help him in the preliminary planning of a new town, Columbia, Maryland, about thirty-five miles from Baltimore. The memorandum tried to predict what life would be like in a new town and what could be done to improve the everyday living conditions. In addition, it sought to react against some proposals in the Work Group with which I disagreed. Rouse wanted to plan Columbia as a small town, with neighborhoods, actually called villages, that would encourage face-to-face relationships, maximal citizen participation, and a strong sense of community; and some of my colleagues in the Work Group wanted Columbia to be an educational community, which would encourage and even require the adult Columbians to seek all kinds of formal and informal schooling.

I felt that most people would not want the village life, intense community participation, and adult education being proposed for them, and that they would be more interested in developing their personal and familial lives, and in getting along with their neighbors. Sharing Rouse's goal that Columbia ought to be "a garden for people," I attempted instead to deal with these interests, and to suggest solutions for all the problems of home, block, and community life which I expected to come up on the basis of what I had observed in Park Forest and Levittown. In other words, I tried to plan the garden in terms of goals and problems which mattered most to the people who would occupy it. As this is written, the first residents of Columbia have moved into their new homes, but it will take some years before anyone can tell whether my memorandum was accurate in predicting the interests and problems of the new towners.

It should be noted that none of these essays deal with the most important problem in planning suburbs and new towns: how to enable the less affluent and nonwhite city residents who want to live in the suburbs to achieve their goal. This omission reflects in part the narrowness of suburban planning ideology—and my own falling in with it—but the problem is discussed at some length in various chapters in Parts IV and V.[2]

NOTES

1. For a more detailed analysis of the pros and cons of popular culture, from which these observations are taken, see Herbert J. Gans, "Popular Culture in America," in Howard S. Becker, ed., *Social Problems: A Modern Approach* (New York: Wiley, 1966), pp. 549–620.
2. It is also dealt with in a paper not reprinted here, Herbert J. Gans, "The White Exodus to Suburbia Steps Up," *The New York Times Magazine,* January 7, 1968.

10

The Suburban Community and
Its Way of Life

I

This chapter discusses primarily, although not exclusively, the low-density, single-family housing areas that have sprung up outside the city limits of most Canadian and American cities since World War II to house the young white middle class. Some of these areas are what S. D. Clark calls packaged suburbs; and since I have studied one of the Levittowns, these are what I know best. Others are small subdivisions which are scattered all over the once rural landscape. Although there are some significant differences between these two types of suburban subdivision, they do not loom large in the kind of analysis I shall attempt, and I shall treat them as one.

From a historical perspective, the packaged suburbs are perhaps the most novel element of the suburban growth, for while there have been company towns and large subdivisions before, the preplanned community (which is not a company town) is a new combination of old elements. But beyond that, postwar suburbia is really not novel at all; it is only the latest phase of the urban growth process, the expansion of the city—albeit outside the city limits—in a normal pattern. As always, this expansion follows the major transportation routes, and as always the move is made by young people, who find that raising a family in the city has become difficult or undesirable. In times past, the people who moved to the outer edges of the urban areas were the rich. Today, the availability of the automobile and the improvements in mass production and mass financing of housing have made it possible for less affluent people to move into single-family houses.

In addition to the fact that people get much more space for relatively

Abridged version of a paper read at the 1963 Eastern Canadian Sociological Association Conference, and later published in Italian in L. Balbo and G. Martinotti, eds., *Metropoli e Sottocomunità* (Padua: Marsilio Editori, 1966), pp. 3–20.

little more expenditure, they seem to feel that renting is a waste of money; owning a house gives them an equity or the promise of one. But perhaps even more important than the financial equity is the emotional one: the desire to be the owner of four walls within which one is in control of one's destiny. Privacy from the rest of the world and the freedom to do what one wishes within these walls are perhaps especially important to people whose privacy and freedom are limited in their work and in many other spheres of life as well. Finally, there is a desire to own some land and a garden to work in, which can be traced to the rural tradition of people of Anglo-Saxon background and of the children of European peasants as well. In short, most people come to suburbia because of the house and the land around it. Thus the rest of the chapter will discuss the community and the ways of life that are associated with house, home, and land.

II

Sociology has always paid a great deal of attention to the concept of community: the idea of an aggregate of people who occupy a common and bounded territory in which they establish and participate in shared institutions. This emphasis perhaps reflects the fact that the pioneers of American sociology stemmed from and favored rural and small-town America. When and where the economy was based on land, the communities that grew up around the production or marketing of agricultural goods played a significant role in people's lives. Moreover, the technology of that era required that people be relatively close to their work, both in the rural areas and in the cities, so that economy, community, and, for that matter, way of life were interrelated and affected by the costs and frictions of space. But today, most of our economic institutions are little concerned with spatial factors: they need to be accessible to the large markets, but even then they have considerable freedom of location. The same is true of workers who have a relatively high amount of job security. Once the fear of job loss is gone, people can reside in what are called bedroom communities, although it would be more correct to call them child-rearing ones.

But what kinds of communities are these? I have already noted that most people buy a house, with only a sidelong glance at the people who are to be their neighbors to make sure that they appear to be compatible. Upper-middle-class people are likely to consider the quality of the schools; Catholics, the presence of a church; and Jews, the availability of coreligionists; but for the most part, nonhouse concerns are minor in the purchase decision.

Once people have moved into the house, their horizon broadens to the spaces beyond. Women, restricted in their mobility by children and in many cases by a little noticed difficulty in using the automobile, become involved with the block or the street front, both for social contact with neighbors, so as to escape at least temporarily the long hours of childish conversation, and for mutual aid in everyday life. Homeowners, who are concerned with maintaining the value and status image of their house, must make sure that their neighbors share their concern, and thus there develops on every block a social system devoted to exerting the social control necessary to maintain the houses and front lawns on the street to a common standard of upkeep.

Some people, especially in the working class, find many of their friends on the block as well, so that for them the block is a vital part of their social universe. But most people realize that too much social intimacy with close neighbors can have undesirable results as easily as desirable ones, and they look elsewhere for new friends. They go to churches, clubs, and civic organizations to find friends, and this explains much of the hyperactivity in many new suburbs. Voluntary associations, be they secular or sacred, classify people not only by subtler divisions of age and class than house price does initially but also by norms affecting leisure time. A Methodist has somewhat different recreational standards than an Episcopalian, and so does a person who joins an organization set up to benefit children as compared with one who joins a lodge or a veterans organization—especially since the latter is in some ways the suburban equivalent of the neighborhood tavern. Regardless of where friends are found, however, the suburban resident eventually establishes a set of friendships that may be scattered all over the subdivision or even over adjacent ones, thus involving him in life beyond the house and the block.

Most people do not remain active in the organizations to which they have flocked in the search for friends, but the organizations persist, and they are an important part of life in the suburbs, at least for an active minority. Some residents participate for occupational reasons: lawyers and insurance salesmen, for example, who can establish new contacts as well as a reputation for community service. Others enjoy organizational activity in itself, because it permits them to have the feeling of usefulness or power they do not get on the job or in the kitchen. And for yet others, notably in the upper-middle class, community activity is an accepted part of a way of life that stresses activity and service as ends in themselves.

But beyond what these organizations do for their active members, they exist because there are public services which either cannot be carried out by the local government or are furnished by nongovernmental agencies because people enjoy doing them or are unwilling to pay for them— and because they satisfy a desire for service to others based on Judaic-Christian concepts of charity to help those who need it. Moreover, there are national organizations, like the Kiwanis, Lions, or Boy Scouts, which function largely through local branches. Most of these organizations want to grow, and thus they make considerable effort to establish branches in the new suburbs. In this process, they hasten—as well as rationalize—the formation of organizations. This is also true of the churches, whose planning is more total and effective than that of most secular organizations in America. In Levittown, for example, the major Protestant denominations had the churches all but built before people had moved in.

The final level of social organization is the government and the political-party system. This also involves a minority of the people: usually those who are professional politicians, if not by vocation, then by temperament. As long as the parties provide the municipal services that are required by law or consensus, the average resident pays little atttention to them or to the government. If he is middle-class, he will vote even when there are no issues that touch him; but when there are such issues and controversies develop, he may become active, putting pressure on the government and his party to bend the final solution his way. This kind of protest is perhaps more common in the suburb than in the city; but even so it is rare, partly because politicians run the government so as to minimize controversy and partly because even in a small suburb, the average person will find that although he can protest to the politician in person, he will not get much personal satisfaction if the politician's constituency is at all heterogeneous.

In most cases, the constituency is heterogeneous. If the subdivision is as large as a Levittown—which may mean 17,000 families—it is heterogeneous because it is so big. If the subdivision is small, it is usually one of many within a politician's constituency. And if there is heterogeneity, there is likely to be difference of opinion, reflecting the values and the incomes of the different types of resident. Thus, upper-middle-class people are very much concerned that the public school prepare their children for a good college and want it to be a prep school. Working-class people, on the other hand, expect the school to prepare their children for the kind of white-collar work that requires only a high-school education. They want the public school to be more vocational.

Lower-middle-class parents are in the middle; they expect their children to go to college, but to a state or community college rather than to a Harvard, and are unwilling, if not unable, to pay for more than this.

But even more fundamental values come into play here. Upper-middle-class people, who start teaching their children at home long before they are of school age, want nursery schools, kindergartens, and small classes to give their children individual attention. Working-class people, especially if they are Catholic, think of the school as helping them to discipline their children so that they will stay out of trouble, and they see no disadvantages in the large, sternly run classroom. Lower-middle-class people, who live much more through their children than others, want to keep them at home as long as possible and reject the upper-middle-class notion that children are ready to learn at age three or four. Thus, when these groups form a single constituency for a school system there is apt to be disagreement about how to allocate public funds and how to design the curriculum. Since the school is the most costly, and in some ways the most important, public agency in the suburbs, it is the major source of governmental conflict. But one must not exaggerate this: I was amazed by how little attention lower-middle-class parents in Levittown paid to the school and what their children were or were not learning. But then the Levittown school system and its personnel were by and large lower-middle-class themselves.

These observations can be coalesced to suggest that the community as a spatially defined unit of social organization is really not very important in the life of the suburbanite. The vital center of suburban life is the home and, to a lesser extent, the block and the network of friends. Only a minority of people are involved in organizations and in the day-to-day activities of the government. Moreover, the relations which people develop with neighbors and other residents are for the most part voluntary; there is no necessary tie between homeowners beyond house maintenance and lawn upkeep. Also, many of the services provided by government could be, and sometimes are, supplied by private enterprise.

In short, the community is really little more than a set of administrative and political organizations for the provision of public services—and for gaining agreement as to how these should be run—as well as a set of voluntary associations which carry out other services that cannot be provided either by private enterprise or the individual homeowner. I do not mean to denigrate these functions but to suggest that the concept of community and the reality contained in the concept are much less significant than they have been considered by sociologists, planners, and other public officials. Perhaps the clearest indication of this is the fact that the boundaries of suburban communities are on the whole arbitrary; they were made in the days when rural needs and horse-and-buggy transportation set definite spatial limits, but they remain intact today. There are, of course, good reasons for this. Not only have political systems developed around them that are hard to alter, but because home-owners are taxpayers, they find it to their interest to maintain the small-ness of suburban municipalities.

The minor role of the community does not mean that the suburbs lack what is commonly called a sense of community. This term is used in two ways; it refers to primary or quasi-primary relations between people and to the feelings of loyalty for the institutions contained within the political boundaries. Community exists in the suburb in both senses. People do relate to neighbors, and there is a considerable amount of mutual trust and mutual aid among people who did not know each other before they became neighbors. Moreover, suburbanites get to know many people other than immediate neighbors; they say hello to a large number of them, and in the informal chitchat that goes on between them, storekeepers, and other local functionaries, the suburb is much like the small town. People do not know one another's ancestors, of course, but that is the major difference. The second sense of community is also present. It is expressed usually through a feeling of loyalty for the place when it is spoken ill of, but some of that is personal self-defense. There is also some identification with the high-school athletic team, the one community institution about which consensus is most easily obtained, and, of course, when hostile elements—be these acts of God or the in-flux of low-status people—threaten the community, people do band together to save the reality and the image in which they have invested their savings.

III

The notion of a suburban way of life has been emphasized in the mass media and in the social criticism of the literary intellectuals, but most of this amateur sociology reports myth, rather than reality. The myth is well known by now: the suburbs are dominated by homogeneity, conformity, hyperorganization, and hypersociability, creating ennui and malaise which result in excessive drinking, adultery, divorce, and mental illness. Although this picture has been corrected by a series of sociological studies, it continues to exist, largely because the upper-middle-class people who write mass-media entertainment and social criticism live in the city—or would if their wives and children would let them—and confuse the suburb with the ways of life of the upper-middle class and lower-middle class. In attacking the homogeneity, conformity, and pettiness of the suburbs, they are really attacking the lower-middle class; in depicting alcoholism, adultery, and intense social competition in suburbia, they are commenting on a highly exaggerated version of the life of upper-middle-class people in such competitive occupations as show business, advertising, architecture, and academia. Their confusion of settlement with way of life is no different from that of Anglo-Saxon critics one hundred years ago, who blamed the city for the existence of the crime, vice, and degradation that are found among lower-class populations wherever they live. When the small-town society of the Anglo-Saxon elite was endangered by immigration, the critics attacked the city; now that the city is losing its power to the suburbs, the critics shoot at the suburb.

Since the large majority of the people who have settled in postwar suburbia are lower-middle-class, their way of life has generally been identified as the suburban one. But whether they live in the city or in the suburb, child-rearing lower-middle-class people are strongly home-oriented. Their major recreation is the care of home and children; their social life is focused on friends and neighbors, rather than on relatives; and they swell the membership rolls of churches and voluntary social organizations. Their culture has always been antiurban even when they lived in the city, and they made little use of city culture even when it was easily accessible. Indeed, in some ways, lower-middle-class culture is ideally suited to suburbia, because the nuclear family is so important, the tie to the extended family weak, and the lack of need for the city so marked.

But the other classes move to suburbia, too. Berger's study of California factory workers has shown that working-class groups can maintain their way of life in the suburbs, and working-class suburbs are therefore quite different from middle-class ones. In them, house upkeep is usually poorer, but the gardens are more densely planted—though more with vegetables perhaps than lawn. Organizations and churches are fewer and less sparsely attended, friendships are closer to home, and wherever possible social life is taken up largely with relatives. The schools are usually poorer in quality; the football teams are better; and taverns or roadhouses usually spring up in the environs of working-class suburbs. It is perhaps true that working-class culture is less congruent with suburbia than middle-class culture. This is especially so for women, and if my findings in Levittown are generally applicable, some of them miss the daily contact with their mothers, the closeness to childhood friends, and the hustle and bustle of working-class neighborhood street life.

The upper-middle classes lived in the suburbs before anyone else could afford to do so, and their way of life differs from both the previous ones. This way is marked by more extensive and intensive participation in community activities, be they social, cultural, or civic; less emphasis on the home as the center of life; even fewer ties to relatives than in the lower-middle class; more shared activities as well as partying with friends; greater demands on the children to do well in school and outside of it; and more interest in culture and civic virtue.

These class-based ways of life are not visible from looking at suburban subdivisions, but they become quite evident on closer inspection, and they stand out especially clearly when they are found side by side in uneasy harmony, as is the case in a heterogeneous suburb. At close view, one can also see what has been found in several studies of people who moved from city to suburb: that these ways of life are independent of suburbia, for they exist in the city as well as in the suburb, even though they are less easily seen in the bigger community. Thus, it is evident that there is no one suburban way of life, or for that matter an urban one. Rather, there are ways of life that are best distinguished by class and to a lesser extent by age, and these are found in all settlement types.

I am oversimplifying somewhat for the purpose of emphasis; one cannot reduce ways of life entirely to functions of age and class; for example, religion and ethnicity must be considered, too. This comes out clearly in my Levittown data, for Jews, Irish Catholics, and Italian Catholics report that life has changed more since they left the city or that the move has brought some discomfort, whereas Protestants report this less often. Some of the former had been socialized to live in urban ethnic-religious enclaves, although most of them soon became enthusiastic suburbanites. Yet this does not alter my basic point: the things which matter most in people's lives are influenced not so much by place of residence as by national and regional changes in the economy, society, and culture of which both city and suburb are an intrinsic part.

IV

It should be clear that I conceive the suburban community and its ways of life as nothing especially unusual, but rather as a more visible expression of behavior patterns and attitudes that are found in all settlement types.

Because people have been able to move voluntarily and to choose where they would live, social relationships between them are superior to those in the city. Not only is family life somewhat freer and less tense, largely because people have acquired more space, but child-rearing is considerably less strained than it is in apartments, and children are more of a joy and less of a burden. The somewhat greater homogeneity of age and class makes it easier for people to find friends, to get along with neighbors, and generally to trust and help each other more, to be kinder to each other and more tolerant of differences and to work with each other for common aims. Suburbia is not the Garden of Eden, however, and conflicts between neighbors, organizations, and political opponents are as frequent as in any other social group.

Suburbanites also have their normal share of personal and familial problems, but their general level of contentment with suburbia is so high that it is safe to say that they will remain in suburbia and, more important, that the next generation of young people will want to live there as well. Since their numbers will be large, and the time when they will start looking for housing will soon be upon us, it is not too early to begin thinking about the next suburban building boom. Two problems are particularly relevant: the shortage of land for low-density housing and the increasing distance of it from the city. The land shortage will probably force builders to develop new housing types that provide the advantages of single-family housing at a somewhat higher density: possibly a row house that offers more privacy than those that have been built in the past. The increasing decentralization of industry will mean that many of the next generation's breadwinners will not have to travel to the city every day, but even so, I think the time has come for the development of high-speed mass transit systems between city and suburb. The technology has long been available, but the tougher problem has not yet been solved: of persuading politicians and voters that the government must make the initial—and high—capital investment necessary to develop a system good enough to persuade people to leave their cars at home.

More suburban housing will also mean more urban sprawl, but this does not strike me as a real problem. The arguments against it have been based on the need to save agricultural land (even though there are more farms and farmers than we can possibly use today) and on aesthetic grounds. While urban sprawl is not very pretty, I think it is less desirable (or feasible) to force people to raise their children in high-rise apartment houses. Moreover, I do not feel that we have a right to even think seriously about the aesthetics of urban sprawl until we do away with the urban slums, which not only are infinitely more ugly but, unlike urban sprawl, produce so much human misery and degradation.

11

Diversity and Homogeneity in American Culture

I

Educated Americans are eager customers for national self-analysis, especially for studies which compare the present unfavorably with the past. They flock to writers like Vance Packard, who see America in the throes of a decline in ethics, individualism, thrift, culture, and other virtues.

One of the favorite topics of the decline-and-fall school of social analysis is the homogenization of American life. Once upon a time, the story goes, America was diverse in peoples and cultures, but today it is a society of middle-class conformists, in which men and women are increasingly less distinguishable puppets run by Hollywood, Madison Avenue—and their children.

There is some truth to this image; some of the past founts of diversity are drying up, notably regional economies and ethnic subcultures. But there are other diversifying influences, some of equally long standing. Of these, the most significant is class. Whatever the pros and cons of economic and social stratification, class differences today provide the most important source of diversity in American life.

II

Before the advent of mass production, ways of living and making a living in America were closely tied to the natural resources and to the geographical characteristics of the environment. Moreover, communication and trade were limited by the existence of natural barriers

Submitted version of a paper which appeared under the title "Diversity Is Not Dead," *New Republic*, CXLIV, No. 14 (April 3, 1961) 11–15. I am indebted to John Dyckman and David Riesman for critical comments on an earlier draft.

and by the lack of transportation facilities. As a result, variations in the country's geography created a set of relatively isolated regions, each with a distinctive economy and social structure. These regions produced either what the land or its tenants could grow best, what could be manufactured from resources within the earth, and what could be marketed. In the first centuries of American life, the regions were almost self-sufficient; later they specialized in contributing distinctive products to the American economy. Textiles and hard goods came from the East, grain and iron from the Midwest, cattle from the Far West, and cotton from the South.

Modern industrialization obliterated the historical tie between geography and economy; modern forms of transportation eliminated the boundaries between regions; and mass production did away with much regional product specialization and with differences in methods. The assembly line moves without respect for regional variations in craftsmanship, and even industrialized farming is much the same, whether the crop is lettuce or cotton. Service occupations, which today employ more people than farming or manufacturing, require no raw materials. They are divorced from the physical environment and are thus not subject to regional variation.

Today, then, regions are sectors of a national economy, and the regional economic differences that remain are due primarily to differences in rates of growth or decline. The Far West differs from the Northeast more in the speed of its recent economic development than in the nature of its products. Only areas like Texas and the Minnesota or western mining regions remain somewhat distinctive because of the raw materials they contribute to the economy.

The social systems and ways of life which were nurtured by the regional economies—and by the isolation of regions from each other—are also disappearing, though at a less rapid rate. The New England merchant and manufacturing aristocracy still exists, but its economic and political power and its prestige are much reduced. The family farm society continues to symbolize the Midwest, but it loses most of its young people to the cities. Even the southern feudal system, which has outlived most of its regional peers, is now on the way out. Differences in geography and climate continue to affect the tempo of life, the remainders of old traditions persist in everyday routines, and small towns still hesitate for many years before they admit newcomers to the inner social circle. But these are minor differences; the mobile employees of the large corporations need no cultural retraining when they are transferred from one region to another.

The decline of regionalism was already under way when the great European immigration of the late nineteenth century began. The ethnic cultures of Catholic peasants and Jewish shopkeepers introduced a new and highly visible diversity to American life and transformed the cities overnight. But these cultures began to disappear almost immediately; their languages, ethnic organizations, newspapers, and arts lasted barely into the second generation. American versions of these institutions took their place, especially among the Jews, and less visible social arrangements, such as the clanlike extended family system of the eastern and southern European migrants, have remained in attenuated form. The southern Negroes and Puerto Ricans who replaced the immigrants in the economy added little new ethnic diversity. The plantations from which they came had permitted them only minimal ways of life, and these fell by the wayside even more quickly than peasant traditions.

III

The diversity of regional economies and ethnic groups was highly visible and overshadowed the less visible fact that people in them were stratified into classes. The classes themselves resulted from differential incomes, occupations, and educational opportunities, and these created differences in ways of life from class to class. The class differences were usually greater than those based on regional factors. Indeed, equally placed classes lived in much the same way in all the regions. The families of southern plantation owners and New England merchants had little in common with their own employees, but much in common with each other: wives devoted to charitable activities and conspicuous consumption; sons trained to continue the family enterprise or to enter the law, the ministry, or the services; and daughters taught to choose husbands who would maintain the family status and possibly aid its business fortunes. Likewise, farm families in one region differed little from those in others. The lowest strata lived a marginal existence that often did not permit family life. This was true in the western ranch areas, the New England textile mills, the plantations, and later in the mines, the stockyards, and the railroad gangs as well.

Class had much the same effect among ethnic groups. Working-class Poles, Italians, and Irish lived in much the same way and in the same tenements, even though they spoke different languages and ate different foods. They had more in common with each other than with ethnic peers who had become middle-class, as in the case of the lace-curtain and shanty Irish. The role of class is most clearly illustrated by the considerable differences between the Jews and the other ethnic groups who came to America at the same time. The Jews have been an urban middle-class people for several centuries, and even though the immigrants worked in sweatshops or small retail stores, they sent their children to college and into the professions. Meanwhile, the children of the peasant immigrant groups were expected to leave school as early as possible in order to contribute to the family income.

The diversifying function of class has not changed significantly in the contemporary era. The class system has virtually become uniform the nation over, and changes have taken place in the nature of the classes. In the nineteenth century and until the Great Depression, occupation and income were the two most important determinants of class position and of the ways of life associated with each class. The traditional division of American society into lower, middle, and upper classes reflected the differences between blue-collar, white-collar, and managerial or professional occupations and incomes. Today, these occupational divisions have less meaning. The skilled worker is able to live like a white-collar one, at least in good times. The differences between white-collar and professional work have been blurred by the professionalization, real or spurious, of many occupations, and the demand for professionals and managers has been so great that it can no longer be filled from the upper class alone.

The ever-growing specialization of our economy has increased the significance of education, or at least of the diploma and the degree, as a prerequisite for employment and as a determinant of occupational status. Moreover, in a changing society, traditional patterns of life fall by the wayside, so that the habits and the wisdom which the adult generation passes on to its offspring are often anachronistic. Other institutions, such as the school, attempt to provide more up-to-date solutions and thus become more influential in shaping work, play, family life, and community participation. Today and in the future, the amount and type of education obtained by parents and aspired to for their children will increasingly distinguish the classes from each other—assuming, of course, that the economic opportunity to achieve the aspirations is available. Consequently, education will probably be, after income, the most important source of diversity in American life.

IV

Education is likely to play an especially significant role in diversifying family life. In an agrarian society, the family is usually the basic economic unit. Its members all have specific duties, which help to assure the family's economic survival and also hold it together as a social entity. In an industrial society, the family is no longer an economic unit; either the man supports it alone or family members work wherever they can find employment. Consequently, if the family is to be a meaningful social unit, other joint activities, aside from the universal sexual, procreative, and child-rearing ones, take the place of economic ones. A review of family life in the present class system will illustrate how education provides a basis for joint activities and for diversity.

When education is minimal, as in the working class, such activities are absent. Husband, wife, and children live together under the same roof, and although love and affection are exchanged, there is little close communication, in the cultural and emotional sense. The few years of elementary-school education have had little effect on the peasant tradition, which trained family members to associate with peers, but made them unable to communicate effectively across age and sex barriers. If there is a family circle, as among the ethnic groups, it is segregated sexually and chronologically; the men spend their nonwork hours with male relatives; the women, with female ones. Where there is no family circle, the men congregate at clubs and taverns; the women, at the neighbors. The absence of close communication between the sexes extends even to the most intimate relationships; working-class sexual life is often a case of the husband taking his pleasure without knowing or caring to know the wife's wishes and feelings, and these are frequently based on lack of interest or simple resignation.

Parent-child relationships are marked by a similar communication gap. The working-class family is *adult-centered*; that is, family life revolves around the adults' preferences. Activities which benefit only the children are rare, and there is little of the self-conscious deliberate child-bearing that is so important in the middle class. Children are expected to act like miniature adults at home, and as a result they spend most of their time away from home. Only on the street and in their clubs can they really behave like children.

The school was traditionally expected to draw children away from working-class culture, but it often failed to do so because the child was not encouraged to learn at home. Today, the decline in unskilled work has dispelled the parental lack of interest in education, and an ever larger proportion of working-class families now urge their children to stay in school. However, the parents' inability to communicate with their children and the failure of the schools to cope with their working-class students maintain the dropout rate at levels higher than justified by economic conditions. In the Negro community, the situation is complicated by financial need; the problem of family communication is compounded by the widespread existence of households without husbands.

The description of working-class family life applies also, though not entirely, to the so-called lower class. In the latter, financial and job insecurity, as well as even more extreme lack of education, ill-health, and emotional problems, result in family instability of a kind less frequently found in the working class.

Middle-class family structure is quite different. The family circle is either totally absent or limited to occasional Sunday afternoon get-togethers. As a result, husband, wife, and children are more dependent on each other for affection and companionship.

In the lower-middle class of the present generation, husband and wife are likely to have finished high school, perhaps even the same one. This shared background helps them to communicate with each other and creates some common interests, although much spare time is still spent with peers of the same sex. The most easily shared interest is the children, and the parents communicate best with each other through joint child-rearing. This family is clearly *child-centered*. Parents play with their children—which is rarer in the working class—raise them with some degree of self-consciousness, and give up many of their adult pleasures for them. Family size is strongly influenced by educational aspirations. If the parents are satisfied with their own occupational and social status and feel no great urgency to make their children into Ph.D.'s, they may have as many children as possible, for each one adds to their shared pleasures and to family unity, at least while the children are young. Parents expect their children to attend college. Even so, the home life and the companions to whom they expose their offspring do not always create either the motivation or the intellectual ability required to stay until graduation.

Among college-educated parents, who are usually found in the middle and upper-middle class, education and educational aspirations shape family life. (This is creating a gap between the college-educated population and the rest of society which replaces the earlier gap between blue- and white-collar workers.) College education adds immeasurably to the number of common interests, including activities other than child-rearing. Consequently, these parents are not as child-centered as lower-middle-class ones. Family life is *adult-directed*; child-rearing gives more priority to what the parents think is desirable than to what the children themselves want. Educated parents devote much time and effort to assuring their children's education. They limit the size of their families for this purpose; they choose their place of residence more by the quality of the local school system than other people; they ride herd on the school authorities to meet their standards; and, of course, they exert considerable pressure on their children to do well in school.

These appear to me the dominant family-life trends. My typology and analysis are oversimplified; they overemphasize the independent role of education as a lever of social change, and they neglect the potent influence of other sources of diversity. Income remains the most important factor, for lack of money discourages not only the achievement of aspirations but also the incentive to seek aspirations and the perseverance to pursue them. Regional variations in economic vitality affect the amount of opportunity for educational and occupational mobility, especially for people outside the middle class. Minor and sometimes subtle differences in family relationships and child-rearing methods still exist among ethnic groups, among regional subcultures, and between people from urban and small-town or farm backgrounds. Moreover, the increasing amount of intermarriage between ethnic and religious groups and between mobile people from different regions, coupled with the increasing ability of family members to communicate with each other and to develop new joint aspirations, is likely to result in less visible, but nevertheless important, kinds of diversity in family life.

The impact of educational diversity makes itself felt throughout American society. For example, since most people no longer live in the neighborhoods in which they work, class distinctions in the residential community are based increasingly on educational differences, as well as on consumer behavior patterns, taste, and leisure-activity preferences which follow in their wake. Community life itself is increasingly structured by educational differences, especially in the suburbs. Social and cultural organizations frequently recruit on the basis of educational background, although not openly or even intentionally so, and by whether the members want to continue to improve themselves or not. Neighborhood conflicts over child discipline and community deliberations about juvenile delinquency and teen-age recreation programs continually reflect class differences of opinion about how children should be reared and how much adult standards and adult supervision should guide their lives. The diversity of educational aspirations appears most clearly in bitterly fought tax battles, which usually pit parents who want a school system that will prepare their children for college against neighbors who want or need to give lower priority to educational expenditures.

The diversifying role of education is likely to increase in the future.

Already, sociological studies show that education is becoming the most important variable, aside from income, in explaining differences in behavior, attitudes, and taste. Recent cultural phenomena such as art theaters, off-Broadway, summer stock, foreign travel, and the mass marketing of contemporary design are a direct result of the new tastes spawned by rising college enrollment. As college attendance becomes a median rather than a minority statistic, diversity will be measured not by amount of education, but by type of college attended. There are many kinds of colleges and universities, each of which prepares its students somewhat differently for work, family life, leisure, and community participation, if not in the classroom, then in dormitories and extracurricular activities. The extent to which this diversity persists—and, hopefully, multiplies—is likely to determine the amount of diversity in the middle class of the future.

V

Given the existence of these diversities in the family and in other sectors of American life as well, why is there so much fear of homogenization? I think there are three reasons. First, diversity is usually measured by the amount of regionalism and ethnicity, and their decline can easily lead to the impression that all diversity is, therefore, on the wane. Second, class was for a long time an uncomfortable topic for students of American life, and the relationship between class differences and diversity has not been explored sufficiently.

Finally, the frame of reference used in evaluating recent social change results in a narrow perspective. Those who fear homogenization look at society from the point of view of culture. They study America as they do works of art, and they evaluate it by how and what it contributes to a cultural record called civilization.

This perspective may be compared to that of a tourist. The tourist is on vacation; he seeks variety and aesthetic pleasure in the physical and human landscape, but he is little concerned with the functioning or the everyday problems of the society he is visiting. Nor does he participate in that society, except with the detachment of the visitor. Consequently, the slum that is odoriferous at home may become exotic abroad, and backward agricultural practices are seen as culturally valuable expressions of tradition and the simple life. But one does not need to go abroad to adopt this perspective. The upper-class observer in America—and many of our critics and observers have come from this class—often expects America itself to provide him with ways of life which are varied, aesthetically satisfying, and culturally diverse from his own.

By such criteria, the ethnic and regional subcultures were highly desirable. When New England villages are overwhelmed by suburban subdivisions, and Italian or Jewish street markets are replaced by chainstore shopping centers, the landscape is undoubtedly denuded, and no one feels it more deeply than the visiting observer. But the cultural perspective gives only half the picture. Society is not only a landscape, and it cannot be judged on aesthetic grounds alone. Social change must also be evaluated from the point of view of people—especially those people whose lives and aspirations are the raw material of social change.

From this perspective, the patterns of family life described here do not represent a decline in diversity, but just the opposite. For the ancestors of the present middle classes and the upper level of the working class, neither regionalism nor ethnicity was an unmixed blessing. The former often meant an involuntary adaption to environmental conditions over which they had no control; the latter, a set of traditional ways which were frequently inappropriate for the economic and social situations with which they had to cope in America. Many—and perhaps even the majority—of the people who are now at or just below the median in income, occupational status, and education have been liberated economically, culturally, and politically by the social changes that accompanied modern industrialization and led to the decline of regional and ethnic diversity. Their contemporary situation is hardly perfect, but it represents a vast improvement over the past.

To paraphrase Nelson Foote, much of the declining diversity was based on tradition and on constraint; much of the present diversity is a result of the enlargement of choice. Americans of all classes, except perhaps the upper class, have more opportunity than their ancestors to make choices in family life and in most other areas of life. The woman who bore nine children a generation or two ago rarely did so by choice. Having children was her traditional role, even though it meant exhaustion, ill-health, and probably a short life span. Moreover, the nature of her marital relationship was such that she had little say in the matter. The woman who bears children today is able to choose, and because of her equal status and her ability to communicate with her husband, she can plan the size of the family with him.

From a cultural perspective, the choices that result are often similar. It is, therefore, easy to jump to the conclusion that these are being made by homogeneous people motivated by conformity, even though in actual fact the choices represent fairly thoughtful compromises between aspirations and opportunities. Young middle-class couples today choose to have two or three children if they want them to have a college education; three or four if they place more value on their pleasures in child-rearing and less on education. Consequently, the over-all statistics show that Americans as a whole generally have two or four children and that few have the large families common in the past. The result is a decrease in cultural diversity, but the dissatisfaction of the observer who mourns for a wider range of family size is surely matched and overridden by the increased satisfaction of those who now have some control over their destiny. The ability to choose between alternatives does not guarantee wise choices, and choices that are wise for individuals do not always serve the public interest. Nor does choice-making eliminate problems; greater awareness of alternatives may even increase them for some people. The fact that the proportion of bachelors and spinsters is declining sharply suggests, however, that American family life is more attractive now than it was in the past.

The change in type of diversity can be illustrated by another example. The extension of equality to women has been viewed by some observers as the incipient homogenization of the sexes. From the cultural perspective, the greater equality of the marriage partners may appear as sameness, but there is no evidence that men are becoming socially or physiologically more effeminate or women more masculine. Indeed, the opposite is true; women who want careers no longer need to have masculine drives in order to succeed. Although middle-class husbands who wash dishes and diapers to help their wives may reduce some of the cultural diversity between the sexes that prevailed when women were second-class citizens, new kinds of diversity are created because women are now able to choose from a wider range of activities.

The old diversity encouraged cultural variety; the new diversity enhances individual difference. The opportunity for making choices allows people to develop their personalities, which are individual to them, more than ever before. To be sure, the ability to make choices is at present a novel experience for most people, and few are trained to take full advantage of the potential, even those that now go to college. Their individualism bears little resemblance to that traditionally promulgated by the highly educated person; the mere fact that it presently focuses on family life, rather than on artistic creativity, does not enhance its visibility. It would be a mistake, however, to identify the striving for individual expression as either homogeneity or conformity.

VI

There is a fourth reason for the fear of homogenization, which reflects anxieties over the future of high culture. The new diversity rests on a mass base, and its cultural forms express "low-brow" or "middle-brow" taste levels. These cultural forms have grown rapidly in the last thirty years, because the lower-middle- and working-class population has achieved the wherewithal to express its preferences for cultural goods and ideas on a market place previously reserved for the upper-middle and upper classes. Moreover, the growth of commercial and private popular culture has wiped out the ethnic and regional folk cultures for which high culture advocates have always had considerable affection.

The new diversity is democratic; it offers an opportunity for the rank-and-file members of society to make choices at all taste levels; it allows them to imitate or borrow from high culture; and it enables them, partly by sheer weight of numbers in the cultural market place, to question the prestige and power of high culture. As a result, the new diversity is seen as a threat to high culture.

There can be no doubt that the power and prestige of high culture has declined in the twentieth century, but decline is qualitatively different from disappearance, and the decline which has occurred does not represent a threat to its existence. In fact, respect for high culture increases as educational levels rise, and imitation is a form of flattery, however discomforting its results. American society is open enough to provide room for all cultures and wealthy enough to support them as well.

The ideal solution is diversity at all levels of taste. The achievement of this ideal is not aided by mourning past forms of diversity which cannot be brought back to life or by deprecating the new kinds of diversity as homogeneity. I believe that Americans are currently seeking to expand their newly found ability to make choices, and I feel that this expansion should be encouraged by all means possible. If wider opportunities for a truly liberal education can be made available in the future, the ability to make choices is likely to improve, and this in turn promises to stimulate additional diversity, social as well as cultural, in the years to come.

12

Planning and Social Life: Friendship and Neighbor Relations in Suburban Communities

Studies of wartime housing projects and postwar suburban subdivisions have shown that the residents of these developments do a considerable amount of visiting with the nearest neighbors and may select their friends from among them. Social relationships appear to be influenced and explained by *propinquity*.[1] As a result, they are affected by the site plan and the architectural design, which determine how near people will live to each other. In fact, the authors of one study of social life have suggested: "The architect who builds a house or designs a site plan, who decides where the roads will and will not go, and who decides which directions the houses will face and how close together they will be, also is, to a large extent, deciding the pattern of social life among the people who will live in those houses."[2]

Conversely, other studies of social life have shown that people tend to choose friends on the basis of similarities in background, such as age and socioeconomic level; values, such as those with respect to privacy or child-rearing; and interests, such as leisure-activity preferences.[3] These findings suggest that social relationships are influenced and explained by people's *homogeneity* with respect to a variety of *characteristics*, although it is not yet known exactly what combination of characteristics must be shared for different social relationships. This explanation would imply that the planner affects social life, not through the site plan, but through decisions about lot size or facility standards that help to determine, directly or indirectly, whether the population of an area will be homogeneous or heterogeneous with respect to the characteristics that determine social relationships.[4]

Reprinted from the *Journal of the American Institute of Planners*, XXVII, No. 2 (May 1961), 134–140. I am indebted to Paul Davidoff, John W. Dyckman, Lewis Mumford, Janet and Tom Reiner, Melvin M. Webber, and William L. C. Wheaton for helpful critiques of earlier versions of this paper.

The two explanations raise a number of issues for planning:

1. Whether or not the planner has tł e power to influence patterns of social life.

2. Whether or not he should exert this power.

3. Whether some patterns of social life are more desirable than others and should, therefore, be sought as plaⅼning goals. For example, should people be encouraged to find their friends among neighbors, or throughout or outside their residential area? Should they be politely distant or friendly with neighbors?

If propinquity is most important in determining friendship formation and neighbor relations, the ideal patterns—if such exist—would have to be implemented through the site plan. If homogeneity of characteristics is most important, the planner must decide whether to advocate homogeneous residential areas, if he wishes to encourage friendliness and friendship among neighbors, or heterogeneous ones, if he wishes to encourage more distant neighbor relations and spatially dispersed friendship.

Although the available research does not yet permit a final explanation of the patterns of social life, a preliminary conclusion can be suggested. This permits us to discuss the implications for planning theory and practice.

Propinquity, homogeneity, and friendship

The existing studies suggest that the two explanations are related, but that homogeneity of characteristics is more important than propinquity.[5] Although propinquity initiates many social relationships and maintains less intensive ones, such as "being neighborly," it is not sufficient by itself to create intensive relationships. Friendship requires homogeneity.

Propinquity leads to visual contact between neighbors and is likely to produce face-to-face social contact. This is true only if the distance between neighbors is small enough to encourage one or the other to transform the visual contact into a social one.[6] Thus, physical distance between neighbors is important. So is the relationship of the dwellings—especially their front and rear doors—and the circulation system.[7] For example, if doors of adjacent houses face each oⅎher or if residents must share driveways, visual contact is inevitable.

The opportunity for visual and social contact is greater at high densities than at low ones, but only if neighbors are adjacent horizontally. In apartment buildings, residents who share a common hallway will meet, but those who live on different floⱼrs are less likely to do so, because there is little occasion for visual contact.[8] Consequently, propinquity operates most efficiently in single-family and row-house areas, especially if these are laid out as courts, narrow loops, or cul-de-sacs.

Initial social contacts can develop into relationships of varying intensity, from polite chats about the weather to close friendship. (Negative relationships, varying from avoidance to open enmity, are also possible.) Propinquity not only initiates relationships but also plays an important role in maintaining the less intensive ones, for the mere fact of living together encourages neighbors to make sure that the relationship between them remains positive. Propinquity cannot determine the intensity of the relationship, however; this is a function of the characteristics of the people involved. If neighbors are homogeneous and feel themselves to be compatible, there is some likelihood that the relationship will be more intensive than an exchange of greetings. If neighbors are heterogeneous, the relationship is not likely to be intensive, regardless of the degree of propinquity. *Propinquity may thus be the initial cause of an intensive positive relationship, but it cannot be the final or sufficient cause.*

This is best illustrated in a newly settled subdivision. When people first move in, they do not know each other or anything about each other, except that they have all chosen to live in this community and can probably afford to do so.[9] As a result, they will begin to make social contacts based purely on propinquity, and because they share the characteristics of being strangers and pioneers, they will do so with almost every neighbor within physical and functional distance. As these social contacts continue, participants begin to discover each other's backgrounds, values, and interests, so that similarities and differences become apparent. Homogeneous neighbors may become friends, whereas heterogeneous ones soon reduce the amount of visiting and eventually limit themselves to being neighborly. (This process is usually completed after about three months of social contact, especially if people have occupied their homes in spring or summer, when climate and garden chores lead to early visual contact.) The resulting pattern of social relationships cannot be explained by propinquity alone. An analysis of the characteristics of the people will show that homogeneity and heterogeneity explain the existence *and the absence* of social relationships more adequately than does the site plan or the architectural design. Needless to say, the initial social pattern is not immutable; it is changed by population turnover and by a gradual tendency to find other friends outside the immediate area.[10]

If neighbors are compatible, however, they may not look elsewhere for companionship, so that propinquity—as well as the migration patterns and housing-market conditions which bring homogeneous people together—plays an important role. Most of the communities studied so far have been settled by homogeneous populations. For example, Festinger, Schachter, and Back studied two student-housing projects whose residents were of similar age, marital status, and economic level. Moreover, they were all sharing a common educational experience and had little time for entertaining. Under these conditions, the importance of propinquity in explaining visiting patterns and friendship is not surprising. The fact that they were impermanent residents is also relevant, although if a considerable degree of homogeneity exists among more permanent residents, similar patterns develop.

Propinquity, homogeneity, and neighbor relations

Although propinquity brings neighbors into social contact, a certain degree of homogeneity is required to maintain this contact on a positive basis. If neighbors are too diverse, differences of behavior or attitude may develop which can lead to coolness or even conflict. For example, when children who are being reared by different methods come into conflict, disciplinary measures by their parents will reveal differences in ways of rewarding and punishing. If one child is punished for a digression and his playmate is not, misunderstandings and arguments can develop between the parents. Differences about house and yard maintenance or about political issues can have similar consequences.

The need for homogeneity is probably greatest among neighbors with children of equal age and among immediately adjacent neighbors. Children, especially young ones, choose playmates on a purely propinquitous basis. Thus, positive relations among neighbors with children of similar age are best maintained if the neighbors are comparatively homogeneous with respect to child-rearing methods. Immediately adjacent neighbors are likely to have frequent visual contact, and if there is to be social contact, they must be relatively compatible. Some people minimize social contact with immediately adjacent neighbors on principle, in order to prevent possible differences from creating disagreement. Since such neighbors live in involuntary propinquity, conflict might result in permanently impaired relationships which might force one or the other to move out.

Generally speaking, conflicts between neighbors seem to be rare. In the new suburbs, current building and marketing practices combine to bring together people of relatively similar age and income, thus creating sufficient homogeneity to enable strangers to live together peaceably. In the communities which I have studied, many people say that they have never had such friendly neighbors. Where chance assembles a group of heterogeneous neighbors, unwritten and often unrecognized pacts are developed which bring standards of house and yard maintenance into alignment and eliminate from the conversation topics that might result in conflict.

The meaning of homogeneity

I have been stressing the importance of resident characteristics without defining the terms *homogeneity* and *heterogeneity*. This omission has been intentional, for little is known about what characteristics must be shared before people feel themselves to be compatible with others. We do not know for certain if they must have common backgrounds, or similar interests, or shared values, or combinations of these. Nor do we know precisely which background characteristics, behavior patterns, and interests are most and least important or about what issues values must be shared. Also, we do not know what similarities are needed for relationships of different intensities or, for any given characteristics, how large a difference can exist before incompatibility sets in. For example, it is known that income differences can create incompatibility between neighbors, but it is not known how large these differences must become before incompatibility is felt.

Demographers may conclude that one community is more homogeneous than another with respect to such characteristics as age or income, but this information is too general and superficial to predict the pattern of social life. Social relationships are based, not on census data, but on subjectively experienced definitions of homogeneity and heterogeneity which terminate in judgments of compatibility or incompatibility. These definitions and judgments have received little study.

Sociologists generally agree that behavior patterns, values, and interests—what people think and do—are more important criteria for homogeneity than background factors.[11] My observations suggest that in the new suburbs, values with respect to child-rearing, leisure-time interests, taste level, general cultural preferences, and temperament seem to be most important in judging compatibility or incompatibility.

Such interests and values do reflect differences in background characteristics, since a person's beliefs and actions are shaped in part by his age, income, occupation, and the like. These characteristics can, therefore, be used as clues to understanding the pattern of social relationships. Life-cycle stage (which summarizes such characteristics as age of adults, marital status, and age of children) and class (especially income and education) are probably the two most significant characteristics. Education is especially important, because it affects occupational choice, child-rearing patterns, leisure-time preferences, and taste level. Race is also an important criterion, primarily because it is a highly visible—although not necessarily accurate—symbol of class position.[12]

Background characteristics provide crude measures that explain only in part the actual evaluations and choices made by neighbors on a block. Until these evaluations themselves are studied and then related to background data, it is impossible to define homogeneity or heterogeneity operationally. Since considerable criticism has been leveled at the new suburbs for being overly homogeneous, at least by demographic criteria, such research is of considerable importance for the planner's evaluation of these communities and for the planning of future residential areas.

Variations in homogeneity

The degree of population homogeneity varies from suburb to suburb. Moreover, since residents usually become neighbors by a fairly random process, for example, by signing deeds at the same time, many combinations of homogeneity and heterogeneity can be found among the blocks of a single subdivision.[13] In some blocks, neighbors are so compatible that they spend a significant amount of their free time with each other and even set up informal clubs to cement the pattern. In other blocks, circumstances bring together very diverse people, and relationships between them may be only polite, or even cool.

Whyte's studies in Park Forest led him to attribute these variations to site-planning features. He found that the small "courts" were friendly and happy; the larger ones, less friendly and sometimes unhappy. He also found that the residents of the smaller courts were so busy exchanging visits that, unlike those of the larger ones, they did not become active in the wider community.[14] My observations in Park Forest and in Levittown, New Jersey, suggest, however, that homogeneity and heterogeneity explain these phenomena more effectively.[15] When neighbors are especially homogeneous, blocks can become friendly, regardless of their size, although the larger blocks usually divide themselves into several social groupings. Block size is significant only insofar as a small block may *feel* itself to be more cohesive because all sociability takes place within one group. In the larger blocks, the fact that there are several groups prevents such a feeling, even though each of the groups may be as friendly as the one in the smaller block.

Community participation patterns can be explained in a similar fashion. If the block population is heterogeneous and residents must look elsewhere for friends, they inevitably turn to community-wide clubs, church organizations, and even civic groups in order to meet compatible people. If participation in these organizations is based solely on the need to find friends, however, it is likely to be minimal and may even cease once friendships are established. This type of membership differs considerably from civic or organizational participation proper. The distinction between the two types is important. Whyte recommends that site planners encourage participation by making blocks large enough to discourage excessive on-the-block social life. While this might increase the first type of participation, it cannot affect the second type. People who are inclined to be really active in community-wide organizations are a self-selected minority who will desert the social life of the block, regardless of the block's layout or of the neighbors' compatibility. They are usually attracted to community participation by pressing community problems and by interest, ambition, or the hope of personal gain. Site-planning techniques cannot bring about their participation.

The role of propinquity

Given the importance of homogeneity in social relationships, what role remains for propinquity? Since propinquity results in visual contact, whether voluntary or involuntary, it produces social contact among neighbors, although homogeneity will determine how intensive the relationships will be and whether they will be positive or not. Propinquity also supports relationships based on homogeneity by making frequent contact convenient. Finally, among people who are comparatively homogeneous and move into an area as strangers, propinquity may determine friendship formation among neighbors.

In addition, some types of people gravitate to propinquitous relationships more than others. Age is an important factor. As already noted, children choose their playmates strictly on a propinquitous basis, though decreasingly so as they get older. This is why parents who want their young children to associate with playmates of similar status and cultural background must move to areas where such playmates are close at hand.

Among adults, the importance of propinquity seems to vary with sex and class. Women generally find their female friends nearby, especially if they are mothers and are restricted in their movements. In fact, young mothers must usually be able to find compatible people—and therefore, homogeneous neighbors—within a relatively small radius. Should they fail to do so, they may become the unhappy isolated suburban housewives about whom so much has been written. My observations suggest that most women are able to find the female companionship they seek, however. In addition, the increase in two-car families and women's greater willingness to drive are gradually reducing the traditional immobility of the housewife.

The relationship between propinquity and class has received little study. Generally speaking, the "higher" the class, the greater the physical mobility for visiting and entertaining. Thus, working-class people seem to be least mobile and most likely to pick their friends on a propinquitous basis. However, since they visit primarily with relatives, they may travel considerable distances if relatives are not available nearby.[16] Upper-middle-class people seem to go farther afield for their social life than do lower-middle-class ones, in part because they may have specialized interests which are hard to satisfy on the block.

Propinquity is also more important for some types of social activities than others. In America, and probably everywhere in the Western world, adolescents and adults socialize either in peer groups—people of similar age and sex—or in sets of couples. Peer groups are more likely to form on the basis of propinquity. For example, the members of that well-known suburban peer group, the women's Kaffeeklatsch, are usually recruited in the immediate vicinity. Since the participants indulge primarily in shop talk—children, husbands, and home—the fact that they are all wives and mothers provides sufficient homogeneity to allow propinquity to function.[17] For couples, homogeneity is a more urgent requirement than propinquity, since the two people in a couple must accept both members of all other couples. The amount of compatibility that is required probably cannot be satisfied so easily among the supply of neighbors within propinquitous distance.

The role of propinquity also varies with the size of the group and with the activities pursued. The larger the group, the less intensive are the relationships between participants and the less homogeneity is required. If the group meets for a specific activity, such as to celebrate a major holiday or to play cards, the behavior that takes place is sufficiently specialized and habitual that the participants' other characteristics are less relevant. If the group meets for conversation, more homogeneity of values and interests is required.[18]

Limitations of these observations

The foregoing comments are based largely on observations and studies in new suburban communities. Little is known about the role of propinquity and homogeneity in established communities, although there is no reason to expect any major differences.[19] Whatever differences exist are probably due to the reduction of much of the initial homogeneity in established communities through population turnover. The same process is likely to take place in new communities. Moveouts create a gap in established social groupings. Newcomers may be able to fill this gap, provided they are not too different from those they have replaced. Even so, it is hard for a newcomer to break into an established Kaffee-klatsch or card party, and only people with a little extra social aggressiveness are likely to do so. In addition, there is the previously noted tendency of the original residents to find new friends outside the immediate area and to spend less time with neighbors. As a result of these processes, patterns of social life in new communities will eventually resemble those in established areas.

Most of my observations are at present only hypotheses that need to be tested by more systematic research. Two types of studies are especially important. The first should investigate the influence of resident characteristics by analyzing the existence of propinquitous relationships among a variety of blocks, all similar in site plan and architectural design, but differing in the degree of homogeneity among neighbors. The second study should analyze the impact of site plans and housing design on propinquity, by studying subdivisions which differ in physical layout, but are occupied by similar kinds of residents.

Conclusions

At the beginning of this paper, I raised three questions: whether the planner had the power to influence patterns of social life; whether he ought to use this power; and if so, whether ideal patterns existed which should be advocated as planning goals. These questions can now be answered in a preliminary fashion.

The planner has only limited influence over social relationships. Although the site planner can create propinquity, he can only determine which houses are to be adjacent. He can thus affect visual contact and initial social contacts among their occupants, but he cannot determine the intensity or quality of the relationships. This depends on the characteristics of the people involved.

The characteristics of the residents can be affected to some small degree by subdivision regulations, lot-size provisions, facility standards, or any other planning tools which determine the uniformity of the housing to be built and the facilities to be provided and can therefore affect the degree of homogeneity or heterogeneity among the eventual occupants. The planner has considerably less influence, however, than the private and public agencies which combine to finance, build, and market houses. These in turn respond to housing demand—and to the fact that most buyers are willing to accept similarity in house type and want a fair degree of homogeneity in their neighbors.

Consequently, within the context of present planning powers and practices, the planner's influence on social relationships is not very great. Whether or not it should be greater can be decided only on the basis of value judgments about patterns of social life.

Needless to say, a wide variety of value judgments can be formulated. My own judgment is that no one ideal pattern of social life can be, or should be, available with respect to both neighbor relations and friendship formation.

Neighbor relations should be positive; no benefits, but many social and emotional costs, result from life in an atmosphere of mutual dislike or coolness. Beyond this point, however, the intensity of relationships should not be a subject for planning values. Whether neighbors become friends, whether they remain friendly, or whether they are only polite to each other should be left up to the people who come to live together. Each type of relationship has its pros and cons, but none is so much more desirable than another that it should be advocated by the planner.

Friendship formation is a highly personal process, and it would be wrong for anyone to presume to plan another person's friendships. Moreover, one pattern of friendship does not seem to me to be preferable to any other. Finding one's friends on the block is convenient, although propinquity may encourage so much social contact that no time is left for friends who live farther away. Also, propinquity may make life on the block difficult if the relationship should cease to be friendly. Dispersal of friendship over a larger residential area may help people to know their community a little better, but unless they are already interested in gathering and using such knowledge, this is not likely to make much difference to them or to the community.

Prescribing the opportunity for choice requires also that no one should be forced into any social relationship not of his own choosing. For example, no site plan should so isolate blocks from one another that residents must find it too difficult to maintain social contacts outside the block. Likewise, no residential area should be so heterogeneous in its population make-up that it prevents anyone from finding friends within the area; nor should it be so homogeneous that residents socialize only on their own block.

Implications for planning practice

Detailed implications cannot be spelled out until considerably more data are available on the relative roles of propinquity and homogeneity. Some guides can be suggested, however.

The site planner should not deliberately try to create a specific social pattern, but he should aim to provide maximum choice. If possible, the site plan should contain a variety of house-to-house relationships, so that residents who desire a large group of visual and social contacts and those who prefer relative isolation can both be satisfied. If density requirements permit, however, the site planner should not locate dwelling units within such close physical and functional distance to each other that the occupants are constantly thrown together and forced into social contact. In areas of single-family houses, the planner should avoid narrow courts. In row-house developments, soundproof party walls are necessary. In addition, some type of separation between houses should be provided to shield front and rear doors from those of adjacent houses. Since Americans seem to dislike complete and permanent separation from neighbors, however, something less irrevocable than a solid wall is desirable.

Blocks and courts should be so laid out that they do not become prisons. At the same time, however, they should not be spread out in such a fashion that all visual and social contact between neighbors is prevented. This is a problem in areas of very low density, where lots are so large that neighbors have difficulty in meeting each other.[20]

If and when sufficient research has been done to establish the relationship between site planning and social life on a sounder empirical basis, the concept of voluntary resident placement should be explored. Thus, if the studies indicate that some locations in a site plan will inevitably result in greater social contact than others, potential occupants should be informed, so that they can take this fact into account in choosing their houses.[21]

Since homogeneity is an important determinant of social relationships, some degree of homogeneity on the block would seem to be desirable. This would encourage positive relationships among neighbors and would allow those who want to find friends in the immediate vicinity to do so without impairing the ability of others to seek friends on the outside. If blocks are too homogeneous, however, people who differ from the majority are likely to be considered deviants and may be exposed to social pressure to conform or sentenced to virtual isolation. Conversely, heterogeneous blocks would produce cool and possibly negative relations among neighbors and would eliminate the chance to make friends on the block.

The proper solution is a moderate degree of homogeneity, although at this point no one knows how to define this degree operationally or how to develop planning guides for it. Moreover, the planner lacks the power to implement such guides. *My observations suggest that, by and large, the present crop of suburban communities provides the degree of homogeneity described here. Consequently, the planner need not worry about his inability to intervene, at least with respect to social life.*

NOTES

1. The principal postwar studies are: R. Merton, "The Social Psychology of Housing," in Wayne Dennis, ed., *Current Trends in Social Psychology* (Pittsburgh: University of Pittsburgh Press, 1947), pp. 163–217; T. Caplow and R. Foreman, "Neighborhood Interaction in a Homogeneous Community," *American Sociological Review,* XV (1950), 357–366; L. Festinger, S. Schachter, and K. Back, *Social Pressures in Informal Groups* (New York: Harper, 1950); L. Festinger, "Architecture and Group Membership," *Journal of Social Issues,* VII (1951), 152–163; L. Kuper, "Blueprint for Living Together," in L. Kuper, ed., *Living in Towns* (London: Cresset Press, 1953), pp. 1–202; W. H. Whyte, Jr., "How the New Suburbia Socializes," *Fortune* (August 1953), pp. 120–122, 186–190, and *The Organization Man* (New York: Simon and Schuster, 1956), Chapter 25. See also the earlier researches and some negative findings cited by I. Rosow, "The Social Effects of the Physical Environment," *Journal of the American Institute of Planners,* XXVII (May 1961), 127–133. The discussion that follows draws on these studies and on my own research and observations in two suburban communities, Park Forest, Illinois, and Levittown, New Jersey.
2. Festinger, Schachter, and Back, *op. cit.,* p. 160. See also Merton, *op. cit.,* p. 208.
3. See, for example, P. Lazarsfeld and R. Merton, "Friendship as a Social Process: A Substantive and Methodological Analysis" (Part I: Substantive Analysis, by R. Merton), in M. Berger, T. Abel, and C. Page, eds., *Freedom and Control in Modern Society* (New York: Van Nostrand, 1954), pp. 21–37.
4. Hereafter, when I describe a population as homogeneous or heterogeneous, I always mean with respect to the characteristics that are relevant to the particular aspect of social life under discussion, although for stylistic reasons, the qualifying phrase is usually left out.
5. The relationship between propinquity and homogeneity is considered in most of the studies cited in note 1. See, for example, the discussion by Kuper, *op. cit.,* pp. 154–164, and by Rosow, *op. cit.,* p. 131.
6. If the physical distance is negligible, as between next-door neighbors, social contact is likely to take place quickly. When neighbors are not immediately adjacent, however, one or the other must take the initiative, and this requires either some visible sign of a shared background characteristic or interest or the willingness to be socially aggressive. This is not as prevalent as sometimes

imagined. Although the new suburbs are often thought to exhibit an inordinate amount of intrablock visiting, I found that on the block on which I lived in Levittown, New Jersey, some of the men who lived three to five houses away from each other did not meet for over a year after initial occupancy. The wives met more quickly, of course.

7. Festinger, Schachter, and Back call this "functional distance." *Op. cit., pp.* 34–35.

8. Festinger, *op. cit.,* p. 157. See also A. Wallace, *Housing and Social Structure* (Philadelphia: Philadelphia Housing Authority, 1952). In urban tenement areas, where neighbors are often related or from the same ethnic background, there may be considerable visiting between floors. A high degree of homogeneity can thus overcome physical obstacles.

9. Home buyers do not, however, move into a new area without some assurance that neighbors are likely to be compatible. They derive this assurance from the house price (which bears some correlation to purchasers' income level), from the kinds of people whom they see inspecting the model homes, and from the previous class and ethnic image of the area within which the subdivision is located.

10. See W. Form, "Stratification in Low and Middle Income Housing Areas," *Journal of Social Issues,* VII (1951), 116–117.

11. For one study which deals with this problem, see Lazarsfeld and Merton, *op. cit.* They concluded that the sharing of values is more important than the sharing of backgrounds.

12. Studies such as M. Deutsch and M. Collins, *Interracial Housing* (Minneapolis: University of Minnesota Press, 1951), and E. and G. Grier, *Privately Developed Interracial Housing* (Berkeley: University of California Press, 1960), suggest that where people are relatively homogeneous in class and age, race differences are no obstacle to social relationships and race is no longer a criterion of heterogeneity. This is especially true in middle-class residential areas occupied by professional people.

13. This is true of the larger subdivisions. Smaller ones are sometimes not settled randomly, but are occupied by groups; for example, related households or members of an ethnic group moving en masse from another area.

14. Whyte, *The Organization Man,* pp. 333–334.

15. These comments are based on observations, however, rather than on systematic studies. Macris studied visiting patterns in Park Forest in 1957 and found considerably less intrablock visiting than did Whyte. He also found that there was almost no visiting at all between tenants and homeowners, even though they were living in physical propinquity in the area he studied. This suggests the importance of neighbor homogeneity. D. Macris, "Social Relationships among Residents of Various House Types in a Planned Community," unpublished master's thesis, University of Illinois, 1958.

16. M. Young and P. Willmott, *Family and Kinship in East London* (London: Routledge and Kegan Paul, 1957).

17. There must, however, be general agreement about methods of housekeeping, getting along with husbands, and child-rearing. Since these methods vary with education and socioeconomic level, some homogeneity of class is necessary even for the Kaffeeklatsch.

18. The kinds of gathering which Whyte studied so ingeniously in Park Forest were mainly those of peer groups indulging in single-purpose activities. This may explain why he found propinquity to be so important.

19. See Rosow, *op. cit.,* p. 131.

20. Erich Lindemann (in a personal conversation) has reported that this resulted

in an upper-income community which he and his associates have studied. The large lots which satisfy the status needs of their owners also create loneliness for women who have no social contacts in the larger community. See also L. Thoma and E. Lindemann, "Newcomers' Problems in a Suburban Community," *Journal of the American Institute of Planners*, XXVII (1961), 185–193.

21. See the discussion of this proposal by Whyte, *The Organization Man*, p. 346.

13

The Balanced Community:
Homogeneity or
Heterogeneity in Residential Areas?

I

In Chapter 12, I discussed the influence of propinquity and homogeneity on social relations. I tried to show that architectural and site plans can encourage or discourage social contact between neighbors, but that homogeneity of background or of interests or values was necessary for this contact to develop into anything more than a polite exchange of greetings. Without such homogeneity, more intensive social relations are not likely to develop, and excessive heterogeneity can lead to coolness between neighbors, regardless of their propinquity. Homogeneity is even more fundamental in friendship formation, and its presence allows people to find friends nearby, whereas its absence requires them to look farther afield for friends.

These observations can be combined with a variety of value judgments, each resulting in alternative planning recommendations. I argued that positive, although not necessarily close, relations among neighbors and maximal opportunity for the free choice of friends both near and far from home were desirable values and concluded that a moderate degree of homogeneity among neighbors would therefore be required.

The advocacy of moderate homogeneity was based on a single set of values: those concerning the quality of social life. Communities have many other functions besides sociability, however, and planning must therefore concern itself with other values as well. With such values in mind, many influential planners have advocated the balanced residential area, containing a typical cross-section of dwelling-unit types and population characteristics, notably age groups and socioeconomic levels.[1]

Reprinted from *Journal of the American Institute of Planners,* XXVII, No. 3 (August 1961), 176–184.

Population heterogeneity has generally been advocated for at least four reasons.[2]

1. It adds variety as well as demographic "balance" to an area and thus enriches the inhabitants' lives. Conversely, homogeneity is said to stultify, as well as to deprive people of important social resources, such as the wisdom of the older generation in the suburbs.

2. It promotes tolerance of social and cultural differences, thus reducing political conflict and encouraging democratic practices. Homogeneity increases the isolation between area residents and the rest of society.

3. It provides a broadening educational influence on children by teaching them about the existence of diverse types of people and by creating the opportunity for them to learn to get along with these people. Homogeneity is thought to limit children's knowledge of diverse classes, ages, and races and to make them less capable of association with others in later years.

4. It encourages exposure to alternative ways of life; for example, by providing intellectually inclined neighbors for the child from a bookless household, or by offering the mobile working-class family an opportunity to learn middle-class ways. Homogeneity freezes people in present ways of life.

These are actually ends to be achieved through population heterogeneity and should be discussed as such. Two questions must, then, be answered:

1. Are the ends themselves desirable?

2. Is the balanced community a proper means for achieving them; that is, is it a logically and empirically verifiable means, free of undesirable by-products or consequences?

No one can quarrel with the ends. A society of diverse people taking pride in their diversity, enriching their own and their children's lives by it, and co-operating to achieve democracy and so alleviate useless social conflict is a delightful and desirable vision. I believe that the achievement of this vision is a legitimate planning goal, and the means to achieve it should be explored.

Whether or not the goal can be achieved simply by requiring diverse people to live together is debatable, however. Even if the planning or legislating of population heterogeneity could be implemented, which is doubtful at present, it is questionable whether a heterogeneous and balanced community would result in the envisaged way of life. Many other societal conditions would have to be altered before such a way of life were possible, notably the present degree of economic and social inequality that now exists in the typical metropolitan area's population.

The data needed to determine the ends–means relationships I have suggested are not yet available, so that only tentative conclusions can be reached. The discussion will be limited to heterogeneity of age, class, and race, these being the most important criteria affecting and differentiating community life.[3]

II

Heterogeneity and social relations

The belief in the efficacy of heterogeneity is based on the assumption that if diverse people live together, they will inevitably become good neighbors or even friends and, as a result, learn to respect their differences. The comments about the importance of homogeneity in social relations in Chapter 12 suggest that this assumption is not valid. A mixing of all age and class groups is likely to produce at best a polite but cool social climate, lacking the consensus and intensity of relations that are necessary for mutual enrichment. Instances of conflict are as probable as those of co-operation. For example, some old people who live in a community of young couples may vicariously enjoy their neighbors' children, and vice versa, but others will resent the youngsters' noise and the destruction they wreak on flower beds. Likewise, some older residents may be founts of wisdom for their younger neighbors, but others are insistent advocates of anachronistic ideas. In a rapidly changing society, the knowledge that the older generation has gathered by virtue of its experience is outdated more quickly than in the past, when social change was less rapid.

Class differences also result in a mixture of good and bad consequences. I noted in the previous chapter that most neighbor disputes arise about the children and that they stem from differences in child-rearing norms among the classes and among parents of different educational backgrounds. People who want to bring their children up one way do not long remain tolerant of the parents of a playmate who is being reared by diametrically opposed methods. People with higher incomes and more education may feel that they or their children are being harmed by living among less advantaged neighbors. The latter are likely to feel equally negative about the "airs" being put on by the former, although some may want to keep up, especially in matters concerning the children. This can wreck family budgets and, occasionally, family stability as well. Social and cultural mobility is difficult enough when it is desired, but it may become a burden to families who are forced into it involuntarily.

The negative consequences of heterogeneity are not inevitable, but they occur with regularity, even among the most well-intentioned people. As a result, a markedly heterogeneous community that spells enrichment to the planner—especially to the one who sees it only through maps, census reports, and windshield surveys—may mean endless bickering and unsettled feuds to the people who actually live in it.

Indeed, the virtues ascribed to heterogeneity are more often associated with the degree and type of population homogeneity found in the typical new suburb. Much has been written about the alleged dangers of homogeneity, but frequently these allegations are based on the false assumption that, because the suburbs as a whole are statistically more homogeneous than cities as a whole, suburbanites are all *alike*. Even if they were alike in age and income, which is not true, they would still be different in occupation, educational level, ethnic and religious background, and regional origin, as well as temperament.

In actual fact, many suburban subdivisions are more heterogeneous than the urban neighborhoods from which some of their residents came. For example, in Levittown, New Jersey, many people felt that they were encountering a greater mixture of backgrounds than where they had lived before.[4] The fact that most people were similar enough in age and, to a lesser extent, income enabled them to become friendly with people of different occupations, religions, ethnic backgrounds, or regional origins for the first time in their lives. Many felt that they had been enriched by experiencing this diversity. This would not have been possible if marked differences in age and income had also been present. It would seem, therefore, that in the large "brand name" suburbs, at least, the relatively greater homogeneity of age and income provides the cultural and social prerequisites which allow people to enjoy their neighbors' heterogeneity with respect to other, less basic characteristics.

Heterogeneity and democracy

Heterogeneity is also thought to engender the tolerance necessary for the achievement of local democracy and for the reduction of social and political conflict. When differences between people are small, residents of an area can develop tolerance toward each other; they can even agree to ignore some important differences that stand in the way of consensus. More extreme population heterogeneity is not likely to have the same result.

Sizable differences, especially with regard to fundamental social and economic interests, are not erased or set aside by the mere fact of living together. For example, many suburban communities today are split over the question of school expenditures. Upper-middle- and middle-class residents, for whom high-quality schooling is important regardless of price, cannot often find a common meeting ground with lower-middle-class residents, who may have different definitions of quality and place less urgent priority on getting their children into a "good" college, or with working-class residents for whom tax economy is often—and of sheer necessity—the most important consideration.[5] Under such conditions, heterogeneity is not likely to encourage greater tolerance, and the struggle between competing points of view may be so intense that the relatively fragile norms of democratic procedure sometimes fall by the wayside. Homogeneity facilitates the workings of the democratic process, but this is no solution for a pluralist society such as ours. Nevertheless, heterogeneity itself does not facilitate the achievement of the democratic norms of community decision-making.

Heterogeneity and the children

The value of population heterogeneity for children is based on the assumption that they discover other age groups and classes through visual contact and that they learn how to live with them through the resulting social contact. In actual fact, however, children develop their conceptions of society and the ability to get along with diverse types from the actions and attitudes of the persons with whom they come into close and continual social contact—especially parents, playmates, and teachers. Mere visual contact does not, however, result in close contact. Although a city child may see all segments of society, he is not likely to come into close contact with them. Even if he does, there is no guarantee that he will learn to be tolerant of differences, especially if he has learned to evaluate these differences negatively at home or elsewhere. Parental attitudes or direct prohibitions can thus discourage a child from playing with other children whom he sees every day. Conversely, a suburban child, who may not see diverse people in his community, is still likely to learn about them—and to evaluate them—from comments made by his parents. If these parents are well educated, the child may even learn to become tolerant of people he has never seen. (In reality, city children get out of their own neighborhoods much less often than is sometimes imagined, and they may not see people of other ages, classes, and races unless they happen to live in particularly heterogeneous or changing residential areas.)

This issue may be illustrated by the relationship between the races. White city children probably see more nonwhites, at least from a distance, than do suburban children, although even in suburbs like Levittown and Park Forest, enough families hire domestic help to insure some visual contact with nonwhites. If community heterogeneity had the positive effects attributed to it, we should expect that city children, who do see more nonwhites, would exhibit greater racial tolerance than suburban ones. This has not happened, however.

In fact, the opposite is probably true. Children exhibit little or no racial intolerance until they are old enough to understand the attitudes and behavior patterns of their parents and other adults. These reactions reflect the current economic and social inequality of the white and nonwhite populations. If children could be isolated from such reactions, they might grow up with more tolerance than they now do. This is, of course, not possible. Consequently, until the inequality between the races is removed, there is little hope for a pervasive change in interracial understanding, either in the city or in the suburb.

The older city child differs from his suburban peer in that he is more likely to have close contact with children of diverse background (for example, of class and race) because urban schools usually draw from a wider variety of residential areas than suburban ones. Although researchers are still undecided whether close contact will increase tolerance and understanding—or under what conditions it is likely to have more positive than negative effects—such contacts should be encouraged wherever possible.[6] This would suggest the desirability of heterogeneous schools, in the suburbs as well as in the city.

Heterogeneity and exposure to alternatives

Heterogeneity is also valued for the opportunity it provides for exposure to alternative and, by implication, better ways of life. Elizabeth Wood's recent argument for the balanced neighborhood stresses this value. She is concerned primarily with public housing and argues that middle-class people have generally provided working-class ones with organizational leadership and with models to inspire them to accept middle-class standards. If public housing projects and the neighborhoods in which they are located are homogeneously working-class or lower-class, the population is deprived of the two functions supposedly performed by the middle class.[7]

Middle-class people have traditionally supplied leadership in settlement houses and similar institutions located in working-class neighborhoods; however, these institutions have not attracted large working-class clientele except from among the socially mobile and from children.[8] The latter tend to use the facilities, while ignoring the middle-class values being propagated by the staff. Middle-class people are also likely to be more active in voluntary associations, such as clubs, civic groups, and tenant organizations, than working-class people, but their activity is usually limited to organizations with middle-class goals, and these are shunned by working-class people. Such organizations do, however, provide leadership to the latter by offering guidance to the socially mobile and by pursuing activities which may benefit every class in the area. Occasionally, a middle-class person may also function as a leader of a predominantly working-class organization, although this is rare.

Instances of middle-class leadership abounded in the annals of public housing during the 1930's and the 1940's. Today, however, public housing attracts or accepts mainly the deprived lower-class population, which stays away from middle-class institutions and does not often join voluntary associations of any kind. The deprived population needs and wants help, but so far, it has not often accepted leadership from the types of middle-class institutions and person who offer it.

No one knows what motivates working-class people to adopt middle-class standards or whether the presence of middle-class neighbors is likely to do so.[9] The new suburban communities could be studied advantageously from this viewpoint. My own impression is that heterogeneity enables those already motivated toward social mobility to learn from their middle-class neighbors and that, in some instances, the exposure to such neighbors can inspire previously unmotivated individuals to change their ways. As previously noted, close contact can have negative as well as positive consequences, for working-class people are as likely to resent the "uppity" behavior of middle-class residents as they are to adopt it. Success in teaching alternative ways of life seems to be dependent on three conditions. First, the people involved must have the necessary economic wherewithal and the social skills required for the new way. Second, sociologists of social stratification have found that ideas and values are diffused from one class to the one immediately "above" or "below" it, rather than between classes that diverge sharply in income, education, and other background characteristics. Consequently, positive effects are more likely to be achieved under conditions of moderate population heterogeneity. Extreme heterogeneity is likely to inhibit communication and to encourage mutual resentment, whereas moderate heterogeneity provides enough compatibility of interests and skills to enable communication, and therefore learning, to take place. Third, the "teachers" must be sympathetic to the needs and backgrounds of their students, and must have sufficient empathy to understand their point of view.

Wood suggests that heterogeneity be implemented through community facilities and neighborhood institutions and that these be used to encourage the exposure to alternative ways, since the mixture of classes can be accomplished more easily than in residential arrangements. (A similar use of community facilities has recently been proposed by some planners and community-organization officials concerned with the social aspects of urban renewal, in order to aid slum dwellers to adapt to life in nonslum urban surroundings.)

I have already noted, however, that such agencies have had little success so far in converting working-class clients to middle-class points of view. Although the lack of success can be explained on the basis of cultural differences between the classes, the existing research has not yet led to policy suggestions as to how these differences may be bridged. My impression is that much of the emphasis—and hope—placed on community facilities and professionally trained staff is naïve. These two elements are important, but success is likely only if the persons chosen to work in such facilities have empathy for their clients' culture and needs. This quality may be more important than professional training, but it is not easily learned, for it entails much more than sympathy and good intentions. Unfortunately, empathic personalities are rare. Consequently, the encouragement of heterogeneity in community facilities is desirable, but it cannot by itself motivate people to expose themselves to new alternatives. Nor is it clear that they should so expose themselves.

III

Implications for planning

I have tried to show that the advantage of heterogeneity and the disadvantages of homogeneity have both been exaggerated and that neither is unqualifiedly good or bad. Extreme forms of either are undesirable. Complete, or near-complete homogeneity, as in a company town where everyone has the same kind of job, is clearly objectionable. Total heterogeneity is likely to be so uncomfortable that only those who want no social contact with neighbors would wish to live under such conditions. Even then, it would be tolerable only in apartment buildings in which visual contact between residents was minimal. Both extremes are rarely found in actual communities. In considering planning implications, we need concern ourselves primarily with more moderate forms.

Specific implications for planning policy are best discussed in two steps: at the level of block life and at the level of area-wide community life. At the block level, the arguments of this and the earlier article suggest that the degree of heterogeneity advocated in the balanced-community concept—which comes close to total heterogeneity—is unlikely to produce social relationships of sufficient intensity to achieve either a positive social life or the cultural, political, and educational values sought through the balanced community. The ideal solution is sufficient homogeneity with respect to those characteristics that will assure:

1. Enough consensus between neighbors to prevent conflict;
2. Positive although not necessarily intensive relationships between neighbors with respect to common needs and obligations;
3. The possibility for some mutual visiting and friendship formation for those who want it in the immediate vicinity.

This should provide sufficient heterogeneity to create some diversity as well. At the present time, no one knows how this solution could be defined operationally, that is, what mixture of specific characteristics would be likely to provide the kind of homogeneity suggested above. Consequently, existing subdivisions with differing degrees of homogeneity and heterogeneity should be studied, and adventurous builders should be encouraged to experiment with mixing people and house types. Planners and students of urban life could observe the results systematically and provide the evidence needed for more specific guides for planning. These guides would not spell out detailed dwelling-unit or population mixtures, but would indicate only the types of population compositions which should be avoided because they bring about the undesirable effects of too much homogeneity or heterogeneity.

At the community level, and especially at the level of the politically defined community, population heterogeneity is desirable.[10] It is not a proper means to the ends for which it has been advocated, although a moderate degree of heterogeneity may aid in the achievement of the educational and exposure values. Rather, its desirability must be argued in relation to two other values. First, ours is a pluralistic society, and local communities should reflect this pluralism. Second, and more important, as long as local taxation is the main support for community services, homogeneity at the community level encourages undesirable inequalities. The high-income suburb can build modern schools with all the latest features; the low-income suburb is forced to treat even minimal educational progress as a luxury. Such inequity is eliminated more efficiently by federal and state subsidy than by community heterogeneity, but the latter is essential as long as such subsidies are so small.

The ideal amount and type of heterogeneity can only be guessed at, since so little is known about the impact of population characteristics within various sectors of community life. Two general statements can be made, however.

First, enough homogeneity must be present to allow institutions to function and interest groups to reach workable compromises. In areas with a wide range of population types, the balanced community—that is, a local cross-section of the entire area—would probably experience intense political and cultural conflict. Since local institutions, including government, have little power to affect and to ameliorate the basic causes of such conflict, they would be unable to handle it constructively. Conflict itself is not unhealthy, but irreconcilable conflict is socially destructive, and nothing would be gained by instituting population heterogeneity within political units which cannot deal with the negative consequences of conflict.

Second, enough heterogeneity must be provided in the community so that important facilities and services can be financed and enabled to find sufficient clients to allow them to function. Economic or social ghettos, either of the very rich or of the very poor, are thus not desirable. (Cultural ghettos, such as those of ethnic groups, are not a problem, as long as they are voluntary ones and are able to provide nonethnic facilities for those who want to get out of the group.)

The generality of these proposals illustrates clearly how little is known about the consequences of homogeneity and heterogeneity. More specific planning guides require a thoroughgoing research program that would explore the consequences of different types and degrees of population mixture for a variety of planning values. No one can now predict the conclusions of such research. For example, I have suggested that schools with heterogeneous student bodies are desirable. Systematic studies may show, however, that children learn better among homogeneous peers. The tracking system that exists in many high schools, and even in elementary schools, suggests this possibility. Moreover, such studies might also show that the heterogeneous elements of the student body come into visual contact, but do not achieve any real social contact. If the learning benefits resulting from homogeneity are greater than the social benefits of a mixed student body, a more homogeneous school system might be desirable. Such a system would, however, conflict with yet another value: that of the school as a symbol and an institution of democratic pluralism. Needless to say, comparison of different types of values is not an easy task. Nevertheless, the importance of the balanced-community concept in contemporary planning thought, and the constant rejection of the concept in the housing market, suggest that policy-oriented research along this line is badly needed.

An appraisal of present conditions

It should be clear from the preceding comments that I place little value on heterogeneity as an end in itself. Consequently, I see no overwhelming objections against the patterns of population distribution that exist in today's suburban subdivisions and new communities. I noted earlier the beneficial effects of the kind of population mixture found in Levittown. In addition, the fact that most developments are built in or near older towns, and therefore fall into existing political subdivisions, usually creates additional heterogeneity at the community level.

Thus it would seem that the present system, in which the housing industry supplies subdivisions which are homogeneous in price and where the buyer decides what he can afford or wants to pay, makes for a degree of heterogeneity that is satisfactory both from the point of view of the residents and from that of society as a whole. Three qualifying comments must be added, however. First, acceptance of house-price homogeneity should not be interpreted as a justification for accompanying by-products and especially for racial or religious discrimination. Specifically, if an individual chooses to move into an area where the residents differ from him in age, income, race, religion, or ethnic background, he has not only the right to do so but also the right to governmental support to uphold his action. If this wreaks havoc with the block's social life or the community's consensus, it is an unfortunate but irrelevant consequence. Freedom of choice, civil rights, and the protection of minority interests are values of higher priority than peaceful social life or consensus. Second, the homogeneity of population that results from the homogeneity of house price is on the whole voluntary, differing radically from the enforced homogeneity of slums and public-housing projects which force deprived people into clearly labeled economic ghettos. Third, the fact that the present suburban housing-market arrangements may be satisfactory with respect to population mixture does not excuse their inability to house low- and even medium-income families.

Toward a reformulation of the issue

At the present time, population heterogeneity as advocated by planners is not workable. Neither home purchasers nor tenants seem to want it, and the housing market is not organized to provide it. (Planners themselves rarely practice what they preach and usually reside in areas inhabited by people of like values and class background.) Consequently, it is unlikely that heterogeneity can be implemented through planning or other legislative and political means. Lack of feasibility is not a legitimate objection per se. However, I have tried to show that heterogeneity does not really achieve the ends sought by its advocates.

Moreover, even if it could be implemented, it would not solve the problems that currently beset our communities. *Indeed, the opposite is closer to the truth; population heterogeneity cannot be achieved until the basic metropolitan area social problem is solved.* This I believe to be the economic and social inequalities that still exist in our society, as expressed in the deprivations and substandard living conditions of the lowest socioeconomic strata of the metropolitan area population. These conditions in turn produce some of the residential patterns that restrict population heterogeneity. For example, the present homogeneity of age and class in cities and suburbs results in part from the desire of middle-class and working-class families to avoid contact with the deprived population and with the way it is forced to live. Thus the city, and especially its inner areas, becomes the abode of the very rich, the very poor, and those who cannot get away.

The planner's advocacy of heterogeneity is in part a means for dealing with this problem; he hopes that the mixing of classes will iron out these inequalities. The intent is noble, but the means are inappropriate. What is needed instead is the raising of substandard incomes, the provision of greater occupational and educational opportunities to the deprived population, and the development of institutions that will create opportunities tailored to their needs and cultural wants. These programs should receive first priority in future metropolitan area policy-making.

The elimination of deprivation cannot be implemented solely or even primarily by city planning as now practiced. Nor are physical planning methods of much relevance. Some policies may fit into the newly emerging field of local social planning, but many can be achieved only through economic and legislative decisions at the national level. Some of the programs in which city planners are involved do, however, bear a direct relation to the basic goal; and changes in city-planning policies would, therefore, be helpful in achieving it. For example, urban-renewal programs that give highest priority to the improvement of housing conditions of the poorest city dwellers would be more desirable than, and considerably different from, those presently supported by the city-planning profession.[11] Similarly, school planning which seeks better methods and facilities for educating lower-class children—the average as well as the gifted—is more important than concern with space standards that are currently applicable only to high-income, low-density communities.[12] Also, a more serious attempt to solve the recreation problems of inner-city children should complement, if not replace, the current preoccupations with marinas and with regional parks for well-to-do suburban residents.

I am suggesting that the city-planning profession should pay less attention to improving the physical environment of those who are already comparatively well served by private and public means and pay more attention to the environmental conditions of the deprived population. Such a change in planning emphasis will not by itself solve the problem (even an intensive national program geared to reduce all inequality cannot erase immediately the inequities of a century), but it will be making a contribution toward the eventual solution.

The reduction of inequalities may also have some positive consequences for population heterogeneity. At first, greater social and economic equality would result in greater homogeneity of income, education, and the like. This homogeneity would, however, extend to a larger number of people the opportunity to make choices, and this in turn is likely to result in more heterogeneity of attitude and behavior. Thus, if more people have the discretionary income and the skills to make choices, they will begin to express and to implement preferences. This can create a demand for greater diversity in housing, recreation, taste, and many other aspects of life.

It must be stressed, however, that the resulting heterogeneity would be qualitatively different from the type that exists today. The disappearance of ways of life based on deprivation would do away with such phenomena as the street life of the overcrowded slum which now provides a measure of variety to the social and physical landscape of a middle-class society. Thus, there would undoubtedly be less clearly visible *cultural diversity*, especially since ethnic differences and exotic immigrant neighborhoods are also disappearing. Conversely, the ability of people to make choices should result in greater expression of *individual preferences*.[13] Even now, homeowners in the Park Forests and the Levittowns make more individual changes in their houses than do the owners of urban row houses.

There is no reason to expect that homogeneity of class and age will ever be totally eliminated in residential areas. But it is possible that a somewhat closer approximation to the kind of residential heterogeneity advocated by planners may be realized when the extreme cultural differences have disappeared and when a greater number of people have more freedom of choice with respect to residence.

IV

Heterogeneity for aesthetic values

My argument has dealt primarily with population heterogeneity, but planners have also advocated heterogeneity of house types, primarily for aesthetic reasons. In the past, it was thought that aesthetic values could be achieved only through custom-built housing, and the discussions of the topic stressed the evils of mass production. Today the issue is: how much heterogeneity should be provided in mass-produced housing to create aesthetic values? No one, including the builder himself, is opposed to beauty; but considerable disagreement exists over priorities and about the definition of aesthetic standards.

The issue of priorities is basically economic, and the debate rages about the price consequences of house-type heterogeneity. I feel that the aesthetic benefits of house-type diversity are not sufficient to justify depriving anyone of a new house because he cannot afford to pay for variations in floor plans or elevations. No one wants what Vernon De Mars has called cooky-cutter developments, although the home buyer with limited means may have no alternative, and he may subsequently build his own individuality into the house when he can afford to do so. Builders of mass-produced housing should, of course, be encouraged to vary designs and site plans as much as possible, as long as the added cost does not price anyone out of the market who would otherwise be able to buy. Planners and architects should be able to use their professional skills to help builders to achieve variety; but, too often, their recommendations add too much to costs and prices.

In recent years, planners have advocated a mixture of dwelling-unit types, mainly to cut down suburban sprawl but also to provide aesthetic variety. Unfortunately, architects have not yet designed salable row houses or duplexes and the universal dislike of these house types among most home buyers has not created the incentives necessary for experimentation by builders or their designers. Some sophisticated consumer research to discover what people dislike about the higher-density dwelling-unit types is necessary before acceptable new versions can be developed.

The second issue results from the lack of agreement on aesthetic standards. Although everyone seeks beauty, concepts of beauty and of what is beautiful or ugly differ between professionals and laymen as well as between people of different socioeconomic backgrounds and educational levels. Unfortunately, the American dedication to cultural pluralism specifically excludes aesthetic pluralism. As a result, demands for more beauty in housing usually favor the aesthetic standards of a single group, the well-educated, upper-middle-class professional.[14] Indeed, much of the critique of suburban housing and of suburbia generally is a thinly veiled attack by this group on the aesthetic principles and over-all taste level of the middle- and working-class population.

There is at present no democratic method for reconciling the aesthetic disagreement. Since differences of taste have not been proven to be socially or emotionally harmful or inimical to the public interest, there is no justification for an undemocratic implementation of a single aesthetic standard. In a democracy, each person is, and should be, free to pursue his concept of beauty. Aesthetic pluralism may hurt the aesthetic sensibilities of the better-educated people, but until everyone has the opportunity to acquire their level of education, such hurts must be borne as a price—and a small one—of living in a democracy. No one should be discouraged from advocating and propagating his own aesthetic standards, but public policy must take the existence of taste differences into account. Needless to say, this does not justify promoting ugliness or taking architectural short cuts under the guise of aesthetic pluralism. Architectural and site designs should, however, respect the aesthetic standards of the people for whom they are primarily intended. This requires some knowledge—little of it now available—about diverse aesthetic standards and cannot be based on uninformed guesses about such standards by either architect or builder. Public buildings exist for the benefit of all cultural groups and should therefore appeal to what is common in all aesthetic standards or, better still, promote architectural innovation. Cognizance of the diversity of aesthetic standards will, of course, add more heterogeneity to the landscape.[15]

NOTES

1. See, for instance, Catherine Bauer, "Social Questions in Housing and Community Planning," *Journal of Social Issues*, VII (1951), 23; Lewis Mumford, "The Neighborhood and the Neighborhood Unit," *Town Planning Review*, XXIV (1954), 267–268; Howard Hallman, "Citizens and Professionals Reconsider the Neighborhood," *Journal of the American Institute of Planners*, XXV (1959), 123–124; Elizabeth Wood, *A New Look at the Balanced Neighborhood* (New York: Citizen's Housing and Planning Council, December 1960). Reginald Isaacs' critique of the neighborhood plan is based on a similar point

of view. See, for example, "The Neighborhood Theory," *Journal of the American Institute of Planners*, XIV (1948), 15–23.

2. A fifth reason, the contribution of heterogeneity to aesthetic values, is discussed at the end of the article. I shall not deal at all with economic reasons; for example, the desirability of age heterogeneity in order to prevent tax burdens resulting from the flood of school-age children in suburban communities.

3. Comments made in Chapter 12 about race as a symbol of class differences apply here also.

4. Communities like Park Forest and Levittown may be more heterogeneous in class than smaller and higher-priced subdivisions. The low house price attracts two types of owners: mobile young couples who will eventually buy more expensive houses as the husband advances in his career; and somewhat older families in which the husband has reached the peak of his earning power and who are buying their first, and probably last, house. These communities are also more likely than smaller subdivisions to attract newcomers to the metropolitan area, which creates a greater diversity of regional origins.

5. In some suburbs, this conflict is complicated by religious differences. Moreover, Catholic families, who may have to support two school systems, often have lower family incomes than do the members of other religious groups.

6. For an interesting study of the attitudes which young children bring to an interracial nursery school, and of the role of close contact in affecting the interracial relationship, see Mary E. Goodman, *Race Awareness in Young Children* (Cambridge: Addison-Wesley, 1952). The general problem is discussed in George E. Simpson and J. Milton Yinger, "The Sociology of Race and Ethnic Relations," in Robert K. Merton, Leonard Broom, and Leonard S. Cottrell, Jr., eds., *Sociology Today* (New York: Basic Books, 1959), pp. 397–398.

7. Wood, *op. cit.*, pp. 18–21.

8. For an analysis of the working-class client's view of the settlement house, see Albert K. Cohen, *Delinquent Boys: The Culture of the Gang* (Glencoe, Ill.: Free Press, 1955), pp. 116–117.

9. There is some evidence that students react positively to the exposure to alternatives. Alan B. Wilson found that some working-class high-school students adopt middle-class standards if they attend a predominantly middle-class school and that some middle-class students adopt working-class standards if they attend a predominantly working-class school. See his "Class Segregation and Aspirations of Youth," *American Sociological Review*, XXIV (1959), 836–845. Students are socially more impressionable than adults, however, and the school is a more persuasive social environment than a residential area of a voluntarily attended neighborhood institution.

10. The planner has traditionally concerned himself more with the neighborhood than with either the block or the political community. The neighborhood is not a meaningful social unit, however, since the significant face-to-face relationships occur on the block. Moreover, it is not a political unit and thus cannot make decisions about its population composition. The neighborhood is therefore not a relevant unit for considering this issue.

11. For details, see Herbert J. Gans, "The Human Implications of Current Redevelopment and Relocation Planning," *Journal of the American Institute of Planners*, XXV (1959), 23–25. In contrast, it may be noted that the recent A.I.P. policy statement on urban renewal refers only to the removal of blight and has nothing to say about the improvement of housing conditions of those who live in blighted areas. "Urban Renewal," *ibid.*, p. 221.

12. See John W. Dyckman, "Comment on Glazer's School Proposals," *Journal of the American Institute of Planners,* XXV (1959), especially p. 199.
13. The two types of heterogeneity and their implications for American society are explored more fully in Herbert J. Gans, "Diversity Is not Dead," *New Republic,* CXLIV (April 3, 1961), 11–15.
14. It is therefore no coincidence that the illustrations of aesthetically desirable blocks in most planning reports are usually from high-income residential neighborhoods. See, for example, Henry Fagin and Robert C. Weinberg, eds., *Planning and Community Appearance* (New York: Regional Plan Association, Inc., May 1958).
15. For a discussion of aesthetic differences and taste levels, see Russell Lynes, "Highbrow, Lowbrow, Middlebrow," in *The Tastemakers* (New York: Harper, 1954), Chapter 13. For an excellent discussion of aesthetic pluralism in a democracy, see Lyman Bryson, *The Next America* (New York: Harper, 1952), Chapter 10. Some of the policy implications of my point of view are discussed in Herbert J. Gans, "Pluralist Esthetics and Subcultural Programming," *Studies in Public Communication,* No. 3 (Summer 1961).

14

Planning for the Everyday Life and Problems of Suburban and New Town Residents

This paper attempts to describe and predict the everyday life and problems to be faced by the future residents of Columbia, Maryland, and to propose solutions to some of these problems. The paper is in four parts: some brief comments on how life will change for people after they move to Columbia; the problems they and the community are likely to come up against; a list of criteria for what I call a mentally healthy social structure; and some recommendations based on expected problems and these criteria.[1]

I. LIFE IN COLUMBIA: HOW LIFE WILL CHANGE
   FOR ITS RESIDENTS

1. Basically, life will be marked by maintenance of old patterns, which are based on enduring influences of class and position in the life cycle. For most people, life will change relatively little as a result of the move.

2. The change that will take place is a combination of aspirations sought in Columbia and the impact of Columbia on its residents. The main changes are likely to be:

   (a) Satisfaction with homeownership and with new house; increased contentment and higher morale.

   (b) Increased social life, especially if neighbors are compatible.

   (c) Greater organizational participation, especially in clubs and social groups. This does not mean intensive activity, nor does it mean a high amount of civic or political participation.

   (d) More community activity of an informal nature, such as barbecues, bowling, swimming, and so on.

Previously unpublished. Prepared in February 1964 for James Rouse, the developer of the new town of Columbia, Maryland.

(e) Formation of innumerable organizations which sort people by background, especially class, education, religion, and age.

3. Unless the community social structure is radically different from that of any other community, the participation in civic, cultural, and educational activities now limited largely to the *upper-middle class* (the graduates of name colleges, in professional and highly technical jobs) should not be expected from either the *lower-middle class* (the high-school educated and those who have attended state or local colleges and work in white-collar jobs, including technical ones) or from the *working class* (those with a high-school education or less, employed in factory or service jobs requiring little "intellectual" skill).

4. If the upper-middle-class population is large enough, it may, perhaps, exert some influence on the rest of the population and encourage the more mobile among it to accept some upper-middle-class ways. But the majority of people from other classes or styles of life will retain their own ways.

II. SOME POSSIBLE PROBLEMS OF COLUMBIA RESIDENTS

1. *Social Isolation.* The inability to get along with neighbors, find compatible friends, and participate in the dominant community activities. This will be most prevalent among women, and especially the following:

   (a) Those who are culturally different and in a minority and thus have difficulty in finding compatible people.

   (b) People who have come from ethnic enclaves and have lived among childhood friends and close to parents and other relatives and find it difficult to make *new* friends, even while they are homesick for the close social ties they left behind.

   (c) People of working-class background who have difficulty in making friends and joining organizations.

   (d) Negroes, especially if they are a minority and find it difficult to make social contact with whites, whether because of their own hesitancy or white resistance.

2. *Physical Isolation.* The feeling of being "stuck" in the house and the community, felt more strongly by women who are socially isolated or are alone with small children all day (especially those who had grandparent baby-sitters near at hand before), those whose husbands are away from the home for several days, and those who cannot drive or are otherwise immobilized in the house.

3. *Financial Problems.* Experienced by people whose income is not

enough to pay the costs of homeownership, raising the children, unexpected medical expenses, and so on. Financial problems also result in worry, family tension, and protests against public expenditures and rising taxes.

4. *Adolescents' Problems.* Teen-agers will feel bored and socially isolated in a town dominated by couples with young children, especially if Columbia lacks the soda shops, bowling alleys, and movie theaters which serve as their social centers in the city, or if access to such facilities is difficult due to lack of public transportation and the great distances resulting from low density.

5. *Community Conflicts.* These are inevitable, but their form and expression are unpredictable now, for they depend on the nature of political organization, the amount of feedback between residents, government, and developers, and the cost of public services, tax methods, and the like. The probable types of conflict to be expected are:

   (*a*) Block conflicts between neighbors who do not get along together. Children, and the way they should be raised and disciplined, are often the source of conflict among parents, and the conflicts usually reflect class and age differences in norms of child-rearing and child-disciplining. Other conflicts may emerge when old people live next to young ones (and object to their noise or children's destructive impact on flowerbeds) or among next-door neighbors with vastly different norms of lawn maintenance. These, too, are usually based on class differences, and conflict generally results after a long series of minor disagreements over specific norms and activities.

   (*b*) Economic conflicts, between haves and have-nots, reflecting differences in styles of life and the economic difficulties of the latter.

   (*c*) Interest conflicts resulting from diverse and incompatible interests held by residents. Such conflicts may be among old residents versus new ones, parents of school children versus childless couples, "conservatives" versus "liberals," one neighborhood versus another, and so on. The source of conflict may depend on community issues, and the locale of conflict will be in the government, in political and social organizations, and only rarely on the block. This type of conflict is inevitable and by no means undesirable in a pluralistic society; it is undesirable only if it cannot be resolved properly, leaves grudges, and results in continuing repetition of conflict.

(d) Resident-builder conflict. Some residents are likely to object to some practices of the builders and developers, especially if they do something which is against the interests of these residents.

(e) "Newness conflict," that is, conflicts reflecting the newness of the community and the unsettled state of communications, government-resident relations, and builder-resident communications. Such conflicts are likely to come at the start of the new community's life, as people test out the feedback mechanisms and the willingness of various institutions and agencies in the community to be responsive. At that time, there may also be a need for a community scapegoat to act as target for these tensions. Newness conflict is not serious or lasting.

6. *Persisting Individual and Family Problems.* A number of residents will come with existing problems, such as marital difficulties, drinking, children's school and discipline problems. Some people will move to Columbia hoping that newness and change of community will resolve their problems; this hope is likely to be disappointed. Persisting problems are not very visible except to next-door neighbors and friends, but they are a major source of neighbor and block difficulties.

III. CRITERIA FOR A "MENTALLY HEALTHY SOCIAL STRUCTURE"

1. The criteria that follow are intended to help achieve a social structure that encourages the mental health of the residents, or at least does not add to existing individual, family, and group tensions and problems. The assumption is that if the social structure is so set up that it does not create additional major tensions and conflicts, it will be supportive of mental health. Such a social structure will not create mental health; it will only reduce those community influences that make life difficult for some people and strengthen tendencies toward mental illness in others. Perhaps the concept of mental health is too all-embracing; what I am suggesting are criteria which encourage a satisfactory morale among the residents or do not add pressures that reduce morale. They attempt to define sociologically what Rouse calls "a garden for people," with major stress on the resolution of problems, and especially on those conditions in which developers, social planners, and policy-makers can exert some leverage.

2. Columbia should aim for a social structure which:

(a) provides for the needs of the family, and of each family member, on the assumption that if this is done, causes of intrafamilial conflict will be ameliorated, or at least not increased.

(*b*) does not set neighbor against neighbor.

(*c*) creates no financial pressures on residents that can result in family tension, fights with neighbors, or community conflict.

(*d*) reduces social and physical isolation and provides for the lonely, the culturally different minority resident, and the people Nelson Foote calls the unelected.

(*e*) provides freedom of choice in block and community activities, including the freedom not to participate.

(*f*) recognizes the inevitability of community conflict and seeks to cope with the undesirable aspects of such conflict by

(1) eliminating as much as possible in the preplanning of the community those problems that are likely to be insoluble.

(2) encouraging the search for solutions and compromises as a source of solutions.

(3) treating politics as inevitable and desirable, rather than as "dirty," and encouraging political communication and feedback, so as to prevent the distorting and scapegoating that result from poor communication and interfere with the solution of problems.

(4) recognizing the pluralism of the community and creating tolerance for alternative views on community issues. This tolerance can best be achieved by preventing conditions in which alternative views and solutions impose severe social or financial costs and emotional threats on other residents. For example, it would be desirable to prevent a situation in which public services *not* used by low-income residents must be paid for by them at a cost which creates financial difficulties for them.

(*g*) provides not only overt or direct mental-health services but also, and more important, indirect or covert services which Leonard Duhl describes as consultation. These latter are intended to encourage community agencies to act in ways that are supportive of mental health and not to act in ways that would increase the problems of their clients. They are also intended to provide services supportive of mental health to people who are not likely to use mental-health clinics. The assumption is that the people who need to use such agencies most are least likely to do so, but will accept similar services from institutions not labeled as mental-health agencies, like doctors, ministers, and lawyers.

IV. SOME RECOMMENDATIONS FOR COLUMBIA

The recommendations and suggestions below relate to previously mentioned problems, but are keyed to the seven criteria for a mentally healthy social structure.

1. *Family Life and Some Suggestions for Housing*

(*a*) For the man: job, job satisfaction, and job security are most important, as is freedom from financial pressure. He wants his wife and children to be happy, the children to grow up properly, not get in trouble, and not be discipline problems. The more they are satisfied, the happier he is. He will want some all-male company, especially if he is of working-class background.

His interest in the house is primarily in the satisfaction of homeownership (unless renting is considerably cheaper) and in the chance for "puttering" in the garage, yard, den, or study.

(*b*) For the wife: welfare and happiness of husband and especially children are most important, with opportunity for easily accessible contact with other, and compatible, women next.

Her interest is in the house less than in ownership. The house is hers; it is a stage on which she presents herself and expresses herself and her sense of aesthetics and efficiency. She must like the house; it must be easy to take care of.

Differences in role priorities must be considered. Many women, especially in the lower-middle class, want to minimize (but not eliminate) the housekeeping role and maximize the mother role. This is perhaps less important to working-class women. Others, especially in the upper-middle class, want to reduce the routine parts of the mother role, that is, being a supervisor of or a chauffeur for the children. They may also appreciate the chance to reduce burdensome parts of the household routine. Levittown women find ironing most boring and depressing, and a cheap, easily accessible laundry might be popular and successful.

(*c*) For the children: they need most a place to be and a place to play without interfering with adults and being interfered with by them. Small children need play space close to home that does not create noise or danger to property and where they will not be harassed by adults or older children. This is also true of older children, who want ball parks next to the house, ideally. The provision of play spaces close by, yet not obnoxious to adults, is a real site planner's challenge. Teen-agers need privacy *in* the house: a room in which they can entertain free from adult interference; for example, play rock-and-roll records at high volume for their friends.

(*d*) For the family as a unit: my assumption is that if the spatial and facility needs of each family member can be taken care of —if all family members are satisfied and do not have to get in one another's way—the planner will be helping to reduce those causes of intrafamilial conflict over which he has leverage.

(*e*) Implications for housing: maximum space is most important; this is Levitt's reason for success. Privacy for each family member must be available, as well as a chance to minimize household routines and maximize opportunity for creativity—in play, in gardening, in cooking, sewing, and so forth. Some people like to garden and need a large yard; others do not and want a small one; different lot sizes may be desirable.

2. *Neighbor Relations, Block and Neighborhood Life, and Implications for Site Planning.*[2]

(*a*) Neighbor relations: Neighbors are important to each other for social life and mutual aid, especially among lower-middle- and working-class women. Neighbors must be accessible, yet not without loss of privacy for each house, so as to minimize the chance of neighbor being set against neighbor.

(*b*) Block homogeneity: Conflict between neighbors is ever present, and since they are spatially tied to each other, it must be minimized. As noted before, much conflict is based on class differences. Block homogeneity is necessary; putting well-educated with poorly educated people or working-class with upper-middle-class people creates such conflicts. One cannot segregate by education or by child-rearing values, so price, which reflects income, is the only form of leverage. Mixing rich with poor puts terrible pressures on the latter to keep up, especially since children make demands they learn on the block.

(*c*) Importance of block: The block is the major social arena, the major source of friends for working and even lower-middle-class residents. Since people live most of their lives in the house and much of the rest in the block, this must be emphasized.

(*d*) The block and other areas: The block is very important as a social unit; other areas, such as the neighborhood, much less so. The neighborhood is too large to be a social unit; hello-exchange is a nice but unimportant form of face-to-face relationship. Neighborhoods have meaning only if they are political units or if they are different from each other, so people can have a sense of that neighborhood. This sense is often negative; for instance, "Our neighborhood is better than yours." If the schools are set up so that parents have a compulsory, vital, and time-consuming role in them, and if most of the neighborhood has children in that school, then the neighborhood may be a social unit. I doubt that this will happen, and undue emphasis on the neighborhood is illusory. Neighborhoods may function as catchment areas for women and teen-age clubs since these groups have low mobility.

(e) Block homogeneity and community heterogeneity: The more homogeneous the block, the greater the opportunity for heterogeneity in the neighborhood and in community institutions, although even here, social stratification will develop.

(f) Some planning and site-planning suggestions:

(1) On the block there must be a compromise between privacy and accessibility; too much of either is bad. Privacy is most important; houses cannot be sited so as to put people on top of each other socially and visually. Small courts and narrow cul-de-sacs are undesirable for this reason.

(2) Social contact is determined to some extent by accessibility and, if the area is occupied by young families, by where the children play, where there is pavement.

(3) Homogeneous blocks can be separated from other blocks of a different price level if a clearly visible social boundary is available, probably one that is also expressed physically, though it cannot be a wall.

(4) A range of $3,000 in house prices will probably work on any given block, providing the lowest-price house does not look "cheap." A $5,000 range is problematical. Higher-priced houses probably need their own neighborhood, both because of property-value considerations and because their purchasers are buying status and must be socially and physically separated from lower-priced houses.

(5) It would be desirable to prevent the development of an "across-the-tracks" area; this can be done by scattering enclaves of higher-priced houses throughout Columbia and by giving areas of lower-priced houses some of the choice sites, such as on hills, near lakes.

(6) It is very important to prevent the possibility of any part of Columbia from becoming a slum. Since different builders will be building in Columbia, strict performance standards are necessary, especially for low-priced housing. Such houses must be cheaper to maintain than higher-priced housing.

(7) It might be desirable to segregate some blocks or larger areas by population characteristics and interests: groups of houses suitable for families with teen-age children, or houses with large yards for enthusiastic gardeners, or houses for retired couples might form enclaves for those people who want neighbors of similar age and interest. This does not prevent the planning of other blocks in which such houses are mixed with those likely to be occupied by young families.

(8) Neighborhood shopping areas should include soda-shop hangouts for teen-agers—perhaps one for young teen-agers, another for older ones—with a public subsidy to the owner for providing this service if the store is not profitable. Living-room type clubs, as suggested by Leonard Duhl, might include places where women can come to have morning coffee with their children and other neighbors, providing the coffee could be a source of funds for community organizations. There might also be garages or gas stations that would serve as social centers for men and boys interested in cars. Commercial areas and especially gas stations are poison to the property-value conscious and to status-conscious homeowners; they must be very clearly separated from residential blocks, preferably without reducing access. The same applies to children's play areas, as noted in IV–1–(c), above.

3. *Financial Pressures*

    (a) The existence of financial pressures on residents is perhaps the clearest illustration of the way in which a social or political structure can cause personal, familial, and even community conflict.

    (b) Solutions:

        (1) Tenant selection on the basis of income: One method is not to admit people who cannot afford to live in Columbia. This extends not only to affording the price of the house but to meeting the cost of living in a new community,

especially with a growing family. If a reasonable estimate of the cost of living can be developed, it is possible to decide who should not be allowed to live in Columbia. The determination must be based not only on present income but on expected income in the future.

This solution has several drawbacks. First, it discourages the goal of having all those working in Columbia living there. Second, builders who must sell a quota of houses are likely to resent any restriction on their market. Here the developer must make a policy decision, which ought to ensure that builders will not be punished financially by such market restrictions, but also that the long-term welfare of the person and the community is considered. To my mind, letting people buy in Columbia who clearly cannot afford it and are not likely to be able to is to hurt them and the community.

(2) Subsidies: People who work in Columbia but cannot afford to live there ought to be given some sort of subsidy so they can live there. Who they are depends on the wages and salaries, as well as house costs, and cannot now be determined.

(3) As noted earlier, people with financial problems can release their frustration only on themselves, the family, or the community. Tax policy must make sure that this consequence is minimized. Taxes are only a scapegoat, of course, but rapid increases in taxes at a time when other family expenditures are rising will surely lead to the appearance of the scapegoat. The more public and other expenditures are programed prior to occupancy—perhaps built into the house price or rent—the more this can be avoided.

4. *Social and Physical Isolation: Some Possible Remedies*

(*a*) Social and physical isolation affect only a minority of the population; most people in Columbia will probably report just the opposite. Yet if the goal is a garden for people, the isolation that does occur ought to be minimized. Solutions depend on the type of isolate and the cause of the problem.

(*b*) Social isolation. Solutions for types of social isolates:

(1) Families used to close ties with parents, siblings, or extended family, and people who have lived all their lives in one neighborhood: People—especially women—who have been used to daily contact with parents (this will be

mostly ethnic and working-class women with a close tie to mothers) should be told that once the novelty of the house and community wears off, they will be quite lonely for their mothers and should take this into account before they buy. However, since the men will want to get away from in-laws in many cases, and the women do want the new house (often it is a matter of having one's cake and eating it too), more positive solutions are desirable. There are at least three. First, the phone system should be set up so that calls to Baltimore and Washington will not be toll calls, enabling women to call their mothers daily if they wish. Second, good and fast public transportation to reach these cities should be available. Third, housing for the older generation, and particularly for parents of Columbia residents, should be provided. In most cases, parents will not leave their present neighborhoods or exchange an inexpensive old house for a more costly new house or apartment unless they are given subsidies.

(2) The culturally different who are in a minority and cannot easily find friends,[3] and working-class people who lack the social skills for making new contacts, particularly older people, poorly educated ones, and ethnic-group members: They will be difficult to reach, but a few solutions are worth trying. One would be to have the local newspaper and TV station present full descriptions of suitable organizations; not just to give the names and activities of these organizations, but to describe their membership in class and other terms so that isolated people will realize where they can find compatible people. Another solution would be a column in the paper in which people who want to find others with common interests or want to start new organizations can express their need. A third solution is to make doctors, ministers, and other counselor-caretakers, as well as leaders of existing organizations, aware of the problem of social isolation and encourage them to contact such people or advise them when they come for help. A kind of "welcome wagon" that sells organizations and not just merchants might be in order if it is designed to encourage the socially isolated.

(3) Reaching the socially most isolated: The solutions listed in (2) above are likely to attract the more easily reached;

the most isolated will be difficult to reach. There is no easy solution to this problem. If possible, counselors and leaders—and all residents—should be given to understand that social isolation is often a social structural problem, and not a personal failing. In addition, the community should make it as easy as possible for people to form organizations and to get into those already formed. Socially unskilled people are often fearful of formal organizations and formal meeting places. One solution—desirable for other reasons as well—is Leonard Duhl's living-room club, where a more informal atmosphere for organizational activity than is possible in a community center can be obtained. Such clubs might especially encourage the formation of block or subneighborhood social or game clubs (card-playing) which attract the women not "ready" for formal organization. (See also IV–5, below.)

Some of the socially isolated will be people with marital or personal emotional problems. Probably they cannot be reached by organizations, but eventually they will take their problems to physicians and ministers. These should be made sensitive to the nature of this type of social isolation and should be given a list of what might be called "helping neighbors" who can try to integrate such people into a formal or informal organization. Ministers often find such helping neighbors in their congregations.

(4) The "racial isolate": Although Columbia will be racially integrated, it is quite likely that much of the informal social life will remain segregated. Well-educated Negroes will be able to find white friends among the liberal segments of the upper-middle-class group, but others will not. If sufficient numbers of Negroes are easily accessible to each other, there should be no problems; if not, some Negroes, especially women and children, may feel socially isolated. Like the people described in (1) above, they will need to have easy contact with their old friends in Baltimore and Washington, or else they may not come to Columbia in the first place. If there is a sizable Negro population, it is quite likely that all-Negro clubs and informal social groups, and probably even churches, will be formed. While it would be desirable, ideally speaking, for integration to be complete, I think it is preferable to have all-Negro social

groups—especially if they are set up voluntarily and do not only reflect rejection by white groups—rather than to force Negro families to live in social isolation.

I raise this problem not because it requires immediate solution, for it does not, but only because it will come up eventually in the community. While it would be undesirable to set up all-Negro neighborhoods, or even all-Negro blocks, I think it would be equally undesirable to have only one Negro family per block, especially in lower-priced areas of Columbia, for this would almost certainly guarantee social isolation for that family.

(5) Teen-agers: If Columbia attracts a large proportion of young families, teen-agers will be a "cultural" minority, and they will be isolated from each other because they have little mobility unless they have cars. As the number of teen-agers increases, they will be less isolated from each other, but they will likely be considered an undesirable minority by the adults. Indeed, in many suburban communities adult–teen-age conflict is more prevalent than class conflict. The teen-agers' right to their own "youth culture" must be acknowledged, and facilities must be provided where they can be free to act as teen-agers and be teen-agers. Moreover, it must be recognized that there are many types of teen-agers, differentiated not only by class but also by age. A fifteen-year-old will not talk easily to or associate with a twelve-year-old. Adults are inclined not only to lump all teen-agers into one group but also to supply them with facilities that are, by adult criteria, good for them, alienating them unnecessarily.

(6) Older people: The elderly are also a cultural minority, in some ways as immobile as teen-agers. Sick older people may need special facilities, but healthy ones do not. They may, however, need opportunities to find compatible people, as do other kinds of social isolates. Some old people will want "senior citizens groups"; others will avoid them like the plague; but in any case, the tendency of young adults to dictate how old people should act must be discouraged. The more the old people, like teen-agers, can be given a useful function in the community, the less likely the possibility of social isolation or the feeling of being useless.

(7) The "useless": Just for the record, it might be relevant to suggest that teen-agers, old people, and especially unemployed people can easily feel useless in the community, and uselessness leads to social isolation and psychological deterioration, among other things. The only real solution is to do away with the cause of social uselessness.

(8) The "organizational" isolate: This term describes people who need organizations that are not likely to exist in Columbia. I am thinking here primarily of members of minority religious groups like the Greek Orthodox church, which may not have enough congregants in Columbia to build a church or even to organize a congregation. The community should set up car pools or provide chartered buses to allow these people to go to Baltimore or Washington where congregations are available.

(c) Physical isolation: Proper house and site planning can help to reduce it; for instance, by providing nearby play spaces for small children which do not need supervision and a porch where children can be put out in bad weather. Equally important is a good intracommunity public transportation system—jitneys, perhaps—which can allow women who do not drive to get out of the house. Since many would (or would like to) head for the main shopping center, there is no reason why such a transportation system cannot be subsidized by the main shopping center if, as I expect, a subsidy is needed. Day and nursery schools will also reduce physical isolation, but only if they are designed to attract the kind of people who now shun them.

5. *Freedom of Choice in Community Life*

(a) It is important to stress again a comment made in I–3 that most people will not participate actively in community organizations, even if they are members. Nor are they likely to come in large numbers to agencies that provide adult education and self-improvement. Unless the developer wants to limit the community to the upwardly mobile, the self-improvement-seeking and tradition-breaking minority, people's right not to join ought to be considered.

(b) Even so, organizational and educational participation should be encouraged. The best way to do this is to be "market-oriented": to know what potential participants want from a group and then provide the incentives that will attract them. Appeals to the duty of community participation and to one's obligation to improve oneself will not work. For example, if mothers are to be encouraged to send children to nursery and day schools, such schools will have to cope with the reason why working- and lower-middle-class mothers who do not work are hesitant now to send their children.

(c) Moreover, preplanning of institutions requiring resident participation ought to be limited as much as possible, perhaps only to those types that, for site-planning and other reasons, must be planned prior to occupancy. In order for institutions to be market-oriented, they cannot be set up until we know what kinds of people they are intended for, which cannot be done until people have moved in. Second, it can be predicted safely that there will be a large number of potential leaders among the residents, some wanting to set up specific organizations, some ready to initiate whatever is being demanded. Although their motives for leadership are unlikely to be purely community-minded, they make effective leaders and should be encouraged. Moreover, many organizations will be formed, partly in order to "sort" people by a variety of background and interest factors —the more so if people of different ages, religions, and so on live side by side. Once these organizations are formed, they will be looking for programs and for things to do in addition to the major activity, sociability. It may then be possible to enroll some in the kinds of educational, self-improvement, and community-service schemes that have been proposed by several Work Group consultants.

6. *Conflict Reduction*

(a) Solutions for conflict reduction are difficult to propose a priori, since sources of conflict cannot now be predicted. As a general principle, two points may be made. First, wherever and whenever possible, pluralism ought to be encouraged. Operationally, this means minimizing the need for one common decision or for unitary solutions to problems where there is disagreement over the nature of the problem or the best solution. This is, of course, an argument for decentralization, but not necessarily a real or spatial decentralization because, as indicated in IV–2–(b), neighborhoods are not social units. In fact, people living together in a small area often find it more difficult to agree on a decision. If they have neighborly obligations toward each other, they are likely to suppress disagreement and to avoid discussing controversial issues or making unpopular decisions. Unless the population is so homogeneous that there is pervasive consensus, the "decision-making area" should be large, since conflicting interests can be translated into compromise solutions more easily among people who are not close to each other, socially and physically.

Second, community decisions which force one group in the community to pay for facilities or services which they will not use, or which they oppose, ought to be minimized. People are willing to live and let live—that is, to be tolerant of diversity— if it does not demand a personal sacrifice or create a threat to their own point of view.

The government of the community, public allocation policies, and taxing procedures ought to be designed with these two points in mind.

(b) Community conflict: Much of this will be class conflict, especially between the have-mores and have-less. The two principles suggested in (a), above, can minimize the kind of insoluble conflict that leads to irreparable and recurring fights. Another principle which ought to be applied in planning for conflict resolution is the minimization of status deprivation, that is, feelings of inferiority on the part of those who have less, be this income, education, prestige, or power. For example, schools and other public agencies should be so designed that the least "desirable" clients are treated as well as the more desirable ones. Of course, national values, which say that in a middle-class community, middle-class people are "better" than working-class ones, will be operating in full force, but public institutions should be designed to fight the tendency to reward the "better" and deprive the "inferior." In the high school, vocational-training programs should not be poor cousins to the academic (college-preparatory) programs. Moreover, opportunities for status should be made available to the former in extra-curricular activity in fields other than athletics; for example, by providing vocational students with a chance to build things needed by the community or rewarded by the national culture, such as cars. Similarly, rock-and-roll combos should be encouraged as much as student symphony orchestras.

(c) Political conflict: Class and area conflicts will express themselves through political conflict, not only between parties but between resident groups and builders and even between organizations, such as the League of Women Voters and veterans groups. This is inevitable; it is undesirable only if the conflict cannot be resolved. Political parties are often good brokers, but they do not participate in conflict resolution when the issue conflicts with other party priorities, when there are divergent opinions about the issue inside the party, and when the issue is so controversial that any party which advocates it would be hurt politically. Under such conditions, the issue is likely to be driven underground, as sometimes happens when a political conflict has religious connotations. Driving an issue underground is undesirable only when the result is to interfere with reaching a solution or when long-lasting grudges are created which interfere with solutions to other issues.

Controversial issues are always difficult to resolve, but attempts to alleviate useless conflict and to direct all conflicts toward the formulation of a compromise decision are worth while. One general principle, described under III–2–(*f*), is to encourage overt discussion of all controversies and conflicts, which can be aided by maximizing feedback and inter- as well as intra-institutional communication. Another possibility is to set up a community ombudsman, or what the Work Group called the "king's representative": a group of community members from all political parties who would have the responsibility of opening up those issues that are in danger of being driven underground and airing them—perhaps in a quasi-judicial institution, a kind of community supreme court.

Finally, conflict, and especially underground conflict, encourages the restriction of information, and this in turn leads to rumor. Rumor has positive functions, but it also has negative ones. A weekly column in the local paper and a program on the TV station might be set up to discuss the rumors that are current, explain why they came about, provide information that would eliminate falsehoods, and thus reduce unnecessary tensions that interfere with the solutions of conflicts and disagreements.

7. *Mental Health and Community Consultation Services*

(*a*) Agencies such as clinics and family-counseling agencies which provide overt mental-health services ought to be set up in such a way that people will be encouraged to come to them. This may require a number of clinics differentiated by type of clientele, and notably by level of education. Present agencies reach only the most easily reached, especially the upper-middle-class population. New clinics, staffed with people who understand lower-middle- and working-class culture, problems, and clients should be provided.

(b) A more feasible method of attracting the hard-to-reach is to make sure that the agencies to which these people now take their problems can provide mental-health services indirectly or covertly. The major agencies are physicians and ministers, and both ought to have training in psychiatry and counseling so that they can provide mental-health services.

  (1) If churches are given free land, the developer should require that ministers selected by the national denominations are trained in pastoral counseling.

  (2) If the developer has some control over the entry of physicians—for example, if group practice and other agencies are preplanned—physicians who have some training in psychotherapy should be given priority. (Psychiatrists might be part of the group agency, but this will not solve the problem of reaching those who now resist approaching them, even on referral.) If possible, medical practice, whether in the group or by an individual, should be so set up that the more routine tasks—giving shots and taking care of minor illnesses like flu—are left to nurses or "assistant doctors," partly to reduce the costs of medical service and partly to make sure that physicians spend their time and energy on the kinds of service for which they have been trained.

(c) Public officials who deal with social and individual problems should be encouraged to accept some training in social psychiatry and sociology that would make them sensitive to the "real" problems with which they are dealing. For example, policemen should be trained to realize that improper action on their part toward juvenile offenders is a major cause of making them feel and become delinquent; judges who sit on domestic-relations cases should understand, rather than punish, cases of intra-familial conflict that come to court. Government officials should be trained to look for the real causes of community conflict. Needless to say, the agencies in which these officials operate should be so set up that the tendency to punish the emotionally disturbed individual, or the individual who commits antisocial acts because the social structure does not minister to his needs (such as the teen-ager who expresses his boredom or his resentment against a poor school system through delinquent acts), is minimized.

NOTES

1. My observations and predictions are based on my empirical research in existing bedroom new towns, especially Park Forest, Illinois, and Willingboro (Levittown), New Jersey. Thus, I am sensitive to the issues and problems that developed in these communities and perhaps insensitive to others. I assume, however, that the everyday life of the Columbia resident will not be very different from that of the Levittowner or Park Forester, especially since everyday life is not affected significantly by the structure of the formal, physical, and public community. Moreover, I assume that the dominant population of Columbia will be a young, lower-middle-class family-raising one, with smaller proportions of upper-middle- and working-class people as well as middle-aged and older families in their midst. By average, then, I mean to refer to that dominant population.

   Park Forest and Levittown are, of course, bedroom communities, and the paper makes no comments about the everyday work life of the breadwinner or on the relationship between work and residential life. Since most middle-class residential areas are, even in the city, bedroom communities which the breadwinners leave during the work period, I assume that the inferences I have made from my studies of bedroom communities will be applicable to life in Columbia.

2. I use *block* as a generic term, not a site-planning concept. I mean that area, in a single-family-house community, that encompasses the four to six houses on either side of a given house with which some social contact is possible and likely. Presumably one can identify "blocks" for different house types; for example, for apartment houses with many apartments on one floor.

3. Well-educated people who are a cultural, ethnic, or religious minority usually have the social skills and the mobility to find compatible people and probably do not need help in relieving social isolation.

Part IV

Part IV PLANNING AGAINST URBAN POVERTY AND SEGREGATION

Introduction

The essays of Parts IV and V have a more urgent tone than the rest of the book; they appeal for immediate action to deal with the urban crisis, and with poverty and segregation which I consider to be the fundamental causes of that crisis.

My concern about the problems of the city developed out of a serendipitous set of occurrences. When I first began to think about studying a future Levittown in the mid-1950's, I was particularly interested in working-class culture and the changes it was undergoing as a result of postwar affluence. (In fact, at one point, I planned to concentrate on a study of the acculturation of working-class Levittowners to the middle-class life they would find in suburbia.) My interest in this topic came from two sources: from a long-standing interest in acculturation, nurtured partly by my studies of American Jewry, and from my first wife, who was concerned about poverty long before I had begun to think about this problem.

She had often encouraged me to do a study of a poor community, and as luck would have it, I was given the opportunity to carry out such a study in the West End, a Boston neighborhood of low-income people. In 1957, when the opening of Levittown, New Jersey, was postponed for a year, I was able to accept an invitation from Leonard Duhl, Erich Lindemann, and Marc Fried—the former the sponsor, the latter two the principal investigators—of a study of how the West Enders would adapt to the crisis of relocation when the area was torn down as a slum.

At that time, I was not very much interested in slum clearance; I had come to the West End to study working-class culture. I carried out my study, but with slum clearance only a year away and a source of worry among the West Enders, I began to share their concern. Living in the

West End, I could see clearly the injustices slum clearance was about to wreak on the hapless West Enders, and I became so angry that at one point during my field work, I considered dropping the study and joining the small band of West Enders who were trying to halt the bulldozer. After much soul-searching, I decided against this move because I knew that it was too late to halt the clearance and I felt that my activities might endanger the long-term study of the effects of relocation. Instead, I waited till my field work was ended and then met with one of the commissioners of the Boston Redevelopment Authority to offer him my critique of the clearance project. At his request, I wrote a memorandum which listed a number of policies that could still be instituted to improve the relocation process and reduce the injustices which would soon be meted out to the West Enders. The memorandum was never even acknowledged, and later that summer I was urged by Melvin Webber and other colleagues to publish it. An expanded version of that memorandum is the first essay reprinted here.[1]

The ideas expressed in that essay were not original, and later I discovered that a number of others had come to similar conclusions earlier. While theirs went unheeded, my essay, together with several others and reinforced a hundredfold by the political protests of the victims of urban renewal in many cities, had some effect on federal legislation and local practices. Today, the critique of relocation has become part of the conventional wisdom of the planning and housing professions, and relocation procedures have been improved; although the main defect of urban renewal, its inability to build low-income housing for the people it displaces, is as serious as ever.

The article about the West End never once mentioned poverty, partly because most West Enders, although not affluent, were not that poor, partly because I was no more concerned about poverty at that time than most other social scientists. In the early 1960's, however, my perspective changed. By 1960, slum clearance was predominantly "Negro removal," and the displacement of poor Negroes without adequate relocation housing was adding significantly to their troubles. Although Michael Harrington's *The Other America* was not published until March 1962, he and others were already talking about the need to do something about poverty.

In 1961, the Ford Foundation launched the so-called human renewal or gray area projects. Initiated by Paul Ylvisaker, then director of public affairs for the Foundation, the human renewal projects sought to help slum dwellers in the urban-renewal areas of a half-dozen cities by providing them with social services and other resources they were thought to need, particularly community organization, counseling, and remedial education, but sometimes also jobs and job training. The Ford Foundation's projects received much favorable publicity, and, together with somewhat similar programs launched by the federal government to help cities fight juvenile delinquency, they eventually became prototypes for the Community Action Programs of the Office of Economic Opportunity.

City planners were, on the whole, favorably inclined to human renewal, partly because it promised to aid the slum dwellers, and partly because it relieved the planners of the responsibility for those displaced under urban renewal and allowed them to continue with the rebuilding of the cities. The hope was that human renewal and urban renewal would work hand in hand to eliminate both the slums and the problems of their occupants —a hope that was never quite fulfilled but was later written into the federal Model Cities legislation.

I welcomed the human-renewal projects in principle, but was critical of them in practice, for I felt that they were not addressing themselves to the fundamental problems. More often than not, they tried to change the slum dweller's behavior, to make him live by middle-class ways, rather than to change the economic and social conditions that forced him to live in the slums. By 1962, I was arguing that the best way of eliminating the slums was to eliminate poverty, and I recall presenting this idea at a government conference in Washington that year, shocking some planners and housing officials present who had not begun to question the traditional housing approach.

In October 1962, I wrote the essay reprinted as Chapter 16 to criticize the direction human renewal was taking, and to urge a direct attack on poverty instead. In the final section of this paper, I went one step further, and argued that most of the problems of the city were caused by poverty, and that planners ought to concern themselves with basic causes. (Many of these ideas appear again, better formulated, in later chapters, but I decided to include the paper in the collection because it is one of my favorites. Readers who want to avoid the repetition can skip the chapter.)

This essay was addressed to city planners, for I was then still interested mainly in the thinking and practice of the profession. I also wrote a slightly different version for sociologists, however, to interest them in becoming involved in the human renewal projects. I believed all too naïvely that they knew more about the needs of the poor than the planners, and could help to alter the projects in the direction I favored.[2]

Chapter 17, which I wrote a few months later, paralleled Chapter 16. Addressed to social workers, it suggested that the settlement house, that nineteenth-century anti-poverty agency, was even less relevant than human renewal in dealing with urban poverty and segregation, and I proposed that the settlement movement devote itself to more limited claims and goals.

In 1965, I returned to the critique of urban renewal. By then, the dissatisfaction with this approach had permeated outside the planning profession, and there was talk that the federal government would soon propose a new method of dealing with the slums (which turned out to be Model Cities). When I was asked by the editor of *Commentary,* an influential magazine that I knew was read in high Washington circles, to review Martin Anderson's highly critical and somewhat unfair attack on the federal urban renewal program, I requested permission to go beyond a review, and wrote the essay reprinted as Chapter 18. While I discussed the pros and cons of urban renewal, my primary aim was to present a program for rehousing the urban low-income population—although I also related it, albeit tangentially, to a more general attack on poverty. As it turned out, President Johnson proposed the new federal approach, which later became the Model Cities program, just before the article appeared, but it failed to provide for a significant amount of rehousing.

Chapters 16 to 18 argued a common thesis; they criticized the illusion that the traditional methods of planners, social workers, community organizers, and other reformers could do away with urban poverty. In 1966, I was asked to testify at Senator Abraham Ribicoff's hearings on the crisis of the city, and decided to talk not about the subject I had been invited to talk about, urban renewal and other planning solutions, but about the basic causes of the crisis. I suggested that most of the so-called urban problems had nothing to do with the city, or with city planning; that these problems were largely the result of the poverty and segregation faced by the rural population that had streamed to the city; that the crisis was national, having to do with economic and social inequality in America; and that the best solution to the urban crisis was a national attack on poverty and segregation. Unrestricted by the space limitations of magazines and professional journals, I presented a fairly detailed set of programs to mount this attack. My testimony, which appears in Chapter 19, is thus my most complete statement on the "urban" problem, although in reprinting it here, I have abridged the description of rehousing programs to prevent overlap with Chapter 18.

NOTES

1. A more detailed description of my reactions to the urban-renewal process in the West End and of how I came to write this paper can be found in Herbert Gans, *The Urban Villagers* (New York: Free Press of Glencoe, 1962) pp. 305–307.

2. This paper, and a critical analysis of what the human renewal projects and the successor community action programs of the War on Poverty had accomplished between 1962 and 1965, appeared as "Social Planning and Urban Poverty," in P. Lazarsfeld, W. Sewell, and H. Wilensky, eds., *Uses of Sociology* (New York: Basic Books, 1967) pp. 437–475.

15

The Human Implications of Slum Clearance and Relocation

Author's note

This evaluation of slum clearance is based on data from an eight-month-long sociological community study which I made in the West End of Boston between October 1957 and May 1958, shortly before the beginning of relocation from the area. During this period, I lived in the neighborhood as a participant-observer, conducting formal and informal interviews with many West Enders as well as with redevelopment officials. After the West End was torn down, I gathered some additional data through visits to old friends and neighbors, now scattered throughout the Boston area.

The community study was conducted under the auspices of the Center for Community Studies, affiliated with the Department of Psychiatry, Harvard Medical School, and Massachusetts General Hospital as part of a larger, long-term research project, Relocation and Mental Health: Adaptation under Stress.

My own conclusions were based on observational and interview evidence; from a scientific standpoint, they were hypotheses and preliminary findings. The long-term research project measured the effects of clearance and relocation on the people of the West End in a systematic manner, principally through a set of before-and-after relocation interviews with a sample of five hundred West End residents. Many of the findings of this study have now been published, and they substantiate the observations and predictions I made about the economic, social, and psychological effects of slum clearance and relocation on the West Enders.[1]

When this article appeared, its conclusions were greeted with considerable skepticism and even hostility from city planners and renewal officials. After the larger West End study and research in other cities produced similar findings, however, they developed a new argument: that the West End project was one of the most poorly handled clearance

Reprinted from *Journal of the American Institute of Planners*, XXV, No. 1 (February 1959), 15–25, where it appeared under the title "The Human Implications of Current Redevelopment and Relocation Planning." I have revised the "Author's Note" to include references to later findings of the West End study.

and relocation projects of the 1950's and that its effects could therefore not be considered as applicable to other, supposedly more adequately handled, renewal projects. Hartman's careful comparative analysis of a number of relocation studies[2] and my own observations in several cities indicate, however, that the relocation of the West Enders was handled relatively well and was certainly no worse than relocation projects in other large cities. Thus, the findings of the West End studies cannot be explained away. Moreover, because the West Enders were white and of a somewhat higher socioeconomic level than most of the people displaced by renewal elsewhere, the West End findings may actually understate the negative impact of clearance and relocation activities in other cities. Indeed, Negroes probably suffered considerably more from slum clearance without proper relocation than the West Enders. Their incomes were lower, their housing choices after displacement were even more limited because of segregation, and they lacked the wide familial contacts of the West Enders, so that they were more dependent on the people they had come to know and trust in the neighborhood.

I. Boston's West End

A number of large American cities are currently initiating or carrying out renewal projects which involve the clearance of a neighborhood and the relocation of a large number of families. This paper attempts to analyze and evaluate some of the social and planning problems in this process, as they were observed in the redevelopment of Boston's West End. It is submitted as a case study, because many of the conditions described exist also in other American cities.

The forty-eight-acre West End project area[3] is part of a seventy-two-acre working-class residential district in downtown Boston.[4] The project area is covered almost solidly with five-story apartment buildings, which replaced older three-story single- and multifamily structures around the turn of the century. The land coverage is very high, as is the ground density.[5] However, the apartments were built at a time when families were much larger, so that for many households the floor density is low. In the last twenty-five years, the West End has been mainly an area of first and second settlement for Italian and Polish families. In 1950, the area was estimated to have 12,000 residents. At the time of the city's "taking" the land under eminent domain in May 1958, about 2,800 households and 7,500 residents remained.[6]

The redevelopment plan proposes total clearance, except for a half-dozen community-wide institutions and buildings of architectural interest. The area is to be redeveloped with up to 2,400 apartments, most of them in elevator buildings, at rents currently estimated to be $45 per room, and with parks, shops, and parking areas for the new tenants. Massachusetts

General Hospital is also expanding its plant and parking areas on an adjacent site.

II. The redevelopment plan

A planning analysis of this redevelopment project must begin with the question of whether or not the area is a slum. The term *slum* is an evaluative, not an empirical, one; and any definition must be related, implicitly or explicitly, to the renewal policy in which it is used. Popular definitions of the slum include two criteria: the social image of the area and its physical condition. Federal standards for determining eligibility for renewal funds focus almost exclusively on the latter. However, it is the local agency which selects the area to be proposed for clearance; and, in most communities, the area's physical condition is a necessary but not sufficient criterion. What seems to happen is that neighborhoods come to be described as slums if they are inhabited by residents who, for a variety of economic, cultural, and psychological reasons, indulge in overt and visible behavior considered undesirable by the majority of the community.[7] The community image of the area gives rise to feelings that something should be done, and subsequently the area is proposed for redevelopment.[8] Usually, the physical condition of the area is such that it is eligible for redevelopment; however, there are areas, such as Boston's North End, which meet physical criteria but are socially and politically strong enough to discourage any official or politician from suggesting them for clearance.[9]

The federal and local housing standards which are applied to slum areas reflect the value pattern of middle-class professionals. These professionals, like the rest of the middle class, allot a higher value to housing (as measured by percentage of income to be spent for shelter) and place greater emphasis on the status functions of housing than does the working class. Their evaluation of the behavior of slum residents is also based on class-defined standards, and these often confuse behavior which is only culturally different with pathological or antisocial acts.[10]

Generally speaking, these standards are desirable bases for public policy, despite their class bias; and many of them should be applied to the poorer areas of the city, if they were followed by a program which provided the residents of these areas with better housing. Presently, however, these standards are used to tear down poor neighborhoods; but the better housing for the residents is not provided. This assertion will be supported by the analysis that follows.

Slum and low-rent districts: a redefinition

Consequently, unless urban-renewal policy is drastically altered, other definitions of the slum should be developed. Existing physical standards fail to make a distinction between *low-rent* and *slum* districts, or low-rent and slum housing, community facilities, street patterns, and so on. This distinction is an important one. *Slum dwellings and the like may be defined as those which are proved to be physically, socially, or emotionally harmful to their residents or to the community at large. On the other hand, low-rent dwellings and so forth, provide housing and the necessary facilities which are not harmful, to people who want, or for economic reasons* must *maintain, low rental payments and are willing to accept lack of modernity, high density, lack of privacy, stair climbing and other inconveniences as alternative costs.*[11]

A set of equitable social standards is more difficult to define, because of the problem of causality. In most cases, people move into what are known as slum areas because they have problems or unacceptable behavior patterns; economic, social, and psychological conditions, rather than the slum, cause these. The social environment may "infect" a few people previously without problems, but this is much rarer than commonly thought. However, for purposes of definition in connection with renewal policy, it is possible to distinguish between undesirable patterns which are related causally to the neighborhood and those which are not. *Thus, for renewal purposes, a slum may also be defined as an area which, because of the nature of its social environment, can be proved to create problems and pathologies, either for the residents or for the community at large.*

For example, if children are drawn into illegal activities and it can be *proved* that the neighborhood, rather than conditions of lower-class life, was responsible, that neighborhood might be called a slum.[12] The same would apply if residential overcrowding inhibited privacy and led to intra- or interfamilial conflict. However, overcrowding is probably caused by socioeconomic deprivations that force people to live under such conditions, rather than by the neighborhood itself; and clearance does not solve this problem.

The West End as a low-rent district

In my opinion, and given existing renewal policies, most of the West End cannot be described as a slum. I would estimate that at the time of the land taking, probably from 25 to 35 per cent of the buildings in the project area were structurally unsound, uninhabitable because they had been vacant for some time, or located on alleys too narrow for proper sanitation and fire prevention.[13] Some of the deterioration was due to the fact that in 1950, when the plans for redevelopment were first announced, landlords were advised not to make extensive repairs on their properties. Many residents claimed—with some justification—that parts of the area deteriorated rapidly as a result, especially where apartments or entire buildings became and remained vacant in the years that followed.[14] However, reduction of maintenance during the period of rent control and the housing shortage, especially by absentee landlords with big holdings, also contributed to the decay.[15]

Nevertheless, the majority of the structures provide low-rent rather than slum dwellings. Rents are extremely low—often below those charged in public housing; and during the postwar prosperity, most West Enders were able to modernize the interiors of their apartments.[16] The low rents enable the many people in the area who have never escaped the threat of work layoffs to keep their fixed housing costs low enough to survive such a layoff, and the location of the area is within walking distance of the central business district where most of the residents are employed. Also, the minimal rents and the familiar neighbors enable the many old people in the area who retired on social security and some income from a building to maintain independent households.

The exteriors of the buildings have not been well maintained. This is in part because West Enders pay little attention to the status symbols connected with housing. The proximity of family and ethnic group and the availability of local institutions catering to their needs are valued by residents more highly than the status image of the neighborhood.[17] Nor do they regard the high density as a problem, except for parking. Privacy is not evaluated here as highly as it is in middle-class culture, and West Enders consider it more important to have large numbers of relatives, friends, and neighbors at hand. Cultural differences between middle- and working-class families thus affect the applicability and validity of some of the planner's housing standards.

Nor does the West End satisfy the social criteria which would make it a slum. There are "problem residents" in the area, because of the spillover from the adjacent skid row and because the low rents have attracted transients, broken families, and new immigrants. For some years now the West End has been the main first area of settlement for newcomers to Boston, and it has thus served an important, though unrecognized, function in the city.[18] Problems and pathologies associated with ethnic and economic status are also present.[19] But these problems are not created by the neighborhood. In fact, for the newcomers the West End has provided an opportunity to avoid the problems that they would have faced in the other major location for first settlement, the South End. Moreover, the highly developed system of informal social control in the West End makes it possible for people with different standards of living and ethnic backgrounds to live together peaceably, tolerant of those with problems.

Some other reasons for the redevelopment decision

The certification of the West End for redevelopment was not due solely to its physical and social characteristics. Because of its central location adjacent to Beacon Hill and near the downtown retail area, real-estate men had long felt the West End was "ripe for higher uses." The Charles River frontage was considered desirable for high-rent apartments. Moreover, the desire of the hospital and other powerful Boston institutions that the low-income population be moved out of the area, the city's desperate need for a higher tax base and its equally urgent search for some signs of economic revival,[20] and the belief that the shrinkage of the central retail area could and should be halted by settling "quality shoppers" nearby—all contributed to justify clearance of the area. The fact that a developer was available made the plan a potential reality. Meanwhile, other Boston neighborhoods in which the housing is more deteriorated and even dangerous received a much lower priority for renewal, because they are not suitable for high-income housing or because there is less interest among the community's major decision-makers.

Costs and benefits of redevelopment

The proposed redevelopment will be profitable for the builders and will add to Boston's tax base; and it should provide a psychological lift to the city. Several questions can be raised, however, about its over-all benefit to the community, especially when some generally unrecognized and perhaps unintended consequences are taken into consideration. An examination of some of these probable consequences follows:

1. The project has been planned on the assumption that high- and middle-income residents are of benefit to the city, whereas low-income residents are only a burden and a source of public expense. This assumption ignores the vital economic and social functions played in the city economy by low-income people and by the availability of low-rent housing. The reduction of the city's low-rent housing supply by close to 3,000

units makes it more difficult for the present and future industrial force of a low-wage city to find centrally located, economic housing. The need to relocate 2,800 households in the reduced supply will thus overcrowd the remainder, or increase further the outmigration from the city.

2. The economic benefits from the redevelopment may be counteracted by the loss of property values and tax yields in the areas from which tenants will be drawn. Moreover, the central business district which is intended to benefit by the redevelopment may actually lose because (a) the redevelopment plan calls for a sizable shopping center; (b) the people likely to rent the new apartments probably already do much of their shopping downtown; and (c) the West Enders who will leave the city will probably shop in outlying centers, whereas previously they did all but their food buying in the downtown stores.

3. West Enders with social, economic, and other problems are faced by yet further problems brought on by the need to move from a familiar, permissive, and inexpensive neighborhood. Although some will undoubtedly find better housing, others will be forced to the real slums of the city or will overcrowd other low-rent districts to the point where they become slums. The need to move and to pay higher rents will increase the burdens of these West Enders and of the community agencies helping them now.

More detailed analyses of the project would have to be made to determine whether or not the benefits outweigh the costs for the community as a whole and for the sectors of the population affected by the project.

The hidden costs

However, such analyses would not take into consideration the hidden social, economic, and other costs paid by the West Enders in being forced out of their neighborhood with nothing more than the $100 moving allowance.

1. West Enders must bear the financial burdens that result from having to pay higher rentals for new apartments that are unlikely to be better in quality than the old ones. For many West Enders, this will require drastic budgetary changes with consequent deprivations in other spheres of life.[21] Because of the shortage of rental housing, some people will be encouraged to buy houses in the suburbs at prices beyond their ability to pay. Moreover, because of the negative publicity leveled at the West End by the press, apartment-hunting tenants from there are likely to be faced with rent gouging by landlords who know that West Enders are at the

mercy of the market as well as with discrimination or refusals because they are "slum dwellers."[22]

2. Landlords who were able to live modestly from the rentals of one or more West End buildings will lose their incomes; the amount of money they will receive for these buildings is not likely to be large enough to allow them to purchase others.

3. Many small businessmen in the area will lose their incomes and livelihood. Although federal relocation regulations allot them $2,500 for moving expenses if they re-establish their business, many will be unable to find a new location, since Boston is already oversupplied with small stores.[23] Many of these businessmen are too old to be hired by employers, so both economically and psychologically their future is grim.

4. There are social and psychological losses that result from the breakup of the neighborhood. Clearance destroys not only housing but also a functioning social system, the existence of which is not even recognized by current relocation procedures. The scattering of family units and friends is likely to be especially harmful to the many older people. The younger West Enders feel that they can adjust to a new neighborhood, but they expect that many of the older ones will not be able to do so and will die during the process.[24]

The variety of costs which West Enders will pay as a result of clearance and relocation (to be discussed below) represent hidden subsidies to the redevelopment program. In effect, the present low-income population will subsidize the clearance of their neighborhood and the apartments of their high-income successors, both by their own losses and by their share of the federal and local tax money used to clear the site. To balance these costs, the only benefit to be received by most residents is the moving allowance.

Some West Enders, especially the most poorly housed, will undoubtedly benefit from the development by being able to find better apartments. Others will gain by being given a push toward a move to the suburbs they had wanted to make anyway, but which they had delayed because of inertia; however, many of the families in this position had already left the West End between 1950 and 1958.[25]

III. The relocation plan

While considerable attention has been devoted to the planning of the physical redevelopment phase of the project, less planning has been done for the relocation of the present West End residents. The local relocation plan, approved by federal officials, is based on the assumption that the

60 per cent of the population eligible for public housing will accept such units and that private housing is available for the remainder. Neither of these assumptions has yet been tested, and both were open to serious question in May 1958.

Many eligible West Enders are unwilling to go into public housing. This is so in part because they have been affected by the negative image given public housing by the Boston newspapers, because they will be unable to live with relatives, friends, and neighbors from their own ethnic group, because they consider public-housing tenants to be below them in status, and because they do not wish to be subjected to administrative regulation of their activities.[26] Nor is it entirely clear whether there are sufficient vacant public-housing units for even those West Enders who will accept them.[27]

As a result, considerably more than the 40 per cent estimated by the relocation planners will be competing for low-rent and low-cost *private* housing. Moreover, no adequate study has been made of the private-housing market,[28] so at the time of the land acquisition, no one knew how much of such housing was available.[29] In addition, since most West End people are used to living amidst their own ethnic group, those of Italian descent (approximately 45 per cent of the present population) would like to move to a handful of Italian communities in the Boston area. However, these probably cannot house more than a small percentage of the relocatees.

As a result, many people inside and outside the West End believe that there is not sufficient relocation housing to meet either the needs of the 2,800 West End households or the federal regulations calling for their rehousing in decent, safe, and sanitary dwellings.[30]

Consequences of relocation

The relocation procedures that have been developed from the nation-wide experience of the past few years also present some problems in relation to the culture and the needs of the West End residents. These problems are discussed below and are in addition to the four types of problems described earlier.

1. Relocation procedures were developed by middle-class professionals and thus assume the self-sufficiency of the nuclear family household. In the West End, however, many of these physically individual households are tied to those of other families by strong bonds, either of kinship or peer-group membership. If households are relocated individually, so they are not accessible to these other households with whom they live, nega-

tive social and emotional consequences may result. For many of the old people, accessibility means pedestrian accessibility, and thus they will suffer most from being separated from West End relatives and neighbors. Younger people can come together again by car or public transportation, but only if they are relocated in relatively accessible neighborhoods.[31]

2. Differences exist between relocation officials and West End residents in the evaluation of physical and social "standardness" of housing. Thus, what the former define as physically standard may be located in areas which the latter will consider socially undesirable. Since social criteria are more important to many West Enders than physical criteria, they may reject on this basis the units offered to them by relocation officials. Conversely, they may relocate themselves in dwelling units that are substandard by federal provisions, but not by the West Enders' priority of social over physical values.

3. As presently indicated, the scheduling of relocation is based on the requirements of the clearance program. If relocation takes longer than expected, this may force officials to interpret the federal relocation provisions as written and limit the apartment choices of the relocatees to the number required by law.[32] Given the differences in housing standards between officials and residents, some people may be forced to move into dwelling units and neighborhoods they do not want. Others may be hurried into panicky voluntary relocation with much the same results.

4. Since relocation procedures do not allow for the transfer of the social system, the shock of the relocation process itself is likely to affect negatively a number of people who have never lived anywhere except in the West End and whose social and emotional ties are entirely within the neighborhood.

Cultural and political obstacles to communication

A fifth problem involves communication difficulties between the redevelopment agency and the West End residents that threaten to make the prospective relocation even more painful. This problem deserves more elaborate discussion than accorded others because these difficulties are an expression of more fundamental problems.

During the eight years in which the Housing Authority and its successor, the Redevelopment Authority, endeavored to implement the redevelopment plan, considerable hostility developed among the residents toward the city agencies. This hostility was based primarily on opposition to the destruction of the West End. However, there were other causes. Working-class people are frequently hostile toward governmental authority in general and feel that the politicians as well as the city officials seek to deprive them of things they value or are trying to cheat them out of their belongings.[33] This attitude was strengthened in the West End by the fact that in a city inhabited by people of Italian and Irish descent in about equal numbers, the latter retain control over its government and political life. Moreover, as a result of the transformation of the Boston City Council from a ward to an at-large system in 1950, the West End was for all practical purposes disfranchised.[34]

The Housing and Redevelopment Authorities acted as strict administrators of the law and failed to take residents' attitudes into consideration. For example, their communication with the West End followed local and federal regulations, and they were extremely careful not to give out any information about which they were not absolutely certain or which was not required by the rule books. The informational vacuum thus created in the West End was filled with rumors. Moreover, the officials assumed that West End residents were as expert as they in understanding the complex administrative processes of redevelopment and could thus interpret properly the cryptic news releases which the agency issued periodically.[35]

However, since West Enders have little contact with bureaucratic procedure, they tend to interpret such procedure in personal terms. Because of their generally suspicious view of city governmental activities, they reinterpreted the agency's communications accordingly. For example, the long years of delay between the announcement of redevelopment and the final taking were generally assumed to be due to the city's desire to confuse the residents, scare them out of the West End, and thus reduce the acquisition costs of property and the relocation problem.

The redevelopment officials did not seem to consider the effects of their announcements, especially since vocal opposition to the redevelopment was minimal. This was interpreted by the agency as a general acquiescence on the part of West Enders toward the fate of their neighborhood.

Actually, since 1950, the residents had read so many news stories announcing an early start of the redevelopment that many were convinced it would never take place. Although a small group of determined West Enders had begun to fight the city's plan in 1954, they received little support from residents for this reason.[36]

The pattern of poor communication on the part of the redevelopment officials and the negative interpretation of any communication by the residents continued after the Authority had set up a project area relocation office and had announced the taking of the properties by eminent domain. The agency continued to be vague on those topics of most importance to the residents; for example, on the relocation and clearance schedules. This was particularly frustrating to those people who, finally relieved of eight years of uncertainty, now wanted to plan ahead.[37] Other West Enders took admonitions to move as soon as possible to mean that the relocation office was set up to scare people out of the area. Suggestions about the availability of vacant housing in areas of lower socioeconomic status than the West End were reinterpreted to mean that the city wanted to push West Enders into the worst slums of Boston. The redevelopment agency's official notification to landlords that their structures had been purchased for one dollar under eminent-domain procedures, plus its failure to include this token payment or to explain why it was not included, convinced many people that the city was not keeping its promises to treat them fairly and was going to cheat them out of their payments. Likewise, the way in which the redevelopment agency took the land caused considerable hurt among the older immigrants. They could not understand how the buildings they had worked so hard to own could suddenly be taken away from them, with no assurance as to when they would be paid or how much. Moreover, at the same time they were told to pay rents for their own apartments in these buildings or face eviction. Thus, many of the landlords who earned their livelihood from the rents they collected were at the same time deprived of both a source of income and the funds with which to pay the rent demanded from them.[38]

Although the residents and redevelopment officials attributed the communication failure to each other's negative motivations, the difficulties were based on cultural factors. The redevelopment agency was concerned mainly with following local and federal regulations governing relocation. These regulations said nothing about understanding the consequences to the residents of its official acts. Thus, the agency had no real opportunity for learning how the West End received its letters and announcements or interpreted its actions. However, it is questionable whether such an opportunity would have been exploited. The officials concerned were not policy-makers; they were hired to carry out their prescribed duties. They felt sorry for some of the West Enders, especially those with serious problems; and they tried to help them in various ways not required by their job. But, since they believed that relocation would improve the living conditions for most of the residents and that the redevelopment was for the good of the city, they could not really understand why the West Enders were hostile and often unwilling to co-operate.

These beliefs about the virtues of relocation and the unilateral desirability of redevelopment are written into existing local and federal renewal policy. *As a result, when redevelopment officials take action affecting project area residents, they are not required to take into account the at-*

titudes and the situation of the residents. There is no opportunity for the correction of such actions by feedback from the residents. As a result, the relocation procedures developed so far in most American cities include no techniques that would ease the burden of the people who are to be moved.

Relocation, the residents' subsidy of redevelopment

American redevelopment planning so far has proceeded on the assumption that relocation is secondary to redevelopment. Thus, great pains are taken with planning for clearance and the reuse of the site, but plans for the present occupants of the site are treated as by-products of the redevelopment proposal. For example, the local and federal redevelopment agencies had detailed maps of the West End's street and utility system, but they did not seem to know the simple fact that a number of owners living in the area depended on the rents they collected for their income.

Perhaps the clearest indication of the relatively low priority of relocation in the redevelopment process is the fact that the funds allocated to relocation are less than 5 per cent of the total cost of taking and clearing the land, and this represents only about 1 per cent of the cost of clearance and redevelopment. The real cost of relocation is very much higher, but is paid in various ways by the people being moved out. Under present conditions, the redevelopment of American cities is economically possible only because of the hidden subsidies provided by the residents of the areas to be cleared.

IV. Some recommendations

This critique is not directed either at renewal or at relocation per se, but at the present policies which use public funds to subsidize—if only indirectly—the erection of high-rent housing and penalize the low-income population, without clear proof that these policies are in the public interest.

Moreover, the specific criticisms made of Boston procedures are not intended as "blame" of any individuals within the local or federal agencies. It is important to emphasize that what has happened cannot be attributed to evil motives. No laws have been broken, and many officials have acted with only the best intentions toward the West Enders![39] However, good intentions can lead to harmful consequences if the basic procedures are at fault. Thus, the responsibility for what has happened rests to a considerable extent on the system of procedures that has emerged from years of legislative and administrative decision-making since the passage of the 1949 Housing Act and on the unintended or unrecognized consequences of these procedures when they are actually implemented. However, this system is tied to the economic and political structure, which must therefore also be implicated. For example, since redevelopment agencies must provide sufficient incentives to attract a redeveloper, some of their policies, such as site selection, must be shaped by the demands, or the anticipated demands, of these redevelopers.

Proposals for redevelopment

Urban renewal and the rehousing of slum dwellers are necessary and desirable objectives. However, the means of achieving them ought to be chosen in relation to these objectives, rather than to extraneous ones.[40] Thus, redevelopment should be pursued primarily for the benefit of the community as a whole and of the people who live in the slum area, and not for that of the redeveloper or his eventual tenants.[41] The recommendations that follow are based largely on this principle. Although they stem from the Boston observations, many of them are undoubtedly applicable to renewal and relocation procedures in other large cities.

1. Renewal projects should be located first in those areas which are slums as defined above, that is, in which it can be proved that the housing and facilities present social and physical dangers to the residents and to the larger community. The availability of a redeveloper ought to be a consideration, but one of lesser priority.

2. Before areas for renewal are finally determined, independent studies should be made which provide proof of the area's character, but take into account the values and living patterns of the residents.[42] These studies should be made by persons who have no connection with either the project area or the redevelopment agency.

3. Renewal proposals which call for the clearance of an entire neighborhood should be studied closely to determine whether the existing social system satisfies more positive than negative functions for the residents. If this is the case, planners must decide whether the destruction of this social system is justified by the benefits to be derived from clearance.

4. Projects which require large-scale relocation[43] should be studied in a similar manner. Such projects should not be initiated until the community has built sufficient relocation units to assure the proper[44] rehousing of the residents. If private enterprise is unable to provide them, city, state, and federal funds will have to be used. Moreover, if relocation housing is built prior to the renewal project, and in sufficient quantity, and if it is attractive, it is likely to draw enough people out of the

slum areas to reduce the market value of slum structures. Consequently, some of the costs of providing such relocation housing will be returned by reduced acquisition costs at the time of renewal.

5. If a community is unwilling or unable to provide the required relocation housing, it should not be permitted to engage in renewal operations.

6. City planners ought to recognize the functions performed in the city by the low-income population. They should make sure that sufficient housing is available for them and in the proper locations (including some near the central business district) for their needs and those of the city. The federal government should encourage the renewal of such housing by increasing its subsidies when the renewal plan calls for the rehabilitation or construction of low-income dwellings.

7. Greater emphasis should be placed on the rehabilitation of low-rent housing, and less on its clearance. Such rehabilitation should be based on standards that provide decent, safe, and sanitary—but economically priced—dwelling units. In order to make this possible, existing standards should be restudied, to distinguish requirements which bring housing up to a standard but low-rent level from those which are "fringe benefits" that price rehabilitated units out of the low-rent market.[45]

8. In the future, when renewal becomes an accepted urban governmental activity, experiments should be made with:

(a) Flexible subsidies, so that federal contributions are increased if the reuse is low- or middle-income housing; and reduced if it is luxury housing.

(b) Requirements that the redeveloper construct or finance some relocation housing, especially if he proposes to redevelop the site with housing out of the price range of the present site residents.

Proposals for relocation

If the purpose of urban renewal is to improve the living conditions of the present slum dwellers, relocation becomes one of the most important phases, if not the most important, of the renewal process. This principle suggests a number of proposals for procedural change:

1. The relocation plan should take priority over the renewal phases of the total plan, and no renewal plan should be approved by federal or local agencies until a proper relocation plan has been developed.

2. This relocation plan should be based on a thorough knowledge of the project area residents, so that the plan fits their demands and needs and so that officials have some understanding of the consequences of their actions before they put the plan into effect. The federal agency ought to

re-evaluate its relation to the local agencies, raising its requirements for approval of the local relocation plan and relaxing its requirements for such phases as rent collection. The latter would make it possible for the local agency to be more sensitive to certain needs of the project area residents.

3. Any renewal plan which requires the clearance of an area and large-scale relocation should contain provisions for the rehabilitation of site structures if changes in market conditions suddenly reduce the amount of land required by the redeveloper.[46]

4. Local and federal agencies should provide interest-free or low-interest loans to relocatees who wish to buy new homes.

5. These agencies should provide similar loans to project area landlords whose present buildings provide decent, safe, and sanitary housing, to allow them to purchase new buildings in other areas or to rehabilitate such buildings and to make them available to project area residents.

6. Landlords with units eligible for relocation housing anywhere in the community should be encouraged to rent to relocatees through such incentives as rehabilitation loans, subsidies for redecorating, and the like.

7. When project area rents have been low, so that residents' housing costs are raised sharply as a result of relocation, the federal and local agencies should set up a rent moratorium to allow relocatees to save some money for future rentals. The length of this moratorium should be based on the gap between project area and relocation area rentals.

8. Liquidation funds in lieu of moving allowances should be provided to small-store owners and other businessmen who will not be able to reopen their firms elsewhere. Other federal and local programs should be made available to provide occupational retraining and other vocational aids to those who want them.

9. Communication between the redevelopment agency and the residents should be set up so that:

(*a*) The amount of information given to site residents is maximized, and the development of rumors due to information vacuums is prevented.

(*b*) Officials are trained to understand the inevitably deprivatory nature of relocation for the residents, so that they have more insight into what relocation means to the residents and can develop a more tolerant attitude toward their reactions of shock and protest.

10. The relocation staff should be strengthened by the addition of:

(*a*) Social workers who can provide aid to residents faced with additional problems resulting from relocation and can make referrals to other city agencies that deal with such problems.[47]

(*b*) Real-estate technicians who can develop a thorough inventory of the city's housing supply and can also weed out unscrupulous landlords who are likely to exploit the relocatees.

11. In relocation projects that involve the destruction of a positive social system, experiments should be conducted to:

(*a*) Find ways of relocating together extended families living together in separate but adjacent households, provided they want to be moved en masse.

(*b*) Make it possible for important project area institutions and organizations to re-establish themselves in those neighborhoods which have received the majority of relocatees or in central locations where they are accessible to scattered relocatees.

(*c*) Develop group relocation methods to allow members of an ethnic group who want to stay together to move into an area as a group. This is especially important if there are neighborhoods with available relocation housing in which there are presently no members of that ethnic group.

12. Previous relocation projects suggest that most people relocate themselves, and only a small proportion are relocated by the agency. In the future, procedures should be revised on this basis. Then, the major functions of the relocation agency should be:

(*a*) To make sure that the supply of relocation housing is sufficient to give relocatees a maximal choice of decent, safe, and sanitary dwelling units at rents they are willing to pay and in neighborhoods in which they want to live.

(*b*) To provide information and other aids that will enable relocatees to evaluate these dwelling units and to make the best housing choice in relation to their needs and wants.

(*c*) To offer relocation service to those who want to be moved by the agency.

Implications for the future of urban renewal

Many of these proposals will increase the cost of relocation, which will in turn raise the cost of renewal. This is equitable, since project area residents should not be required to subsidize the process, as they do presently. In time, the higher cost of renewal will become the accepted rate. Moreover, since redevelopers often stand to make considerable profit from their renewal operation, they should eventually be asked to bear part of this increased cost.[48]

Current renewal and relocation procedures have been discussed mainly in terms of the inequities being borne by the project area residents. However, these procedures can be shown to have undesirable consequences for renewal itself. For example, projects based on inadequate relocation plans simply push site residents into the next adjacent low-income area and create overcrowding that leads to the formation of new slums. Thus, the city is saddled with additional problems and new costs, which eventually overwhelm the apparent short-run benefits of the renewal project. Moreover, poorly handled relocation frequently results in political repercussions which can endanger the community's long-range renewal plans. Consequently, the critique and proposals suggested here have implications not only for the site residents but for the future of urban renewal itself.[49]

NOTES

1. Among the principal publications are: Marc Fried and Peggy Gleicher, "Some Sources of Residential Satisfaction in an Urban 'Slum,' " *Journal of the American Institute of Planners,* XXVII (November 1961), 305–315; Marc Fried, "Grieving for a Lost Home," in Leonard J. Duhl, ed., *The Urban Condition* (New York: Basic Books, 1963), pp. 151–171; Chester Hartman, "The Limitations of Public Housing: Relocation Choices in a Working Class Community," *Journal of the American Institute of Planners,* XXIX (November 1963), 283–296; Chester Hartman, "The Housing of Relocated Families," *ibid.,* XXX (November 1964), 266–286; and Marc Fried, "Transitional Functions of Working Class Communities: Implications for Forced Relocation," in Mildred B. Kantor, ed., *Mobility and Mental Health* (Springfield, Ill.: Charles C Thomas, 1965), pp. 123–165.
2. Hartman, "The Housing of Relocated Families."
3. The terms *West End* and *project area* will hereafter be used interchangeably.
4. The eastern boundary of the project area fronts on Massachusetts General Hospital and the back of Beacon Hill; the northern, on the Charles River; the southern, on a number of blocks much like the West End, although in poorer condition, and on Scollay Square. This is one of Boston's major skid-row areas, soon to be redeveloped as a government center. The western boundary faces a major railroad station and a wholesaling-industrial area which separates the West End from the North End.
5. "Buildings now cover 72 per cent of the net land area in the West End, excluding streets and vacant lots. Of the total of 48 blocks, 11 have building coverages of over 90 per cent." Boston Housing Authority, "West End Project Report" (Boston: 1953), p. 5. This refers to the 72-acre study area. An unpublished Housing Authority report indicated that according to the 1950 census, the ground density was in excess of 152 dwelling units per net residential acre. "Supporting Documentation to the Redevelopment Plan" (Boston: September 1955), p. 7.
6. This paper is based largely on conditions at the time of the taking; the figures

are from a survey made by the Boston Redevelopment Authority just prior to the taking.

7. For an analysis of the kinds of people who live in the slums and the ways in which they deviate from the rest of the urban population, see John Seeley, "The Slum: Its Nature, Use, and Users," *Journal of the American Institute of Planners*, XXV, No. 1 (February 1959), 7–14.

8. Consequently, the planning reports which are written to justify redevelopment dwell as much on social as on physical criteria and are filled with data intended to show the prevalence of antisocial or pathological behavior in the area. The implication is that the area itself causes such behavior and should therefore be redeveloped (see, for example, Boston Housing Authority, *op. cit.*).

9. Actually, a considerable number of West End families had moved into the area from the North End during the 1930's and 1940's, since West End apartments were more spacious and modern and had their own, rather than shared, bathrooms.

10. The latter point is developed further in the author's unpublished paper, "Some Notes on the Definition of Mental Health: An Attempt from the Perspective of the Community Planner," 1957.

11. Planners like to describe such housing as "obsolescent." However, it is obsolescent only in relation to their own middle-class standards and, more important, their incomes. The term is never used when alley dwellings of technologically similar vintage are rehabilitated for high rentals, as in Georgetown, Washington, D.C.

12. A number of West End mothers want to isolate their children from the culture of "the street." Since peers are a strong influence on older children and teen-agers, the conflict between the norms of home and street within the child may be resolved in favor of the latter. Only systematic research can determine whether or not such neighborhood characteristics as high density and the mixture of "respectable" and "rough" working-class residents are responsible for any subsequent delinquency. I suspect that relations within the family, and the external socioeconomic and cultural factors creating them, are probably more important.

13. Because of the high land coverage, the first- and second-floor apartments of many buildings received less air and sunlight than desirable, although there is no evidence that this had deleterious effects. This may be owing in part to the fact that many West Enders spent much time outside, since the street is a major location for neighborhood sociability. I would not defend such apartments as desirable, but I can understand the preferences of low-income West End residents for these dwellings at rentals of $30 a month over those with more air and sunlight at $75.

14. The eight-year interim period was taken up by the usual technical and political problems that make up the "natural history" of a redevelopment project. However, owing to poor newspaper coverage and the West Enders' inability as well as unwillingness to understand the complex administrative process, many of the residents were convinced until the last minute that what they called "the steal" of their neighborhood would never go through. The less sanguine suffered greatly from the uncertainty as to whether the project would or would not go through, as did the landlords and the businessmen, who lost tenants and customers during this period. This is one of the hidden costs of redevelopment paid by the West Enders.

15. The stereotype of the "greedy" slum landlords who fail to maintain their buildings applied mainly to the absentee owners. The resident owners with

one or two buildings generally kept up their buildings until the land taking. Most of the vacancies in the area were in absentee-owned buildings; the resident owners had been able to hold their tenants, partly because many of them were friends or relatives.

16. Visitors were often surprised that West End apartments differed little from those in lower-middle-class neighborhoods and could not easily reconcile this with the stereotype of slum housing.

17. Because most of the residents are of Italian or Polish descent, some aspects of life in the West End resembled that of the European villages from which they or their parents came. The extended family plays an important role, since relatives often reside in adjacent apartments. People here live within an intricate social network and a multitude of informal groups which are crucial to the functioning of people in a culture in which the individualism of the middle-class professional is unknown. Despite published statistics, antisocial behavior among permanent West End residents was low, in part because of the strict (though decreasing) parental control over children and of the persuasive sanctions against any kind of nonconformity.

18. Some of the people who left the West End after 1950 were young people who participated in the suburban boom. They were replaced by people of lower incomes and more transitional living habits, single transients, gypsies, and families with obvious pathological characteristics. Such people found a home in the West End because landlords with vacant units could no longer afford to reject what they defined as "undesirable tenants." The arrival of the new kinds of tenants also helped to convince the community at large that the West End was a slum. Despite this self-fulfilled prophecy, the majority of the West Enders who lived there before 1950 remained until the time of the land taking. Many had lived in the area for from twenty to forty years.

19. The Redevelopment Authority claimed that delinquency statistics in the area were among the highest in the city, but these figures were questioned by local sources, including the police. The disparity is due in part to the fact that youngsters from other neighborhoods perpetrated their antisocial acts in the West End, just as some West End teen-agers, true to the code of protecting the in-group and hurting only the stranger, were delinquents in other neighborhoods.

20. For the past few years, politicians and other community leaders have used West End redevelopment as a major symbol of Boston's emergence from its economic doldrums. This may be a false hope, since the apartments to be built in the area will probably draw tenants primarily from other parts of Boston and there is little indication that the project represents any significant amount of new growth.

21. Many of these people were being subsidized by low rentals. However, the proportion of their total income paid for rent was not lower than that of the average high-income Bostonian.

22. Evidence of both types of discrimination came to my attention even before relocation had formally begun.

23. Thus the businessmen who are economically strong enough to relocate will receive funds for the move, but those who are most in need of aid will receive nothing. Redevelopment officials justify this by the argument that the small stores are already marginal and are being driven out by economic processes, not by redevelopment policies. However, these stores are less marginal in their present neighborhoods; and in addition, they serve a variety of social and communication functions. There are also a number of small businessmen and semiprofessionals in the area who were able to escape from factory jobs by

being able to rely on low residential rentals. These will also be forced out of business when their rent bills go up.

24. Several deaths among older residents at the time that West Enders realized the area would be cleared were attributed by informants to the shock of this recognition.

25. The other beneficiaries will be the absentee landlords, who were losing money on partly or totally vacant buildings and will now be able to sell their buildings to the city. Since they have the funds for legal fees and the political know-how to choose the right lawyers, they can go to court and may be able to get higher prices for their buildings than can the small resident owners.

26. This is owing in part to the animus against authority and middle-class bureaucracy in Italian-American working-class culture. West Enders are particularly opposed to the review of income and to the raising of rents with increases in earnings.

27. The West Enders I talked with were willing to accept units in the small projects in or near middle-class districts, but were violently opposed to the large institutional projects built in recent years. Since the former already have long waiting lists, the Housing Authority plan was to move West End people into vacancies in the latter.

28. The Authority based its estimate on newspaper rentals, without knowing whether or not these were eligible to be used for relocation. Federal provisions require that relocatees must be moved into decent, safe, and sanitary (that is, standard) housing.

29. The more West Enders go into public housing, the more competition there will be among those leaving public housing and the remaining West Enders for the limited supply of private low-rent or low-cost housing.

30. Since the relocation will take several years, the trickling-down process may throw some low-cost units on the regional housing market and thus reduce somewhat the discrepancy between supply and demand for relocation housing.

31. One of the reasons families like to live in the West End is its central location with respect to other Italian neighborhoods in the Boston area, so that family members scattered over them can be visited easily.

32. At the start of relocation, officials indicated that they would be more liberal than the law requires in allowing West Enders to reject apartments offered to them.

33. Thus, many West Enders were convinced that the redevelopment was just another instance of government action to benefit those with greater economic resources and political influence. Since a member of the redeveloper firm had managed the mayor's election in 1950 and had subsequently served in his office, they believed that the redevelopment project was set up to pay off a political debt and also to fatten the mayor's purse before he left office. Such beliefs can arise in Boston more easily than in other cities, since the city government has been unusually inefficient and in recent years more attentive to the demands of the business interests than to those of the rest of the population.

34. Although one of the city's nine councilors came from the West End, and another from the North End, there were not enough voters in the West End to make it politically possible for these representatives to support the West End at the expense of other districts.

35. The Boston press was of little aid to the West Enders, since it was very much in favor of the redevelopment and also seemed to assume that West Enders do not read the papers.

36. There were other reasons. First, many working-class people rarely think in

community-wide terms, since they believe that the community is exploiting them. Second, they are not inclined to, or skilled in, the middle-class pattern of community participation; and they expect their political representatives to take care of this function. Finally, the protest organization was led by a Beacon Hill resident and a small group of West Enders of middle-class background, who were not "natural leaders" by the standards of most of the residents of Italian and Polish descent.

37. However, many residents were not planning ahead. Since they have traditionally suffered from economic uncertainty, they have adjusted to this by a flexible and fatalistic day-to-day philosophy of living. The kind of planning familiar to middle-class households would have raised too many false hopes and left them psychologically unprepared to accept sudden job losses and the like.

38. Kindly relocation officials attempted to soften the hurt by allowing owners to postpone their rent payments until they had been reimbursed for their buildings.

39. Needless to say, more farsighted and analytically oriented officials might have ameliorated the process to some extent. Moreover, if there had been some criticism of the program on the part of planners (commissioners as well as professionals), some changes might now be under way. However, some planners seem to feel that relocation is not their responsibility, even though it is a direct consequence of their plans.

40. For example, objectives such as attracting middle- and upper-income citizens back from the suburbs, contributing potential shoppers to a declining central retail area, creating symbols of "community revival," or providing more statusful surroundings (and parking lots) for powerful community institutions.

41. This statement is based on a comment made by Ruth Glass, the British planner, after her observations of American renewal. She described it as primarily for the benefit of the redeveloper and his tenants, whereas British renewal tries to aid mainly the present residents of the slum area.

42. Studies made by redevelopment agencies rarely concern themselves with the characteristics and needs of the project area residents or the ways in which they live. Instead, they try to prove, on the one hand, how undesirable the area is in order to persuade the federal and local agencies to provide funds for renewal and, on the other, how desirable the area is for potential redevelopers. Thus, they judge the area from the narrowly class-determined values of their clients and ignore the neighborhood's positive functions. The previously cited West End Project Report is a particularly blatant example. The fault here lies not so much with the local agency that writes such a report as with the federal procedures which permit no real alternative.

43. This is defined as any relocation proposal that requires the rehousing of more people than is possible, given the existing low-rent housing supply of the community.

44. "Proper" should be defined by the standards of the residents who are to live in the relocation units as well as by those of the housing and planning officials.

45. Current rehabilitation frequently takes low-rent apartments and transforms them into dwellings that fit the demands, tastes, and pocketbooks of middle- and upper-class people, but not those of their present residents.

46. For example, where the reuse is luxury housing, clearance of existing housing should be scheduled so that if the market for high-rent units suddenly shrinks, the remaining stock of existing housing can be rehabilitated for low- or middle-income tenants or redeveloped for them if necessary.

47. The relocation office in the West End has done some pioneering work in this

respect. The relocation staff should also call on resource persons in those areas to which site residents are moving and employ them to facilitate the adjustment of the relocatees in their new neighborhoods.

48. Thus, the redeveloper could be asked to include some proportion of relocation expenses in his costs and pass them on to his tenants as their share of the renewal charges. Alternatively, the city could bear relocation costs initially and require the redeveloper to repay part of them if his project shows more than an agreed-upon reasonable profit. In either case, the lower the rentals of the redevelopment housing, the lower should be the share of relocation costs to be paid by the redeveloper.

49. Many of the conclusions and recommendations described here were reached also by a thorough Philadelphia study, "Relocation in Philadelphia" (Philadelphia Housing Association, November 1958), which was published after this article had been written.

16

Social and Physical Planning for the Elimination of Urban Poverty

I

City planning has traditionally sought community betterment through so-called *physical* methods, such as the creation of efficient land-use and transportation schemes, the sorting out of diverse types of land use, and the renewal of technologically obsolescent areas and buildings to achieve functional, as well as aesthetically desirable, arrangements of structures and spaces. This paper deals with a new planning concept which places greater emphasis on economic and social methods of improving community life. In some places it is called human renewal; in others, community development; in yet others, social planning. Although none of the names is quite appropriate, the programs to which they refer are of crucial importance to the future of the city, for they seek to do away with—or at least to decimate—urban poverty and the deprivation that accompanies it. If these programs succeed, they are likely to have a lasting impact on city planning and on the other professions concerned with planning for community welfare.

The fight against poverty is not new, of course, and, in fact, the elimination of urban deprivation was one of the goals of the founders of modern city planning. The planning movement itself developed partly in reaction to the conditions under which the European immigrants who came to American cities in the mid-nineteenth century had to live. The reduction of their squalor was one of Frederick Law Olmsted's goals when he proposed the building of city parks so that the poor—as well as the rich—might have a substitute rural landscape in which to relax from urban life. It motivated the Boston civic leaders who first built playgrounds in the slums of that city and the founders of the settlement-

Reprinted from B. Rosenberg, I. Gerver, and W. Howton, eds., *Mass Society in Crisis: Social Problems and Social Pathology* (New York: The Macmillan Co. 1964), pp. 629–644. Copyright © The Macmillan Company, 1964. The paper was originally prepared for the 1962 conference of the American Institute of Planners.

house movement, notably Jane Addams, who argued strongly for city planning. It also sparked the efforts of those who built model tenements to improve the housing conditions of the poor. And Ebenezer Howard had this goal in mind when he proposed to depopulate the London slums through Garden Cities.

Most of these planning efforts were not aimed directly at the reduction of poverty and deprivation, but sought to use land planning, housing codes, and occasionally zoning to eliminate slums and reduce densities in the tightly packed tenement neighborhoods. The apotheosis of this approach—slum clearance—followed upon the arrival of the newest wave of poor immigrants: the southern Negroes, Puerto Ricans, and Mexicans who came to the city during World War II and in the postwar era. After a decade of noting the effects of the federal slum-clearance program, however, some observers became concerned because while this method was eliminating slums, it was not contributing significantly to the improvement of the slum dwellers' living conditions.

In many cases, the reduction in the already short supply of low-cost housing brought about by slum clearance, together with faulty or non-existent relocation planning, sent slum dwellers into adjacent slums or forced them to overcrowd declining areas elsewhere. But even where slum clearance was accompanied by adequate relocation programs, the housing of poor people in decent low-cost dwellings did not solve other —and equally pressing—problems, such as poverty, unemployment, illiteracy, alcoholism, and mental illness. Nor could rehousing alone do away with crime, delinquency, prostitution, and other deviant behavior. In short, it became clear that such physical changes as urban renewal, good housing, and modern project planning were simply not enough to improve the lives of the poverty-stricken.

As a result, planners and "housers" began to look for nonphysical planning approaches.[1] In this process, they made contact with other professions that are concerned with the low-income population; for example, social workers. Working in tandem with them and others, they have developed new programs, bearing the various names indicated above. Most often they have been referred to as social planning, a term that had been coined by social workers to describe the co-ordination of individual social-agency programs carried out by such central planning and budgeting agencies as the United Fund.[2]

Although the term has already received considerable attention in city-planning circles, I prefer to use another term. Insofar as the programs seek to aid low-income people to change their fortunes and their ways of living, they are attempts to guide them toward the social and economic mobility that more fortunate people have achieved on their own. For this reason, the programs might best be described as planning for *guided mobility*.

Such programs are now under way in many American cities. Some are designed as programs in juvenile-delinquency prevention, which have come into being under the aegis of the President's Committee on Juvenile Delinquency and work mainly with young people.[3] Others are oriented toward low-income people of all ages, and since planners have been most active in these, the rest of the article will deal primarily with such programs.[4] Although most of the programs are just getting started, some over-all similarities between them are apparent. Needless to say, any generalizations about them are preliminary, for the programs are likely to change as they progress from initial formulation to actual implementation.

The guided mobility plans and proposals which I have examined have four major programatic emphases:

1. To develop new methods of education for children from low-income and culturally deprived homes, so as to reduce functional illiteracy, school dropouts, and learning disabilities which prevent such children from competing in the modern job market in adulthood.

2. To reduce unemployment by new forms of job training among the young, by the retraining of adults, and by the creation of new jobs in the community.

3. To encourage self-help on an individual and group basis through community-organization methods that stimulate neighborhood participation.

4. To extend the amount and quality of social services to the low-income population. Among the latter are traditional case-work services, new experiments for giving professional help to the hard-to-reach, multi-problem family, and the provision of modern facilities and programs of public recreation, public health, and community-center activities.

The educational phase of guided mobility includes programs such as Higher Horizons, which attempt to draw bright children from the culturally restrictive context of low-income environments and to offer them the academic and cultural opportunities available to bright middle-class children. There are also programs to help average and backward youngsters, using remedial reading and other devices to guide them during the early school years, so that they will develop the skills and motivations to stay in school until high-school graduation. The occupational phase of the plans includes job programs which will employ young people in useful community projects and in quasi-apprentice programs in private industry, as well as various vocational-training and retraining programs for young and old alike. Meanwhile, added effort is scheduled to attract new industries and thus to bring new jobs to the community.

The extension of social services and the community-organization phase of the programs use decentralization as a means of reaching the high proportion of low-income people who usually abstain from community contact. The provision of social services to the hard-to-reach will be attempted by bringing programs to the neighborhood level, with neighborhood directors to supervise the process. In addition, the social agencies plan to co-ordinate their services, so that individual agencies working with the same individual or family know what the other is doing and duplication and contradictions can be avoided. More neighborhood facilities will also be established, including community schools, public-health clinics, and recreation centers, sometimes grouped in a "services center," so that people will be encouraged to come there when they need help.

The decentralizing of community-organization activities is intended to create a sense of neighborhood and an interest in neighborhood self-help. Community organizers will work in the neighborhood for this purpose and will try to involve "natural leaders" living in the area, who can act as a bridge between the professionals, the city, and the neighborhood population.

This is a very general description of the programs. In actuality, each community has a somewhat distinctive approach, or a different emphasis in the selection of programs, depending partly on the line-up of sponsoring agencies. But some city planners who have become interested in guided mobility programs are still preoccupied—and sometimes too much so—with traditional physical planning approaches, notably two: the realization of a neighborhood scheme—originally devised by Clarence Perry[5] and consisting of a small, clearly bounded residential area, built up at low density, with auto and pedestrian traffic carefully separated, considerable open space, and a combination elementary school and neighborhood meeting place in its center; and the provision both in such neighborhoods and in the larger community of a standard array of public facilities for recreation, health, education, culture, and other community services.

The concern with neighborhood is, of course, traditional in city planning, and even the new challenge of finding nonphysical ways of helping the low-income group has not diverted the planner from it. In some cities, guided mobility plans are thus almost appendages to physical planning programs, based on the traditional belief that the rebuilding of the city into a series of separate neighborhoods to encourage a small-townish middle-class form of family life is a proper solution even for poverty. Elsewhere, the program may be an appendage of urban-renewal activities, the main intent still being the upgrading of the physical neighborhoods. Thus, guided mobility is used partly to organize the neighborhood into undertaking—or helping the city with—this task. But in most cases, the neighborhod emphasis is based on a genuine concern that one of the causes of urban deprivation is to be found in the poor quality of neighborhood life.

The provision of public facilities is also a traditional planning emphasis, dating back to the days when the planner was an ally of the reformers who were fighting for the establishment of these facilities. Out of this has come the belief that public facilities are crucial agencies in people's lives, that up-to-date facilities and programs will encourage intensive use of them, and that this in turn will help significantly in achieving the aims of guided mobility planning.

Despite the intensity of the planner's belief in neighborhood and public facility use, there is no evidence that these two planning concepts are as important to low-income people as they are to planners. Consequently, it is fair to ask whether such concepts are as crucial to the elimination of urban poverty and deprivation as is signified by their appearance in some guided mobility plans. The answer to this question requires a brief discussion of the nature of contemporary urban poverty.

II

The low-income population may be divided into two major segments, which sociologists call the *working class* and the *lower class*.[6] The former consists of semiskilled and skilled blue-collar workers who hold steady jobs and are thus able to live under stable, if not affluent, conditions. Their way of life differs in many respects from that of the middle class; for example, in the greater role of relatives in sociability and mutual aid, in the lesser concern for self-improvement and education, and in their lack of interest in the good address, cultivation, and the kinds of status that are important to middle-class people. Although their ways are culturally different from the dominant middle-class norms, these are not pathological, for rates of crime, mental illness, and other social ills are not significantly higher than in the middle class. This population, therefore, has little need for guided mobility programs.

The lower class, on the other hand, consists of people who perform the unskilled labor and service functions in the society. Many of them lack stable jobs. They are often unemployed or forced to move from one temporary and underpaid job to another. Partly because of occupational instability, their lives are beset with social and emotional instability as well, and it is among them that one finds the majority of the emotional problems and social evils that are associated with the low-income population.[7]

In past generations, the American economy had considerable need for unskilled labor, and the European immigrants who performed it were able to achieve enough occupational stability to raise themselves, or their children, to working-class or even middle-class ways of living. Today, however, the need for unskilled labor is constantly decreasing and will soon be minimal. Consequently, the Negro, Puerto Rican, and Mexican newcomers who now constitute much of the American lower class find it very difficult to improve their condition.[8]

Guided mobility planning is essentially an attempt to help them solve their problems and to aid them in changing their lives. This makes it necessary to find out what causes their problems, what they themselves are striving for, and how they can be helped to achieve their objectives.

The nature of the problem is not difficult to identify. For economic reasons, and for reasons of race as well, the contemporary lower class is often barred from opportunities to hold well-paid, stable jobs, to receive a decent education, to live in good housing, or to get access to a whole series of choices and privileges that the white middle class takes for granted.

In addition, some lower-class people lack the motivations and skills that are needed not only to participate in contemporary society but, more important, to accept the opportunities if and when they become available. Moreover, the apathy, despair, and rejection which result from lack of access to crucial opportunities help bring about the aforementioned social and emotional difficulties.

There are a number of reasons for these reactions.[9] When men are long unemployed or underemployed, they feel useless and eventually become marginal members of the family. This has many consequences. They may desert their families and turn to self-destructive behavior in despair. If male instability is widespread, the woman becomes the dominant member of the family, and she may live with a number of men in the hope of finding a stable mate. The result is a family type which Walter Miller calls female-based; it is marked by free unions, illegitimate children, and what middle-class people consider to be broken homes.[10] Boys who grow up in such families may be deprived of needed male models and are likely to inherit some of the feelings of uselessness and despair they see in their fathers. In addition, the children must learn at an early age how to survive in a society in which crisis is an everyday occurrence and violence and struggle are ever-present. Thus, they may learn how to defend themselves against enemies and how to coexist with an alcoholic parent, but they do not learn how to read, how to concentrate on their studies, or how to relate to the teacher.[11] Those that do must defend their deviant behavior—and it is deviant in the lower class —against their peers, who, like peers in all other groups, demand that they conform to the dominant mode of adaptation. Also, many children grow up in households burdened with mental illness, and this scars their own emotional and social growth. Out of such conditions develops a lower-class culture with a set of behavior patterns which is useful for the struggle to survive in a lower-class milieu, but makes it almost impossible to participate in the larger society. And since the larger society rejects the lower-class individual for such behavior, he can often develop self-respect and dignity only by rejecting the larger society. He blames it for his difficulties—and with much justification—but in this process rejects many of its values as well, becoming apathetic, cynical, and hostile even toward those that seek to help him.

This overly brief analysis is at present mostly hypothetical, for we do not yet know exactly what it is that creates the lower-class way of life. We know that the nature of family relationships, the influence of peers, the kind of home training, the adaptive characteristics of lower-class culture, the high prevalence of mental illness, and the need to cope with one crisis after another are all important factors, but we do not yet know exactly which factors are most important, how they operate to create the way of life that they do, and how they are related to the lack of opportunities that bring them about.

Similarly, we know that lower-class people are striving to change their condition, but we do not know exactly for what they are striving. It is clear that they want stable jobs and higher incomes, and there is considerable evidence of an almost magical belief in education and high occupational aspirations for the children, especially among Negroes.[12] The lack of opportunity and the constant occurrence of crises frustrate most of these aspirations before they can be implemented, but they do exist, especially among the women. On the other hand, the failure of settlement houses, social workers, and other helping agencies to reach the majority of the lower-class population suggests that these people either cannot or do not want to accept the middle-class values which these professionals preach and which are built into the welfare activities they carry out. Such programs attract the small minority desirous of or ready for middle-class life, but they repel the rest. A number of social scientists suggest that what lower-class people are striving for is the stable, family-centered life of working-class culture, and at least one delinquency-prevention program is based on such an assumption.[13]

These observations about the nature of lower-class life have many implications for guided mobility planning. As a result of the sparsity of knowledge, much research, experiment, and evaluation of experience will be necessary in order to learn what kinds of program will be successful. It is clear that the most urgent need is to open up presently restricted opportunities, especially in the occupational sphere. The guided mobility programs which stress the creation of new jobs, the attack on racial discrimination, education, and occupational training as highest-priority items are thus on the right track. Even so, new ways of bringing industry and jobs to the community must be found, for conventional programs have not been sufficiently productive. Then, ways of channeling lower-class people into new jobs, and keeping them at work even if their initial performance is not so good as that of other people or of labor-saving machines, must be invented. Racial barriers will also have to come down more quickly, especially in those spheres of life and activity most important to lower-class people, so that they can begin to feel that they have some stake in society. This too is easier said than done.

Not only is desegregation difficult to implement, but the most successful programs so far have benefited middle-class nonwhites more than their less fortunate fellows. For lower-class people, access to jobs, unions, and decent low-cost housing is most important, as is the assurance of fair treatment from the police, the courts, city hall, storeowners, and helping agencies. The integration of high-priced suburban housing, expensive restaurants, or concert halls is for *them* of much less immediate significance.

Also, methods of encouraging motivations and skills and of maintaining aspirations in the face of frustration must be found. If the matriarchal lower-class family is at fault, ways of providing boys with paternal substitutes must be developed. Where the entire lower-class milieu is destructive, children may have to be removed from it, especially in their formative years. Treatments for mental illness, alcoholism, and narcotics addiction that will be effective among lower-class people have to be discovered and the causes of these ills isolated so that prevention programs may be set up. Schools must be created which can involve lower-class children. This means that they must teach the skills needed in a middle-class society, yet without the middle-class symbols and other trappings that frighten or repel the lower-class student.[14] Finally, it is necessary to develop urban-renewal or other housing programs that will make livable dwellings available to the low-income population, within its price range, and located near enough to its places of employment so as not to require unreasonable amounts of travel time and expenditures.

These program requirements demand some radical changes in our ways of doing things. For example, if lower-class people are to find employment, there will need to be economic enterprises geared not solely to profit and to cost reduction but also to the social profits of integrating the unemployed. In short, eventually we shall have to give up the pretense that nineteenth-century free-enterprise ideology can cope with twentieth-century realities and learn to replan some economic institutions to help the low-income population, just as we are now redesigning public education to teach this population's children. Likewise, if lower-class people are to become part of the larger society, there must be changes in the way the police, the courts, and political structures treat them. To cite just one instance, lower-class people must be represented more adequately in local party politics, and their needs and demands must receive more adequate hearing at city hall than has heretofore been the case. Similarly, the professions that now seek to help lower-class people will have to be altered so as to be more responsive to how lower-class people define their needs, and this may mean the replacement of some professionals by skilled nonprofessionals who are more capable of achieving rapport with lower-class clients. Also, urban-renewal policy must concern itself less with "blight" removal, or with the use of new construction to solve the city's tax problems, and more with improvement of the housing conditions of the slum dwellers. Changes such as these, which require redistribution of power, income, privileges, and the alteration of established social roles, are immensely difficult to bring about. Even so, they are necessary if urban poverty and deprivation are to be eliminated.[15]

III

Proper guided mobility planning must be based on methods that will achieve the intended goal. If the hypotheses about the causes of urban deprivation are correct, the basic components of guided mobility planning must be able to affect the economy, the political and social structures that shore up poverty and racial—as well as class—discrimination, the focuses of lower-class culture that frustrate the response to opportunities, notably the family, the peer group, the milieu in which children grow up, and the helping agencies that now have difficulty in reaching lower-class people, especially the school. Any programs which lack these components and cannot bring about changes in the position of the lower-class population vis-à-vis the institutions named are unlikely to contribute significantly to the aim of guided mobility.

The list of basic components does not include the two that have been especially emphasized by planners: the belief in neighborhood and the importance of public facilities. This omission is not accidental, for I do not believe that these two concepts are of high priority. Indeed, it is possible that they may divert guided mobility programs from the direction they ought to take.

By focusing programs on neighborhoods as spatial units, planners are naturally drawn to what is most visible in them—the land uses, buildings, and major institutions—and their attention is diverted from what is hardest to see, the people—and social conditions—with problems. It should be clear from the foregoing analysis that the program must concentrate on the people and on the social and economic forces which foster their deprivation, rather than on neighborhood conditions which are themselves consequences of these forces.

Moreover, too much concern with neighborhoods may cause the programs to seek out the wrong people: the working-class segment of the low-income population, rather than the lower-class one. This may happen for two reasons. First, the planner often finds it difficult to distinguish between areas occupied by working-class people and those occupied by lower-class people, mainly because his concept of standard housing blinds him to differences between low-rent areas, usually occupied predominantly by the former, and slums, which house the latter. Also, working- and lower-class people sometimes live together in the same planning area, especially if they are nonwhite, and a neighborhood focus makes it difficult to reach one without the other. This is undesirable because, as noted earlier, the working-class population does not need guided mobility, whereas the lower-class population needs it so badly that all resources ought to be allocated to it.

Even so, these drawbacks would not be serious if neighborhood planning could achieve the aims of guided mobility. But this is not the case, mainly because people's lives are not significantly influenced by the physical neighborhood. The important aspects of life take place within the family, the peer group, and on the job, and the neighborhood does not seem to affect these greatly. Moreover, although middle- and working-class people do sometimes participate in neighborhood activities, this is not true of lower-class people.[16] Not only do they shy away from organizational partcipation generally, but because of their great transience they do not spend much time in any one area. More important, since life is a constant struggle for survival and an endless series of crises, lower-class people are often suspicious of their neighbors and even more so of the landlord, the storeowner, the police, and the local politician. They harbor similar feelings toward most other neighborhood institutions and local public facilities.

Thus, the lower-class population's involvement in the neighborhood is at best neutral and more often negative. Yet even if it were more positive, the components of neighborhood planning and the provision of the entire range of modern public facilities could contribute relatively little to solving the problems which concern lower-class people the most. To a poverty-stricken family, the separation of car and pedestrian traffic or the availability of park and playground within walking distance are not very crucial; their needs are much more basic.

This is not to reject the desirability of such planning concepts, but only to say that given the present conditon of lower-class life, they are of fairly low priority. The location and equipment of the school are much less important than the presence of the kind of teacher who can communicate with lower-class children, and a conventional public-health facility is much less vital than an agency that can really help a mother deserted by her husband, or a person who must cope with mentally ill family members.

The standard neighborhood-and-facilities planning package cannot even contribute significantly to the improvement of the lower-class milieu. The significant components of this milieu are other people, rather than environmental features, and until these other people are socially and economically secure enough to trust each other, the milieu is not likely to improve sufficiently to prevent the perpetuation of past deprivations on the young growing up within it.

In short, it seems clear that the kind of neighborhood scheme sought through traditional planning and zoning methods cannot be implemented among lower-class people until the basic components of guided mobility programs have been effectuated. A stable, peaceful neighborhood in which there is positive feeling between neighbors assumes that people have good housing, the kind of job that frees them from worrying about where the next meal or rent money will come from, the solution of basic problems so that the landlord, the policeman, or the bill collector is no longer threatening, and the relief from recurring crises so that they can begin to pay some attention to the world outside the household. Similarly, only when people feel themselves to be part of the larger society, and when they have learned the skills needed to survive in it, will they be able to take part in school or community-center activities or to develop the ability to communicate with the staff of a health clinic.

Neighborhood planning is necessary, of course, but a social and political type which supports the community, state, and federal programs for the elimination of poverty. Thus, the methods required to help the low-income population develop the skills and attitudes prerequisite to survival in a modern society must reach into the neighborhood and the street in order to recruit people who do not, for one reason or another, come by themselves into public facilities established for such programs. Also, local political activity must be stimulated so that low-income people can use the one power they have—that of numbers and votes—to make their wishes heard at city hall and in Washington. This differs considerably from the need for "citizen participation" often called for by planners and community-organization experts; that has usually been defined as citizen consideration of—and consent to—professionally developed programs, or civic activity which is decidedly nonpolitical. The kind of local citizen participation that is needed is quite political, however, and since its aim must be to change the political status quo, it is unlikely that community organizers, who are after all employees of the existing political institution or of establishment-dominated welfare agencies, will be able to encourage such activity even if they are personally willing to do so. Hopefully, enlightened civic leaders and politicians will eventually realize that the low-income population must be more adequately represented in the political process, but in all likelihood, they will resist any change in the existing political alignments until they have no other choice. Thus, the initiative for local political activity must come from the areas in which low-income people live. But whoever the initiating agencies may be, these are the types of neighborhood planning that are required to do something about urban poverty.

IV

The incompatibility of traditional city-planning aims and the basic components of guided mobility programing is not to be blamed on one or another set of planners, nor indeed is it a cause for blame at all. Rather, it stems from the history and nature of modern city planning and from the basic assumptions in its approach. The description of two of these assumptions will also shed some light on the relationship between social and physical planning and their roles in the improvement of cities.

The first of these assumptions is the belief in the ability of change in the physical environment to bring about social change. Planners have traditionally acted on the assumption that the ordering of land uses, and improvements in the setting and design of buildings, highways, and other physical features of the community, would result in far-reaching improvements in the lives of those affected. The validity of this assumption has been seriously questioned in recent years, and indeed, the rise of what has been called social planning is one expression of this questioning.

But the traditional city-planning approach can also be described in another way, as being *method-oriented*. By this I mean that it has developed a repertoire of methods and techniques which have become professionally accepted and which distinguish planning from other service-giving professions. As a result, the planner concerns himself largely with improvements in these methods. In this process, however, he loses sight of the goals which his methods are intended to achieve or the problems they are to solve. Thus, he does not ask whether the methods achieve these goals or whether they achieve *any* goals.

This concern with method is not limited to the planning profession; it can be found in all professions. The attempt to maintain and improve existing methods is useful if the goals are traditional ones or if the profession deals only with routine problems. But it does not work as well when new goals are sought and when new problems arise. As I have already noted, improvements in neighborhood planning cannot contribute significantly to the new problems of the city or to the new goal of eliminating urban poverty.

What is needed instead is a *goal-oriented* or problem-oriented approach which begins, not with methods, but with the problems to be solved or the goals to be achieved. Once these are defined and agreed upon, the methods needed to achieve them can be determined through the use of professional insight, research, and experiment until the right methods—those which will solve the problem or realize the goal—are found. This approach was used in the foregoing pages, in which I questioned the usefulness of traditional planning methods and proposed instead programs to cope with the problems of the lower-class population—and their causes—as well as programs which would lead toward the goals this population was seeking for itself.

This approach is more difficult to implement than a method-oriented one, because it does not respect accepted methods—unless they work—and because it rejects the claims of professional traditions or professional expertise that are not supported by empirical evidence. It may require new methods and new approaches and thus can wreak havoc with the established way of doing things. However much the goal-oriented approach may upset the profession in the short run, in the long run it improves its efficiency and thus its expertise and status, because its methods are likely to be much more successful, thus reducing the risk of professional failure. In an effort as pioneering and difficult as guided mobility planning, a problem- and goal-oriented approach is therefore absolutely essential.

The conception of method-oriented and goal-oriented planning can also aid our understanding of the relationship between physical and social planning. In the professional discussions of this relationship, the subject has frequently been posed as social planning versus physical planning. Although it is not difficult to understand why the subject has been framed in this competitive way, the resulting dichotomy between social and physical planning is neither meaningful nor desirable. There are several reasons for rejecting this dichotomy.

First, social planning is said to deal with the human elements in the planning process. When planners talk of the human side of renewal or of the human factors in planning, they are suggesting by implication that physical planning is inhuman, that in its concern with land use, site design, the redevelopment of cleared land, and the city tax base it has no concern for the needs of human beings. I would not blame physical planners for objecting to this implication and am surprised that they have not done so.

But even if this implication is inaccurate, the dichotomy has led to another, even more unfortunate implication, which has some truth to it. Every planning activity, like any other form of social change, creates net benefits for some people and net costs for others. These may be nonmaterial as well as material. Whether intentionally or not, physical planning has tended to provide greater benefits to those who already have considerable economic resources or political power, be they redevelopers or tenants who profit from a luxury housing scheme, central business district retailers who gain, or expect to gain, from the ever-increasing number of plans to "revive downtown," or the large taxpayers who are helped most when planning's main aim is to increase municipal revenues. The interest in social planning is a direct result of this distribution of benefits, for it seeks to help the people who are forced to pay net costs in the physical planning process. Too often, these are poor people; for example, residents of a renewal or highway project who suffer when adequate relocation housing is lacking. Needless to say, this political bifurcation, in which physical planning benefits the well-to-do and social planning the less fortunate ones, is not a desirable state of affairs either for the community or for planning.

Finally, in actual everyday usage, the dichotomy refers to skills possessed by different types of planners. Physical planning is that set of methods which uses the traditional skills of the city planner and zoning official; social planning, that set favored by sociologically trained planners, social workers, and other professionals concerned with welfare aims. Yet if the planning activities of each are examined more closely, it becomes evident that the terms *social* and *physical* are inaccurate labels. Zoning is considered a physical planning method, but an ordinance which determines who is to live with whom and who is to work next to whom is as much social—as well as economic and political—as it is physical. So is a transportation scheme which decides who will find it easy to get in and out of the city and who will find it difficult. Conversely, social planners who urge the construction of more low-rent housing, or argue for scattered units rather than projects, are proposing physical schemes even while they are ostensibly doing social planning. Since all planning activities affect people, they are inevitably social, and the dichotomy between physical and social methods turns out to be meaningless. Moreover, in actual planning practice, no problem can be solved by any one method or any one skill. In most instances a whole variety of techniques are needed to achieve the goal.

The social-physical dichotomy is a logical consequence of viewing planning as method-oriented, because when methods are most important, there is apt to be competition between people who are skilled in the different methods. All successful professions want to apply the methods they know best, for this permits them to maintain their power and social position most easily.

If planning is conceived as goal-oriented, however, goals become most important, and methods are subordinated to the goal. In such a planning process, in which a large number of different methods are used in an integrated fashion, any single method loses its magical aura. Moreover, no goal can be defined so narrowly that it is only physical or only social. In a goal-oriented approach, then, there can be no social or physical planning. There is only *planning:* an approach which agrees upon the best goals and then finds the best methods to achieve them.

But it is not only the methods which must be reconsidered. Even the goals which are built into these methods are turning out to be less important today. The neighborhood concept has received little support from the clients of planning; the same is true of the planner's insistence on a reduction in the journey to work, which has not been accepted by the journeying populace. Also, in an age of automation and increasing unemployment, the need for economic growth, even if it is disorderly, is becoming more vital than the ordering of growth and the planner's desire for stability. It is, of course, still important to have efficient transportation schemes and to locate noxious industry away from residences; but there is less noxious industry than ever before, and for those who are affluent, the inefficiency of the automobile seems to matter little, especially if it is politically feasible to subsidize the costs of going to work by car. And even the concern with land use per se is becoming less significant. In a technology of bulldozers and rapid transportation, the qualities of the natural environment and the location of land are less important—or rather, more easily dealt with by human intervention—and increasingly, land can be used for many alternatives. The question of what is the best use, given topography and location, is thus less important than who will benefit from one use as compared to another, and who will have to pay costs, and how is the public interest affected.

V

One of the most important tasks in the improvement of cities is the elimination of urban poverty and of the deprivations of lower-class life. Poverty is fundamentally responsible for the slums we have been unable to eradicate by attacking the buildings and for the deprivations which ultimately bring about the familiar list of social evils. Moreover, poverty and deprivation are what makes cities so ugly and depressing, and they hasten the flight of more fortunate people into the suburbs. This in turn contributes to economic decline, the difficulties of financing municipal services, political conflict, corruption, and many of the other problems of the contemporary city.

I would not want to argue that all the city's problems can be laid at the doorstep of poverty. There are technological changes that affect its economic health and result in the obsolescence of industrial areas and street patterns. There are political rigidities that inhibit its relations with its hinterland. And the desire of most families to raise their children in low-density surroundings suggests that suburbia is not produced solely by the flight from the city and would exist without urban poverty. Even so, many of the suburbanites have come to hate the city because of the poverty they see there, and this in turn helps to create the hostility between city and suburb and the political conflict that frustrates schemes for metropolitan solutions.

If planners are genuinely concerned with the improvement of cities, the fight against poverty becomes a planning problem and one that needs to be given higher priority than it has heretofore received. A beginning is being made in the guided mobility programs that are now in operation, but a much greater effort is needed, on both the local and the federal scene, before these programs can achieve their aim. If such efforts are not made, all other schemes for improving the city will surely fail.

NOTES

1. Another impetus came from the fact that several cities scheduled urban-re-newal projects in their skid-row areas, and programs to "rehabilitate" its residents were developed as part of the relocation plan.
2. The term has also been applied to plans which attempt to outline social—that is, nonphysical—goals for the entire society, a procedure that would be more aptly called *societal* planning.
3. Of these, the leading program is New York's Mobilization for Youth. This is described in Mobilization for Youth, Inc., *A Proposal for the Prevention and Control of Delinquency by Expanding Opportunities* (New York: December 1961—mimeographed).
4. Examples of the many such plans are: Action for Boston Community Development, *A Proposal for a Community Development Program in Boston* (Boston: December 1961—mimeographed); Action Housing, Inc., . . . *Urban Extension in the Pittsburgh Area* (Pittsburgh: September 1961—mimeographed); City of Oakland, *Proposal for a Program of Community Development* (City of Oakland, Calif.: June and December 1961—mimeographed); Community Progress, Inc., *Opening Opportunities: New Haven's Comprehensive Program for Community Progress* (New Haven, Conn.: April 1962—mimeographed); and Department of City Planning, *A Plan for the Woodlawn Community: Social Planning Factors* (Chicago: January 1962—mimeographed). My comments about the plans below are based on a number of published and un-published documents which I have examined as well as on discussions about existing and proposed plans in which I have participated in several cities. My description of these plans is, in sociological terminology, an ideal type and does not fit exactly any one of the plans now in existence.
5. Clarence A. Perry, "The Neighborhood Unit," in *Regional Survey of New York and Its Environs* (New York: Committee on Regional Plan of New York and Its Environs, 1929), VII, 22–140.
6. Herbert J. Gans, *The Urban Villagers* (Glencoe, Ill.: Free Press, 1962), Chapter 11. See also S. M. Miller and Frank Riessman, "The Working Class Subculture: A New View," *Social Problems,* IX (1961), 86–97. The nature and extent of urban poverty are described in Michael Harrington, *The Other America* (New York: Macmillan, 1962), Chapters 2, 4, 5, 7, 8.
7. An excellent brief description of lower-class culture may be found in Walter B. Miller, "Lower Class Culture as a Generating Milieu of Gang Delinquency," *Journal of Social Issues,* XIV (1958), 5–19. The everyday life of the lower class is pictured in Oscar Lewis, *Five Families* (New York: Basic Books, 1959), and *The Children of Sanchez* (New York: Random House, 1961). Although Lewis' books deal with the lower class of Mexico City, his portrait applies, with some exceptions, to American cities as well.
8. For an analysis of the occupational history of the European immigrants and the more recent immigrants, see Oscar Handlin, *The Newcomers* (New York: Anchor Books, 1962).

9. For a more detailed analysis, see Gans, *op. cit.,* Chapter 12; Mobilization for Youth, Inc., *op. cit.;* and Walter B. Miller, *op. cit.*

10. Walter B. Miller, *op. cit.* This family type is particularly widespread in the Negro lower class, in which it originated during slavery.

11. The educational and other problems of the lower-class child are described in more detail in Patricia C. Sexton, *Education and Income* (New York: Viking, 1961), and Frank Riessman, *The Culturally Deprived Child* (New York: Harper, 1962).

12. For a recent example of this finding, see R. Kleiner, S. Parker, and H. Taylor, *Social Status and Aspirations in Philadelphia's Negro Population* (Philadelphia: Commission on Human Relations, June 1962—mimeographed).

13. Mobilization for Youth, Inc., *op. cit.*

14. See Sexton, *op. cit.,* and Riessman, *op. cit.*

15. For other programatic statements, see Peter Marris, "A Report on Urban Renewal in the United States," and Leonard J. Duhl, "Planning and Poverty," in Leonard J. Duhl, ed., *The Urban Condition* (New York: Basic Books, 1963), pp. 113–134 and 295–304, respectively. See also Harrington, *op. cit.*

16. Generally speaking, middle-class people participate in formal neighborhood organizations to a much greater extent than other classes, although their social life often takes place outside the neighborhood. Working-class people are less likely to participate in formal organizations, but most of their social activities take place close to home. For a discussion of working-class attitudes toward the neighborhood, see Marc Fried and Peggy Gleicher, "Some Sources of Residential Satisfaction in an Urban 'Slum,'" *Journal of the American Institute of Planners,* XXVII (November 1961), 305–315.

17

Redefining the Settlement's Function for the War on Poverty

I

Almost a hundred years have passed since the settlement house was founded in America as part of an earlier generation's attempt to do something to remove the deprivations of urban poverty. This paper examines the role of the settlement house today and the contribution it has made—and can make—to the attack on urban poverty. Although much of this analysis is based on observations of three settlement houses in a low-income neighborhood of Boston, gathered in connection with a broader study of the area, the conclusions may be relevant to many other settlements elsewhere.[1] Some of the comments also apply to the other helping professions—Erich Lindemann has called them caretakers—which seek to provide welfare, health, recreation, and other services to low-income people.[2]

II

The settlement house, like most other helping professions, is currently going through a fundamental and often agonizing reappraisal of its functions, an important part of which concerns its ability to reach the client. By "reaching" is meant involving the client in the settlement program and encouraging him to develop values and behavior patterns favored by the settlement staff. Doubts about the ability to reach the client have developed only recently, largely as the European immigrant population served by the settlement has been replaced by Negroes, Puerto Ricans, and white Appalachians. Difficulties in reaching clients have a long his-

Reprinted from *Social Work,* IX, No. 4 (October 1964), 3–12. Section IV of the paper has been cut to reduce repetition. The paper is a revised version of the keynote address to the 1963 Northeastern Regional Conference, National Federation of Settlements and Neighborhood Centers, Philadelphia, May 2, 1963.

tory, however, and are intimately related to the nature of the helping professions.

These professions emerged out of nineteenth-century reform movements, set up by middle- and upper-class "Yankee" Americans who not only wanted to do something about urban poverty but also hoped to make the then ethnic poor into middle-class Americans and allies against corrupt political machines and incipient socialist organizations. The reformers viewed the poor as weak and therefore unable to resist the taverns, brothels, and other negative influences of the slums in which they lived. They hoped that this proclivity to temptation could be corrected in the public schools and, after hours, in the settlement houses and other facilities where the children could participate in "character-building" programs and come into close contact with staff members who could help them change their ways.

This conception of the clients failed to take into account that the slum dwellers had a culture of their own and that, despite economic and even emotional exploitation, and amidst the squalor and vice, most people continued to live by the peasant ways they had brought with them from Europe. This peasant culture—transformed into a working-class one here —was well suited to coping with poverty and provided satisfaction as well as dignity to lives marked by hard work and little hope of anything better.[3]

The cultural blindness of the settlements did not prevent them from providing useful services and from attracting many children and some adults to their facilities. There are several reasons for their success: they offered information about American ways; they supplied recreational and other services not available elsewhere; and, most important, their middle-class programs and staffs gave poor children an opportunity to learn how to become middle-class themselves. This opportunity was taken, however, only because the settlements were initially able to draw on a highly mobile set of clients, the Jews. The hypothesis presented here is that the early success of the settlement was due to the predominance of Jewish clients and that the subsequent decline of the settlement's impact was associated with their departure from the slums.

Data to test this hypothesis are hard to come by, but it is interesting to note that the settlement-house movement began at the height of Jewish immigration, that the first settlement—Toynbee Hall in London—was located in a Jewish ghetto, and that many American houses were also located in or near Jewish neighborhoods. Indeed, an analysis of neighborhood descriptions in the 1911 *Handbook of Settlements* suggests that a disproportionate number of settlements had Jewish neighbors.[4] For example, in Boston, where 10 per cent of the population was Jewish in 1910, 27 per cent of the settlements named Jews as principal neighbors; in Chicago, with a 5 per cent Jewish population, 11 per cent of the houses did so; and in New York, where between 16 and 26 per cent of the residents were Jews, 38 per cent of the settlements reported them as neighbors.[5]

There are also some data that suggest that Jews were more likely to come to the settlements than other immigrants. In 1922, Woods and Kennedy wrote that "more than any other immigrant, the Jew manifests a willingness to take advantage of educational and recreational opportunities,"[6] and a 1935 study of eighteen representative New York settlements showed that 56 per cent of their members were Jews, as compared to 20 per cent Italians, 10 per cent Irish, and 14 per cent "Other."[7] In 1930, 26 per cent of the city's population was Jewish.[8]

There is general agreement among sociologists that the Jews were different from their fellow immigrants.[9] Most of them were not peasants, but retailers or artisans, and in many instances of urban origin. More important, they had great faith in education, both as an end in itself and as a means to obtaining white-collar and professional jobs. Jewish parents made many sacrifices to keep their children in school, and as part of this process they encouraged them to attend the settlement houses as well.

When the Jews achieved sufficient prosperity to leave the slums, the settlements had to draw their clientele from the other immigrant groups, fewer of whom were aspiring to middle-class status. With this change, both the attendance and the impact of the settlement-house project began to wane. As European peasants, these immigrants had traditionally subsisted on unskilled work that required no schooling; and as long as such work was plentiful in America, they saw no need for education and took their children out of school as soon as the law permitted. Consequently, they had equally little interest in the settlement house. Moreover, they lived within an extended family which monopolized their social life and even handled many of the caretaking functions the settlement offered. In addition, they stayed out of formal institutions, partly because they distrusted anyone not of their own ethnic origin, partly because they had not been served well by such agencies in Europe. As a result, most of them came to the settlement only to make transitory use of recreational and athletic facilities not available elsewhere or did not come at all.[10]

Because the aims of the settlement house—and most of the other caretaking professions—were well defined, there was little curiosity about who the clients were and why they behaved as they did. The caretakers wanted to change the slum dwellers, not understand them, and as a result they made few attempts to find out whom they were and were not serving and why so many people who lived close to the settlements never came. They thought they were reaching most of the low-income population and converting it to middle-class ways, but they deceived themselves into overestimating their impact.

Another of the settlement's historic goals was the establishment of neighborhood democracy in the slums. This too was based on an inaccurate perception of its clients. Like other caretaking movements, the settlement sought to bring the New England town-meeting democracy into the city, but, unfortunately, it held a highly romanticized image of that institution, failing to realize that in many New England communities the town meeting was less an expression of direct democracy than a public forum in which the upper-income townspeople expressed their wishes to the other residents, many of whom were their employees or tenants.

The settlement house tried to transplant the ideal image of the town meeting by treating the urban slum as a small town, which it called a neighborhood, and in which citizens could better themselves and their area by uniting in civic pursuits. Although this goal interested some of the Jews, it aroused little enthusiasm among the other European immigrants and especially those of peasant background. They participated in common activities with family members and, to a lesser extent, joined ethnic institutions, but they had little to do with the people who lived next door unless these were relatives, and, as already indicated, they distrusted neighborhood organizations set up by other ethnic groups or middle-class "Yankees."

The amount and intensity of interaction among family and ethnic-group members led the settlement-house workers to think that the slum was a warm and cohesive neighborhood, and they celebrated this communion in the sentimental prose of their annual reports and other writings. But the intimacy was not based on neighborhood feeling; what brought people together was family and ethnic ties, not common residence on a block or in an area. Moreover, the problems that concerned the slum dwellers most were not neighborhood deficiencies; they wanted jobs and financial aid, and these were most easily obtained from the ward political organization.

The settlement's belief in neighborhood had some useful functions, however. The workers acted on their belief and put pressure on the politicians to improve their areas, using their high social status and the political influence it gave them to good purpose. Indeed, many of the finest achievements of the settlement-house movement are embodied in the neighborhood and city-wide improvements and in the local, state, and federal legislation for which it fought.

III

Although this analysis of the settlement's limitations in reaching the clients has been historical, most of these conclusions still apply equally well today. Of course, a number of improvements have taken place: some houses have moved their programs out of the building, often through the use of detached workers; others have employed the so-called indigenous leaders; and many have developed new programs to deal with the problems of the Negro and Puerto Rican people who have become their major clients.[11]

Increasing recognition has also been given to the cultural narrowness of the settlement, and a significant proportion of the professional literature is now devoted to the description of low-income culture and to the understanding of cultural differences between the profession and its clients. Nevertheless, there has been no real change in point of view, for even the writers who appeal to their colleagues for cultural awareness still view their function as changing the culture. They express little sympathy for the behavior of their clients or for the reasons for that behavior and do not side with them in their grievances and needs.

For example, a recent survey of neighborhood-center activities reports extensively on new programs and on what these ought to do for the clients. It describes what programs were offered, but it gives no evidence that these programs were wanted by the clients or that the clients' wants had any role in shaping the program.[12] The reports include considerable detail on methods of organization, on the use of volunteers, on the relationships with other agencies, but nary a word on the settlements' relationships with their populations, such as how many people came, who they were, and how they reacted to the offered programs.

If the Boston agencies observed by this author are representative, the settlement house often may not know the impact of its programs on the client. For example, one settlement attempted to assist the area's residents with their relocation problems, but much of the program it developed and reported bore little relevance to the need.[13] The people were desperately trying to find low-cost apartments, preferably in neighborhoods where others of their ethnic group lived; the settlement imported a social worker to tell them about the variety of public agencies that were ready to help them once they had found a place to live. But she even misperceived the agencies they needed, for she told them about the high quality of specialists at various area hospitals, yet could not answer questions about the outpatient clinics which were most frequently used among this population.[14]

The settlement house never realized how little it understood its neighborhood. Nor did it perceive that most of the residents had never been in the house and saw it as irrelevant to their concerns. The house was not even aware of the neighborhood's resentment because its board had supported the city's renewal scheme that was soon to drive them out of their neighborhood. A settlement house may thus delude itself into thinking that it is effective when it is not. Perhaps the lower-echelon workers who have the most contact with residents see through this delusion, but only at the cost of considerable personal frustration and low professional morale. This result is not unique to the settlement; it exists in most other caretaking professions.

The problem is not lack of good intentions or dedication on the part of the settlement-house worker, for few people work harder for low pay and little prestige. Nor is it simply a function of the fact that the workers are middle-class, although admittedly, for middle-class people, understanding and making contact with low-income people is quite difficult, as is any contact with people of another culture. The major source of the problem is in the nature of the profession and particularly in its central assumption that the program, rather than the client, is its primary function. The settlement house sees itself as a provider of programs, determined by professional standards, rather than as a place where people may come to be, to do, and to learn.

The overcommitment to program blinds the settlement to the fact that agencies whose clients come voluntarily can reach only those who want to be reached and that program-centered facilities will reach only a predisposed minority. Awareness of this fact is also hindered by the various methods that settlement workers and other caretakers have developed to repress or ignore it; for example, by retreating into administrative work and endless meetings with colleagues and by leaving the contact with clients to neophyte professionals or volunteers. Moreover, since the failure to reach a larger proportion of the low-income population is viewed as a reflection on the workers' personal ability, discussion of the problem is avoided, even though it is an institutional rather than a personal failure that is shared by most of their colleagues.[15]

IV

Nevertheless, the realization that something is wrong and that the role of the settlement house has to be reappraised is beginning to make itself felt in the profession, especially among its younger members. This realization has come from increased sophistication and improved professional training, from the participation of social scientists in schools of social work, and, most important, from the changes taking place in the urban low-income population and the clients that come to the settlement house. Indeed, the major impetus for reappraisal has come from the settlement house's new neighbors: the Negroes and the Puerto Ricans.

Today, unskilled labor is fast becoming superfluous in the country's automating economy, and the low-income population has increasing difficulty in finding jobs.

In addition, the new low-income population is largely nonwhite and thus is being discriminated against in the access to jobs, housing, good education, and other facilities and opportunities.

Also, new difficulties have developed in the residential pattern. Not only is the housing often worse than that which housed the European immigrants—in many cities it is exactly the same housing, only now thirty years older—but the housing standards of the society and the housing accommodations of the affluent have improved tremendously. In addition, in a number of cities, urban renewal has in practice been Negro removal. Moreover, for Negroes, the ethnic tie that kept the earlier generations of the poor together is lacking. The end result is that the slum of today is even less of a neighborhood than it was in the past, and this complicates the settlement house's already difficult task of reaching the people who live around it.

In past decades, the failure of the settlement house and the other caretaking professions to reach the majority of the low-income population was not too serious. The help that caretakers gave was useful, but for most people it was not urgent. Today, however, the situation has changed drastically. Thus, if anything is to be done about poverty, new ways of helping the low-income population are required. The poor need better jobs, higher incomes, the elimination of racial segregation, and the improvement of schools and other public services—and such programs cannot be supplied by the settlement house.

V

The changes now taking place in the American city require the settlement house to make fundamental decisions about its own future. There are a number of directions in which it could move. For instance, it could make a radical turnabout, giving up its present role as a middle-class institution to join with the poor in their struggle for economic advancement and social equality. Alternately, it could become an antipoverty community action agency and devote itself to organizing as many of its low-income neighbors as possible, developing whatever new programs are needed to help them. And finally, it could continue to maintain its present programs, but carry them out in a more effective manner.

The first alternative would mean a total overhaul, with the settlement house becoming a protest agency of the poor. The second alternative would require an almost equally drastic change, for the new programs would force it to accept many if not all of the positive elements of low-income culture. Its staff members would have to be chosen on the basis of their ability to empathize and communicate with the poor and most likely from among the poor themselves.

The settlement house cannot—and should not—move in either direction. Institutions can alter themselves radically only when they cannot survive otherwise, and even then change is rarely complete. Assuming that the settlement house should survive, it can do so best by continuing with its present functions, but by performing these more rationally and effectively than it has done in the past.

The typical settlement house, serving an urban low-income neighborhood, ought to have three major functions: to be a source of intensive help to people aspiring to middle-class ways; to provide less intensive services to a larger proportion of its neighborhood population, especially those not offered by other agencies; and to offer whatever other aid it can as a neighborhood institution that is at least physically close to its population.

The first function would require a retooling of the settlement-house program to discover how socially mobile people can be helped in their efforts to become middle-class. Sociological research on the processes of mobility and past experience in aiding clients who became middle-class ought to be reviewed for this purpose. The program would probably involve intensive staff contact and informal teaching of middle-class patterns to a small number of self-selected clients.

The second function would depend in part on what other facilities are available, but in most cases, it would require recreational and other programs for people who simply want to come to the settlement to use facilities they cannot obtain or afford elsewhere. Such programs should be user-oriented, that is, developed to meet the preferences and needs of the clients, without demanding that they participate in educational or other behavior-transforming activities not of their own choosing. The programs would probably require little client-staff contact, and they should probably be staffed largely by people from the neighborhood who can lead activities in a client-centered way.

This second function should be strictly demarcated from the first one (perhaps even through separate buildings), so that the two types of clients—who are quite different in their characteristics and needs—do not get in each other's way or, more important, do not stay away from the settlement house because each believes that the house is only interested in the other.

The third function would be an interstitial one and would draw on the settlement's long acquaintance with the people of its area. It might involve case work and other forms of aid to a small number of well-known clients, especially those who fail to get help from city-wide agencies, but it might also mean activities for a much larger number; for example, for the remaining members of an ethnic group whose institutions have moved out to other areas.

VI

The suggested redefinition of the settlement's function does not mean that it should cease to fight for the national and local policies necessary to eliminate poverty, racial discrimination, or other restrictions on opportunity. But here, too, some reappraisal of traditional approaches is necessary.

Although the settlement-house movement can take credit for much desirable legislation, individual settlements in some cities have occasionally supported local policies that did not really help the low-income population. Cited earlier was the fact that the three settlements in the Boston neighborhood all supported the city's renewal scheme for the area, even though it meant the destruction of a neighborhood in which many of the residents had lived all their lives, causing many of them grievous suffering. They supported the project because their boards included business and civic leaders who helped to draw it up, because they did not realize that the residents were willing to put up with outwardly shabby housing because of its low cost and in order to participate in a vital social life, and because they believed relocation to neighborhoods better by middle-class standards would honestly help the residents.[16] Also, they found it much easier to communicate with city-renewal officials—middle-class people like themselves—than with the residents and accepted their claims that the project would improve the condition of the residents, even though these claims turned out to be false.[17]

Other government policies may be more beneficial to the low-income population than urban renewal, but if the settlement houses wish to aid this population through support of new legislation, they must make sure that the legislation is what the poor need and want, and not just middle-class estimates of what is best for them. Such a position is as difficult to take as the programatic changes suggested earlier; it forces the middle-class professional to deny his own culture and may alienate him from friends and colleagues, especially those whose first loyalty—lip service aside—is to the interests of a middle-class constituency. Perhaps it is unreal to expect the settlement-house worker to ally himself with points of view that contradict his own values, but in that case, he, like many other caretakers, must expect to be pushed aside as the growing political vitality of the low-income population makes itself felt in the years to come.

NOTES

1. The Boston observations are reported in more detail in Herbert J. Gans, *The Urban Villagers: Group and Class in the Life of Italian-Americans* (New York: Free Press of Glencoe, 1962), especially Chapter 7. William F. Whyte, Jr., had reached similar conclusions twenty years earlier about two settlements in an adjacent area. See his *Street Corner Society* (2d ed.; Chicago: University of Chicago Press, 1955), pp. 99–104.

2. The term *caretaker* is used here as a label to encompass the professions that provide help, services, education, as well as specific care. It is a descriptive term rather than a normative one. Care-giver would be equally appropriate, and neither term should be taken to mean that the professions named give only care. See also Gans, *op. cit.*, pp. 142–143.

3. The viability of working-class culture has been well described by John Seeley when he wrote about a Polish-American group with whom he once lived: "No society I have lived in before or since seemed to me to present so many of its members . . . so many possibilities and actualities of fulfillment of a number at least of basic human demands." John Seeley, "The Slum: Its Nature, Use, and Users," *Journal of the American Institute of Planners*, XXV (February 1959), 10.

4. The survey is based on ethnic descriptions of the neighborhood served by the settlement. When areas were multiethnic, the author tabulated only the first ethnic group mentioned on the assumption that it was dominant either in the area or in the settlement. The data are taken from Robert A. Woods and Albert J. Kennedy, eds., *Handbook of Settlements* (New York: Charities Publication Committee, 1911).

5. The population data are taken from the *American Jewish Yearbook*, the U.S. Census for 1910 and C. Horowitz and L. Kaplan, *The Jewish Population of the New York Area* (New York: Federation of Jewish Philanthropies, 1959), Table 6. For 1910 this report shows the Jewish population as 26.3 per cent of the total, while a comparison of *American Jewish Yearbook* and census figures for 1910 results in a proportion of 16 per cent Jews.

6. Robert A. Woods and Albert J. Kennedy, eds., *The Settlement Horizon* (New York: Russell Sage Foundation, 1922), p. 333.

7. Albert J. Kennedy *et al.*, *Social Settlements in New York City* (New York: Columbia University Press, 1935), chart 9, p. 462.

8. Horowitz and Kaplan, *op. cit.*
9. For a recent statement, see Nathan Glazer and Daniel P. Moynihan, *Beyond the Melting Pot* (Cambridge: Massachusetts Institute of Technology Press, 1963), especially Chapter 3.
10. The 1935 study of New York settlements showed that "a large proportion of members are participating in one activity, clubs and athletics attracting the largest number of single activity members . . . turnover is high and the majority of members retain their affiliation over a short period." Kennedy *et al., op. cit.,* p. 483. In five settlements for which data were available, from 45 to 71 per cent of members enrolled in one year were not registered the following year. *Ibid.,* p. 481.
11. More than sixty such projects are reported in National Federation of Settlements and Neighborhood Centers, *Summary of Research and Demonstration Projects in Process or Proposed by Members of the National Federation of Settlements, Reported as of February–May 1962* (New York: May 1962— mimeographed).
12. National Federation of Settlements and Neighborhood Centers, *Neighborhood Centers Today* (New York: 1960).
13. For a telling illustration of the settlement's conception (or reportage) of its effectiveness and what actually happened among the clients, see "Assisting with Relocation," in Fern M. Colborn, *The Neighborhood and Urban Renewal* (New York: National Federation of Settlements and Neighborhood Centers, 1963), pp. 60–63; and the author's account of the same settlement's activities in Gans, *op. cit.,* pp. 148–151, 154, 284.
14. The settlement house reported this meeting as follows: "A staff member from United Community Services was invited to meet with parents to tell of resources in neighborhoods to which they might move and to tell about old neighbors happily settled in their new communities." Colburn, *op. cit.,* p. 62. An extended description of how this meeting appeared to the residents is in Gans, *op. cit.,* p. 154. Some of the other services extended by the settlement were more useful, however, especially its policy of keeping the house open until the last days of the neighborhood's existence.
15. Whyte reported his findings about the actual role of the settlement house in Boston's North End to its directors in the hope that this would help them to achieve their goals more adequately. The cool reception which he encountered is described in Whyte, *op. cit.,* pp. 354–356. This author originally reported to a settlement-house workers' conference quite similar conclusions and met with the same reaction from a number of the professionals, although others felt the author had described many settlement houses quite accurately.
16. One solution would be to reduce the participation of such leaders on settlement boards and to give the majority of memberships to residents.
17. In recent years, settlements in another Boston neighborhood undergoing renewal have, in the words of one informant, "carried on a pretty vigorous campaign on behalf of the residents. It is true that they have been swinging on a tight rope between trying to get renewal and protecting resident interests and it may be that they have fallen on one side more than another but . . . [they] have tried to reconcile contradictory values."

18

The Failure of Urban Renewal:
A Critique and Some Proposals

I

Suppose that the government decided that jalopies were a menace to public safety and a blight on the beauty of our highways and therefore took them away from their drivers. Suppose, then, that to replenish the supply of automobiles, it gave these drivers a hundred dollars each to buy a good used car and also made special grants to General Motors, Ford, and Chrysler to lower the cost—although not necessarily the price —of Cadillacs, Lincolns, and Imperials by a few hundred dollars. Absurd as this may sound, change the jalopies to slum housing, and I have described, with only slight poetic license, the first fifteen years of a federal program called urban renewal.

Since 1949, this program has provided local renewal agencies with federal funds and the power of eminent domain to condemn slum neighborhoods, tear down the buildings, and resell the cleared land to private developers at a reduced price. In addition to relocating the slum dwellers in "decent, safe, and sanitary" housing, the program was intended to stimulate large-scale private rebuilding, add new tax revenues to the dwindling coffers of the cities, revitalize their downtown areas, and halt the exodus of middle-class whites to the suburbs.

For some time now, a few city planners and housing experts have been pointing out that urban renewal was not achieving its general aims, and social scientists have produced a number of critical studies of individual renewal projects. These critiques, however, have mostly appeared in academic books and journals; otherwise there has been remarkably little public discussion of the federal program. Slum dwellers whose homes were to be torn down have indeed protested bitterly, but their outcries have been limited to particular projects; and because such outcries have

Reprinted from *Commentary*, XXXIX No. 4 (April 1965), 29–37, by permission. Copyright © 1965 by the American Jewish Committee.

rarely been supported by the local press, they have been easily brushed aside by the political power of the supporters of the projects in question. In the last few years, the civil-rights movement has backed protesting slum dwellers, though again only at the local level, while rightists have opposed the use of eminent domain to take private property from one owner in order to give it to another (especially when the new one is likely to be from out of town and financed by New York capital).

Slum clearance has also come under fire from several prominent architectural and social critics, led by Jane Jacobs, who have been struggling to preserve neighborhoods like Greenwich Village, with their brownstones, lofts, and small apartment houses, against the encroachment of the large, high-rise projects built for the luxury market and the poor alike. But these efforts have been directed mainly at private clearance outside the federal program, and their intent has been to save the city for people (intellectuals and artists, for example) who, like tourists, want jumbled diversity, antique "charm," and narrow streets for visual adventure and aesthetic pleasure. (Norman Mailer carried such thinking to its furthest point in his recent attack in *The New York Times* magazine section on the physical and social sterility of high-rise housing; Mailer's attack was also accompanied by an entirely reasonable suggestion—in fact, the only viable one that could be made in this context—that the advantages of brownstone living be incorporated into skyscraper projects.)

II

But if criticism of the urban-renewal program has in the past been spotty and sporadic, there are signs that the program as a whole is now beginning to be seriously and tellingly evaluated. At least two comprehensive studies, by Charles Abrams and Scott Greer, are nearing publication,[1] and one highly negative analysis—by an ultraconservative economist and often free-swinging polemicist—has already appeared: Martin Anderson's *The Federal Bulldozer*.[2] Ironically enough, Anderson's data are based largely on statistics collected by the Urban Renewal Administration. What, according to these and other data, has the program accomplished? It has cleared slums to make room for many luxury-housing and a few middle-income projects, and it has also provided inexpensive land for the expansion of colleges, hospitals, libraries, shopping areas, and other such institutions located in slum areas. As of March 1961, 126,000 dwelling units had been demolished and about 28,000 new ones built. The median monthly rental of all those erected during

1960 came to $158, and in 1962, to $192—a staggering figure for any area outside of Manhattan.

Needless to say, none of the slum dwellers who were dispossessed in the process could afford to move into these new apartments. Local renewal agencies were supposed to relocate the dispossessed tenants in "standard" housing within their means before demolition began, but such vacant housing is scarce in most cities and altogether unavailable in some. And since the agencies were under strong pressure to clear the land and get renewal projects going, the relocation of the tenants was impatiently, if not ruthlessly, handled. Thus, a 1961 study of renewal projects in 41 cities showed that 60 per cent of the dispossessed tenants were merely relocated in other slums; and in big cities, the proportion was even higher (over 70 per cent in Philadelphia, according to a 1958 study). Renewal sometimes even created new slums by pushing relocatees into areas and buildings which then became overcrowded and deteriorated rapidly. This has principally been the case with Negroes who, for both economic and racial reasons, have been forced to double up in other ghettos. Indeed, because almost two-thirds of the cleared slum units have been occupied by Negroes, the urban-renewal program has often been characterized as Negro clearance, and in too many cities this has been its intent.

Moreover, those disposssesed tenants who found better housing usually had to pay more rent than they could afford. In his careful study of relocation in Boston's heavily Italian West End,[3] Chester Hartman shows that 41 per cent of the West Enders lived in good housing in this so-called slum (thus suggesting that much of it should not have been torn down) and that 73 per cent were relocated in good housing—thanks in part to the fact that the West Enders were white. This improvement was achieved at a heavy price, however, for median rents rose from $41 to $71 per month after the move.

According to renewal officials, 80 per cent of all persons relocated now live in good housing, and rent increases were justified because many had been paying unduly low rent before. Hartman's study was the first to compare these official statistics with housing realities, and his figure of 73 per cent challenges the official claim that 97 per cent of the Boston West Enders were properly rehoused. This discrepancy may arise from two facts: renewal officials collected their data after the poorest of the uprooted tenants had fled in panic to other slums; and officials also tended toward a rather lenient evaluation of the relocation housing of those actually studied in order to make a good record for their agency. (On the other hand, when they were certifying areas for clearance, these officials often exaggerated the degree of "blight" in order to prove their case.)

As for the substandard rents paid by slum dwellers, these are factual in only a small proportion of cases, and then mostly among whites. Real-estate economists argue that families should pay at least 20 per cent of their income for housing, but what is manageable for middle-income people is a burden to those with low incomes who pay a higher share of their earnings for food and other necessities. Yet even so, low-income Negroes generally have to devote about 30 per cent of their income to housing, and a Chicago study cited by Hartman reports that among non-white families earning less than $3,000 a year, median rent rose from 35 per cent of income before relocation to 46 per cent afterward.

To compound the failure of urban renewal to help the poor, many clearance areas (Boston's West End is an example) were chosen, as Anderson points out, not because they had the worst slums, but because they offered the best sites for luxury housing—housing which would have been built whether the urban-renewal program existed or not. Since public funds were used to clear the slums and to make the land available to private builders at reduced costs, the low-income population was in effect subsidizing its own removal for the benefit of the wealthy. What was done for the slum dwellers in return is starkly suggested by the following statistic: *only one-half of 1 per cent* of all federal expenditures for urban renewal between 1949 and 1964 was spent on relocation of families and individuals, and 2 per cent if payments to businesses are included.

Finally, because the policy has been to clear a district of all slums at once in order to assemble large sites to attract private developers, entire neighborhoods have frequently been destroyed, uprooting people who had lived there for decades, closing down their institutions, ruining small businesses by the hundreds, and scattering families and friends all over the city. By removing the structure of social and emotional support provided by the neighborhood, and by forcing people to rebuild their lives separately and amid strangers elsewhere, slum clearance has often come at a serious psychological as well as financial cost to its supposed beneficiaries. Marc Fried, a clinical psychologist who studied the West Enders after relocation, reported that 46 per cent of the women and 38 per cent of the men "give evidence of a fairly severe grief reaction or worse" in response to questions about leaving their tight-knit community. Far from "adjusting" eventually to this trauma, 26 per cent of the women remained sad or depressed even two years after they had been pushed out of the West End.[4]

People like the Italians or the Puerto Ricans who live in an intensely group-centered way among three-generation "extended families" and ethnic peers have naturally suffered greatly from the clearance of entire neighborhoods. It may well be, however, that slum clearance has inflicted yet graver emotional burdens on Negroes, despite the fact that they generally live in less cohesive and often disorganized neighborhoods. In fact, I suspect that Negroes who lack a stable family life and have trouble finding neighbors, shopkeepers, and institutions they can trust may have been hurt even more by forcible removal to new areas. This suspicion is supported by another of Fried's findings: that the socially marginal West Enders were more injured by relocation than those who had been integral members of the old neighborhood. Admittedly, some Negroes move very often on their own, but then they at least do so voluntarily and not in consequence of a public policy which is supposed to help them in the first place. Admittedly also, relocation has made it possible for social workers to help slum dwellers whom they could not reach until renewal brought them out in the open, so to speak. But then only a few cities have so far used social workers to make relocation a more humane process.

These high financial, social, and emotional costs paid by the slum dwellers have generally been written off as an unavoidable by-product of "progress," the price of helping cities to collect more taxes, bring back the middle class, make better use of downtown land, stimulate private investment, and restore civic pride. But as Anderson shows, urban renewal has hardly justified these claims either. For one thing, urban renewal is a slow process: the average project has taken twelve years to complete. Moreover, while the few areas suitable for luxury housing were quickly rebuilt, less desirable cleared land might lie vacant for many years because developers were—and are—unwilling to risk putting up high- and middle-income housing in areas still surrounded by slums. Frequently, they can be attracted only by promises of tax write-offs, which absorb the increased revenues that renewal is supposed to create for the city. Anderson reports that, instead of the anticipated four dollars for every public dollar, private investments have only just matched the public subsidies, and even the money for luxury housing has come forth largely because of federal subsidies. Thus, all too few of the new projects have produced tax gains and returned suburbanites or generated the magic rebuilding boom.

Anderson goes on to argue that during the fifteen years of the federal urban-renewal program, the private housing market has achieved what urban renewal has failed to do. Between 1950 and 1960, twelve million new dwelling units were built, and fully six million substandard ones disappeared—all without government action. The proportion of substandard housing in the total housing supply was reduced from 37 to 19 per cent, and even among the dwelling units occupied by nonwhites, the proportion of substandard units has dropped from 72 to 44 per cent. This comparison leads Anderson to the conclusion that the private market is much more effective than government action in removing slums and supplying new housing and that the urban-renewal program ought to be repealed.

III

It would appear that Anderson's findings and those of other studies I have cited make an excellent case for doing so. However, a less biased analysis of the figures and a less tendentious mode of evaluating them than Anderson's leads to a different conclusion. To begin with, Anderson's use of nationwide statistics misses the few good renewal projects, those which have helped both the slum dwellers and the cities, or those which brought in enough new taxes to finance other city services for the poor. Such projects can be found in small cities and especially in those where high vacancy rates assured sufficient relocation housing of standard quality. More important, all the studies I have mentioned deal with projects carried out during the 1950's and fail to take account of the improvements in urban-renewal practice under the Kennedy and Johnson administrations. Although Anderson's study supposedly covers the period up to 1963, many of his data go no further than 1960. Since then the federal bulldozer has moved into fewer neighborhoods, and the concept of rehabilitating rather than clearing blighted neighborhoods is more and more being underwritten by subsidized loans. A new housing subsidy program, known as 221 (d) (3), for families above the income ceiling for public housing has also been launched, and in 1964 Congress passed legislation for assistance to relocatees who cannot afford their new rents.

None of this is to say that Anderson would have had to revise his findings drastically if he had taken the pains to update them. These recent innovations have so far been small in scope—only 13,000 units were financed under 221 (d) (3) in the first two years—and they still do not provide subsidies sufficient to bring better housing within the price range of the slum residents. In addition, rehabilitation unaccompanied by new construction is nearly useless because it does not eliminate overcrowding. And finally, some cities are still scheduling projects to clear away the nonwhite poor who stand in the path of the progress of private enterprise. Unfortunately, many cities pay little attention to federal pleas to improve the program, using the local initiative granted them by urban-renewal legislation to perpetuate the practices of the 1950's. Yet even with the legislation of the 1960's, the basic error in the original design of urban renewal remains: it is still a method for eliminating the slums in order to "renew" the city, rather than a program for properly rehousing slum dwellers.

Before going into this crucial distinction, we first need to be clear that private housing is not going to solve our slum problems. In the first place, Anderson conveniently ignores the fact that if urban renewal has benefited anyone, it is private enterprise. Bending to the pressure of the real-estate lobby, the legislation that launched urban renewal in effect required that private developers do the rebuilding, and most projects could therefore get off the drawing board only if they appeared to be financially attractive to a developer. Thus, his choice of a site and his re-building plans inevitably took priority over the needs of the slum dwellers.

It is true that Anderson is not defending private enterprise per se, but the free market, although he forgets that it only exists today as a concept in reactionary minds and dated economics texts. The costs of land, capital, and construction have long since made it impossible for private developers to build for anyone but the rich, and some form of subsidy is needed to house everyone else. The building boom of the 1950's which Anderson credits to the free market was subsidized by income-tax deductions to homeowners and by F.H.A. and V.A. mortgage insurance, not to mention the federal highway programs that have made the suburbs possible.

To be sure, these supports enabled private builders to put up a great deal of housing for middle-class whites. This in turn permitted well-employed workers, including some nonwhites, to improve their own situation by moving into the vacated neighborhoods. Anderson is quite right in arguing that if people earn good wages, they can obtain better housing more easily and cheaply in the not-quite-private market than through urban renewal. But this market is of little help to those employed at low or even factory wages, or the unemployed, or most Negroes who, whatever their earnings, cannot live in the suburbs. In consequence, 44 per cent of all housing occupied by nonwhites in 1960 was still substandard, and even with present subsidies, private enterprise can do nothing for these people. As for laissez faire, it played a major role in creating the slums in the first place.

IV

The solution, then, is not to repeal urban renewal, but to transform it from a program of slum clearance and rehabilitation into a program of urban rehousing. This means, first, building low- and moderate-cost housing on vacant land in cities, suburbs, and new towns beyond the suburbs and also helping slum dwellers to move into existing housing outside the slums; and then, *after* a portion of the urban low-income population has left the slums, clearing and rehabilitating them through urban renewal. This approach is commonplace in many European countries, which have long since realized that private enterprise can no more house the population and eliminate slums than it can run the post office.

Of course, governments in Europe have a much easier task than ours in developing decent low-income projects. Because they take it for granted that housing is a national rather than a local responsibility, the government agencies are not hampered by the kind of real-estate and construction lobbies which can defeat or subvert American programs by charges of socialism. Moreover, their municipalities own a great deal of the vacant land and have greater control over the use of private land than do American cities. But perhaps their main advantage is the lack of popular opposition to moving the poor out of the slums and into the midst of the more affluent residents. Not only is housing desperately short for all income groups, but the European class structure, even in Western socialist countries, is still rigid enough so that low- and middle-income groups can live near each other if not next to each other and still "know their place."

In America, on the other hand, one's house and address are major signs of social status, and no one who has any say in the matter wants people of lower income or status in his neighborhood. Middle-class homeowners use zoning as a way of keeping out cheaper or less prestigious housing, while working-class communities employ less subtle forms of exclusion. Consequently, low-income groups, whatever their creed or color, have been forced to live in slums or near-slums and to wait until they could acquire the means to move as a group, taking over better neighborhoods when the older occupants were ready to move on themselves.

For many years now, the only source of new housing for such people, and their only hope of escaping the worst slums, has been public housing. But this is no longer a practical alternative. Initiated during the Depression, public housing has always been a politically embattled program; its opponents, among whom the real-estate lobby looms large, first saddled it with restrictions and then effectively crippled it. Congress now permits only 35,000 units a year to be built in the entire country.

The irony is that public housing has declined because, intended only for the poor, it faithfully carried out its mandate. Originally, sites were obtained by slum clearance; after the war, however, in order to increase the supply of low-cost housing, cities sought to build public housing on vacant land. But limited as it was to low-income tenants and thus labeled and stigmatized as an institution of the dependent poor, public housing was kept out of vacant land in the better neighborhoods. This, plus the high cost of land and construction, left housing officials with no other choice but to build high-rise projects on whatever vacant land they could obtain, often next to factories or along railroad yards. Because tenants of public housing are ruled by a set of strict regulations—sometimes necessary, sometimes politically inspired, but always degrading—anyone who could afford housing in the private market shunned the public projects. During the early years of the program, when fewer citizens had that choice, public housing became respectable shelter for the working class and even for the unemployed middle class. After the war, federal officials decided, and rightly so, that public housing ought to be reserved for those who had no alternative and therefore set income limits that admitted only the really poor. Today, public housing is home for the underclass—families who earn less than $3,000 to $4,000 annually, many with unstable jobs or none at all, and most of them nonwhite.

Meanwhile the enthusiasm for public housing has been steadily dwindling and, with it, badly needed political support. Newspaper reports reinforce the popular image of public housing projects as huge nests of crime and delinquency—despite clear evidence to the contrary—and as the domicile of unregenerate and undeserving families whose children urinate only in the elevators. The position of public housing, particularly among liberal intellectuals, has also been weakened by the slurs of the social and architectural aesthetes who condemn the projects' poor exterior designs as "sterile," "monotonous," and "dehumanizing," often in ignorance of the fact that the tightly restricted funds have been allocated mainly to make the apartments themselves as spacious and livable as possible and that the waiting lists among slum dwellers who want these apartments remain long. Be that as it may, suburban communities and urban neighborhoods with vacant land are as hostile to public housing as ever, and their opposition is partly responsible for the program's having been cut down to its present minuscule size.

The net result is that low-income people today cannot get out of the slums, either because they cannot afford the subsidized private market or because the project they could afford cannot be built on vacant land. There is only one way to break through this impasse, and that is to permit them equal access to new subsidized, privately built housing by adding another subsidy to make up the difference between the actual rent and what they can reasonably be expected to pay. Such a plan, giving them a chance to choose housing like all other citizens, would help to remove the stigma of poverty and inferiority placed on them by public housing. Many forms of rent subsidy have been proposed, but the best one, now being tried in New York, is to put low- and middle-income people in the same middle-income project, with the former getting the same apartments at smaller rentals.

Admittedly, this approach assumes that the poor can live with the middle class and that their presence and behavior will not threaten their neighbors' security or status. No one knows whether this is really possible, but experiments in education, job-training, and social-welfare programs do show that many low-income people, when once offered *genuine* opportunities to improve their lives and given help in making use of them, are able to shake off the hold of the culture of poverty. Despite the popular stereotype, the proportion of those whom Hylan Lewis calls the clinical poor, too ravaged emotionally by poverty and deprivation to adapt to new opportunities, seems to be small. As for the rest, they only reject programs offering spurious opportunities, like job-training schemes for nonexistent jobs. Further, anyone who has lived in a slum neighborhood can testify that whatever the condition of the building, most women keep their apartments clean by expenditures of time and effort inconceivable to the middle-class housewife. Moving to a better apartment would require little basic cultural change from these women, and rehousing is thus a type of new opportunity that stands a better chance of succeeding than, say, a program to inculcate new child-rearing techniques.

We have no way of telling how many slum dwellers would be willing to participate in such a plan. However poor the condition of the flat, the slum is home, and for many it provides the support of neighborhood relatives and friends and a cultural milieu in which everyone has the same problems and is therefore willing to overlook occasional disreputable behavior. A middle-income project cannot help but have a middle-class ethos, and some lower-class people may be fearful of risking what little stability they have achieved where they are now in exchange for something new, strange, demanding, and potentially hostile. It would be hard to imagine an unwed Negro mother moving her household to a middle-income project full of married couples and far removed from the mother, sisters, and aunts who play such an important role in the female-centered life of lower-class Negroes. However, there are today a large number of stable two-parent families who live in the slums only because income and race exclude them from the better housing that is available. Families like these would surely be only too willing to leave the Harlems and Black Belts. They would have to be helped with loans to make the move and perhaps even with grants to buy new furniture so as not to feel ashamed in their new surroundings. They might be further encouraged by being offered income-tax relief for giving up the slums, just as we now offer such relief to people who give up being renters to become homeowners.

Undoubtedly there would be friction between the classes, and the more affluent residents would likely want to segregate themselves and their children from neighbors who did not toe the middle-class line, especially with respect to child-rearing. The new housing would therefore have to be planned to allow some voluntary social segregation for both groups, if only to make sure that enough middle-income families would move in (especially in cities where there was no shortage of housing for them). The proportion of middle- and low-income tenants would have to be regulated, not only to minimize the status fears of the former but also to give the latter enough peers to keep them from feeling socially isolated and without emotional support when problems arise. Fortunately, nonprofit and limited-dividend institutions, which do not have to worry about showing an immediate profit, are now being encouraged to build moderate-income housing; they can do a more careful job of planning the physical and social details of this approach than speculative private builders.

If the slums are really to be emptied and their residents properly housed elsewhere, the rehousing program will have to be extended beyond the city limits, for the simple reason that that is where most of the vacant land is located. This means admitting the low-income population to the suburbs; it also means creating new towns—self-contained communities with their own industry which would not, like the suburbs, be dependent on the city for employment opportunities and could therefore be situated in presently rural areas.

To be sure, white middle-class suburbanites and rural residents are not likely to welcome nonwhite low-income people into their communities, even if the latter are no longer clearly labeled as poor. The opposition to be expected in city neighborhoods chosen for mixed-income projects would be multiplied a hundredfold in outlying areas. Being politically autonomous, and having constituencies who are not about to support measures that will threaten their security or status in the slightest, the suburbs possess the political power to keep the rehousing program out of their own vacant lots, even if they cannot stop the federal legislation that would initiate it. On the other hand, experience with the federal highway program and with urban renewal itself has demonstrated that few communities can afford to turn down large amounts of federal money. For instance, New York City is likely to build a Lower Manhattan Expressway in the teeth of considerable local opposition, if only because the federal government will pay 90 per cent of the cost and thus bring a huge sum into the city coffers. If the rehousing program were sufficiently large to put a sizable mixed-income project in every community, and if the federal government were to pick up at least 90 per cent of the tab, while also strengthening the appeal of the program by helping to solve present transportation, school, and tax problems in the suburbs, enough political support might be generated to overcome the objections of segregationist and class-conscious whites.

Yet even if the outlying areas could be persuaded to co-operate, it is not at all certain that slum dwellers would leave the city. Urban-renewal experience has shown that for many slum dwellers there are more urgent needs than good housing. One is employment, and most of the opportunities for unskilled or semiskilled work are in the city. Another is money, and some New York City slum residents recently refused to let the government inspect, much less repair, their buildings because they would lose the rent reductions they had received previously. If leaving the city meant higher rents, more limited access to job possibilities, and also separation from people and institutions which give them stability, some slum residents might very well choose overcrowding and dilapidation as the lesser of two evils.

These problems would have to be considered in planning a rehousing program beyond the city limits. The current exodus of industry from the city would, of course, make jobs available to the new suburbanites. The trouble is that the industries now going into the suburbs, or those that would probably be attracted to the new towns, are often precisely the ones which use the most modern machinery and the fewest unskilled workers. Thus, our rehousing plan comes up against the same obstacle—the shortage of jobs—that has frustrated other programs to help the low-income population and that will surely defeat the War on Poverty in its present form. Like so many other programs, rehousing is finally seen to depend on a step that American society is as yet unwilling to take: the deliberate creation of new jobs by government action. The building of new towns especially would have to be co-ordinated with measures aimed at attracting private industry to employ the prospective residents, at creating other job opportunities, and at offering intensive training for the unskilled after they have been hired. If they are not sure of a job before they leave the city, they simply will not leave.

The same social and cultural inhibitions that make slum residents hesitant to move into a mixed-income project in the city would, of course, be even stronger when it came to moving out of the city. These inhibitions might be relaxed by moving small groups of slum residents en masse or by getting those who move first to encourage their neighbors to follow. In any case, new social institutions and community facilities would have to be developed to help the erstwhile slum dweller feel comfortable in his new community, yet without labeling him as poor.

Despite its many virtues, a rehousing program based on the use of vacant land on either side of the city limits would not immediately clear the slums. Given suburban opposition and the occupational and social restraints on the slum dwellers themselves, it can be predicted that if such a program were set in motion it would be small in size and would pull out only the upwardly mobile—particularly the young people with stable families and incomes—who are at best a sizable minority among the poor. What can be done now to help the rest leave the slums?

The best solution is a public effort to encourage their moving into existing neighborhoods within the city and in older suburbs just beyond the city limits. Indeed, a direct rent subsidy like that now given to relocatees could enable people to obtain decent housing in these areas. This approach has several advantages. It would allow low-income people to be close to jobs and to move in groups, and it would probably attract the unwed mother who wanted to give her children a better chance in life. It would also be cheaper than building new housing, although the subsidies would have to be large enough to discourage low-income families from overcrowding—and thus deteriorating—the units in order to save on rent.

There are, however, some obvious disadvantages as well. For one thing, because nonwhite low-income people would be moving into presently white or partially integrated areas, the government would in effect be encouraging racial invasion. This approach would thus have the effect of pushing the white and middle-income people further toward the outer edge of the city or into the suburbs. Although some whites might decide to stay, many would surely want to move, and not all would be able to afford to do so. It would be necessary to help them with rent subsidies as well; indeed, they might become prospective middle-income tenants for rehousing projects on vacant land.

Undoubtedly, all this would bring us closer to the all-black city that has already been predicted. For this reason alone, a scheme that pushes the whites further out can be justified only when combined with a rehousing program on vacant land that would begin to integrate the suburbs. But even that could not prevent a further racial imbalance between cities and suburbs.

Yet would the predominantly nonwhite city really be so bad? It might be for the middle class which needs the jobs, shops, and culture that the city provides. Of course, the greater the suburban exodus, the more likely it would become that middle-class culture would also move to the suburbs. This is already happening in most American cities—obvious testimony to the fact that culture (at least of the middle-brow kind represented by tent theaters and art movie houses) does not need the city in order to flourish; and the artists who create high culture seem not to mind living among the poor even now.

Nonwhite low-income people might feel more positive about a city in which they were the majority, for if they had the votes, municipal services would be more attuned to their priorities than is now the case. To be sure, if poor people (of any color) were to dominate the city, its tax revenues would decrease even further, and cities would be less able than ever to supply the high-quality public services that the low-income population needs so much more urgently than the middle class. Consequently, new sources of municipal income not dependent on the property tax would have to be found; federal and state grants to cities (like those already paying half the public-school costs in several states) would probably be the principal form. Even under present conditions, in fact, new sources of municipal income must soon be located if the cities are not to collapse financially.

If nonwhites were to leave the slums en masse, new ghettos would eventually form in the areas to which they would move. Although this is undesirable by conventional liberal standards, the fact is that many low-income Negroes are not yet very enthusiastic about living among white neighbors. They do not favor segregation, of course; what they want is a free choice and then the ability to select predominantly nonwhite areas that are in better shape than the ones they live in now. If the suburbs were opened to nonwhites—to the upwardly mobile ones who want integration now—free choice would become available. If the new ghettos were decent neighborhoods with good schools, and if their occupants had jobs and other opportunities to bring stability into their lives, they would be training their children to want integration a generation hence.

In short, then, a workable rehousing scheme must provide new housing on both sides of the city limits for the upwardly mobile minority and encouragement to move into older areas for the remainder. If, in these ways, enough slum dwellers could be enabled and induced to leave the slums, it would then be possible to clear or rehabilitate the remaining slums. Once slum areas were less crowded and empty apartments were going begging, their profitability and market value would be reduced and urban renewal could take place far more cheaply and quickly. Relocation would be less of a problem, and with land values down, rebuilding and rehabilitation could be carried out to fit the resources of the low-income people who needed or wanted to remain in the city. A semi-suburban style of living that would be attractive to the upper-middle class could also be provided.

At this point, it would be possible to begin to remake the inner city into what it must eventually become: the hub of a vast metropolitan complex of urban neighborhoods, suburbs, and new towns in which the institutions and functions that have to be at the center—the specialized business districts, the civil and cultural facilities, and the great hospital complexes and university campuses—would be located.

Even in such a city, there would be slums—for people who wanted to live in them, for the clinical poor who would be unable to make it elsewhere, and for rural newcomers who would become urbanized in them before moving on. But it might also be possible to relocate many of these in a new kind of public housing in which quasi communities would be established to help those whose problems were soluble and to provide at least decent shelter for those who cannot be helped except by letting them live without harassment until we learn how to cure mental illness, addiction, and other forms of self-destructive behavior.

V

This massive program has much to recommend it, but we must clearly understand that moving the low-income population out of the slums would not eliminate poverty or the other problems that stem from it. A standard dwelling unit can make life more comfortable, and a decent neighborhood can discourage some antisocial behavior, but by themselves, neither can effect radical transformations. What poor people need most is decent incomes, proper jobs, better schools, and freedom from racial and class discrimination. Indeed, if the choice were between a program solely dedicated to rehousing and a program that kept the low-income population in the city slums for another generation but provided for these needs, the latter would be preferable, for it would produce people who were able to leave the slums under their own steam. Obviously, the ideal approach is one that co-ordinates the elimination of slums with the reduction of poverty.

As I have been indicating, an adequate rehousing program would be extremely costly and very difficult to carry out. But its complexity and expense can both be justified, however, on several grounds. Morally, it can be argued that no one in the Great Society should have to live in a slum, at least not involuntarily.

From a political point of view, it is urgently necessary to begin integrating the suburbs, and to improve housing conditions in the city before the latter becomes an ominous ghetto of poor and increasingly angry Negroes and Puerto Ricans and the suburbs become enclaves of affluent whites who commute fearfully to a downtown bastion of stores and offices. If the visible group tensions of recent years are allowed to expand and sharpen, another decade may very well see the beginning of open and often violent class and race warfare.

But the most persuasive argument for a rehousing program is economic. Between 50 and 60 per cent of building costs go into wages and create work for the unskilled who are now increasingly unemployable elsewhere. A dwelling unit that costs $15,000 would thus provide as much as $9,000 in wages—one and a half years of respectably paid employment for a single worker. Adding four and a half million new low-cost housing units to rehouse half of those in substandard units in 1960 would provide almost seven million man-years of work, and the subsequent renewal of these and other substandard units yet more. Many additional jobs would also be created by the construction and operation of new shopping centers, schools, and other community facilities, as well as the highways and public transit systems that would be needed to serve the new suburbs and towns. If precedent must be cited for using a housing program to create jobs, it should be recalled that public housing was started in the Depression for precisely this reason.

The residential building industry (and the real-estate lobby) would have to be persuaded to give up their stubborn resistance to government housing programs, but the danger of future underemployment, and the opportunity of participating profitably in the rehousing scheme, should either convert present builders or attract new ones into the industry. As for the building-trades unions, they have always supported government housing programs, but they have been unwilling to admit nonwhites to membership. If, however, the rehousing effort were sizable enough to require many more workers than are now in the unions, the sheer demand for labor—and the enforcement of federal nondiscriminatory hiring policies for public works—would probably break down the color barriers without much difficulty.

While the federal government is tooling up to change the urban-renewal program into a rehousing scheme, it should also make immediate changes in current renewal practices to remove their economic and social cost from the shoulders of the slum dwellers. Future projects should be directed at the clearance of really harmful slums, instead of taking units that are run down but not demonstrably harmful out of the supply of low-cost housing, especially for downtown revitalization and other less pressing community-improvement schemes. Occupants of harmful slums, moreover, ought to be rehoused in decent units they can afford. For this purpose, more public housing and 221 (d) (3) projects must be built, and relocation and rent-assistance payments should be increased to eliminate the expense of moving for the slum dweller. Indeed, the simplest way out of the relocation impasse is to give every relocatee a sizable grant, like the five hundred dollars to one thousand dollars paid by private builders in New York City to get tenants out of existing structures quickly and painlessly. Such a grant is not only a real incentive to relocatees but a means of reducing opposition to urban renewal. By itself, however, it cannot reduce the shortage of relocation housing. Where such housing now exists in plentiful supply, renewal ought to move ahead more quickly, but where there is a shortage that cannot be appreciably reduced, it would be wise to eliminate or postpone clearance and rehabilitation projects that require a large amount of relocation.

VI

Nothing is easier than to suggest radical new programs to the over-worked and relatively powerless officials of federal and local renewal agencies who must carry out the present law, badly written or not, and who are constantly pressured by influential private interests to make decisions in their favor. Many of these officials are as unhappy with what urban renewal has wrought as their armchair critics and would change the program if they could—that is, if they received encouragement from the White House, effective support in getting new legislation through Congress, and, equally important, political help at city halls to incorporate these innovations into local programs. But it should be noted that little of what I have suggested is very radical, for none of the proposals involves conflict with the entrenched American practice of subsidizing private enterprise to carry out public works at a reasonable profit. The proposals are radical only in demanding an end to our no less entrenched practice of punishing the poor. Yet they also make sure that middle-class communities are rewarded financially for whatever discomfort they may have to endure.

Nor are these suggestions very new. Indeed, in March 1965 President Johnson sent a housing message to Congress which proposes the payment of rent subsidies as the principal method for improving housing conditions. It also requests federal financing of municipal services for tax-starved communities and aid toward the building of new towns. These represent bold and desirable steps toward the evolution of a federal rehousing program. Unfortunately, however, the message offers little help to those who need it most. Slum dwellers may be pleased that there will be no increase in urban-renewal activity and that relocation housing subsidies and other grants are being stepped up. But no expansion of public housing is being requested, and to make matters worse, the new rent subsidies will be available only to households above the income limits for public housing. Thus, the President's message offers no escape for the mass of the nonwhite low-income population from the ghetto slums; in fact it threatens to widen the gap between such people and the lower-middle-income population which will be eligible for rent subsidies.

On the other hand, as in the case of the War on Poverty, a new principle of government responsibility in housing is being established, and evidently the President's strategy is to obtain legislative approval for the principle by combining it with a minimal and a minimally controversial program for the first year. Once the principle has been accepted, however, the program must change quickly. It may have taken fifteen years for urban renewal even to begin providing some relief to the mass of slum dwellers, but it cannot take that long again to become a rehousing scheme that will give them significant help. The evolution of federal policies can no longer proceed in the leisurely fashion to which politicians, bureaucrats, and middle-class voters have become accustomed, for unemployment, racial discrimination, and the condition of our cities are becoming ever more critical problems, and those who suffer from them are now considerably less patient than they have been in the past.

NOTES

1. Charles Abrams, *The City is the Frontier* (New York: Harper and Row, 1965); Scott Greer, *Urban Renewal and American Cities* (Indianapolis: Bobbs Merrill, 1965).
2. Cambridge: Massachusetts Institute of Technology Press, 1964.
3. "The Housing of Relocated Families," *Journal of the American Institute of Planners*, XXX (November 1964), 266–286. This paper also reviews all other relocation research and is a more reliable study of the consequences of renewal than Anderson's work.
4. Marc Fried, "Grieving for a Lost Home," in Leonard J. Duhl, ed., *The Urban Condition* (New York: Basic Books, 1963), pp. 151–171.

19

The Federal Role in
Solving Urban Problems

I. The real causes of the urban crisis

Cities today have many critical problems, but two are uppermost: poverty and segregation. My studies have convinced me that the urban crisis is that our cities are becoming the major place of residence for poor Americans, many of them nonwhite. I argue that this is *the* urban crisis partly because poverty amidst affluence, and segregation in a democracy, are social evils, but also because poverty and segregation cause, directly or indirectly, all the other problems of the city.

Poverty and segregation are the basic causes of slums, for when people cannot afford to pay for decent housing and are kept out of some areas by their color, they cannot help but live in overcrowded circumstances in the oldest and least desirable buildings of the city. And when men are unemployed or underemployed, whatever their race, they cannot play their proper familial roles, and this results in the broken families, illegitimacy, and welfare dependency currently found in both white and nonwhite poor families. Poverty and segregation breed despair and alienation, feelings of hopelessness that are soon translated into actions that then become social problems. Youngsters who see their elders without jobs or who discover that segregation means poor jobs even for the educated have little incentive to learn; they become school dropouts. Despair and hopelessness also express themselves in juvenile delinquency, sexual promiscuity, and crime, as well as in pathological forms of escape—mental illness, alcoholism, and drug addiction—and the latter leads directly to yet more crime. Recently, despair has also produced rioting and looting, violence and property destruction.

A slightly abridged version of my testimony to the "Ribicoff Committee on the crisis of the cities," December 8, 1966. The full statement appears in *The Federal Role in Urban Affairs,* Hearings Before the Subcommittee on Executive Reorganization, Committee on Government Operations, U.S. Senate, 89th Congress (Washington: Government Printing Office, 1967), Part 11, pp. 2400–2417.

These consequences of poverty and segregation are costly for the people who are driven to despairing behavior, for their fellow citizens, and for their communities. Poor people do not want to become school dropouts, unwed mothers, drug addicts, or rioters; they are literally forced into self-destructive and antisocial acts because, seeing no other choice, they grow desperate. These acts make for unsafe neighborhoods and streets, particularly in the slums, but also in more affluent neighborhoods. Our institutional ways of coping with desperate acts and desperate people —public welfare payments, police protection, prisons and rehabilitation centers, mental hospitals and addiction-treatment centers, among others —are expensive and must be funded from the public treasury, even though the poor people whom they "serve" pay little in taxes. An increase in the number of poor city dwellers thus means lower tax receipts and at the same time more costly municipal services. As a result, cities find themselves in financial straits.

Moreover, the spread of slums and of despairing acts by poor people encourages the suburban exodus of more affluent city dwellers, thus causing a further loss of tax revenue to the cities. The exodus also deprives central business districts of their most profitable customers, thus creating problems for downtown. And the more the cities become the home of the nonwhite poor, the less willing are the suburbs to co-operate in solving the problems of the metropolitan area. They become more resistant to racial integration, oppose metropolitan government and regional planning, and even refuse to participate in mass transit schemes for fear that they will bring in the urban poor. And this in turn accelerates the extent of suburbanization and the problems of physical and governmental sprawl.

In short, there are few urban problems which cannot somehow be traced to the twin evils of poverty and segregation. Moreover, these evils are not limited to the cities. The urban crisis is also a rural one, for many of the urban poor have come from rural areas to escape greater poverty and segregation there. The crisis is thus not urban, but national, both in origin and scope; it has little to do with the city and much more with social and economic inequalities in our society. Indeed, the crisis is, above all, economic, for many of the negative consequences of segregation are in reality the consequences of poverty. It is poverty, not race, that breaks up families, and it is poverty, not race, that creates the fears which drive more affluent whites to the suburbs. These fears are not of the Negro per se, but of the slum dweller, the poor Negro. It is a class fear more than a racial fear—the same class fear that led to discrimination against the Irish, Jews, Italians, and other European immigrants when they were poor.

That the fear is class-based is perhaps best illustrated by the fact that much of the opposition to present government efforts against poverty and segregation comes from people whom I would call the "not-so-affluent"—blue-collar and lower-level white-collar workers in the cities and suburbs who become anxious about the antipoverty program and the extension of equality to nonwhites and express it in counterdemonstrations, violence against civil-rights demonstrators, or backlash voting to force retrenchment in public efforts. If a person, whatever his color, is fearful that he may lose his job to the computer (or to a poorer person), or if he is anxious that the property value of his house (usually an old one) will go down as a result of Negro inmigration or other urban change, he will inevitably feel threatened. This population, which is not half as affluent as we think, also suffers from social and economic inequality, and its protests are also part of the urban crisis. Its problems are less serious than those of the poor, but they are real, and the federal government must help to solve them, particularly if it is to provide political support for a federal program to stamp out poverty and segregation.

Urban poverty in turn is largely the result of unemployment and underemployment—of the lack of jobs and of being eligible only for insecure, underpaid, and dead-end jobs. Of course, some people are poor because they cannot work—for example, the aged and unmarried mothers; but the latter are in this condition mainly because when men are unreliable breadwinners, they have little incentive to marry, and women have equally little incentive to marry them or to stay married. Moreover, many unmarried mothers who raise their children on grants by Aid for Families of Dependent Children would much rather work if they could find jobs and if day-care facilities were available for their children.[1]

Some have argued that the real problems of the urban poor have nothing to do with unemployment; they are the result of slavery or cultural deprivation which has created an apathetic population that is unwilling to work or is incapable of performing on the job. Admittedly, there are such cases, particularly among youngsters, but they are often the result, not of cultural inadequacy, but of two other factors. First, a youngster who has never worked before or has long ago given up the hope that anyone would give him a decent job is frightened, and the slightest sign of failure may cause him to lose hope and to drop out of the job just as he dropped out of school.

Second, and more important, the jobs in which poor youngsters fail most often turn out to be poorly paid or dead-end jobs which under-employ rather than employ them. In a society in which most people expect to have useful and dignified jobs, it should not be surprising that poor people would have similar expectations, and youngsters without family responsibilities may well be uninterested in a dead-end job. Al-though the social and emotional consequences of unemployment are now being recognized, little attention has so far been paid to the consequences of underemployment, even though these may be far worse. According to a finding from the H.A.R.Y.O.U. study, social pathology (delinquency, crime, illegitimacy, and homicide) in Central Harlem was related to and perhaps caused by poor jobs more than by unemployment, particularly since so many more people were holding poor jobs than were unem-ployed. As Kenneth Clark concludes: "Apparently the roots of social pathology in Central Harlem lie not primarily in unemployment [but] in the low status of the jobs held by the residents of the community."[2]

The fact that poor people can perform well in useful and dignified jobs is best illustrated by the experience of World War II, when defense plants hired the poor, the illiterate, the unemployed, and even the allegedly unemployable and put them to work without benefit of elaborate train-ing, counseling, or educational schemes. Moreover, in doing so, the defense plants integrated poor people into the common war effort and thus made them part of American society in a way that we have not yet been able to—but must—duplicate today. Useful and dignified jobs are, after all, the way by which people judge whether or not they are wanted and needed by their society and by their family, and when they are faced with unemployment or underemployment, they realize quickly that they are being excluded from their society and thus turn to despair and des-perate actions. *Ultimately, then, most of the problems of the poor can be traced to unemployment and underemployment, and these in turn are largely responsible for bringing about the crisis of the city.*

It should be stressed that most poor people live law-abiding and re-spectable lives without ever resorting to the desperate acts that become social problems for the city. Most keep their suffering to themselves, expressing it in the prevailing depression that students of slum life have observed or in emotional disturbances that cause pathology in the family, but are invisible outside the home. Moreover, it does not take many people to create a social problem. Only a small percentage of the poor are drug addicts, but they wreak great havoc on themselves and on those from whom they must steal to pay for their daily "fix"—and much of that theft is never reported to the police. Also, only a small proportion of slum dwellers is desperate enough to riot, although the rioters' actions are supported by a much larger number of people who share their feelings, but do not approve of their methods or are just not desperate or foolish enough to risk being arrested or shot at by the police.

II. The goals of a national policy for the cities

This analysis leads logically to the most important goal of future urban, or rather national, policy: *to make sure that the poor, the unemployed, and the underemployed obtain the incomes and jobs that will make them members of the affluent society and entitle them to the rights and privileges and the goods and services which affluent white Americans take for granted.* Once poor people, white and nonwhite, can obtain decent jobs and incomes, they can afford standard housing and will no longer be a captive market for slums and slumlords. Crime, delinquency, addiction, and violence will be reduced drastically; children will grow up in stable, two-parent families and will have the incentive to learn in school and to prepare themselves for a positive future. The cities will derive higher taxes from them; and the central business districts, more free-spending customers.

Moreover, once the majority of nonwhite people are on the way to affluence, they will no longer be so threatening to their white fellow citizens. When they do not need to resort to the desperate acts that stem from poverty, color will no longer be a symbol of poverty, the stereotype of the slum dweller will disappear, and so will many of the current objections to racial desegregation. Nonwhites will be able to move to the suburbs if they wish, and the opposition to a constructive city-suburb relationship will die down.

In effect, I suggest that if unemployment and other causes of poverty can be eliminated, segregation will eventually begin to disappear by itself. This does not mean giving up the struggle for integration, *but national strategy ought to emphasize the abolition of poverty in this generation, so that the children of today's Negro poor will be able to move into the mainstream of American society economically, socially, and politically. If these children can obtain decent jobs and incomes, so that being nonwhite is no longer viewed as equivalent to being lower class, much of the white support for segregation would begin to crumble. Once color is no longer an index of poverty and lower class status, it will cease to arouse white fears, so that open-housing laws can be enforced more easily and ultimately may even be unnecessary. Real integration could then be achieved, possibly even through voluntary means.*

The crucial question, then, is: How can this strategy be achieved?

III. Programs to end poverty and unemployment

Poverty is best eliminated by having more money, and for poor people who cannot work, income grants are the only solution. Old people can be helped by a significant increase in social-security payments and by equivalent grants for those not covered by social security. Other poor people who cannot work should also be supported by direct income grants, for these are not only a more effective way of reducing poverty than welfare or dependency payments but also less punitive and degrading, and they decrease the feeling of poor people that they are being officially labeled and stigmatized as poor and worthless.

Public welfare payments are based on the assumption that their recipients are unwilling to work and must therefore be "encouraged" by low payments to get off the rolls, by regulations which prescribe how the payments must be spent and how their recipients ought to live, and by investigators who invade their lives and their privacy to make sure the regulations are enforced. In a society where poverty is largely a result of job scarcity and racial discrimination, such treatment is unjustifiable. Dependency programs such as Aid to Families with Dependent Children are equally undesirable because they encourage families to separate in order to obtain payments. Since they are given to mothers, rather than to families, they are particularly undesirable in the Negro community, for they maintain the superior economic and familial role of the mother and thus help to keep the Negro man in the inferior and marginal familial role he has occupied since slavery. A much better solution would be to provide job opportunities for the men and even for unmarried mothers who want to work. And all families would be aided significantly by a national program of family allowances, formulated so as to exclude all but the children of the rich. Family allowances, as Daniel P. Moynihan, Alvin Schorr, and others have pointed out, would help children, whether legitimate or illegitimate, and also provide needed aid to large families among the not-so-affluent who cannot afford to keep children in school or send them to college.

Unemployment compensation is superior to public welfare and A.F.D.C. because it goes to the man of the family, but it is presently too low, too short in duration, and it does not take cognizance of family size. Finally, the minimum wage, which is another form of income subsidy, is also too low, for the people who earn such a wage cannot possibly support a family, particularly in the cities, and those who receive it are in effect subsidizing the more affluent customers of the resulting goods or services. The minimum wage must either be raised or, in essential industries and public agencies which cannot operate at higher wage levels, be complemented by federal wage supplements which function like the recently approved rent supplements. Of course, new jobs will have to be found for those who are laid off when the minimum wage is raised.

Despite the need for family allowances and income grants for those who really cannot work, the most important program for abolishing poverty is eliminating unemployment and underemployment: for providing decent, useful, and well-paying jobs for all who want them. Job training, job counseling, better vocational education, are all necessary, but they are all secondary; as I noted before, when useful jobs are available, people flock to them, and if the jobs pay well enough, they can find their way out of poverty with only little additional help.

Where will more and better jobs come from, particularly in an automating society which no longer needs unskilled and even semiskilled workers in large numbers? One source is in the present shortage of skilled workers. Existing job-training and retraining programs should be expanded to give the unemployed and the underemployed a chance to fill these vacancies. This is no easy task, for job-training schemes work best on site, when the trainees have obtained the job. If they are only promised the hope of a job after they undergo training, they are likely to be less motivated, especially since they have often been disappointed by promises before. The job must be given before training begins, with some guarantee that the trainee will not be laid off for the slightest infraction of rules or malperformance. Some unemployed people need only to be taught new skills, but others have become so discouraged and cynical that they lack the faith in themselves and in their employers that is necessary to perform in and hold a job. Consequently, job-training programs must build in "tolerance," both for the youngster who is doubtful about himself and the job and for the employer who can, after all, not afford to pay a poorly performing worker. Building in tolerance means, essentially, providing enough federal funds to help worker and employer in the early period when there are problems, giving both incentive and time to remain in the program. The opportunity to train for a guaranteed job should be given first to the presently unemployed, but it should be extended also to the underemployed who want better jobs, including people in the not-so-affluent category. Indeed, in the long run, all efforts should be made to eliminate jobs that provide only underemployment, using the blessings of automation to do away with as much of the dirty work of our society as possible.

Another, perhaps more important, source of employment is in newly created jobs of two types. One is "nonprofessional" jobs in what are often called the helping or caretaking services—in schools, hospitals, clinics, libraries, recreation centers, welfare and legal agencies, and the like—which would improve the quality of service by providing trained nonprofessionals to help understaffed, overworked professionals. For example, most hospitals are now run to reduce the work load on their harried staffs, rather than to extend maximum help to patients. Hospital staffs should be enlarged so that more attention—which people need as much as they need surgery, medicine, or nursing—can be paid to patients. Hospital aides can help in this process, just as teaching aides can help teachers with large classes, paying more attention to slow learners.

Nonprofessionals are especially useful in agencies that provide services to poor people, for if the former are themselves poor people, they can understand, communicate with, and help clients more easily than professionals, who are almost always middle-class people. For example, a professional social worker has written about the nonprofessional "indigenous home-makers" hired by New York's Mobilization for Youth:

> Indigenous people could teach professional staff a great deal if the latter were willing to learn. . . . They don't perceive people as problems. . . . I sometimes feel like an inhibiting influence when I go along to introduce a homemaker to a client. When I leave, they break out into their own language and vernacular. . . . Empathy rather than sympathy comes more naturally sometimes to the homemaker than the professional worker.[3]

Many communities, helped by federal grants, are now already hiring nonprofessionals for a variety of services. This program should be expanded greatly, for not only does it raise the quality of public services but it provides highly useful, dignified, and interesting jobs. If such jobs were combined with educational opportunities and scholarships, many high school dropouts may be encouraged to return to school and to prepare themselves for professional careers.[4]

This expansion of nonprofessional job creation should take two forms. First, such jobs should not be limited to the antipoverty program, as is now largely the case, for the work to be done by trained nonprofessionals is needed in all public services, to raise the quality of such services for *all* Americans, rich and poor. Second, the federal government will have to find ways of persuading federal, state, and local agencies to improve their services with nonprofessional aid. This can best be done by developing new concepts of the good school, hospital, library, and the like and by setting federal performance standards for these agencies which would require the use of nonprofessonial workers. In addition, the federal government should provide grants to initiate the process of implementing these performance standards, enabling agencies to redesign their operations and to hire nonprofessionals.

Nonprofessional and other workers are also needed elsewhere. Daniel P. Moynihan has suggested that the United States Post Office restore the twice-a-day mail delivery and create fifty thousand new jobs in the process. Municipal agencies can use aides and researchers for a variety of duties; parks, playgrounds, and community centers could be maintained and serviced better if additional staff were available.

The second type of job to be created is for improving the public facilities in cities, suburbs, and elsewhere. All communities need more schools, hospitals, recreation centers, and parks, more highways and mass transit facilities, to name just a few. But perhaps the most important source of such jobs is in the area of housing and slum clearance and, more generally, in rebuilding our cities.

IV. The failure of urban renewal and public housing as antipoverty programs

We have long believed that clearing slums and providing poor people with good housing and new community facilities alone would improve their living conditions and reduce their poverty. Our experience with urban renewal and public housing has shown, however, that these beliefs are without foundation and that a new housing policy is needed.

No one has yet made a definitive analysis of the urban-renewal program, but the available studies show that in many, although not in all, cities urban renewal tore down slums but could not provide better inexpensive housing to the people it displaced. In cities where such housing was in short supply, the displaced were often forced to move into other slums or into standard housing, but, in both cases, almost always at considerably higher rents.

This observation contradicts the findings of the 1964 Census Bureau study, made for the Housing and Home Finance Agency, which showed, among other things, that fully 94 per cent of the relocated families were relocated in standard housing and that median gross rents rose only from $66 to $74. These data come from an H.H.F.A. summary (the study itself has never been published), but the research has been criticized on several points. First, it surveyed only people relocated by local agencies, and not those who were displaced, thus leaving out the many slum dwellers who flee from a project area when renewal is announced and before the local agency can interview them or offer relocation aid. For example, according to a 1965 report of the New York City Department of Relocation, 47 per cent of the slum dwellers in the Upper West Side renewal project left between the time the city took title to the project area and the start of relocation activities. We know little about the people who flee, but I believe that they are the poorest and most frightened, and most go to other slums. Second, single people were not surveyed, although they are often a third of project populations, and they usually relocate to other slums. Third, the H.H.F.A. summary did not list the cities (there were 132) which were studied, but because the data show that 33 per cent of the people were homeowners even in the slums, it is clear that many and perhaps most of the places studied were small cities and towns.

In some cities, probably small ones with high vacancy rates, urban renewal's relocation program did provide many relocatees with standard housing. In other cities, however—particularly the larger ones, and those with low vacancy rates—the poor were simply shunted to other slums or to other housing for which, thanks to the federally subsidized reduction in the supply of cheap housing, they now had to pay more. As Scott Greer has put it, "At a cost of more than three billion dollars, the Urban Renewal Agency has succeeded in materially reducing the supply of low cost housing in American cities."[5]

Urban renewal was based on another belief which has also been proved false: that the problems of the cities could be solved by luring affluent citizens back from the suburbs in the hope that this would refill the city's tax coffers, recruit new customers for downtown stores, and reduce the proportion of poor people in the city. I have seen no study of how many suburbanites were actually brought back by urban-renewal projects, but my own observations convince me that their number is minuscule.[6] Most renewal projects only enabled affluent people already living in the city to obtain new housing, and with a sizable public subsidy.

Many urban-renewal projects are still being undertaken in the hope of attracting suburbanites, but I am convinced that this hope is illusionary. Most Americans, including those who now live in the slums, want a house in the suburbs, and none of the city's attractions are significant enough to keep them in the city, even in a world metropolis like Manhattan. They can be persuaded to live in the city only if it is made over into a suburb, obviously an impossible solution. City living seems attractive mainly to middle-class single people, and childless couples, and some upper-middle-class professionals with families. The rest of the city dwellers live there to be close to their jobs, because they are middle-aged and older people who want to stay in the homes and neighborhoods to which they have become accustomed, or because they have no other choice. The people who really want to live in the city are numerous enough to fill up the new downtown apartment projects (though not in all cities), but they are too few to add significantly to the city's tax receipts. Ultimately, only sizable federal grants to the cities and payroll or income taxes levied on suburban commuters can provide the funds that cities need. Nor are urbanites numerous enough to change the city's class composition, that is, to make the city a middle-class community (which it never was in the past) in the hope of reducing suburban opposition to metropolitan planning.

Moreover, even if more suburbanites could be lured back to the city, its problems would not be solved. Their presence would perhaps create additional middle-class areas, increase the sales of a few department stores, and add some tax income, but this would not eliminate any of the urban problems that cause poverty, for the poor would still be as poor and numerous as before, and they would still be living in the city. The attempt to bring the middle class back only sidesteps the real problems of the city. Finally, even those cities which have rebuilt their downtowns and have added many new buildings to the tax rolls have not generated enough of an increase in tax income to find the funds to help their poorer residents. New Haven, Connecticut, perhaps the most successful of these cities, is as beset with problems of poverty as it ever was.

Public housing has not helped to reduce poverty either. It provided some people with better apartments before public opposition brought the program to a virtual standstill, but it also demonstrated that putting poor people into good housing is not enough; it does not eliminate their poverty or unemployment and so does not solve their economic, social, and psychological problems. This is no criticism of public housing, for to expect it to reduce poverty is to expect the impossible. A house is only a house, not an agent of social change.[7]

New community facilities alone are not significant either. Opening a clinic next door to a public housing project is a good idea, but the effectiveness of a clinic or any other community facility is not determined by the age or modernity of its building. For one thing, the people who need clinic services most are usually the least likely to enter, because they are frightened by its official aura. They must be persuaded to come, be shown that the staff can and will help them, that the doctor they see can understand their problems and their language, will have the empathy to listen to them—and will be able to see them again the next time they come. They cannot be shunted from doctor to doctor, and they must have money to buy the prescribed medicine. None of these requirements are affected by the clinic building, but only by what goes on inside it.

V. A job-centered housing and urban-development program

Urban renewal and the minuscule public housing program are not the answer: we need a national policy which begins with the assumption that *good housing does not cure poverty, but that curing poverty will enable people to afford good housing.* If poor people can obtain the incomes, jobs, and freedom of choice to allow them to afford decent homes in decent neighborhoods, slums and slum living will be eliminated almost automatically. This ought to be the main goal of national urban policy.

This goal can, however, be achieved in part through a housing and urban-development program, for building and rebuilding houses and community facilities is a labor-intensive activity and will create many jobs, particularly for unskilled and semiskilled people. Consequently, it is possible and desirable to kill two birds with one stone: to replace the slums with good housing and to create jobs in the process—jobs that will help people to move into such housing and into the affluent society.

Some of the new and rebuilt housing should be public housing, preferably on scattered sites, but as much as possible should be exactly the same government-supported "moderate"- and "middle"-income housing that is provided for other Americans, with poor people being enabled to live there through rent supplements. In other words, instead of putting poor people into special kinds of housing, the government should use most of its funds to construct more middle-income housing—and to encourage builders to construct it—and enable poor people to move into it as well through rent supplements to them or to builders.

This program calls for two concurrent schemes: to open the suburbs to some poor and nonwhite citizens and to rebuild the ghettos. Although some have argued that rebuilding the ghetto would perpetuate segregation and that future federally supported housing should be entirely integrated, others have argued that integration is unlikely to happen quickly, that it is principally of interest to middle-class nonwhites, and that if the majority of poor nonwhites is to be helped, the ghetto ought to be rebuilt for them and by them.

I believe that framing the issue in an either-or manner is dangerous and unnecessary; housing and integration are both important goals, and both must be pursued. Rebuilding the slums without integrating the suburbs is wrong, but integrating the suburbs without touching the ghetto means relegating many people to the slums for another generation, ignoring the desire of those who want to remain in familiar neighborhoods even if they are in the ghetto, and neglecting the needs of those who must have access to jobs in the inner city.

Integrating the suburbs is essential, particularly because industries and offices are moving out of the city at a rapid rate, and nonwhite people must have access to these jobs. But building integrated housing in the suburbs is difficult, for the opposition to "open housing" is intense and widespread and is not likely to decrease in the future. There are, however, ways of reducing this opposition. The federal government could make the stepped-up housing program attractive to the suburbs by paying for schools and other community facilities and by offering tax subsidies for municipal services so that suburbanites would receive some relief from rising property taxes. Conversely, the government could withhold school and other funds from the suburbs as long as they are segregated. Moreover, it could provide greater incentives to builders and thus obtain their political support for integrating the suburbs. If the plan to build new housing in the suburbs is massive enough, and builders and suburbs can be given incentives to erect integrated housing all over the metropolitan area, then no suburb can continue to attempt to remain racially "pure." Greater efforts to persuade private enterprise and the unions to integrate suburban job opportunities should also be made; and if all these efforts are co-ordinated, the badly needed federal open-housing requirement, whether by legislation or executive order, would be politically feasible much sooner.

Actually, the white fears over the consequences of suburban integration are highly exaggerated. Until many more suburban jobs for nonwhites are available, the nonwhite families who will be financially able and occupationally secure enough to move to predominantly white areas will be middle-class and will be accepted more readily by whites of equal status. There is considerable evidence that housing integration is successful when whites and nonwhites are both middle-class and the latter are in a minority.[8] Also, there is little likelihood that the nonwhite slum dwellers whom white suburbanites seem to fear will be able or willing to move to the suburbs in the near future in large number. Even if they could afford to do so, many would prefer to remain near inner-city jobs or in or near familiar neighborhoods. Indeed, a goodly number of such people have bought houses outside the ghetto, thus revitalizing older urban areas.

Even though all efforts must be made to hasten integration, probably the fastest and politically most feasible way of providing more employment and better housing to the urban poor is to rebuild the ghettos. This is the intent of the Model Cities program, of the Comsatlike Urban Development Corporation which the President has been asked to establish, and of the Community Development Corporations proposed by Senator Robert F. Kennedy. All three are highly desirable programs. The Model Cities program is at present better in principle than in reality, for the funds now allocated and scheduled are too small to do any significant amount of rebuilding in any ghetto. Indeed, unless the funds are increased quickly, there is a danger that the Model Cities program will fall back on the routine of urban renewal and replace slums with housing for the more affluent, rather than for the poor. Since so little money is being provided to build or rehabilitate housing that poor people can afford, and since rent-supplement appropriations are also minuscule, the Model Cities program may falter, like urban renewal, because of the lack of relocation housing or because local agencies will be forced to rely on private enterprise to do the rebuilding, which means that, as in the case of urban renewal, the resulting housing will be out of the price range of poor people.

When President Johnson first proposed the Model Cities program, he insisted that it must "foster . . . widespread citizen participation—especially from the demonstration area—in planning and execution of the program" and offer maximum occasions for employing residents of the demonstration area in all phases of the program. The proposed Urban Development Corporation would provide the massive funds needed to provide inexpensive housing and ensure the creation of jobs in significant numbers.

Senator Kennedy's Community Development Corporations scheme is more emphatic on the use of housing programs as a source of jobs than even the Model Cities legislation and vests greater control of the rebuilding program with the residents of the slum areas than does the Urban Development Corporation. I am less sanguine than he, however, that "the great financial institutions" will invest their funds readily in Community Development Corporations, at least at the start, and I would question his suggestion that the Corporations "should need and receive no significantly greater subsidy than is ordinarily available to nonprofit housing corporations under present law." I would argue that these Corporations must be eligible for whatever federal subsidy is needed to make them successful, particularly if they are to be organized and managed by ghetto residents.

America's poor have been so often disappointed by government efforts to help them that they have become discouraged and even cynical and are reluctant to raise their hopes once more, for that is an emotionally risky step for people who have to live with constant disappointment. If funds are insufficient to get the Community Development

Corporations off to a flying start and provide no clear evidence that they will improve the living conditions of a large number of people in a foreseeable future, few ghetto residents will have incentive to participate in or support the Corporations. Second, and equally important, the ghetto-rebuilding program has to be massive, whether done by Model Cities, the Urban Development Corporation, or the Community Development Corporations, so that enough jobs are created to make significant inroads on unemployment and underemployment—and so that the building trades unions can be motivated to integrate.

Moreover, building funds should be allocated so as to maximize the number of jobs, rather than to encourage the housing industry (and other industries interested in building housing) to develop new construction technologies that would lead to automated factories and a minimal number of new jobs. Modern methods of construction must be brought into the housing industry, of course, but if it is done in such a manner that the federal government only subsidizes the industry's automation, the job-creating efforts of the housing program will be minimal and the Urban Development Corporation will only be building better kinds of public housing to shelter the unemployed, leaving them as poor as before. This consequence must be avoided at all costs.

Rebuilding the houses and tenements of the ghetto is not enough; better neighborhoods and community conditions must also be created, and this process should be, as Senator Kennedy suggests, correlated with the rebuilding program. The usual physical facilities—schools, playgrounds, community centers, hospitals, and the like—which have often been scarce in the ghetto must be built, but, more important, they must be developed with programs, staffs, and client-involvement techniques so that they will address themselves to their areas' needs.

The most crucial such facility is probably the school. Shiny new buildings alone are insufficient; they must also be schools that will enable poor children to want to learn and to learn. This is no easy task, for since its inception more than a hundred years ago, the public-school system has never learned how to teach poor children, mainly because it has not needed to do so. In the past, those who could not or would not learn what the schools taught dropped out quietly and went to work. Today, such children drop out less quietly, and they cannot find work. Consequently, the schools have to learn how to hold them, not only when they drop out physically, but long before, in the early elementary grades, when they begin to drop out in spirit. At present, many poor children, and not only in the ghetto, come to school knowing already from what they have seen in their neighborhoods that they are unlikely to be admitted to full membership in the affluent economy or the democratic society. As a result, they lack motivation to learn, and this motivation is reduced further by anachronistic, irrelevant, or dull curriculums and texts and by teachers who are either too poorly trained or too harried to understand them or to persuade them that they should learn.

The school's task will be much easier if employment programs are vast enough so that the next generation of children will realize they can obtain jobs—and membership in the affluent society—if they are willing to learn. As the Coleman report[9] points out, a Negro child's achievement is highly correlated with his feeling that he can control his own destiny, and that feeling—and the social and economic changes that are needed to create it—will motivate him more quickly and easily than the best curriculums and teachers. Even so, the schools must develop the teaching methods, the teachers, and, equally important, the school "climate" that will help children to learn. Such schools require smaller classes, better teachers, curriculums more relevant to the ideas and aspirations which the ghetto child brings to school, and more decentralized, less bureaucratized school systems which can permit experimentation and innovation, relate the school to the ghetto-rebuilding program, experiment with joint work-education programs, offer scholarships to adult dropouts who now want to go back to school, and even provide training for nonprofessionals working in the neighborhood agencies.

A quality education also means integrated education, for de facto segregated schools are as unequal as de jure segregated schools, and children who do not feel themselves to be equals cannot learn to become equals. In the ghetto, where school integration is impossible, more effective neighborhood participation in the school may help give the children more feeling that they control their own destinies, but wherever possible schools and school-district boundaries must be located so that the student body will include children from outside the ghetto, particularly beyond the early elementary grades. In the long run, however, the federal government must help cities build educational parks—large campuses where children from many neighborhoods can go to school together and programs are designed for the particular needs and strengths of the park's service area. By centralizing facilities, it will be possible to decentralize services and programs, thus giving the students attending school in an educational park the quality education—special classes, teachers, and courses, for example—which cannot be offered in a set of individual schools, set far apart and isolated from one another.

Furthermore, all schools, inside the ghetto and out, must revamp their social-studies programs to give students an opportunity to learn the problems as well as the ideals of American society. If children are to become intelligent adult citizens, white ones need to learn that the myths and stereotypes with which their elders reject the Negro poor are inaccurate, and Negro children need to learn that poverty and segregation are the result of more complex causes than a white conspiracy.

The rebuilt slum also needs nursery schools, day-care centers, and Headstart schools where working mothers and others can send their children to play and learn. It also needs better, cheaper, and more decentralized medical services: an expanded Medicaid program that covers all poor people, plus neighborhood clinics, group practice, and more hospitals. These should offer medical and psychiatric treatment under the same conditions as are (or ought to be) available to other Americans: no waiting lines, a stable and positive doctor-patient relationship, and the necessary specialists. Poverty and segregation have fostered a great deal of emotional disturbance and mental illness, and the services of psychotherapy, now barely available to middle-class people, must be extended to the poor. Neighborhood clinics must be established for this purpose, and less intensive counseling and helping can be provided by psychiatric aides, homemakers, and social workers able to practice their profession, rather than to act as budget investigators. The ghetto slum needs treatment centers for addicts most urgently, both to help the addicts, and if possible to cure them, and to protect ghetto residents from the problems they cause, although if proper help is provided the addicts, they will no longer need to steal or destroy property to pay for their drugs. Many of these facilities could be provided in one-stop neighborhood service centers, which should be constructed as part of the ghetto-rebuilding process and, wherever possible, staffed with trained nonprofessionals from the neighborhood.

Better shopping facilities are as important as new playgrounds, although, again, new buildings are less necessary than stores which serve their customers honestly and equitably and provide opportunities for ghetto residents to go into retail businesses. Moreover, the ghetto needs better police protection and sanitation, more extensive legal services, to be supplied through neighborhood law firms, and, as Watts has demonstrated, better mass transit facilities. Neighborhood municipal offices must be established to create better communication between city hall and the ghetto; and neighborhood planning offices, staffed in large part by residents to be trained in planning techniques, are essential if the ghetto is actually to rebuild itself. Such offices cannot, however, be mere branches of central agencies, for the ghetto must have power to implement its demands, and authority to develop plans for its future.

VI. Helping rural areas and the not-so-affluent

Many of the urban poor escaped worse poverty in rural areas, and most left voluntarily, for the lure of the city's job opportunities is as strong for people in underdeveloped portions of America as for the people in the "developing" nations. Yet some want to stay in rural areas, and others would want to if they could earn a decent living. Consequently, rural programs are needed as part of the urban ones I have described, some to prevent involuntary city migration and help people stay on the land or in small towns.

Programs are also needed for people whom I called the not-so-affluent. Although they are not poor, they have difficulties in coping with the rising cost of living, with increased property taxes, disappearing jobs, and aging neighborhoods. They too cannot afford adequate medical and psychiatric service, and they worry about their children, for with factory jobs in increasingly short supply, these children must be educated for other kinds of work.

VII. Needed resources for employment and housing programs

The economic, housing, and community programs I have suggested as necessary to help the cities are vast in scope and in the amount of effort, money, and innovation they require. It is easy to propose new programs, but difficult to carry them out, particularly for four reasons: little is really known about the city and its problems; the technical personnel needed to develop and carry out most of the programs I have proposed are in short supply; the federal government is not organized to deal in a co-ordinated fashion with what is essentially a single set of interrelated problems; and it has never before been willing to appropriate the amount of money necessary to really solve these problems.

Although goodly sums have been spent for research in agriculture, defense, health, and other governmental activities, almost nothing has been done to study housing and community problems. Urban renewal has now been in existence for over fifteen years, but we still know little about its effects, its benefits, and its costs. We have not measured the consequences of slum clearance on the displaced; we have no idea how many middle-class people have actually been lured back to the city; and we do not even know how much downtown revitalization can be credited to urban-renewal activities. We debate the virtues of integration versus ghetto rebuilding, but we do not know how many ghetto residents want better housing while remaining in their present neighborhoods, how many want to live in urban areas beyond the ghetto, and how many want to move to the suburbs—or how many can afford any of these options. We know even fewer basic facts about the poor and the Negro populations: how many of them are permanently poor, and how many are just caught in a temporary squeeze. Nor do we know how much the exodus of white families to the suburbs is caused by racial change and racial fears, and how much by the desire to live in low-density new single-family houses that are normally available only in the suburbs. We do not know how many white families leave because of the quality of urban schools, or what kinds of schools would persuade them to stay. In short, we know equally little about the needs and wants of more affluent citizens.

Market researchers know pretty well who likes what kind of soap or aspirin, and the manufacturers of consumer products would not think of planning for their future production without such information; but government, federal, state, and local, knows almost nothing about the citizens for whom it plans and about needs which are much more important than soap or aspirin. And while there are ratings for every last television program, governments have no "ratings" for their "programs"; they must infer from election results how well these appeal to the "audience." We do not know how government programs really affect people at the grass-roots level or whether they ever reach those grass roots. We build elaborate legislative and administrative safeguards into government programs against graft and corruption, but we rarely include research and evaluation techniques to make sure that these programs achieve the goals intended by legislation.

I am a researcher by profession and have a vested interest in more research. But I am not asking for more research per se or for more basic research, but for policy research, studies framed to answer the questions which must be answered to develop programs for the city and its peoples; and for program experimentation, for demonstrations and pilot projects to test many new program ideas.

A second need is for federally supported training activities to recruit and train the people needed to carry out programs. For example, rebuilding the ghetto slums requires not only masons and electricians but planners, manpower specialists, and job creators, doctors, nurses, psychiatrists, social workers, teachers, administrators, educational planners, municipal specialists, and many more. Both professionals (and nonprofessionals) must be trained to work for and with poor people rather than as experts who tell less-informed clients what to do.

A third need is to develop a federal administrative structure that can deal with the urban crisis in an integrated fashion. I am less concerned about internal contradictions within an agency—for example, that within the Housing and Home Finance Agency, the Federal Housing Administration was subsidizing the suburban exodus while the Urban Renewal Administration was trying to bring middle-class people back—than about the more general tendency of redefining social problems so that they fit the division of labor between the executive departments. This tendency may please the departments, but it often fails to solve the original problem and is particularly inappropriate for the urban condition. If the main problem is urban poverty, then it logically "belongs" to the Office of Economic Opportunity, but insofar as poverty is abolished by income grants, it also belongs to Health, Education, and Welfare, and insofar as it is eliminated by job creation and job training, it belongs as well to Labor, Commerce, and H.E.W. And if housing is to be a major source of jobs, then the problem belongs also to Housing and Urban Development, although the federal housing agency has traditionally been more concerned with producing housing than with creating jobs.

Obviously, the urban problem belongs to almost all agencies in the federal government, and because the parts of the problem are intricately interrelated, attempts have been made to co-ordinate the efforts of these agencies. Co-ordination has not been effective, however, because the problems of the city are so large, widespread, and diffuse and those charged with the task of co-ordinating are so powerless that individual agencies have done little more than pay lip service to co-ordination, and, like all agencies in and out of government, have spent most of their time and money pursuing their own favorite programs.

I have little faith in co-ordination and would argue that because the urban problem is in reality a national problem, it must be assigned to a separate governmental body which has the power to determine the needed programs, and the funds to create new ones where necessary, and can use relevant established federal agencies and their programs to help it. This governmental body could be a co-ordinating agency, provided it had the ability to establish needed new programs and to reformulate traditional programs of other federal agencies, but it must have the ability to shape the programs to the problem, rather than the other way around. Moreover, it must have more power than federal agencies do today to influence local activities; not to dictate to the states and the cities, but to set performance standards which would require them to concentrate on the problem if they are to receive funds, rather than, as now often happens, to divert federal funds to less important local concerns. Admittedly, such a governmental body would have tremendous power, but I can see no other solution if the urban-national problem is really to be solved. Moreover, if the job-creation and housing programs will involve private enterprise and the ghetto neighborhoods themselves, these will be able to provide a large measure of decentralization that reduces the power of the federal body.

The last but hardly the least need is for more federal funds. A variety of estimates suggest that it will take between $100 billion and $200 billion to eliminate poverty, but the federal government and the American people are still looking for magical ways of doing it cheaply. The unwillingness to spend what is needed results in large part from the fact that we have not spent very much in the past, and it is difficult to tear ourselves away from that comfortable tradition. For example, we have known for over a decade that huge sums are needed to replace the slums with good housing, but the federal government still spends less on housing than it takes in. William Wheaton writes:

> The truth is that even in these days of reapportionment, the historic rural bias of our state legislatures and the Congress produces annual expenditures exceeding $5 billion each year for agricultural subsidies, largely directed to wealthy landowners, and literally nothing for housing and urban renewal. The President's budget message indicates that all programs of the Department of Housing and Urban Development *will show a net revenue to the federal government of approximately $100 million this year, as they have in almost every year for two decades.* In sum, nothing for housing and urban renewal, but billions for agriculture, highways and other less controversial objects. [Emphasis added.][10]

Admittedly, more money is spent for the poor than the funds allocated to O.E.O., but much of that money is used badly. The funds spent on public welfare do not reduce poverty; they only keep the poor in their present state. Millions are spent to prevent the import of heroin, but much less on the addicts. Every time a cache of heroin is confiscated, the price of the drug is driven up, and those who need it to exist must then drive up the crime rate, which then in turn requires the hiring of more policemen. It costs no more to create a job for a poor youngster than to put and keep him in jail, but we do too little of the former, and eventually we are often forced to do the latter.

Wiser spending, for programs that will reduce rather than maintain poverty, would help, but much more federal spending is essential. Private enterprise can help more with the antipoverty effort than it has so far, but moral appeals to businessmen cannot overcome the fact that the poor often are—or are thought to be—unprofitable or risky customers, even by government itself. After all, slumlords exist only because no one else has sought to house the poor and because respectable private firms can make money more easily by serving the affluent, particularly when government housing programs have been more inclined to subsidize building for the affluent than for the poor. Nor will appeals encourage private enterprise to create jobs, for we live in an era in which profit and productivity are most easily increased by replacing workers with machines.

I am not convinced, however, that poor people are really such unprofitable customers, except when they are treated as such and then revenge themselves by living up to expectations. Consequently, it should be possible to incorporate the poor people into the same production and consumption markets that serve other Americans, provided they have the jobs and incomes to participate in those markets.

The federal government's role ought to be to initiate and support this incorporation: to make the poor better customers and to make private enterprise better suppliers. Since private enterprise has usually been willing to engage in new ventures when financial incentives were available to reduce or eliminate the risks, the federal government ought to provide the funds needed to start private enterprise in the new ventures and continue to provide such funds until private enterprise can make a reasonable profit by its own efforts.

In addition to providing incentives, however, the federal government should also reduce the temptations that now encourage private enterprise to serve mainly the affluent. It can do so by re-evaluating all of its subsidization activities and by withdrawing its subsidies from those activities which can be carried on by private enterprise without federal help, particularly for products and services to the affluent, who need governmental subsidy less than the poor. Federal funds recouped in this fashion could then be diverted to solving the urban problem. But whatever the source of federal money, there is no other choice but for the federal government to fund and to set in motion the economic processes by which the poor and the cities must be helped. If the federal government will not do it, it will not be done.

VIII. The consequences of federal action and inaction

The opponents of federal spending have argued vociferously that America cannot afford to eliminate poverty, that taxes must be spent on the war in Vietnam, or that they must be cut to retain private initiative; but they have been fighting all government programs which extend affluence to the less fortunate for generations. The money to mount an effective war on poverty and slums *is* available; A. Philip Randolph's *Freedom Budget*[11] demonstrates fully and impressively that these funds can come *just* from the increases in national production, what the Budget calls the "economic growth dividend," in the next ten years.

The real issue is not lack of money, but lack of political support to spend a share of American affluence to abolish poverty. All Americans support the War on Poverty in the abstract, but many are against specific programs as soon as these become effective or endanger existing privileges. Programs to help the poor are therefore controversial, and since the poor are a small and powerless portion of the national constituency and of most local constituencies as well, elected officials have little political incentive to propose or to support programs that are likely to generate opposition from larger and more powerful constituencies: the affluent and particularly the not-so-affluent.

How, then, can the massive expenditures needed to solve the urban crisis be justified, and how can the needed new legislation and programs be made politically feasible? One can argue that these programs are required on moral grounds, but the celebrated American generosity leans more toward charity than toward effective action and typically results in the minuscule federal programs now available; for example, for the War on Poverty or public housing. One can argue also that such programs are needed to save the cities, but the balance of power today lies with the suburbs, and with industry and offices streaming out of the city to join the suburbanites, they have less and less reason to feel that they need the city.

Ultimately, I suspect that an effective program must be justified on practical grounds: that the consequences of not mounting it will be far greater than the costs of doing something. If we as a society continue to promise equality to the poor, white and nonwhite, but continue to do little to bring it about, they are likely to give up the patience and self-discipline they have shown in the past. On the one hand, there may be more family breakups, crime, delinquency, and escape into alcohol, drugs, or mental illness; on the other hand, more group violence: more riots, more looting, and more destruction of property.

Coping with more pathology and violence will, of course, require large sums from the public treasury, even for stopgap measures like those we use today. But more important, the rise in pathology, violence, and public expenditures to control them will create a demand from other Americans for repressive action and for retrenchment in federal antipoverty and civil-rights programs. Whether we call it backlash or, with Louis Levine, "the opportunity for the fearful and hostile white to 'legitimately' reveal his bias,"[12] they will demand an end to federal efforts until Negroes stop engaging in desperate acts. But such demands can only generate more Negro hostility, and these will in turn produce yet more pathology and violence.

I believe that we are now at the beginning of such a process, and if it is permitted to continue, the country may be caught in a vicious circle that will spiral and escalate, until eventually America will be divided into a small but growing pathology-ridden and hostile "underclass" and a fearful and revenge-seeking majority, one predominantly Negro, the other mainly white. If this happens, American life may be marked by recurring riots, by full-fledged class warfare between the haves and the have-nots. Then the taste of affluence will be bitter, and the American way of life will not be worth living even for the rich.

NOTES

1. Helen I. Safa, *Profiles in Poverty* (Syracuse: Youth Development Center, 1966—mimeographed).
2. Harlem Youth Opportunities Unlimited, *Youth in the Ghetto* (New York: H.A.R.Y.O.U., 1964), p. 159. The correlation between social pathology and unemployment was only .07, but between pathology and unskilled workers, it was .64.
3. From an unpublished memorandum by Gertrude Goldberg, quoted in Frank Riessman, *The Revolution in Social Work: The New Nonprofessional* (New York: Mobilization for Youth, November 1963—mimeographed), pp. 26, 35.
4. Arthur Pearl and Frank Riessman, *New Careers for the Poor* (New York: Free Press, 1965).
5. Scott Greer, *Urban Renewal and American Cities* (Indianapolis: Bobbs Merrill, 1965), p. 3.
6. It is perhaps not coincidental that such a study has not been made.
7. Lee Rainwater, "Fear and the House as Haven," *Journal of the American Institute of Planning,* XXXII (January 1966), 23–31.
8. See, for example, Housing and Home Finance Agency, *Equal Opportunity in Housing* (Washington: Government Printing Office, June 1964).
9. James S. Coleman, *et al., Equality of Educational Opportunity* (Washington: Government Printing Office, 1966)
10. "Comments on the Demonstration Cities Program," *Journal of the American Institute of Planners,* XXXII (November 1966), 368.
11. *A 'Freedom Budget' for all Americans* (New York: A. Philip Randolph Institute, October 1966).
12. Louis Levine, *The Racial Crisis: Two Suggestions for a National Program* (New York: Center for Research and Education in American Liberties, Columbia University, 1966—mimeographed), p. 12.

Part V THE RACIAL CRISIS

Introduction

Although I believe that the elimination of poverty has to precede the total elimination of segregation, because white Americans will not accept residential integration until the majority of blacks are as affluent as they, it is impossible to discuss the two evils separately. Logically speaking, therefore, Part V is only a continuation of Part IV.

Still, for a variety of reasons, most of them political, the low income urban Negro is the primary target population of the War on Poverty. The next four chapters discuss various aspects of his life and problems, but they also deal with one of the more heated theoretical and policy debates among poverty warriors: whether the underclass status of the Negro is an outgrowth of socioeconomic or cultural factors. Advocates of the socioeconomic explanation argue that black deprivation results from the economy's lack of need for unskilled workers and the society's opposition to racial integration. The advocates of the cultural explanation stress that deprivation results from Negro culture and personality, that slavery and generations of poverty since Emancipation have created social and psychological inadequacies which prevent the Negro from participating in the post-industrial economy and society. The two explanations have significant policy implications: the former would deal with the problem by creating new sources of jobs and income and by attacking segregation; the latter would emphasize programs to acculturate or enculturate the Negro poor.

There is some truth in both explanations but in order to develop viable policy proposals, it is necessary to determine which explanation is more accurate, and how socioeconomic and cultural factors interact. If cultural factors are more important, then the best economic and social policies will falter, but if economic factors are more important, then resources should not be wasted on cultural programs.

As a sociologist, I had been trained to study the noneconomic factors in human behavior, and much of my prior research had been devoted to the role of culture in society. Consequently, I had struggled over this debate even before the advent of the War on Poverty, when I was writing the final draft of *The Urban Villagers* in 1961. Although that book presented a cultural analysis—albeit of a working class rather than a poverty-stricken (or lower-class) population—I hesitated to accept cultural explanations for the West Enders' behavior. Instead I argued (particularly in Chapter 10) that behavior was always a response both to current economic and other opportunities and to cultural norms, but that these norms themselves grew out of past opportunities and that behavior change could be achieved best by improving present opportunities.

This resolution of the debate was already implicit in the paper on the human renewal projects (Chapter 16), but I made it explicit when I began to write about the so-called Negro problem. My first effort, an anxious letter in August 1964 to Richard Goodwin, Special Assistant to President Johnson, was impelled by newspaper articles about the then unpublished "Moynihan Report," which were suggesting that the Report might encourage a shift of federal policies away from economic programs and to social and cultural efforts to alter Negro family structure. I warned Goodwin that such a shift "could maintain the already overly paternalistic and manipulative ways in which we have been dealing with the Negro problem, and more important, it could deflect attention away from the economic causes of the problem."

When the Moynihan Report was published, and *Commonweal* asked me to review it, I wrote the paper which leads off Part V. Questioning Moynihan's conclusion that Negro family structure is itself a cause of Negro poverty, I suggested that whether or not the Negro matriarchy is at fault, it is only a cultural effect of the lack of economic opportunities for the Negro man, and that the best solution was an antipoverty program which emphasized jobs for men. The original paper described this program in some detail, in the hope that my proposals would be considered by the Planning Session of the White House Conference "To Fulfill These Rights," which was to be held a few weeks later.[1] Probably because of the publication of the paper, I was invited to participate in the Planning Session and to write a memorandum for it, but the high hopes of that meeting were shattered by the controversy around the Moynihan Report.[2]

Without intending to do so, the Moynihan Report probably reinforced a popular white image of the Negro as disorganized and promiscuous. Another white image, of the Negro as hipster, was being given new publicity by Claude Brown's best-selling *Manchild in the Promised Land* and by his testimony before the Ribicoff Committee on the crisis of the city. Chapter 21, written at the suggestion of Nelson Aldrich, editor of the *Urban Review,* questions the numerical importance of the Negro hipster and argues, as does the review of the Moynihan Report, that the average Negro, if he exists, differs from other Americans largely in being poor, segregated, and disfranchised. Were he liberated from these burdens, he would become a typical middle- or working-class member of American society, as Ralph Ellison has long pointed out. This essay also touches on a theme explored more fully in the final part of the book: how a stereotype which is only partially true becomes the basis of people's behavior and is thus made all too true as a self-fulfilling prophecy.

Chapter 22 deals in detail with the theoretical question of how much the behavior of the poor and the Negro is induced by poverty or by culture. The essay was written for a seminar on poverty and was stimulated most immediately by a presentation by Walter Miller, an anthropologist, who argues that the poor possess an independent and viable culture which is far from pathological and which they do not want to give up. Although I shared Miller's opposition to middle-class reform efforts to transform lower-class behavior, I rejected his implication that the poor want to remain poor. The essay explores some long-festering doubts about the usefulness of the anthropological concept of culture for understanding a modern society and concludes that while lower-class life may reflect both poverty and culture, culturally ingrained behavior patterns can be given up provided poor people—who, I believe, want the incomes if not necessarily the life-styles of middle-class America—are offered viable alternatives. The best way to test this hypothesis is to set up experiments which offer poor people jobs and incomes that enable them to escape poverty, and then to study the changes that take place in their behavior and values, that is, their culture.

At the time I was writing this paper, governmental policy priorities had begun to shift; the dominant question began to be how to deal with the annual ghetto rebellions. In August 1967, shortly after the Detroit rebellion, I was asked by a high official in the Department of Health, Education, and Welfare—as were other social scientists—to write him a letter offering proposals to prevent further rebellions. (The term is mine; after the summer of 1967, I stopped using the word "riot.") Subsequently, I rewrote the letter into a short paper, which got into the hands of the staff of the then newly formed National Advisory Commission on

Civil Disorders. Several staff members agreed with my analysis, and I was asked to testify before the Commission itself. My testimony, reprinted in Chapter 23, also included twenty-one specific policy proposals, but since I described most of them in Chapter 19, they are not included in the present version.

As a result of the popular opposition to the fight on poverty and segregation, and the elimination, watering down, or subversion of needed programs by the White House, Congress, and local governments, I have become increasingly pessimistic about the possibility of making significant inroads on the two problems. The final essay, written specially for this volume to serve as a partial conclusion to Parts IV and V, expresses my pessimism and explains my feeling that only a change in the structure of American politics will make it possible to deal with the grievances of the deprived minority.

NOTES

1. Many of my recommendations were similar to those Moynihan had in mind but was unable to include in the Report because the interdepartmental competition in the federal executive branch did not permit him to offer policy proposals.
2. See Lee Rainwater and William L. Yancey, *The Moynihan Report and the Politics of Controversy* (Cambridge: Massachusetts Institute of Technology Press, 1967). The context in which I and others reviewed the Report is described in chapters 10 and 11 of that book.

20

The Negro Family:
Reflections on the Moynihan Report

I

In March 1965, the United States Department of Labor published "for official use only" a report entitled *The Negro Family: The Case for National Action*. Written by Daniel Patrick Moynihan and Paul Barton just before the former resigned as Assistant Secretary of Labor to run unsuccessfully for president of New York's City Council, it was soon labeled the Moynihan Report by the Washington officials who were able to obtain copies.

Although not apparent from its title, the report called for a bold and important change in federal civil-rights policy, asking the federal government to identify itself with the Negro revolution and to shift its programs from an emphasis on liberty to one on equality. "The Negro Revolution," says Moynihan, "like the industrial upheaval of the 1930's, is a movement for equality as well as liberty," but the Supreme Court decision for school desegregation, the Civil Rights Acts of 1964 and 1965, and other legislation have only provided political liberty. The War on Poverty, which Moynihan describes as the first phase of the Negro revolution, makes opportunities available, but job-training programs which promise no jobs at their conclusion cannot produce equality. Held back by poverty, discrimination, and inadequate schooling, Negroes cannot compete with whites, so that "equality of opportunity almost insures inequality of results."

Federal policies must therefore be devised to provide equality, "distribution of achievements among Negroes roughly comparable to that of

Submitted version of a paper which appeared, with slight cuts for reasons of space, in *Commonweal*, LXXXIII (October 15, 1965), 47–51. The present version is reprinted from Lee Rainwater and William L. Yancey, *The Moynihan Report and the Politics of Controversy* (Cambridge: Massachusetts Institute of Technology Press, 1967), pp. 445–457, but Section IV, which deals with program proposals already described in Chapter 19, has been sharply abridged.

whites," for otherwise, "there will be no social peace in the United States for generations."

But according to Moynihan, a serious obstacle stands in the way of achieving equality: the inability of Negroes "to move from where they are now to where they want and ought to be." This inability he ascribes to the breakdown of Negro social structure and, more particularly, the deterioration of the Negro family. The remainder of the report is devoted to an analysis of that deterioration.

Soon after the report was published, President Johnson drew extensively on it for a commencement address at Howard University. He placed himself firmly behind Moynihan's proposal for a policy of equality of results, describing it as "the next and more profound stage of the battle for civil rights," and pointed to the breakdown of the Negro family as a limiting factor. He called for programs to strengthen the family and announced that a White House conference would be assembled in the fall for this purpose.

During the summer of 1965, public interest in both the report and the speech declined as new speeches and reports made the headlines, but after the Los Angeles riots, the Moynihan report suddenly achieved new notoriety, for its analysis of Negro society seemed to provide the best and the most easily available explanation of what had happened in Watts. Demand for copies increased, and the government released it to the press. Consequently, it is worth looking more closely at its findings and their implications.

II

From a variety of government and social-science studies, Moynihan concludes that the principal weaknesses of the Negro family are its instability, its proclivity for producing illegitimate children, and its matriarchal structure. Nearly a quarter of married Negro women are divorced or separated, and 35 per cent of all Negro children live in broken homes. Almost a quarter of Negro births are illegitimate, and nearly a quarter of all Negro families are headed by a woman. As a result, 14 per cent of all Negro children are being supported by the Aid for Families of Dependent Children (A.F.D.C.) program.

Although these figures would suggest that a smaller proportion of the Negro community is in trouble than is often claimed, they also underestimate the extent of the breakdown, for more families are touched by it at some time in their lives than at the given moment caught by the statistics. Thus, Moynihan estimates that less than half of all Negro children have continuously lived with both their parents by the time they reach the age of eighteen, and many legitimate children grow up without their real fathers. As Lee Rainwater points out,[1] lower-class Negro women often marry the man who fathers their first or second child in order to obtain the valued status of being married, but thereafter they live in unmarried unions with other men. Also, many households in which a man is present are nevertheless headed by women, for Moynihan indicates that in a fourth of Negro families in which a husband is present, he is not the principal earner. Perhaps the best illustration of the way in which available figures understate the problem comes from unemployment statistics which show that while the average monthly unemployment rate for Negro males in 1964 was 9 per cent, fully 29 per cent were unemployed at one time or another during that year. Moreover, the rates of family instability among whites are considerably lower and still decreasing, while they are on the rise among the Negro population.

The population which bears the brunt of these instabilities is, of course, the low-income one. Although the proportion of stable two-parent Negro families is probably increasing, "the Negro community is . . . dividing between a stable middle class group that is steadily growing stronger . . . and an increasingly disorganized and disadvantaged lower class group."

In that group, a significant minority of the families are broken, headed by women, and composed of illegitimate children. The Negro woman can obtain either employment or welfare payments to support her children, while the Negro man, saddled with unstable jobs, frequent unemployment, and short-term unemployment insurance, cannot provide the economic support that is a principal male function in American society. As a result, the woman becomes the head of the family, and the man a marginal appendage, who deserts or is rejected by his wife when he can no longer contribute to the family upkeep. With divorce made impossible by economic or legal barriers, the women may then live with a number of men in what Walter Miller calls "serial monogamy," finding a new mate when the inevitable quarrels start over who should support and head the family. And because the women value children, they continue to have them, illegitimately or not.

This family structure seems to have detrimental effects on the children, and especially on the boys, for they grow up in an environment which constantly demonstates to them that men are troublesome good-for-nothings. Moynihan's data show that Negro girls do better in school and on the labor market than the boys and that the latter more often turn to delinquency, crime, alcohol, drugs, and mental illness in order to escape the bitter reality of a hopeless future. The girls are not entirely immune from ill effects, however, for many become pregnant in their teens; but since the girls' mothers are quite willing to raise their grand-children, the girls do not become a public and visible social problem.

The fundamental causes of family instability Moynihan properly traces to slavery and unemployment. Drawing on the researches of Frank Tannenbaum and Stanley Elkins, he points out that American slaveowners treated their slaves as mere commodities and, unlike their Latin American counterparts, often denied them all basic human rights, including that of marriage. More important, the structure of southern slave economy also placed the Negro man in an inferior position. He was needed only when the plantation economy was booming, and his price on the slave market was generally lower than that of the woman. Her services were always in demand around the household—or in the master's bed —and until her children were sold away from her, she was allowed to raise them. This established her in a position of economic and familial dominance which she has maintained, willingly or not, until the present day. All the available evidence indicates that since the Civil War, Negro male unemployment has almost always been higher than female. The gap has been widened further in recent years, especially in the cities, as job opportunities have increased for women, while decreasing for men, due to the ever-shrinking supply of unskilled and semiskilled work and the continuing racial discrimination in many trades. Since Negroes are still moving to the cities in large numbers, the trends which Moynihan reports are likely to continue in the years to come.

Slavery made it impossible for Negroes to establish a two-parent family, and its heritage has undoubtedly left its mark on their descendants. Even so, slavery is only a necessary but not a sufficient cause of the problem. Histories of the nineteenth-century European immigration, anthropological studies of the Caribbean matriarchal family, and observations among Puerto Ricans in American cities indicate that whenever there is work for women and serious unemployment among men, families break up as the latter desert or are expelled. The most impressive illustration of this pattern is a chart in the Moynihan report which shows that between 1951 and 1963, increases in the Negro male unemployment rate were followed, a year later, by a rise in the proportion of separated women.

Underemployment, being stuck in a dead-end job, and low wages may have similar consequences, and Moynihan points out that the minimum wage of $1.25 an hour, which is all that too many Negroes earn, can support an individual, but not a family.

In short, Moynihan's findings suggest that the problems of the Negro family which he sees as holding back the achievement of equality are themselves the results of previous inequalities, particularly economic ones that began with slavery and have been maintained by racial discrimination ever since. The report's concluding proposal, that "the policy of the United States is to bring the Negro American to full and equal sharing in the responsibilities and rewards of citizenship" and that "to this end, the programs of the federal government . . . shall be designed to have the effect, directly or indirectly, of enhancing the stability and resources of the Negro American family," therefore requires a drastic change of direction in federal civil-rights activities.

III

The Moynihan report does not offer any recommendations to implement its policy proposal, arguing that the problem must be defined properly first in order to prevent the hasty development of programs that do not address themselves to the basic problem. While this argument was perhaps justified as long as the report remained confidential, it may have some negative consequences now that the contents have been released to the press. The vacuum that is created when no recommendations are attached to a policy proposal can easily be filled by undesirable solutions, and the report's conclusions can be conveniently misinterpreted.

This possibility is enhanced by the potential conflict between the two major themes of the report: that Negroes must be given real equality and that because of the deterioration of the family they are presently incapable of achieving it. The amount of space devoted to the latter theme and the inherent sensationalism of the data make it possible that the handicaps of the Negro population will receive more attention than Moynihan's forthright appeal for an equality of outcomes.

Thus, the findings on family instability and illegitimacy can be used by right-wing and racist groups to support their claim that Negroes are inherently immoral and therefore unworthy of equality. Politicians responding to more respectable white backlash can argue that Negroes must improve themselves before they are entitled to further government aid, and so can educators, psychologists, social workers, and other professionals who believe that the Negro's basic problem is "cultural deprivation" or "ego inadequacy," rather than lack of opportunities for equality. This in turn could lead to a clamor for pseudopsychiatric programs which attempt to change the Negro family through counseling and other therapeutic methods. Worse still, the report could be used to justify a reduction of efforts in the elimination of racial discrimination and the War on Poverty, watering down programs which have only recently been instituted and have not yet had a chance to improve the condition of the Negro population, but are already under concerted attack from conservative white groups and local politicians.

Of course, the deterioration of Negro society is due both to lack of opportunity and to cultural deprivation, but the latter is clearly an effect of the former and is much more difficult to change through government policies. For example, poor Negro school performance results both from inadequate, segregated schools and from the failure of the Negro home to prepare children for school, as well as from low motivation on the part of Negro children who see no reason to learn if they cannot find jobs after graduation. Even so, however difficult it may be to improve and desegregate the schools and to provide jobs, it is easier, more desirable, and more likely to help Negro family life than attempts to alter the structure of the family or the personality of its members through programs of "cultural enrichment" or therapy, not to mention irresponsible demands for Negro self-improvement.

In addition, it must be stressed that at present we do not even know whether the lower-class Negro family structure is actually as pathological as the Moynihan report suggests. However much the picture of family life painted in that report may grate on middle-class moral sensibilities, it may well be that instability, illegitimacy, and matriarchy are the most positive adaptations possible to the conditions which Negroes must endure.

Moynihan presents some data which show that children from broken homes do more poorly in school and are more likely to turn to delinquency and drugs. Preliminary findings of a study by Bernard Mackler, of the Center for Urban Education, show no relation between school performance and broken families, and a massive study of mental health in Manhattan demonstrated that among whites, at least, growing up in a broken family did not increase the likelihood of mental illness as much as did poverty and being of low status.[2]

Families can break up for many reasons, including cultural and personality differences among the parents, economic difficulties, or mental illness on the part of one or both spouses. Each of these reasons produces different effects on the children, and not all are likely to be pathological. Indeed, if one family member is mentally ill, removing him from the family and thus breaking it up may be the healthiest solution, at least for the family.

Likewise, the matriarchal family structure, with the absence of a father, has not yet been proved pathological, even for the boys who grow up in it. Sociological studies of the Negro family have demonstrated the existence of an extended kinship system of mothers, grandmothers, aunts, and other female relatives which is surprisingly stable, at least on the female side. Moreover, many matriarchal families raise boys who do adapt successfully and themselves make stable marriages. The immediate cause of pathology may be the absence of a set of emotional strengths and cultural skills in the mothers, rather than the instability or departure of the fathers. A family headed by a capable if unmarried mother may thus be healthier than a two-parent family in which the father is a marginal appendage. If this is true, one could argue that at present the broken and matriarchal family is a viable solution for the Negro lower-class population, for given the economic and other handicaps of the men, the family can best survive by rejecting its men, albeit at great emotional cost to them.

Similar skepticism can be applied to premature judgments of Negro illegitimacy. Since illegitimacy is not punished in the lower class as it is in the middle class, and illegitimate children and grandchildren are as welcome as legitimate ones, they may not suffer the pathological consequences that accompany illegitimacy in the middle class. Moreover, even the moral evaluation of illegitimacy in the middle class has less relevance in the Negro lower class, particularly when men cannot be counted on as stable family members.

Finally, illegitimacy and the bearing of children generally has a different meaning in this population than in the middle-class one. Rainwater's previously cited paper suggests that adolescent Negro girls often invite pregnancy because having children is their way of becoming adults and of making sure that they will have a family in which they can play the dominant role for which they have been trained by their culture. Although many older Negro women have children because they lack access to birth-control methods they can use or trust, I suspect that others continue to have them because in a society in which older children are inevitably a disappointment, babies provide a source of pleasure and a feeling of usefulness to their mothers. If having children offers them a reason for living in the same way that sexual prowess does for Negro men, then alternate rewards and sources of hope must be available before illegitimacy can be judged by middle-class standards or programs developed to do away with it. Until more is known about the functioning and effects of lower-class Negro family structure, the assumption that it is entirely or predominantly pathological is premature.

It would thus be tragic if the findings of the Moynihan report were used to justify demands for Negro self-improvement or the development of a middle-class family structure before further programs to bring about real equality are set up. Consequently, it is important to see what conclusions and recommendations emerge from the forthcoming White House conference and how the assembled experts deal with the two themes of Moynihan's report. It is also relevant to describe some recommendations which seem to me to be called for by the findings of that report.

IV

The fundamentally economic causes of the present structure of the Negro family indicate that programs to change it must deal with these causes, principally in the areas of employment, income, and the provision of housing and other basic services. The history of the Negro family since the time of slavery indicates that the most important program is the elimination of unemployment and underemployment. If Negro men can obtain decent and stable jobs, then many—and far more than we think—can at once assume a viable role in the family and raise children who will put an end to the long tradition of male marginality and inferiority.

A second set of needed programs must provide equality of income for people who cannot work or cannot earn a living wage. The program for Aid to Families of Dependent Children, which at present fosters the instability of the Negro family, should at once be replaced by a policy of payments to all families in which the men cannot provide support. By giving larger payments to households in which husbands are present, family stability and the two-parent family could be encouraged. But all present forms of welfare payments ought to be replaced by a single system of income grants, based on the concept of the negative income tax, to be paid to all households below a minimum income, whatever the reason for their poverty.

A third set of programs should aim at equality of results in housing and other basic services. The enforcement of effective desegregation laws would at once enable many Negro parents who can afford to live outside the ghetto to raise their children amid other stable families. A massive federal rehousing program, combined with an expansion of the rent-supplement scheme, would make this opportunity available to yet others, including many female-headed households, struggling desperately to keep their children "off the streets" in order to isolate them from early pregnancy, delinquency, and despair. Until this happens, however, independent steps must be taken to desegregate the schools, so that Negro youngsters can escape the culture of inferiority which is endemic to segregated schools.

Some immediate steps can also be taken to change the female-dominated environment in which Negro boys grow up. While little can be done in the home, it is possible to increase the number of men in schools, recreation centers, settlement houses, and social-work agencies in order to give the boys contact with men who have a viable function and reduce the impression—and the fact—that women are the source of all instruction, authority, and reward in their lives. Adolescent boys and adult men can be hired as subprofessionals for this purpose. Similarly, voter-registration and political-organization programs ought to be supported, for politics is, even in the Negro community, a male activity, and the extension of real democracy to the ghetto would do much to make its residents feel that they have some power to change their lives and their living conditions.

Finally, a massive research program on the structure of the Negro family ought to be undertaken, to determine how and where it breeds pathology and to permit the development of therapeutic methods to aid those who cannot adapt to programs for equality of results. There will be men who are so ravaged by deprivation and despair that they cannot hold a job even when jobs are plentiful, but I am confident that if men can be given a viable occupational role, if family income is sufficient to guarantee a decent living, if Negroes are freed from the material and emotional punishment of racial discrimination and allowed to participate as first-class citizens in the political community, a healthy Negro family structure—which may or may not coincide with the middle-class ideal—will develop as a result.

V

The insistence on equality of results in the Moynihan report is therefore the most effective approach to removing the instabilities of the Negro family. Whether or not Moynihan's plea, and that made by President Johnson at Howard University, will be heeded remains to be seen. The economic, social, and political changes required to provide equality are drastic, and both the white and the Negro middle classes, not to mention the white lower class, have a considerable investment in the status quo which condemns the poor Negro to membership in a powerless, dependent, and deprived underclass. Some change can be initiated through federal action, but the implementation of civil-rights legislation and anti-poverty programs also indicates that much of the federal innovation is subverted at the local level and that a significant portion of the new funds are drained off to support the very political and economic forces which help to keep the lower-class Negro in his present position.

Federal and local officials must do all they can to prevent this from happening in the future, but they must be supported—and pressured—by professional, religious, and civic groups dedicated to racial equality. Also, the civil-rights movement must begin to represent and speak for the low-income Negro population more than it has done in the past, for if the Negro revolution and the social peace of which Moynihan speaks are to be won, they must be won by and for that population.

Yet, inescapably, the Negro problem is primarily a white problem, for the ultimate source of change must be the white population. Of the twin ideals of American democracy which Moynihan describes, it has traditionally opted for Liberty rather than Equality, including the liberty to keep the less equal in their place. It would be hard to imagine a sudden ground swell for equality from the white population; but if it really wants to prevent the spreading of violent protest through race riots and the proliferation of the less visible but equally destructive protest expressed through delinquency and drug addiction, it must allow its political leaders to make the changes in the American social, economic, and political structure that are needed to move toward equality. Unfortunately, so far most whites are less touched than titillated by riots and family break-down and more driven to revenge than to reform when Negro deprivation does reach into their lives. In this desert of compassion, the Moynihan report is a tiny oasis of hope and, if properly interpreted and implemented, a first guide to the achievement of equality in the years to come.

NOTES

1. "Crucible of Identity: The Negro Lower Class Family," in Talcott Parsons and Kenneth B. Clark, eds., *The Negro American* (New York: Houghton Mifflin, 1966).
2. Thomas S. Langner and Stanley T. Michaels, *Life Stress and Mental Health* (New York: The Free Press of Glencoe, 1963), Chapter 8.

21

Negro Problems and White Fantasies

White society uses the Negro "underclass" in many ways: from requiring it to do the needed dirty and servile work to borrowing its music, its hip talk, and even its causes. White students help the civil-rights movement to express their own desire for social change, and the mass media recruit Negro leaders for constant discussions of Black Power, as if the political tribulations of the civil-rights movement existed primarily to provide new debating topics for the predominantly white audience. White educators, frustrated in their attempts to teach poor children, create the "culturally deprived" student, which, although an improvement over the earlier image of the genetically inferior child, absolves them of much of the responsibility of learning how to teach these children.

One of the most enduring white images of the Negro is perhaps that of a hedonistic and violent "stud" and his willing, casually promiscuous girl friend. As James Baldwin has often told us, this image was created by the sexual inhibitions of respectable white society—upper, middle, and working class alike—and has its origins in slavery as well as the nineteenth-century American fantasies about the sexual potency of Italian, Greek, Jewish, and other "dark" European immigrants. That this image of the Negro is as prominent as ever is suggested by the popularity of Claude Brown's best seller, *Manchild in the Promised Land,* which has now been given quasi-official recognition by the author's testimony before the Ribicoff hearings on the crises of the cities. This testimony, which appears in the September 26, 1966, issue of *The New Leader,* entitled "Harlem's America," presents the high lights of his book and additional observations by Arthur Dunmeyer, a friend who did not make it out of the ghetto. Dunmeyer shocked the committee of senators by announcing that he, himself illegitimate, had fathered eight children while still unmarried, the first at fifteen, and that this first child, a daughter, had borne *her* first child at twelve, making him a grandfather at the age of

Reprinted, slightly abridged, from *The Urban Review,* I, No. 5 (December 1966), 2–3.

thirty—thus extending the pattern of illegitimacy over three generations within a span of three decades.

I don't know *The New Leader's* readership, but I suspect it consists largely of educated white middle-class people who do not live in sexual anarchy, but sometimes wish they could and so enjoy reading about it. Of course, Brown and Dunmeyer also pointed out that this way of life was not one of untrammeled choice and endless pleasure, as the white reader often imagines it to be. It seems to me that when a youngster can look forward only to segregation, inequality, poverty, and slum life, however, he (or she) naturally looks for an escape route. One is through education, but only a few Negro children are lucky enough to find a good and sympathetic—or even just unharried—teacher in the crucial early years or to meet neighbors (role-models) for whom education has paid off with a decent job. Other escape routes are less scarce, and according to Brown, the first of these is sex, often followed in later years by heroin. Brown also suggests that the only path to a more dignified way of life is equality—of opportunity and of achievement: freedom for Negroes to have the same choices in jobs, education, housing, and so on that affluent whites take for granted every minute of the day. But for most readers, such recommendations are less exciting than the biography of a life of kicks.

Like all descriptions of a large population, Brown's is only a partial one, true of only a small segment of the whole population—probably less than 10 per cent of Harlem's inhabitants. But when facts are lacking or there is a need for fantasy, the partial truth is often overgeneralized and becomes a blanket description which is projected onto the entire population in order to fill the data vacuum or the need for fantasy. If we cannot have sexual paradise in America, we pretend that all French women are like the characters Brigitte Bardot plays in her films. Similarly, when Negro demands for equality begin to require real concessions from white society, we pretend that many Negroes have become advocates of Black Power—and not in Stokely Carmichael's original sense, but in an exaggeratedly racist one, which enables whites to justify the anxiety and hatred they feel toward the Negroes who are demanding equal rights.

Brown can, of course, be faulted for overgeneralizing, but he is no more guilty than other writers, white or Negro, who have resorted to sensationalism to sell their books; and besides, readers, not authors, make best sellers. Many a sensational book has gathered dust on bookstore shelves. Nor is the overgeneralizing process restricted to white (or Negro) notions about "the Negro"; some Negroes have also developed racist stereotypes of "Whitey," and when adults—of all races—become threat-

ened by their teen-agers, they respond with fantasies of an "LSD generation." Now, fantasies are necessary, and no danger is done if we fantasize
about Brigitte Bardot, but when our fantasies are about real people—
as is the case with the Negro stud, the Black Power advocate, and
"Whitey"—they become social and political realities which are reflected
in people's voting patterns, viz. the current backlash, and then inevitably
in government decisions and programs.

In the same issue of *The New Leader,* there also appears the testimony
of Ralph Ellison, the noted Negro novelist, and it offers another picture
of Negro Harlem: of good and kind, quietly desperate but nevertheless
law-abiding and even puritanical people, whose lives revolve around
the elusive search for stability, security, and dignity; not around kicks, but
around the family, neighborhood, and church. The people Ellison describes are not fundamentalist fanatics, and they are not servile, they are
simply poor Americans, whose children imitate "Batman" like anyone
else's children and who are, except in their color and social-economic
condition, not much different from even the readers of *The New Leader.*
Indeed, Ellison suggests, as he has done before, that centuries of adversity
have made the Negro a stronger personality than the average white,
who does not have to cope with lack of security and freedom and does
not have to repress the constant rage generated by inequality and injustice.

There is much more in Ellison's testimony, and it should be required
reading, but I cite from it only to make one point: that there is no one
Negro, any more than there is one white or one teen-ager, and that any
attempt to create a single image of Negro people (or Negro politics) is
a white fantasy which must immediately be suspect. And lest we—educators, social scientists, and intellectuals—consider ourselves immune
from such fantasizing, we should not forget that it is we who invented the
image of the culturally deprived Negro student; it is we who restrict our
social-science studies of Negro life to topics of "disorganization" and
fail to do the research on Negro society that allows other writers to over-
generalize. Few social scientists have investigated the "organization" that
exists alongside the chaos, and fewer still have measured the diversity of
Negro peoples and Negro goals. We do not know how many Harlemites
live as Claude Brown and Arthur Dunmeyer lived, and we have not yet
bothered to find out.

1966 has become the year of the white backlash, and everywhere
there is retrenchment in the public—that is, white—effort to provide
equality to the nonwhite and the poor population. The backlash is blamed
on Black Power and the summer's riots—even though last year's riots

produced no backlash, and the riots themselves were engendered by the miserly efforts made toward equality so far. The retrenchment is blamed on yet another fantasy, one shared by both races: that we need to kill more Vietnamese in order to cope with China's power in Southeast Asia. But the retrenchment only postpones the inevitable, for as in many underdeveloped countries where powerful whites are getting richer and powerless blacks, poorer—the revolution of rising expectations is on. In a brilliant analysis, Ellison points out that for over three hundred years, Negroes have been resigned to the inevitability of slavehood and its quasi-slavehood aftermath, "disciplining" themselves "not to be provoked," even when they were boiling inside. This resignation and discipline may be evaporating, now that Negroes are being teased—and only teased—with the promises of equality being offered them by the civil-rights movement, the New Frontier, and the Great Society. Because "things don't appear to be happening fast enough," a "crisis of optimism" is developing, and, as Ellison sees it, American Negroes are now deciding whether they are justified in remaining optimistic, in patiently waiting for the promises made to them by the democratic rhetoric to be carried out. The revolution of rising expectations can be diverted, as it is now, by pushing some of the most deprived (and the most hopeful) Negroes into acts of desperation, be they addiction or rioting, but it cannot be stopped.

The senators who listened to Brown, Dunmeyer, and Ellison seem to have divested themselves of their fantasies about the Negro, but no one has yet "re-educated" us, their white constituents. Until this happens our present efforts can only increase Negro frustration and deepen the Negro "crisis of optimism," and this can only spawn more Negroes of the type Brown and Dunmeyer described. The thought is horrendous, but maybe this is exactly what white society wants.

22

Culture and Class in the Study of Poverty: An Approach to Antipoverty Research

I. The moral assumptions of poverty research

Poverty research, like all social research, is suffused with the cultural and political assumptions of the researcher. Consequently, perhaps the most significant fact about poverty research is that it is being carried out entirely by middle-class researchers, who differ in class, culture, and political power from the people they are studying. Such researchers—and I am one of them—are members of an affluent society, who, however marginal they may feel themselves to be, are investigating an aggregate which is excluded from that society. Whatever the researcher's political beliefs—and students of poverty span the political spectrum—this difference in class position affects his perspective, particularly at present, when the new social-science literature on poverty is little more than impressionistic. Consequently, the researcher's perspective is often built on random observations and untested assumptions and may include inaccurate folklore about the poor which he has unconsciously picked up as a middle-class person. As a result, "Social science views [of poverty] inevitably grow out of the more common sense views."[1]

Moreover, poverty researchers, like other affluent Americans, have had to grapple with the question of how to explain the existence of an

This paper was prepared for the Seminar on Poverty of the American Academy of Arts and Sciences and will appear in a book edited by Daniel P. Moynihan, to be published by Basic Books in 1969. I am grateful to Mr. Moynihan for permission to include it in this volume. The paper is a revised version of "Poverty and Culture," prepared for the International Seminar on Poverty, University of Essex, April 1967, and draws on an earlier paper, "Some Unanswered Questions in the Study of the Lower Class," written in 1963. All versions are indebted to the work of Hylan Lewis, particularly his paper "Culture, Class and the Behavior of Low Income Families," in *Culture, Class and Poverty* (Washington: Cross-Tell, 1967), pp. 13–42.

underclass in their society. In a fascinating paper, Rainwater has recently described five explanatory perspectives which, as he puts it, "neutralize the disinherited" by considering them as immoral, pathological, biologically inferior, culturally different, and heroic. As his terms indicate, these "explanations" are by no means all negative, but they enable the explainers to resolve their anxiety about the poor by viewing them as different or unreal.[2]

Rainwater's list is a sophisticated and updated version of an older, more familiar explanatory perspective, which judges the poor as deserving or undeserving.[3] This dichotomy still persists today, albeit with different terminologies, for it addresses the basic political question of what to do about poverty. If the poor are deserving, they are obviously entitled to admittance into the affluent society as equals, with all the economic, social, and political redistribution this entails; if they are undeserving, they need not be admitted, or at least not until they have been made or have made themselves deserving.

The history of American poverty research can be described in terms of this moral dichotomy. Most of the lay researchers of the nineteenth century felt the poor were personally and politically immoral and therefore undeserving. Although some researchers understood that the moral lapses of the poor stemmed from economic deprivation and related causes, most offered a cultural explanation, indicting the non-Puritan subcultures of the Irish and eastern and southern European immigrants.[4] These high-born observers, who were struggling to maintain the cultural and political dominance of the Protestant middle and upper classes against the flood of newcomers, proposed that poverty could be dealt with by ending the European immigration and by Americanizing and bourgeoisifying the immigrants who had already come.[5]

Social scientists took up the study of poverty in the twentieth century without an explicit political agenda and also changed the terminology. They saw the poor as suffering from individual pathology or from social disorganization; they treated them as deficient, rather than undeserving, but there was often the implication that the deficiencies had to be corrected before the poor were deserving of help.

This conception of the poor spawned a generation of countervailing research which identified positive elements in their social structure and culture.[6] Although many of the actual studies were done among the working-class populations, the findings suggested or implied that because the poor were not disorganized, socially or individually, they were therefore deserving.

At the present time, the debate over the moral quality of the poor is most intense among the practitioners of public welfare and antipoverty programs. Today's advocates of undeservingness see the poor as deficient in basic skills and attitudes. Educators who share this view describe them as culturally deprived; social workers and clinical psychologists find them weak in ego strength; and community organizers view them as apathetic. Professionals who believe the poor to be deserving argue that the poor are not deficient, but deprived; they need jobs, higher incomes, better schools, and "maximum feasible participation"—"resource strategy equalization" in Lee Rainwater's terms, rather than just services, such as training and counseling in skills and ways of living that lead to cultural change.[7]

Today's social scientists have debated an only slightly different version of the same argument. Some feel that the poor share the values and aspirations of the affluent society and if they can be provided with decent jobs and other resources, they will cease to suffer from the pathological and related deprivational consequences of poverty. According to Beck's review of the recent poverty literature, however, many more social scientists share the feeling that the poor are deficient.[8] Yet others, particularly anthropologists, suggest that poverty and the lowly position of the poor have resulted in the creation of a separate lower-class culture, or a culture of poverty, which makes it impossible for poor people to develop the behavior patterns and values that would presently enable them to participate in the affluent society.

Although few social scientists would think of characterizing the poor as deserving or undeserving, at least explicitly, those who argue that the poor share the values of the affluent obviously consider them as ready and able to share in the blessings of the affluent society, whereas those who consider them deficient or culturally different imply that the poor are not able to enter until they change themselves or are changed. Walter Miller argues that the poor do not even want to enter the affluent society, at least culturally, and his analysis implies that the poor are deserving precisely because they have their own culture. Even so, those who see the poor as deficient or culturally different often favor resource-oriented antipoverty programs, just as those who feel that the poor share the values of the affluent society recognize the existence of cultural factors that block the escape from poverty.

The ghetto rebellions have, however, encouraged a popular revival of the old moral terminology. The Negro poor, at least, are now seen by many whites as undeserving; they have rioted despite the passage of civil-rights legislation and the War on Poverty and should not be rewarded for their ungrateful behavior.[9] Observers who feel the Negro poor are deserving, on the other hand, claim that the rebellions stem from the failure of white society to grant the economic, political, and social equality it has long promised and that rioting and looting are only desperate attempts by the poor to obtain the satisfactions that the affluent society has denied them.

The poor: neither deserving nor undeserving

Because of its fundamental political implications and its moral tone, the debate about whether the poor are deserving or undeserving will undoubtedly continue as long as there are poor people in America. Nevertheless, I feel that the debate, however it is conceptualized, is irrelevant and undesirable. The researcher ought to look at poverty and the poor from a perspective that avoids a moral judgment, for it is ultimately impossible to prove that the poor are more or less deserving than the affluent. Enough is now known about the economic and social determinants of pathology to reject explanations of pathology as a moral lapse. Moreover, since there is some evidence that people's legal or illegal practices are a function of their opportunity to earn a livelihood in legal ways, one cannot know whether the poor are as law-abiding or moral as the middle class until they have achieved the same opportunities, and then the issue will be irrelevant.[10]

It is also undesirable to view the poor as deserving or undeserving, for any judgment must be based on the judge's definition of deservingness, and who has the ability to formulate a definition that is not class-bound? Such judgments are almost always made by people who are trying to prevent the mobility of a population group which is threatening their own position, so that the aristocracy finds the *nouveau riche* undeserving of being admitted to the upper class; the cultural elite believes the middle classes to be undeserving partakers of "culture"; and many working-class people feel that people who do not labor with their hands do not deserve to be considered workers. Still, almost everyone gangs up on the poor; they are judged as undeserving by all income groups, becoming victims of a no-win moral game in which they are expected to live by moral and legal standards which few middle-class people are capable of upholding. Deservingness is thus not an absolute moral concept, but a means of preventing one group's access to the rights and resources of another.

The only proper research perspective, I believe, is to look at the poor as an economically and politically deprived population whose behavior, values—and pathologies—are adaptations to their existential situation, just as the behavior, values, and pathologies of the affluent are adaptations to their existential situation. In both instances, adaptation results in a mixture of moral and immoral, legal and illegal, practices, but the nature of the mix is a function of the existential situation. Since the standards of law, and even of morality, of an affluent society are determined by the affluent members of that society, the poor are, by definition, less law-abiding and less moral, but only because they are less affluent and must therefore adapt to different existential circumstances.

If the poor are expected to live up to the moral and legal standards of the affluent society, however, the only justifiable antipoverty strategy is to give them the same access to resources now held by the affluent and to let them use and spend these resources with the same freedom of choice that is now reserved to the affluent.

The remainder of the paper will elaborate this perspective, particularly around the debate over class and culture among the poor, spelling out some of the implications for both social-science theory and antipoverty policy. I should note that by "the poor" I shall refer principally to people who have presumably been poor long enough to develop cultural patterns associated with poverty and are permanently rather than temporarily poor.

II. Poverty and culture

The argument between those who think that poverty can best be eliminated by providing jobs and other resources and those who feel that cultural obstacles and psychological deficiencies must be overcome as well is ultimately an argument about social change, about the psychological readiness of people to respond to change, and about the role of culture in change. The advocates of resources are not concerned explicitly with culture, but they do make a cultural assumption: whatever the culture of the poor, it will not interfere in people's adaptation to better opportunities for obtaining economic resources. They take a *situational* view of social change and of personality: that people respond to the situations—and opportunities—available to them and change their behavior accordingly. Those who call attention to cultural (and psychological) obstacles, however, are taking a *cultural* view of social change, which suggests that people react to change in terms of prior values and behavior patterns and adopt only those changes which are congruent with their culture.[11]

Since academicians have been caught up in the debate over deservingness and undeservingness as much as the rest of American society, the situational and cultural views of change have frequently been described

as polar opposites, and theorists have battled over the data to find support for one pole or the other. Clearly, the truth lies somewhere between,
but at present, neither the data nor the conceptual framework to find that
truth is as yet available.

The situational view is obviously too simple; people are not automatons
who respond either in the same way or with the same speed to a common
stimulus. Despite a middle-class inclination on the part of researchers to
view the poor as homogeneous, all available studies indicate that there
is as much variety among them as among the affluent. Some have been
poor for generations; others are poor only periodically. Some are down-
wardly mobile; others are upwardly mobile. Many share middle-class
values, others embrace working-class values; some have become so used
to the defense mechanisms they have learned for coping with deprivation that they have difficulty in adapting to new opportunities, and some
are beset by physical or emotional illness, poverty having created pathologies that now block the ability to adapt to nonpathological situations.[12]
Sad to say, there is as yet no research to show quantitatively what proportion of poor people fit into such categories.

The shortcomings of the cultural view of change

The cultural view of social and personal change is also deficient. First,
it uses an overly behavioral definition of culture which ignores the existence of values that conflict with behavior; and second, it sees culture as
a holistic system whose parts are intricately related, so that any individual
element of a culture cannot be changed without system-wide reverbera-
tions.

The behavioral definition identifies culture in terms of how people act;
it views values as *behavioral norms* which are metaphysical and moral
guidelines to behavior and are deduced from behavior. For example,
Walter Miller sees values as "focal concerns" which stem from, express,
and ultimately maintain behavior. As he puts it, "The concept 'focal
concern' . . . reflects actual behavior, whereas 'value' tends to wash out
intracultural differences since it is colored by notions of the 'official'
ideal."[13] This definition, useful as it is, pays little or no attention to
aspirations, values which express the desire for alternative forms of behavior.

The behavioral conception of culture can be traced to anthropological
traditions and to the latent political agenda of anthropological researchers. The field worker who studied a strange culture began by gathering
artifacts, and as anthropology matured, he also collected behavior pat-

terns. The cultural relativist, who wanted to defend these cultures against involuntary change, sought to show that the behavior patterns were functional to the survival of the group. How people felt about their behavior did not interest him unduly. He noted that infanticide was functional for the survival of a hunting tribe, but he did not devote much attention to how people felt about the desirability of infanticide—or about less deadly patterns of culture.

His approach may have been valid at its time; it was in part a reaction against nineteenth-century idealism which identified culture solely with aspirations and was not interested in how people really behaved. The behavioral view of culture was also a useful tool to fight the advocates of colonialism, who viewed all cultures in terms of the aspirations of their own Western society and were ready to alter any culture they encountered to achieve their own goals. Moreover, the approach was perhaps empirically valid; it may have fitted the preliterate group whose culture had developed around a limited and homogeneous economy and ecology. Tribes who devoted themselves exclusively to agriculture or hunting developed cultures which fitted such single-minded economies. Such cultures gave their people little if any choice; they bred fatalists who did not know that alternative ways of behaving were possible, usually because they were not possible, and this left no room for diverging aspirations.

But such a definition of culture is not applicable to contemporary Western society. Many poor people in our society are also fatalists, not because they are unable to conceive of alternative conditions, but because they have been frustrated in the realization of alternatives. Unlike preliterate people—or at least the classic version of the ideal type preliterate —they are unhappy with their state; they have aspirations which diverge from the focal concerns underlying their behavior. Of course, they can justify, to themselves and to others, the behavioral choices they make and must make, and Walter Miller's insightful analysis of focal concerns indicates clearly how they "support and maintain the basic features of the lower class way of life."[14] Even so, people who are forced to create values and justifications for what they must do may also be well aware of alternatives which they would prefer under different conditions.

For generations, researchers made no distinction between norms and aspirations, and most research emphasis was placed on the former. Lay observers and practitioners were only willing to judge; they saw the behavioral norms among the poor which diverged from their own and bade the poor behave like middle-class people. In reaction, social scientists who had done empirical work among the poor defended their behavioral norms as adaptations to their existential situation or as an independent culture, but paid little attention to aspirations diverging from these norms. Walter Miller has taken perhaps the most extreme position; he implies that lower-class aspirations as well as norms are different from those of the rest of society, and if poor people express middle-class values, they do so only because they are expected to endorse the "official ideals."[15] Their real aspirations, he seems to suggest, are those of their own lower-class culture.

Recent research has begun, however, to distinguish between aspirations and behavioral norms. Starting with a debate among anthropologists over whether Caribbean lower-class couples in "living" or consensual relationships preferred formal marriage, several studies have shown that poor people share many of the aspirations of the affluent society, but also develop norms which justify their actual behavior. Rodman conceptualizes the divergence between aspirations and norms as lower-class value stretch; Rainwater argues that poor people share the aspirations of the larger society, which he calls conventional norms, but knowing that they cannot live up to them, develop other norms which fit the existential conditions to which they must adapt.[16]

At present, there are only enough data to affirm the existence of a divergence between aspirations and behavioral norms and to insist on more research, particularly in areas of life other than marriage. In a heterogeneous or pluralistic society, such divergence is almost built in; where a variety of cultures or subcultures coexist, aspirations diffuse freely. Among affluent people, the gap between aspirations and behavioral norms is probably narrower than among poor people; the former can more often achieve what they want. Even if they cannot satisfy occupational aspirations, they are able to satisfy other aspirations; for instance, for family life. The poor have fewer options. Lacking the income and the economic security to achieve their aspirations, they must develop diverging behavioral norms in almost all areas of life. Nevertheless, they still retain aspirations, and many are those of the affluent society.

Consequently, research on the culture of the poor must include both behavioral norms and aspirations. The norms must be studied because they indicate how people react to their present existence, but limiting the analysis to them can lead to the assumption that behavior would remain the same under different conditions, when there is no reliable evidence, pro or con, to justify such an assumption today. As Hylan Lewis puts it, "It is important not to confuse basic life chances and actual behavior with basic cultural values and preferences."[17] Cultural analysis must also look at aspirations, determining their content, the intensity with which they are held, and, above all, whether they would be translated into behavioral norms if economic conditions made it possible.

The second deficiency of the cultural view of change is the conception of culture as holistic and systemic. When a behavior pattern is identified as part of a larger and interrelated cultural system, and when the causes of that pattern are ascribed to "the culture," there is a tendency to see the behavior pattern and its supporting norms as resistant to change and as persisting simply because they are cultural, although there is no real evidence that culture is as unchanging as assumed. This conception of culture is also ahistorical, for it ignores the origin of behavior patterns and norms. As a result, too little attention is paid to the conditions that bring a behavior pattern into being or to the conditions that may alter it. Culture becomes its own cause, and change is possible only if the culture as a whole is somehow changed.

This conceptualization is, once more, a survival of a now inappropriate intellectual tradition. Anthropologists started out by studying small and simple societies, which may have been characterized by a cultural system whose elements were interrelated. Whether or not this was the case, the desire to preserve preliterate cultures encouraged field workers toward holistic functionalism, for if they could argue that any given behavior pattern was an integral part of the system and that the entire system might well collapse if one pattern was changed, they could oppose the colonialists who wanted to change a tribe's work habits or its religion.

Sociology used much the same conceptual apparatus; it became enamored of such terms as Gemeinschaft and community, viewing these as organic wholes which could be changed only with dire results, that is, the creation of a Gesellschaft and the city, which were described as atomized, impersonal, and dehumanized groupings. Like the anthropological concept of folk culture, Gemeinschaft and the organic community bore little relation to real societies, and although these terms were formulated as ideal types, rather than descriptive concepts, still, they were largely romantic fictions generated by nostalgia for the past and by the opposition of earlier sociologists and anthropologists to urbanization and industrialization.[18] It is very doubtful whether any past society ever came close to being a folk culture or a Gemeinschaft or whether any modern society is principally a Gesellschaft.

The systemic concept of culture is also inappropriate. Modern societies are pluralist; whether developed or developing, they consist of a diverse set of cultures living side by side, and researchers studying them have had to develop such terms as subculture, class culture, and contraculture to describe the diversity.[19] Holistic functionalism is irrelevant too; no culture is sufficiently integrated so that its parts can be described as elements in a system. In modern sociology and anthropology, functionalism can survive only by identifying dysfunctions as well as functions and by showing that cultural patterns which are functional for one group may well be dysfunctional for another.

An ahistorical conception of culture is equally inapplicable to modern societies. In such societies, some behavior patterns are persistent, but others are not; they change when economic and other conditions change, although we do not yet know which patterns are persistent, and for how long, and which are not. More important, culture is a response to economic and other conditions; it is itself situational in origin and changes as situations change. Behavior patterns, norms, and aspirations develop as responses to situations to which people must adapt, and culture originates out of such responses. Changes in economic and social opportunities give rise to new behavioral solutions, which then become recurring patterns, are later complemented by norms which justify them, and are eventually overthrown by new existential conditions. Some behavioral norms are more persistent than others, but over the long run, all the norms and aspirations by which people live are nonpersistent; they rise and fall with changes in situations.[20]

These observations are not intended to question the validity of the concept of culture, for not all behavior is a response to a present situation, and not all—and perhaps not even most—behavior patterns change immediately with a change in situation. A new situation will initially be met with available norms; only when these norms turn out to be inapplicable or damaging will people change: first their behavior, and then the norms upholding that behavior. Nevertheless, the lag between a change in existential conditions and the change of norms does not make the norms immutable.

An alternative conception of culture

People's behavior is thus a mixture of situational responses and cultural patterns, that is, behavioral norms and aspirations. Some situational responses are strictly *ad hoc* reactions to a current situation; they exist because of that situation and will disappear if it changes or disappears. Other situational responses are internalized and become behavior norms which are an intrinsic part of the person and of the groups in which he moves and are thus less subject to change with changes in situation. The intensity of internalization varies; at one extreme, there are norms which are not much deeper than lip service; at the other, there are norms which are built into the basic personality structure, and a generation or more of living in a new situation may not dislodge them. They become culture, and people may adhere to them even if they are no longer appropriate, paying all kinds of economic and emotional costs to maintain them.

The southern white reaction to racial integration offers many examples of such intensely internalized norms, although it also offers examples of norms which were thought to be persistent, but crumbled as soon as the civil-rights movement or the federal government applied pressure to eliminate them. Indeed, there are probably many norms which can be toppled by a threat to exert power or to withdraw rewards; the many cultural compromises which first- and second-generation ethnics make to retain the affection of their children is a good example. Conversely, some norms are maintained simply because they have become political symbols, and people are unwilling to give them up because this would be interpreted as a loss of power. Thus, acculturated ethnic groups often preserve ethnic cultural traits for public display to maintain their ethnically based political influence. The role of power in culture, culture change, and acculturation deserves much more attention than it has so far received.

Not all behavioral norms are necessarily conservative; some may make people especially adaptable to change and may even encourage change. Despite what has been written about the ravages of slavery on the southern Negro, he went to work readily during World War II when jobs were plentiful. Similarly, the southern businessman operates with behavioral norms that make him readier to accept racial change than others; he cannot adhere with intensity to any beliefs that will cut into profit.

To sum up: I have argued that behavior results initially from an adaptation to the existential situation. Much of that behavior is no more than a situational response which exists only because of the situation, and it changes with a change in situation. Other behavior patterns become behavioral norms which are internalized and are then held in varying degrees of intensity and persistence. If they persist with a change in situation, they may then be considered patterns of *behavioral culture,* and such norms may become causes of behavior. Other norms can encourage change. In addition, adaptation to a situation is affected by aspirations, which also exist in various degrees of intensity and persistence and form an *aspirational culture.* Culture, then, is that mix of behavioral norms and aspirations that causes behavior, or maintains present behavior, or encourages future behavior independently of situational incentives and restraints.

Culture and poverty

This view of culture has important implications for studying the poor. It rejects a concept that emphasizes tradition and obstacles to change and sees norms and aspirations within a milieu of situations against which the norms and aspirations are constantly tested. Moreover, it enables the researcher to analyze, or at least to estimate, what happens to norms under alternative situations and thus to guess at how poor people would adapt to new opportunities.

With such a perspective, one can—and must—ask constantly: to what situation, to what set of opportunities and restraints, do the present behavioral norms and aspirations respond and how intensely are they held; how much are they internalized, if at all, and to what extent would they persist or change if the significant opportunities and restraints underwent change? To put it another way, if culture is learned, one must ask how quickly and easily various behavioral norms could be unlearned, once the existential situation from which they sprang had changed.

Moreover, supposing this change took place, and opportunities—for decent jobs and incomes, for example—were made available to poor people, what behavioral norms, if any, are so deeply internalized that they interfere, say, with taking a good job? Answers to this question lead directly to policy considerations. One alternative is to seek a change in norms; another, to design the job in such a fashion that it can be accepted without requiring an immediate change in strongly persisting norms. Since such norms are not easily changed, it may be more desirable to tailor the opportunity to fit the norm, rather than the other way around. For example, if the inability to plan, often ascribed to the poor, is actually a persisting behavioral norm that will interfere in their being employable, rather than just an *ad hoc* response to an uncertain future, it would be wrong to expect people to learn to plan at once, just because jobs are now available. The better solution would be to fit the jobs to this inability and to make sure that the adults, once having some degree of economic security, will learn to plan or will be able to teach their children how to do so.

The prime issue in the area of culture and poverty, then, is to discover how soon poor people will change their behavior, given new opportunities, and what restraints or obstacles, good or bad, come from that reaction to past situations we call culture. To put it another way, the primary problem is to determine what opportunities have to be created to eliminate poverty, how poor people can be encouraged to adapt to those opportunities that conflict with persistent cultural patterns, and how they can retain the persisting patterns which do not conflict with other aspirations.

Because of the considerable divergence between behavioral norms and aspirations, it is clearly impossible to think of a holistic lower-class culture. It is perhaps possible to describe a *behavioral lower-class culture,* consisting of the behavioral norms with which people adapt to being poor and lower-class. There is, however, no *aspirational lower-class culture,* for much evidence suggests that poor people's aspirations are similar to those of more affluent Americans. My hypothesis is that many and perhaps most poor people share the aspirations of the working class; others, those of the white-collar lower-middle class; and yet others, those of the professional and managerial upper-middle class, although most poor people probably aspire to the behavioral norms of these groups—to the ways they are living now—rather than to their aspirations.

Under present conditions the aspirations which poor people hold may not be fulfilled, but this does not invalidate them, for their existence, and the intensity with which they are held, can be tested only when economic and other conditions are favorable to their realization. If and when poor people obtain the resources for which they are clamoring, much of the behavioral lower-class culture will disappear. Only those poor people who cannot accept alternative opportunities because they cannot give up their present behavioral norms can be considered adherents to a lower-class culture.

In short, such conceptions of lower-class culture as Walter Miller's describe only part of the total reality. If Miller's lower-class culture were really an independent culture with its own set of aspirations, its practitioners would presumably be satisfied with their way of life. If they are not satisfied, however, if they only adapt to necessity but want something different, then ascribing their adaptation to a lower-class culture is inaccurate. It is also politically undesirable, for the judgment that behavior is cultural lends itself to an argument against change. But if data are not available for that judgment, the researcher indulges in conceptual conservatism.[21]

Miller does not indicate specifically whether the adolescents he studied adhered to both a behavioral and an aspirational lower-class culture. He suggests that "the motivation of 'delinquent' behavior engaged in by members of lower-class corner groups involves a *positive* effort to achieve states, conditions or qualities valued within the actor's most significant cultural milieu,"[22] that is, that the adolescents valued the behavior norms for which they were rewarded by their reference groups.

Perhaps the Roxbury adolescents did not share the aspirations of the larger society; they were, after all, delinquents, youngsters who had been caught in an illegal act and might be cynical about such aspirations. Moreover, the hippies and other "youth cultures" should remind us that adolescents do not always endorse the aspirations of an adult society. The crucial question, then, is how did lower-class adults in Roxbury feel? I would suspect that they were less positive about their youngsters' delinquent activities, partly because they are more sensitive to what Miller calls "official ideals," but partly because they do adhere to a nonlower-class aspirational culture.

My definition of culture also suggests a somewhat different interpretation of a culture of poverty than Oscar Lewis' concept. If culture is viewed as a causal factor, and particularly as those norms and aspirations which resist change, then a culture of poverty would consist of those specifically cultural or nonsituational factors which help to keep people poor, especially when alternative opportunities beckon.

Lewis' concept of the culture of poverty puts more emphasis on the behavior patterns and feelings that result from lack of opportunity and the inability to achieve aspirations. According to Lewis, "The culture of poverty is both an adaptation and a reaction of the poor to their marginal position in a class-stratified, highly individuated society. It represents an effort to cope with feelings of hopelessness and despair which develop from the realization of the improbability of achieving success in terms of the values and goals of the larger society."[23] His conception thus stresses the defense mechanisms by which people cope with deprivation, frustration, and alienation, rather than with poverty alone; it is closer to a culture of alienation than to a culture of poverty. In fact, Lewis distinguishes between poor people with and without a culture of poverty, and in indicating that people can be poor without feeling hopeless, he seems to suggest that the culture of poverty is partly responsible for feelings of hopelessness. Moreover, if poor people can overcome their malaise and resort to political action—or if they live in a socialist society like Cuba, in which they are presumably considered part of the society— they give up the culture of poverty. "When the poor become class-conscious or active members of trade-union organization, or when they adopt an internationalist outlook on the world, they are no longer part of the culture of poverty although they may still be desperately poor."[24]

Lewis' distinction between poverty and the culture of poverty is important, for it aims to separate different kinds of poverty and adaptations to poverty. Lewis' emphasis on alienation suggests, however, that his concept pertains more to belonging to an underclass than to being poor, while his identification of the culture of poverty with class-stratified, highly individuated societies suggests that for him the culture is an effect rather than a cause of membership in an underclass. The various traits of the culture of poverty which he describes are partly social psychological consequences, partly situational responses, and partly behavioral norms associated with underclass membership, but the major causal factor is the class-stratified, highly individuated society. From a causal perspective, Lewis' concept is thus less concerned with culture than with the situational factors that bring about culture; it is less a culture of poverty than a sociology of the underclass.

Whether or not the families who tell their life histories in Lewis' books adhere to a culture which is a direct or indirect cause of their remaining in poverty is hard to say, for one would have to know how they would react under better economic conditions. Such data are almost impossible to gather, so that it is difficult to tell how the Sanchez and Rios families might respond, for example, if Mexico and Puerto Rico offered the men a steady supply of decent and secure jobs. Since almost all the members of the families aspire to something better, my hunch is that their behavioral and aspirational cultures would change under improved circumstances; their culture is probably not a cause of their poverty.

As I use the term *culture of poverty,* then, it would apply to people who have internalized behavioral norms that cause or perpetuate poverty and who lack aspirations for a better way of life; particularly people whose societies have not let them know change is possible: the peasants and urbanites who have so far been left out of the revolution of rising expectations. The only virtue of this definition is its emphasis on culture as a causal factor, thus enabling the policy-oriented researcher to separate the situational and cultural processes responsible for poverty.

If the culture of poverty is defined as those cultural patterns which keep people poor, it would be necessary to include in the term also the persisting cultural patterns among the affluent which, deliberately or not, keep their fellow citizens poor. When the concept of a culture of poverty is applied only to the poor, the onus for change falls too much on them, when, in reality, the prime obstacles to the elimination of poverty lie in an economic, political, and social structure that operates to protect and increase the wealth of the already affluent.

Culture and class

My definition of culture also has implications for the cultural aspects of social stratification. Class may be defined sociologically to describe how people stand in the socioeconomic hierarchy with respect to occupation, income, education, and other variables having to do with the resources they have obtained, but it is often also defined culturally, in terms of their class-bound ways of life, that is, as class culture. Generally speaking, descriptions of class cultures pay little attention to the distinction between behavioral and aspirational culture, on the one hand, and situational responses, on the other hand. Descriptions which determine people's class position on the basis of situational responses, but ascribe them to culture, make *ad hoc* behavior seem permanent and may assign people to class positions on a long-term basis by data which describe their short-run response to a situation.[25] For example, if poor people's inability to plan is a situational response, rather than a behavioral norm, it could not be used as a criterion of lower-class culture, although it might be considered a pattern associated with lower-class position. Class, like culture, should be determined on the basis of norms which restrain or encourage people in adapting to new conditions.

Class-cultural descriptions must therefore focus on behavioral norms, on the intensity with which they are held, and on people's ability to adapt to new situations. Moreover, if culture is defined to include aspirations, assignments of class position would have to take people's aspirations into account. Since these aspirations may be for working-class, lower-middle-class, or upper-middle-class ways of life, it becomes difficult to assign poor people to a single lower-class culture. In addition, if the previous criterion of ability to adapt is also included, those who can adapt to change would have to be classified further on the basis of whether their aspirations are for one or another of the "higher" classes. The resulting classification would be quite complex and would indicate more accurately the diversity within the poverty-stricken population than current concepts of lower-class culture. More important, the number who are, culturally speaking, permanently and inevitably lower-class is much smaller than sometimes imagined, for that number would include only those whose aspirations are lower-class and whose behavioral culture prevents easy adaptation to change.

This approach would, of course, limit the use of current typologies of class. Dichotomies such as working class and lower class, or upper-lower and lower-lower class, can be used to describe the existential condition in which people find themselves and the situational responses they make, that is, as *sociological* typologies of class, but they cannot be used as *cultural* typologies, for people who share the same existential situation may respond with different behavioral norms and aspirations.[26] Combining sociological and cultural criteria into a single holistic category not only underestimates the diversity of people but also implies that they are satisfied with or resigned to being lower-class, so that class culture is used to explain why poor people remain lower-class when in reality their being poor and members of an underclass is responsible. No doubt cultural patterns do play a causal role in class culture, but they must be determined empirically. Any other approach would reify the concept of class culture and give it a conservative political bias which suggests the poor are happy with or resigned to their lot.

Moreover, dichotomies such as working and lower class are in many ways only a sociological version of the distinction between the deserving and undeserving poor, even if their formulators had no such invidious distinction in mind. These labels are also too formalistic; they only chart the social and economic distances between people on a hierarchical scale. The terms lower and middle class are positional; they do not describe people's behavioral or aspirational culture. In fact, they really refer only to the economic, behavioral, and status deviation of poor people from the middle classes, for most current models of the class system are based on the amount of deviation from middle-class norms and aspirations.

Ideally, definitions and labels of class should include substantive elements which refer to the major themes of each class culture and indicate the real differences of culture, if any, between the classes. If the data for a thematic cultural analysis were available, we might discover that there is no distinctive lower-class culture; there are only tendencies toward distinctiveness, many of which are but functions of the situations with which people must cope and might disappear altogether once situations were changed.

Sociologists cannot ignore present situations, however, even if they are undesirable, and despite my reservations about the concepts of class and culture, ultimately I would agree with Lee Rainwater when he writes: "If, then, we take subculture to refer to a distinctive pattern of existential and evaluative elements, a pattern distinctive to a particular group in a larger collectivity and consequential for the way their behavior differs from that of others in the collectivity, it seems to me that there is no doubt that the concept of lower class subculture is useful."[27] I would add only that I am skeptical of the existence of lower-class evaluative elements, or what I have called aspirational culture.

III. An outline of basic research and policy questions

The remainder of this paper attempts to apply the frame of reference I have outlined by suggesting some of the questions that ought to be asked by researchers and by indicating the methodological implications of the approach.

Studies of the poor should give up the notion of culture as largely behavioral, with little concern about divergent aspirations; as holistic; and as persistent causal factor in behavior. Instead, insofar as poverty research should focus on the poor at all—a point I shall consider below —it should deal with behavior patterns, norms, and aspirations on an individual basis, relate them to their situational origin, and determine how much the behavioral norms related to poverty would persist under changing situations. Whether or not there is a persisting and holistic culture (or a set of subcultures) among the poor should be an empirical question.

In studying behavioral norms and aspirations among the poor, the following questions are most important: Does a given behavioral pattern block a potential escape from poverty, and if so, how? Conversely, are there aspirations related to this behavioral pattern, and do they diverge? If so, are they held intensively enough to provide the motivation for an escape from poverty when economic and other opportunities are available? Are there behavioral norms which encourage this escape?

In analyzing the behavior patterns that do block the escape from poverty, one must look for the social and cultural sources of that behavior. Is the behavior a situational response that would change readily with a change in situation, or is it internalized? If it is internalized, how does it become internalized (and at what age), what agents and institutions encourage the internalization, and how intensive is it? How long would a given behavioral norm persist if opportunities changed, and what are the forces that encourage its persistence?

Similar questions must be asked about aspirations: What are their sources, how are they internalized, and how intensely are they held? How responsive are they to changes in situation, and can they enable people to give up poverty-related behavior once economic opportunities are available? And what kinds of noneconomic helping agents and institutions are needed to aid poor people in implementing their aspirations?

Equally important questions must be addressed to the affluent members of society. Indeed, if the prime purpose of research is the elimination of poverty, studies of the poor are not the first order of business; they are much less important than studies of the economy which relegate many people to underemployment and unemployment and nonmembers of the labor force to welfare dependency. They are also less important than studies of the political, social, and cultural factors that enable and encourage the affluent population to permit the existence of a poverty-stricken underclass. In the final analysis, poverty exists because it has many positive functions for the affluent society; for example, by providing a labor force to do the "dirty" work of that society.

Consequently, assuming that lower-class culture is less pervasive than has been thought and that poor people are able and willing to change their behavior if economic opportunities are made available to them, one must ask what kinds of changes have to take place in the economic system, the power structure, the status order, and the behavioral norms and aspirations of the affluent members of society for them to permit the incorporation of the poor into that society? Which of the functions of poverty for the affluent population can be eliminated, which can be translated into functional alternatives that do not require the existence of poverty, and which functions absolutely require the existence of either a deprived or a despised class, or both?

In addition, one must ask questions about the affluent society's attitudes toward behavior associated with poverty. Many behavior patterns may be the result of poverty, but they do not necessarily block the escape from poverty. They do, however, violate working- and middle-class values and thus irritate and even threaten working- and middle-class people. For example, the drinking bouts and extramarital sexual adventures which have been found prevalent among lower-class people may be correlated with poverty, but they do not cause it and probably do not block the escape from poverty.

They might persist if people had secure jobs and higher incomes, or they might not, or they might take place in more private surroundings, as they do in the middle class. But since they shock the middle class, one must also ask which behavior patterns must be given up or hidden as the price of being allowed to enter the affluent society. This question must be asked of affluent people, but one would also have to determine the impact on poor people of changing or hiding the behavior. In short, one must ask: what changes are *really* required of the lower class, which ones are absolutely essential to the escape from poverty and the move into the larger society, and which are less important?[28]

These rather abstract questions can perhaps be made more concrete by applying them to a specific case: the set of behavioral norms around the female-based or "broken" family. The first question, of course, is: Does this family structure block the escape from poverty? Assuming that the answer could be "Yes," how does it happen? Is it because a mother with several children and without a husband or a permanently available man cannot work? Or is the female-based family per se at fault? Does it create boys who do poorly in school and on the job and girls who perpetuate the family type when they reach adulthood? If so, is the matriarchal dominance to blame (perhaps by "emasculating" boys) or is it the absence of a father? Or just the absence of a male role-model? If so, could surrogate models be provided through schools, settlement houses, and other institutions? Or are there deeper, dynamic forces at work which require the presence of a stable father figure? Or is the failure of the boys due to the mother's lack of income, that is, a result of her being poor and lower-class? Or does their failure stem from the feelings of dependency and apathy associated with being on welfare? Or is their failure a result of lack of education among the mothers, which makes it difficult for them to implement their aspirations for raising their children to a better life? (But lack of income and education are not restricted to the female-based family.)

Next, what are the social, economic, political—and cultural—sources and causes of the female-based family, and to what situations, past and present, does this institutional array of behavioral norms respond? Moreover, how persistent are the norms that uphold this family type, and what aspirations exist that would alter or eliminate it if conditions changed? If the female-based family is an adaptive response to frequent and continuing male unemployment or underemployment, as I suspect it is, one must then ask whether the family structure is a situational response which would disappear once jobs were available. But if the norms that underlie this family have been internalized and would persist even with full employment, one would then need to ask: Where, when, and how are these norms internalized? Do the men themselves begin to lose hope and become so used to economic insecurity that they are unable to hold a good job if it becomes available? Do the women develop norms and even aspirations for independence, so that, doubting that men can function as husbands and breadwinners, they become unable to accept these men if they are employed?

Are such attitudes transmitted to the children of female-based families, and if so, by whom, with what intensity, and at what age? Do the boys learn from their mothers that men are unreliable, or do they conclude this from the male adults they see around them? At what age does such learning take place, and how deeply is it internalized? If children learn the norm of male unreliability during the first six years of their life, would they have difficulty in shedding their beliefs under more favorable economic conditions? If they learn it when they are somewhat older, perhaps six to nine, would they be less likely to internalize it? If they learn this norm from their mothers, is it more persistent than if they learn it later from their peers and the male adults they see on the street? And at what age does the boy begin to model himself on these male adults?

It may be that the entire set of norms underlying the female-based family are much less persistent than the questions in the previous paragraph assume. Whether or not they are persistent, however, one would have to go on to ask: Under what conditions is it possible for people, adults and children, to give up the norms of the female-based family? Would it follow quickly after full employment, or would adults who have become accustomed to economic insecurity and female-based families pass on these norms to their children even if they achieved economic security at some time in their lives? If so, the female-based family might persist for another generation. Or are there helping institutions which could aid parents and children to give up irrelevant norms and speed up the transition to the two-parent family? And if it were impossible to help adults to change, how about eighteen-year-olds, or thirteen-year-olds, or six-year-olds?

Moreover, what aspirations exist among the poor for a two-parent family? Do lower-class Negro women really "want" a two-parent family, and are their aspirations intense enough to overcome the behavioral norms that have developed to make them matriarchs?

In addition, one must also ask what functions the female-based family performs for the affluent members of society and what obstacles the latter might put in the way of eliminating this family type. How quickly could they overcome their belief that Negro family life is often characterized by instability, illegitimacy, and matriarchy? Would they permit public policies to eliminate male unemployment and to provide higher and more dignified income grants to those who cannot work? And most important, would they permit the changes in the structure of rewards and in the distribution of income, status, and power that such policies entail?

If such questions were asked about every phase of life among the poor, it would be possible to begin to determine which of the behavioral norms of poor people are causally associated with poverty. I suspect that the answers to such questions would show what Hylan Lewis found among the people he studied: "The behaviors of the bulk of the low income families appear as pragmatic adjustments to external and internal stresses and deprivations experienced in the quest for essentially common values."[29]

Structuring new opportunities

If the major aim of research is to eliminate poverty, one would also have to ask questions about how to structure new economic and non-economic opportunities to enable poor people to accept them, so that the incentives created by these opportunities will overcome the restraints of persisting behavioral norms. Current experiments with providing job training and even jobs to the unemployed have encountered enough refusals to indicate quite clearly that giving unemployed men any kind of job training or any kind of job is not enough. Since unemployed youth do not have lower-class aspirations, but want the kinds of job that are considered decent, dignified, and status-bearing by working- and middle-class cultures, the new opportunities must be designed accordingly.

The first policy question is: What kinds of opportunities have highest priority, economic or noneconomic opportunities? Assuming that the first priority is for economic opportunity, what is most important for whom, a job or an income grant? And what types of jobs and income grants are most desirable? What type of job would actually be considered an opportunity by poor people, both unemployed and underemployed, and what type would be inferior to present methods of earning an income; for example, welfare payments, illicit employment provided by the numbers racket, or various forms of male and female hustling?

This would require an analysis both of job aspirations and of persistent behavioral norms that interfere with holding a job. What elements of a decent job are most important to poor people: the wage or salary, the security of the job, physical working conditions, the conditions, the opportunities for self-improvement, the social characteristics of the work situation, the relationship to the boss, the skills required, the opportunities for self-improvement and promotion, or the status of the job—and in what order of priority?

What behavioral norms function as incentives to holding a job? And what are the obstacles? Is it the lack of skills; the unwillingness to work every day, or an eight-hour day; the pressures to associate with the peer group; or the inability or unwillingness to adapt to the nonwork requirements of the job; for instance, in terms of dress, decorum, or submission to impersonal authority? What kinds of incentives, monetary and otherwise, can overcome these obstacles, and what kinds of training programs, job guarantees, and social groupings on the job would be necessary to "acculturate" people who have never or rarely held a full-time job in the society of workers?

Similarly, for those who cannot work, what kinds of income grants would provide the best means for a permanent escape from poverty for them and particularly their children? Is the amount of income alone important? If not, how important is the release from stigmatization and identification as poor that would be provided by a family allowance, rather than by welfare payments or a negative income-tax grant? What forms of payment will provide the least discouragement and the most encouragement to go to work among people who want to be in the labor force? Would across-the-board grants be more desirable than a set of categorical grants, such as family allowances, rent supplements, and Medicaid?

Also, what kinds of noneconomic opportunities are necessary or desirable? Would jobs and income grants replace the need for social case work, or would people be more likely to ask for help from social workers once they did not depend on them for welfare payments? And what helping milieu is most effective? Should services be provided in special institutions for the poor, or should the poor be given grants so that they can buy the same services purchased by affluent people? Would poor people go more often to a private physician whom they pay like everyone else, or would they be readier to visit a superior clinic or group practice which is set up specially for them? Which alternative would be most compatible with the behavioral norms and aspirations of different kinds of poor people—and what are the benefits and costs of grants to use private medical and other services, as compared to expenditures that would offer improved services expressly for the poor?

Finally, how long must special opportunities be made available before poor people can truly be on their own? How much security, economic and other, must be provided for how long in order for people to take the risk of grasping at new opportunities and to be able to give up present behavioral norms and associations?

Other questions must be asked of the affluent society; for example, of employers and employees who will be working alongside the newly employed poor. Yet other questions arise because many of the poor are nonwhite, and their poverty is a result of segregation. Eventually, questions must also be asked of the voters, to estimate the political feasibility of instituting the needed programs and to determine what program designs have the greatest chance of political acceptance. In the last analysis, the shape of an effective antipoverty program probably depends more on the willingness of affluent voters to accept such a program that on the economic and cultural needs of the poor.

IV. Some methodological implications: the need for social experiments

Many of the questions I have raised about the culture of the poor can be investigated through a combination of presently available empirical research methods, including participant-observation; the mixture of ethnological techniques, participant-observation, and life-history collection used by Oscar Lewis; intensive or depth interviewing; and extensive interviewing of large samples by social surveys.

Yet none of these methods are able to get at the prime question about the culture of the poor: what behavioral norms will and will not persist under changed economic and noneconomic condtions. *This question can be answered best by altering the conditions and then seeing how people respond.* Consequently, the most desirable method of antipoverty research is inducing social change and observing the results.

Researchers lack the power and the funds to undertake social change on a large scale, but they can do it on a small scale, through social experimentation. The best technique is the field experiment, which enables a sample of poor people to live under improved conditions and then measure their response: whether or not they change their behavior and implement their aspirations. Such experiments can determine what effect the provision of a variety of new opportunities has on poverty-related behavioral norms, such as family structure, mental health, physical health, work and work performance, school attendance and school performance, political participation, and the like.

A wide range of experiments is needed to determine (and compare) the response of poor people to different kinds of new opportunities, economic and noneconomic: the efficacy of secure and well-paying jobs, a guaranteed income without employment, income derived from public welfare, the negative income tax or a family allowance, superior education for the children, better housing for families, and yet others. All the alternative policies for eliminating poverty must be tested among various kinds of poor people, with control groups established wherever possible to determine how much the impact is a result of the specific policy or policies being tested. Such experiments are already coming into being; the Office of Economic Opportunity has begun an experiment to test the impact of the negative income tax on work incentives and other behavior and attitude patterns; the Department of Health, Education, and Welfare and the Ford Foundation are considering tests of alternative income grants, such as the family allowance. Other experiments are needed to study various employment, job-training, and noneconomic programs.

Most experiments would have to be set up *de novo,* but others can treat existing social processes as experiments. One approach is historical: to analyze the experience of the European immigrants in America and their descendants as a field experiment, to measure, however imperfectly, the impact of stable jobs and decent incomes on the cultural patterns which they brought with them from Europe. More useful studies could be conducted among people, white and nonwhite, who have recently been able to move out of the slums of American cities, to determine what opportunities were available to them, how they took hold of these opportunities, and what changes in behavior followed. A comparison of an experimental group which escaped from a ghetto and a control group which did not might yield some useful preliminary answers to the questions raised in this paper.[30]

In addition, it is possible to analyze the various antipoverty programs and demonstration projects now going on all over the United States as experiments, to determine how the participants reacted to the opportunities they were offered. Such studies would focus on program elements, on the one hand, and the behavioral norms and aspirations of participants, on the other hand, to determine what program elements and cultural factors were responsible for successes—and failures.

The great need is for more experiments. Most such experiments can be initiated only by the government or by well-endowed private foundations, but they can be undertaken only if social scientists are willing to design them in the first place. If social science is to serve the ends of policy, and particularly to help eliminate poverty, it must place less emphasis on the study of existing conditions and more on experimentation with improved conditions. Such an approach would also be fruitful to social-science theory, for it would answer more reliably than current research methods whether there is a culture of poverty and a lower-class way of life.

NOTES

1. Lee Rainwater, *Neutralizing the Disinherited: Some Psychological Aspects of Understanding the Poor,* Pruitt-Igoe Occasional Paper No. 30 (St. Louis: Washington University, June 1967—mimeographed), p. 2.
2. *Ibid., passim.*
3. See for example, David Matza, "The Disreputable Poor," in Reinhard Bendix and Seymour Martin Lipset, eds., *Class, Status and Power* (2d ed.; New York: The Free Press of Glencoe, 1966), pp. 289–303.
4. For a useful review of these writings, see Robert H. Bremner, *From the Depths* (New York: New York University Press, 1956).
5. See for example, Barbara Solomon, *Ancestors and Immigrants* (Cambridge: Harvard University Press, 1956).
6. William F. Whyte, Jr., *Street Corner Society* (2d ed.; Chicago: University of Chicago Press, 1955); Michael Young and Peter Willmott, *Family and Kinship in East London* (London: Routledge and Kegan Paul, 1957); Walter Miller, "Lower Class Culture as a Generating Milieu of Gang Delinquency," *Journal of Social Issues,* XIV (1958), 5–19; Oscar Lewis, *The Children of Sanchez* (New York: Random House, 1961), and *La Vida* (New York: Random House, 1966); Herbert J. Gans, *The Urban Villagers* (New York: The Free Press of Glencoe, 1962); Hylan Lewis, *op. cit.;* Elliott Liebow, *Tally's Corner* (Boston: Little, Brown, 1967); and Lee Rainwater, "The Problem of Lower Class Culture and Poverty War Strategy," in the same forthcoming Moynihan volume for which this chapter was first prepared (see note page 321).

7. Rainwater, *op. cit.*
8. Bernard Beck, "Bedbugs, Stench, Dampness and Immorality: A Review Essay on Recent Literature about Poverty," *Social Problems,* XV (Summer 1967), 101–114.
9. Some writers have even resurrected Karl Marx's pejorative *Lumpenproletariat* to describe participants in the rebellions, ironically forgetting that Marx applied the term to people who did not share his revolutionary aims. Still, it is interesting that Marx, who apotheosized the working class, nevertheless felt the poor were undeserving, although his pejorative refers to political rather than moral lapses. Conversely, nineteenth-century American observers felt the poor were politically immoral for the opposite reason, because they were drawn to socialist and Communist movements.
10. See, for example, Jerome Carlin, *Lawyers' Ethics* (New York: Russell Sage Foundation, 1966).
11. See, for example, Louis Kriesberg, "The Relationship between Socio-Economic Rank and Behavior," *Social Problems,* X (Spring 1963), 334–353.
12. Hylan Lewis, *op. cit.,* pp. 17–18.
13. Miller, *op. cit.,* p. 7.
14. *Ibid.,* p. 19.
15. *Ibid.,* p. 7.
16. Hyman Rodman, "The Lower Class Value Stretch," *Social Forces,* XLII (December 1963), 205–215; Rainwater, *op. cit.*
17. Hylan Lewis, *op. cit.,* pp. 38–39.
18. See Robert A. Nisbet, *The Sociological Tradition* (New York: Basic Books, 1967).
19. For more extreme examples of the use of the term *culture* see Hylan Lewis, *op. cit.,* pp. 14–15. See also Jack L. Roach and Orville R. Gurselin, "An Evaluation of the 'Culture of Poverty' Thesis," *Social Forces,* XLV (March 1967), 383–392.
20. For a persuasive illustration, see Margaret Mead, *New Lives for Old* (New York: Morrow, 1956).
21. For some illustrations of the policy implications of conceptual conservatism, see Frederick S. Jaffe, "Family Planning and Public Policy: Is the 'Culture of Poverty' Concept the New Cop-Out?", paper presented to the 1967 meeting of the American Sociological Association.
22. Miller, *op. cit.,* p. 18 (emphasis added).
23. Oscar Lewis, *La Vida,* p. xliv.
24. *Ibid.,* p. xlviii.
25. See, for example, Kriesberg, *op. cit.*
26. For excellent discussions of this point, see S. M. Miller, "The American Lower Classes: A Typological Approach," and S. M. Miller and Frank Riessman, "The Working Class Subculture: A New View," in Arthur B. Shostak and William Gomberg, eds., *Blue-Collar World* (Englewood Cliffs, N.J.: Prentice-Hall, 1964), pp. 9–23, 24–35.
27. Lee Rainwater, "The Problem of Lower Class Culture" (St. Louis: Washington University, Pruitt-Igoe Occasional Paper No. 8, September 1966), p. 32; also in Moynihan, *op. cit.*
28. See here S. M. Miller, *op. cit.,* p. 20.
29. Hylan Lewis, *op. cit.,* p. 38.
30. Zahava Blum has suggested studies of American Indians who received large cash payments from the government for their reservations, to determine how they spent these funds and what successes and failures they encountered in escaping from the poverty of reservation life.

23

The Ghetto Rebellions

I. The causes of the rebellions

The events commonly described as riots or civil disorders are in reality *spontaneous rebellions,* carried out impulsively by people fed up with the way they have been treated by white American society. These rebellions are the natural outcome of years and years of anger that have been building up in the ghettoes of our cities, towns, and rural areas.

The first participants in a city's rebellion may be adolescents and young adults, undereducated, unemployed or underemployed. Having few family or community responsibilities, they have the least to lose from rebellious behavior that can land them in jail or in the cemetery. Before long, however, they are joined by people of all classes and ages, including even those with decent and respectable jobs, for almost every ghetto resident has grievances which breed anger.

The most serious grievances are by now familiar to everyone: poverty, unemployment, underemployment, blighted but expensive housing, inadequate schools, recreation facilities and hospitals, exploiting storeowners, insufficient police protection and too much police harassment, and substandard public services of all kinds. The poorer residents must subject themselves to the social worker's direction of their private lives; the more affluent residents are cut off by segregation from achieving the American Dream.

Rich or poor, ghetto residents also have political grievances, for they rarely obtain equal treatment from the courts, the municipal bureaucracies, and elected officials. More often than not, ghetto wards are gerrymandered,

Slightly revised version of sections I to IV of testimony before the National Advisory Commission on Civil Disorders, October 6, 1967. Section V, omitted here, consists of twenty-one programatic proposals to deal with the problems of the ghetto, most of which are described in earlier chapters of this book. The revision of the portion of Section III analyzing the failure of the European immigrants to rebel draws on my memorandum, "Escaping from Poverty: A Comparison of the Immigrant and Negro Experience," prepared for the Commission staff in January 1968, which became Chapter 9 of the Commission's Report.

either through boundary lines or through at-large elections, which reduces the impact of the Negro vote on elected officials. As a result, the demands that Negro residents make on city offices get less attention than those from whites—poor people of any color often get little attention in any case—even when Negroes are close to a majority of the voters. In many of the cities where rebellions took place, the ghetto also had specific grievances. One is urban renewal. Even the most publicized "model" urban renewal program, in New Haven, never built any public housing for the displaced slum dwellers, and in Newark, where the relocation record is even sorrier, the ghetto objected violently to a medical center project which would have deprived people of their homes and their political strength. Added to long-standing grievances about poor public services, the typical ghetto resident is likely to feel that none of the people he has voted for care the least about his needs.

In recent years, a new grievance has developed, the failure of the War on Poverty to deliver aid to the rank-and-file resident of the ghetto. It may not be coincidental that rebellions have broken out in cities which were alleged to have "model" antipoverty programs. The endless publicity about model programs which looked good on paper and in city hall tables of organizations but did not bring better jobs, higher incomes, or better schools to the ghetto only added to the long list of traditional frustrations.

But the one grievance that unites all ghetto residents is racial segregation, which condemns people to an almost certain and permanent inequality in all spheres of life, and brings with it a feeling of powerlessness and frustration over being unable to achieve any aspirations.

I think it is very difficult for affluent whites, cut off by segregation from any direct contact with life in the ghetto, to understand the endless frustrations which stem from poverty, segregation, and inequality. Contemporary America is an affluent society whose economy is organized to increase the wealth of the affluent, but to keep the poor in their economic, political, and social place. America is really rigged against the poor, whether they are white or nonwhite—and then it blames the victims of that rigging for being lazy or immoral or violent.

A few examples will suffice. Many Negroes who are employed hold the dirtiest and most boring jobs in our society, and they work much harder, physically and mentally, than most white-collar workers or professionals. Yet many whites think Negroes are lazy. Similarly, most Negro women work much harder at housework than do most whites, for slum apartments are much harder to keep clean than suburban houses. Yet many whites think that Negroes are dirty.

In our era, education is crucial to a good job, but the affluent neighborhoods get the best schools and the best teachers. The slum areas get the poorest, but the Negro is blamed for being stupid or unwilling to learn.

When affluent people want to gamble, they can play the stock market, a highly respected institution. When Negroes (and other poor people) want to gamble, they have to use the numbers racket, which is illegal, and in which the odds are much worse—and so Negroes are accused of wasting their money on gambling.

When white people express their ethnic political power, it is taken for granted, and many cities and national electoral offices are divided up between ethnic and religious groups as a matter of course. But now that Negroes are developing the same sense of ethnic identity, and are demanding the same ethnic political power, they are attacked for being advocates of Black Power. When that concept was first coined, it was no different from Irish, Jewish, Polish, or Italian Power, and even Stokely Carmichael originally meant little more by the term than a sense of Negro identity and power. The attacks on him from all quarters, white and Negro, as well as the violent reaction to S.N.C.C.'s use of civil disobedience as a political tactic have forced him and H. Rap Brown to shift definitions, and they have made the term a symbol of violent opposition to segregation. I am disappointed by their appeals to violence, but as Father Groppi of Milwaukee once pointed out, these appeals are a result of five long years of violence exerted against them—and who among us can be patient in the face of violence for that length of time.

The inequities which Negroes and other poor people face in this society extend to governmental activities as well. Housing for affluent whites is subsidized by F.H.A., by tax deductions for home ownership, by federal grants for highway programs that take the suburbanite to and from his downtown job, and by urban renewal, but federally aided housing for the poor, be it through public housing or rent supplements, is minuscule and under constant attack as socialistic. In New York, the threat of a rent strike by middle-class residents in the Spring of 1967 brought the city government into the picture to resolve a union-management dispute; the rent strikes of the poor against their landlords have not resulted in productive municipal intervention.

Government programs that aid the affluent, like F.H.A., are well publicized, and all citizens know they are entitled to federal subsidies. Government programs that aid the poor, such as public welfare, are not publicized. The welfare client is not told his rights; more than half the eligible do not receive the welfare payments to which they are entitled, and even the recipients get much less than what the official standards prescribe.

When people are poor, one crisis automatically leads to others; when a man loses his job, he is likely to be unable to pay his rent or his car insurance or his medical bills. Thus his troubles mount geometrically, and he becomes enmeshed in a vicious spiral of difficulties.[1] Yet when he seeks help, he must appeal to many different agencies—and too often they turn him down. No wonder, then, that the people who are enmeshed in this spiral eventually get fed up and are ready to attack the individuals and institutions that make their life miserable.

Few of these inequities are perpetrated by evil or malicious people; they stem from our social and economic system which helps the affluent but rejects the poor, and which encourages the white man but discourages the Negro. Ironically enough, the current rebellions are also a result of the positive steps that have been taken toward the amelioration of poverty and segregation, for the rising incomes of a part of the Negro population and the integration of some middle-class Negroes into the mainstream of American life have highlighted for the rest, the large majority of the ghetto which is denied these advances, the injustice and inequality of their position. The rebellions are the result of gradualism, for while gradualism has meant a better life for some, it has also resulted in increasing frustration for many others. The ghetto's anger has been rising for many years, but in the past it expressed itself mainly in rising rates of juvenile delinquency and social pathology, which we failed to interpret as signs of protest and anger.

II. The rebellion as a social process

The ghetto rebellions must also be understood as a social process which begins with mounting community anger that is expressed at an inciting incident, expands into a community-wide uprising, and often ends with revengeful repression by the forces of law and order.

Grievances obviously lead to anger, but anger must be widely shared, and it must be expressed against a target which is hated by people with different grievances. So far, the target has usually been an incident, either a fight between Negroes and whites in which the latter use unfair tactics, or more often, a police incident in which one or more policemen deal roughly with a ghetto resident who has broken only a minor law—and in front of witnesses. The incident may itself be no different from many others in the past, but this time a bystander may say he is fed up.

At one such incident, other bystanders will agree with him, and then initiate further incidents which may spiral into a full-fledged rebellion. No one knows yet exactly what sets off the spiraling process, for incidents involving interracial conflict or police harassment occur frequently in the ghetto without resulting in a rebellion. A particular serious incident, the location of an incident near an easily assembled crowd, and hot weather may play a role in the process, but most likely the spiral is the outcome of a series of incidents during prior weeks that have raised the community's level of anger to the boiling point.

If enough people are sufficiently angry, the spiraling process spreads so rapidly that it is virtually unstoppable. Even if it can be stopped momentarily, a new inciting incident is almost certain to take place when ghetto and police tempers are frayed, and the temporarily halted rebellion then resumes.

The rebellion is an act of collective behavior in which people behave as part of a group rather than as individuals. It is not the behavior of a mob which acts impulsively however; in most cases, people destroy or loot only the property of those who have exploited them, and they take as few risks as they can. In some cities, they may be joined by more desperate ghetto residents who resort to arson or sniping, and although such people may be few in number, they can create the kind of chaos which makes the rebellion seem more violent and destructive than it actually is, and leads to unrestrained shooting by the police and the troops.

But most of the rebellious activity is property destruction and looting, and often it takes on the mood of a "carnival." This is not because the participants are callous, but because they are happy at the sudden chance to exact revenge against those who have long exploited and harassed them. The rebellion becomes a community event, a community activity; for once, the ghetto is united and people feel they are acting together in a way that they rarely can. But most important, the destruction and looting allows ghetto residents to exert power. The evidence from many cities shows that looting is difficult to stop, and ghetto residents realize that they can do something to overcome their fate; for once they have some control over their environment, if only for a little while.

As in all rebellions throughout history, eventually agitators and professional revolutionaries come into the picture, but only after the ordinary and usually law-abiding ghetto residents have begun the rebellion, and they succeed only because these residents are willing to follow and listen; because they see truth in the desperate message of the revolutionary. Even so, I do not think that the rebellions of the past few years are, as yet, a beginning of a revolution; they are too impulsive, too chaotic, and too home-made; they do not seek to overthrow the city government, and they are not based on a considered strategy which would achieve that, or any other, revolutionary aim. This is why I call them *spontaneous rebellions*.

A rebellion in one city does not automatically cause rebellions in other cities.The mass media do of course diffuse information about rebellions to other cities, but I doubt that this encourages additional ghettos to rebel. Rather, the knowledge that a rebellion is going on elsewhere, particularly in a nearby city, raises tension levels in the ghetto, outside it, and among the police, increasing the likelihood of an inciting incident. Ghetto residents in one city may become angrier when they hear rumors that Negroes in another city are dying, and police officials may unconsciously be tougher with law violators because they know that fellow professionals are under attack in another city. Given the nature of this process, it is unlikely that changes in mass media coverage would do much to prevent additional rebellions; ghetto residents and police need only learn that a rebellion is taking place in another city to raise the tension level, and this information can be transmitted by a handful of intercity phone calls. Only a complete news blackout and the shutting down of phone lines would prevent the diffusion of the needed information, and such solutions are inconceivable in a democratic society.

The mass media can improve their coverage by including more than just the most extreme actions by the rebels and the police, for such "highlighting" gives newspaper readers and television viewers the impression that the rebellion is more violent and more widepread than it really is. This impression builds on already existing stereotypes among ghetto residents, whites, and the police about the mutual readiness to resort to violence; and these stereotypes help heighten the anger of ghetto residents and increase the feeling of threat among the police and in the white community.

Although the mass media have described the rebellious as extremely violent—and although people would probably think of them as violent even without the mass media emphasis on the most extreme incidents—the rebellions have so far been violent mainly against property, and against the property of hated white exploiters at that. I am amazed at how little violence has been exerted by the rebellion participants against human beings, including even white policemen. The evidence suggests that the snipers are few in number, and in many cases, they have only shot into the air to create confusion and chaos. They may escalate the violence, particularly by panicking the police and the National Guard, but they have seemingly not used their many opportunities to kill those whom they consider their enemies.

In fact, as the chronological and other reports from a variety of cities indicate, most of the violence against persons resulted from police and National Guard actions. This does not justify or condone the ghetto's resort to violence, but it indicates that there was violence on both sides. I think there are three important reasons for this exchange of violence. First, a spontaneous mass rebellion, and a community-wide looting rampage is threatening to even the best-trained policeman, and it should not have surprised anyone that some of the policemen and many of the

National Guard troops panicked and shot looters, curfew violators, and even innocent bystanders. Second, and perhaps more important, the police and the troops expect the ghetto to be much more violent than it is, and they acted on their stereotype and on their fantasies rather than on the reality. This was best illustrated in Cambridge, Maryland, where police believed that the burning of a hated ghetto institution was a ruse to draw the firemen away from the central business district, after which, they imagined, the Negroes would rush downtown. As a result, the firemen were told not to enter the ghetto, and fire destroyed many other buildings.

Third, and perhaps most important, the people (and institutions) to whom American society assigns the unpleasant task of maintaining order tend to be drawn from working class, not-so-affluent populations, people who are just one step above the Negro in status, sometimes compete with him for jobs, and are often the most militantly anti-Negro. Moreover, policemen sometimes have to take considerable abuse from ghetto residents whom they arrest. As a result, they are angry at and threatened by ghetto residents even when there is no rebellion. When they are forced to restore order in the ghetto, this anger turns into revenge, and this then results in the wild shooting and property destruction by police and troops during and at the end of the rebellion.

The over-reaction of white working class protectors of "law and order" is also stimulated by the political power of that class. In many cities, the dominant urban political machine, whether old-style or new-style, is caught between the conflicting demands of the white working class population and the ghetto. Usually, however, the former is more powerful, partly because the ghetto is often racially gerrymandered, so that city governments usually draw most of their support from the white working class and therefore tend to be more responsive to its demands. Nor will this change until the Negro population increases in size, the courts extend the one-man, one-vote principle to the cities, and more federal funds become available to subsidize the bankrupt cities. Even in cities with liberal, reform mayors, such as Detroit and New Haven, many of the lower echelon officials are more responsive to the demands of white voters than of nonwhite voters. As a result, seemingly model cities with model governments and model anti-poverty programs are, for ghetto residents—who only meet the underlings —often illiberal and even repressive.

III. The ghetto and the white working class

One can take this analysis one step further to argue that the rebellions represent, at one level, a continuation of an old American tradition: the conflict between the white working class and the Negro population. This conflict began in nineteenth century America with the New York draft riots, and continued with white-initiated race riots in several American cities during the twentieth century. One should remember that the white working class is also a deprived group in American society, relatively speaking, particularly now, when participation in the affluent society requires a college diploma. Thus, the current rebellions are a conflict between two deprived groups, one only slightly better off than the other, but with some measure of power at city hall, which is fighting the rising number and potentially rising power of a group just below it in the socioeconomic hierarchy.

If my analysis is correct, more and more violent Negro rebellions and white reaction can be expected in those cities which have an increasing Negro population and a large white working-class population, either of European or Southern poor white origin. Los Angeles, Newark, Detroit, New Haven, Cambridge, Maryland, and other cities which have experienced rebellions fall into this category—although a few Southern cities of this type have not (yet) experienced them, for example, Dallas and St. Louis. Of the cities with the population mix I have described, the ones most prone to rebellion would probably be those whose major municipal services —and particularly the services with which the ghetto comes into contact— are provided by city officials who are, for political and other reasons, primarily responsive to the white working-class voters.

Urban white working-class antagonism toward the ghetto is based partly on fear. When the ghetto expands, it often expands into white working-class neighborhoods. In addition, Negro workers frequently compete with white working-class people for jobs. In an era when blue-collar jobs are disappearing, the Negro demand for integration of the unions is seen as competition for scarce jobs.

The feelings of fear are reinforced, however, by other grievances, which have nothing to do with Negroes, but for which Negroes become scapegoats. One of the major white grievances is that the government does more for the ghetto than for the not-so-affluent whites, and although governmental expenditures in behalf of the ghetto are small, governmental programs for whites tend more often to benefit the middle classes. Indeed, an analysis of all federal programs which subsidize local communities and institutions would probably show that the largest proportion of these subsidies go to the middle class.

Consequently, the white working class feels that its demands are ignored by the federal government. In addition, this population is anxious because of shrinking blue-collar jobs, and the resulting need to send children to college, which not only causes financial problems, but also makes parents fearful of losing their children to the sophisticated culture of the campus. Also, white working-class people tend to be owners of older homes, and rising maintenance costs as well as rising property taxes present them with further financial problems, as well as the fear that their neighborhoods are going downhill. The young people who have gone to college—as yet still a small proportion among working-class people—may be moving into the mainstream of the affluent society, but their parents, and the young people who do not get to college, undoubtedly experience not only financial strains, but also status strains. Thus they feel, with some justification, that their social position in American society is weaker than it once was, and that they are losing prestige and political power. Although this prestige and power loss must be attributed to the changes in the American economy which have made the college-going white-collar and professional middle class the dominant political and cultural force in the society, the working class tends to hold the Negro population responsible for its decline—but then declining groups always blame the groups below them in the socioeconomic hierarchy for their troubles.

Related grievances are held by the rural and small town populations of America, for their affluence and power are also declining in a rapidly urbanizing and suburbanizing society. And even the suburbanites have their grievances; the less affluent young families who have moved to the suburbs in the last decade find themselves beset with rising taxes and other costs of homeownership so that they too, need to find scapegoats for their problems. Lower middle-class homeowners in the city are in a roughly similar position and although they are usually not as directly threatened by the ghetto as working-class homeowners, they are at best ambivalent about antipoverty and integration programs. Indeed, only the upper middle and upper classes are untouched by the events in the ghetto, and among them can be found the largest proportion with favorable opinions toward antipoverty programs and integration (partly because they know few Negroes can afford to move into their neighborhoods) although these two classes tend to be politically conservative, and therefore are opposed to increase in governmental spending *sui generis*.

If many groups in our society have major problems and grievances, it becomes relevant to ask why so far only Negro groups have rebelled, and also, why the slum dwellers of earlier generations, the European immigrants who came in the nineteenth and early twentieth century, never resorted to spontaneous uprising. Of course, not all rebellions have taken place in the ghetto; some have occurred in Puerto Rican neighborhoods, but not so often, and Mexican-Americans have not rebelled at all. Why the European immigrants never rebelled, except occasionally against Negroes, is worth discussing, for the reasons shed light on why the ghetto is in rebellion today.

The primary reason is that when the immigrants came to America, unskilled work was in relatively large supply. They arrived at a time when the urban-industrial economy was beginning to grow rapidly, and by the sweat of their labor, they built the cities and factories of the modern era. Moreover, they emigrated from much poorer societies with a low standard of living, and they came at a time when job aspirations were minimal. When most jobs in the American economy were unskilled, they did not feel so deprived in being forced to take the dirty and poorly paid jobs. Their families were large, and many breadwinners, including children, contributed to the total family income. As a result, family units could live off even the lowest paid jobs and still put some money away for savings or investment, for example to purchase a house or tenement, to open a store or factory.

Since the immigrants lived in their own ethnic culture and could not speak English, they needed stores which supplied them with ethnic foods and services. It took little capital to start stores and even factories at that time, and the rapid growth of the cities made it possible for them to succeed in these commercial ventures. Also, the immigrant family structures were patriarchal, so that the men could find satisfactions in family life which compensated somewhat for the bad jobs, the hard work, and the poverty they had to endure.

In addition, the immigrants were white and they came into a society in which the Negro was already discriminated against. In fact, had it not been for discrimination, the North might well have recruited southern Negroes after the Civil War. Instead, northern employers recruited workers in Europe. Once the immigrants came, they were able to take jobs away from Negroes, even pushing them out of the few urban occupations they had dominated, such as catering and barbering.

For all these reasons, the immigrants were able to obtain an economic and political foothold in American society, making it possible for their children to obtain better jobs, better housing, and most of the rights and privileges open to other white Americans. This is important, because I suspect that it is always the second generation which rebels, and the second generation, the children of the immigrants, did not have to rebel—at least not against American society, but only against the ethnic culture and values of their own parents.

The Negro came to the city under quite different circumstances. The urban-industrial economy had been built, and the number of unskilled jobs had begun to decline. Negroes were relegated to the jobs which no one else would take, and which paid so little that they could not put away money for savings, houses, or stores. They spoke English and did not need their own stores, and besides, the areas they occupied were by then already well supplied with stores. In addition, Negroes lacked the extended family and employed children so that each household usually had only one or two bread-winners. Moreover, Negro men had fewer cultural incentives to work in a dirty job for the sake of the family, for the matriarchal Negro family provided him few of the cultural and psychological rewards of home life available to the immigrant. Instead, many Negroes took to the male street corner group, which as Elliot Liebow's study of such a group shows so well, often gave them more dignity and respect than the female-dominated society of home and family.[2]

Even so, most Negro men worked as hard as the immigrants to support their families but the payoff was just not the same. Nor could they look to the political machines for help. By the time the Negroes arrived in the city, the power of these machines had been blunted by business reform groups, and the completion of the task of building the city had deprived them of many patronage jobs. As a result, the machines took over the area settled by Negroes but did not share either the political jobs or the power. Discrimination played a role here too; the immigrants and their descendants who controlled the machines were anti-Negro and gerrymandered ghetto neighborhoods so that they would not have to share their power with Negroes.

The differences between the immigrant and the Negro experience should not be exaggerated. Many immigrants suffered intensely from poverty, unemployment, and discrimination. Family breakdown, desertion, alcoholism, and all the other forms of social and individual pathology rampant in the ghetto today were equally prevalent in the ethnic slums of the nineteenth century. Moreover, many white Americans tend to overestimate the speed with which their ancestors escaped from poverty in comparison with Negroes. The fact is that among the various ethnic groups who came to America in the last big waves of immigration, only the Jews, who were already urbanized, have totally escaped from poverty. The Italians, Poles, Greeks, Slovenians—and even the Irish—who, like Negroes, came to America with peasant backgrounds, are only now, after three generations, in the final stages of that escape. Until the last ten years or so, the majority of the members of these ethnic groups were employed in blue-collar jobs, and only a small proportion of their children had entered the college-educated white-collar class. In short, it took these ethnic groups three and sometimes four generations to achieve the kind of middle-class income and status that means affluence in today's America.

Negroes have been in the city for only two generations, and they have come under much less favorable conditions. Indeed, their escape from poverty has been blocked in part by the very slowness of the European ethnic groups in moving up. Their exclusion from the building trades and other unions and their inability to move into better neighborhoods beyond the ghetto has been brought about by the descendants of the European immigrants who control these unions and neighborhoods and have not yet given them up for middle-class occupations and residential areas.

The Negroes who first came to the cities from the South were, like the European immigrants, apathetic, or resigned to their fate. What we see now, I think, is the rebellion of the urban-born second generation against that fate.

Still, statistically speaking, only a small proportion of the Negro second generation has joined in rebellion. We do not even know that further rebellions will occur—although the mere fact that they are expected may help to bring them about. The expectation itself will not cause rebellions, but if federal and local governments pass riot-control legislation, and if local police forces prepare for them physically and emotionally, it is likely that more police-ghetto incidents will take place, and that some will spark future rebellions.

IV. Methods of dealing with the ghetto rebellion

There are two major methods for dealing with the ghetto rebellions: repression, and the redressing of grievances, both in the ghetto and else-where. Repression appears to some a highly desirable method, for it is, relatively speaking, inexpensive and in the short run, seemingly effective —and it requires no significant political and legislative changes. As a result, this method appeals both to many elected officials and to large portions of the electorate.

In the long run, however, this method is not only dangerous but in-effective and expensive. Repression may work in the short run, for the loss of Negro lives in the past rebellions may have made ghetto residents aware of the risks they are taking when their anger leads them into a rebellion, and not even the most militant revolutionary really wants to die. Consequently, ghettoes which exploded in years past have not, so far, exploded for a second time. Since little has been done to redress the ghetto's grievances in any of the other cities which experienced earlier rebellions, however, anger is beginning to mount again and surely, one day it will once more boil over. It may boil over into another rebellion, or it may boil over into self-destructive behavior, resulting in rapidly increasing rates of alcoholism, drug addiction, mental illness, homicide, and suicide. This possibility is suggested by the fact that when the fighting gangs of New York were broken up, many of the gang members became heroin addicts. The social and financial costs of self-destructive behavior are just as high as the property destruction of a rebellion, and the consequences of that behavior affect not only the people who resort to it, but also the people who are its victims—and of course the people who pay the taxes to maintain addiction treatment centers, prisons, and other institutions that deal with the self-destructive individual.

I feel that the future holds more rebellions. If they are met by repression, America will be faced with permanent and expanding guerilla warfare between the races, until the entire country becomes a tinderbox, like South Africa.

The only other alternative solution, and really the only rational alternative, is to deal with the grievances that make the ghetto boil over and that encourage the police, the troops, and their supporters in the white population to resort to excessive repression in return. American society must begin to repair the injustices of slavery and post-slavery, and eliminate the present underclass status of the American ghetto Negro, and of all other poor people on the one hand, and it must find ways of determining and dealing with white grievances and deprivations on the other hand.

NOTES

1. For poignant accounts of this spiral, see Robert Conot, *Rivers of Blood, Years of Darkness* (New York: Bantam, 1967), Part I; and Paul Jacobs, *Prelude to Riot: A View of Urban America from the Bottom* (New York: Random House, 1967).
2. Elliott Liebow, *Tally's Corner* (Boston: Little, Brown, 1967).

24

The Prospects of Eliminating Poverty and Segregation

Several of the essays in the last two parts of the book end on a pessimistic note, for I am increasingly skeptical that the war on poverty and segregation can be won. This pessimism conflicts, I realize, with the optimistic assessment of American society put forward in the essays on suburbia and with my notion that recent changes in American society represent a liberating force for many people. I think that both conclusions are justified, but they raise a disturbing question: whether the new affluence of white lower-middle- and working-class Americans has been achieved at the cost of withholding the same blessings from their poor and nonwhite fellows. Is it possible that America's increasing economic, cultural, and political democracy requires the continuing deprivation of the remaining poor, a foreign policy which actively discourages poor people the world over from improving their condition, not to mention a military machine which kills them systematically and in large numbers for opposing American policy in Southeast Asia? If so, can one still insist that the changes that have taken place in America since World War II have been worthwhile?

At present, I think that all these questions must be answered with a qualified "yes." There can be no doubt that the newly affluent have elected political representatives who have joined with America's old-line conservatives to oppose a genuine antipoverty program, to block legislation that would allow Negroes to leave the ghetto, and to reject programs for better hospitals, schools, and other public services. At the same time, they support an American foreign policy that consistently sides with the defenders of an elitist status quo in Latin America, Southeast Asia, and elsewhere.

This reaction is not surprising: people who have just achieved affluence are not secure enough in their new position to share their blessings with others, particularly when this requires sacrifices on their part, in both money and status. For example, when working-class people become

Written specially for this volume (February 1968).

homeowners, they are more unwilling than ever to pay taxes that would benefit the yet less affluent; they turn into fierce opponents of racial integration and support the most conservative foreign-policy measures. Lower-middle-class Americans are not much different, however, and even upper-middle-class professionals are reluctant to support integration when it threatens a decline in their status or in the academic prestige of the schools to which they send their children, even though they provide political support for the War on Poverty and opposition to the war in Vietnam.

In short, white Americans as a whole—and they vote as a whole—are presently not impelled to do much about either poverty or segregation. Although many whites feel some moral obligation toward the ghetto, such obligation is not an effective source of pressure for change. They are not impelled by other pressures, because the problems of the ghetto do not impinge on their lives in any direct or intimate fashion. So far, most whites see the ghetto, its poverty, and even its rebellions, only on television; their lives are not disrupted by the existence of an unhappy underclass.

The prospects for any immediate change in this state of affairs is bleak. Democracy can be used to prevent equality, and the affluent voters whose standard of living is subsidized by the government they elect can deny similar subsidies to those who are still poor. This is no argument against the increases in affluence or in cultural and political democracy over the past generation however; the parents of those who now oppose antipoverty programs and racial integration were, after all, no kinder to the people below them in income and status. Nor is this an argument for abolishing the welfare state and for returning to the era when the poor were looked after by a philanthropic elite. The welfare state may benefit principally the working and middle classes, but it has brought some material improvement to the poor as well, and the old elites, while perhaps more charitable to the poor than the middle class are, were nevertheless even more unwilling to entertain real antipoverty programs. Their despotism was sometimes benevolent, but it was still despotism, and it created the underclass in which so many poor people find themselves today. Elites are moved only by revolution or appeals to altruism, an unreliable way of achieving social change in significant amounts; democracy provides at least a chance for the poor to fight it out on the political battlefield.

Nor is the current state of affairs an argument for the classical left position, old or new, that a complete transformation of the entire "system" is essential. I agree with most of the goals of that position: domestic equality and a foreign policy that supports fundamental social change in the developing nations, but I do not consider the ways by which these goals are to be achieved feasible or acceptable. I still hold to the methods suggested in the Preface and in many of the preceding chapters: to struggle for large-scale change of, and within, the existing political and economic institutions, and thus to transform them over time. In the long run, as newly affluent Americans become more secure in their status, they will be more favorably inclined to support the poor and the Negro population in their quest for incorporation into the affluent society, provided they do not suffer economically by the advent of widespread automation of jobs. But the brunt of the effort will have to come from the deprived populations themselves.

They must use the arsenal of methods in the democratic repertoire: political organization, block voting, third parties or threats of such parties, coalitions, marches, demonstrations, boycotts, and other forms of protest to put pressure on the officials who are nominally elected to represent every voter. Even rebellion and the threat of rebellion belong in that arsenal.

Of course, such political actions have costs as well as benefits; the targets of political pressure can and will react, as they are now doing, by attempts to roll back the antipoverty program and to stop further racial integration. Still, in sum, political action creates more benefits than costs; a small active minority can wring concessions from an inert majority, and some change toward greater equality has already taken place as a result of the activities of the civil-rights movement. Inroads have been made on seggregation in North and South, and the right of government to mount antipoverty programs has been accepted in principle if not yet very much in practice. Even the ghetto rebellions have not resulted solely in repression; they have also wrung some concessions from government, and they have added to the pressure for change, particularly on the big corporations which have plants in the riot-torn cities.

It is, of course, patently unfair to demand more and more effective political action from the poorest, least-educated, and most disfranchised members of American society. Moreover, there is no assurance that any of these methods will work completely and quickly enough to eradicate the evils in American life. The American political system is rigged against the poor and the black. The structure of democratic politics gives power to the already powerful; majority rule means that a powerless minority must almost always lose when programs that could help it are put to the vote. The radicals of the left know this, and so do the black militants; that is why they despair of conventional democracy, and why they developed the tortured new formulas for representation of the black minority that came out of the Chicago meeting of the Conference of New Politics in the summer of 1967. I am not yet ready to give up hope in the combination of democratic procedures and militant political pressure by minorities, but in addition, some change in the structure of American democracy is required so that the needs of a minority can be granted even if they conflict with the demands of the majority.

Some proposals are politically feasible; for example, the enforcement of the one-man, one-vote principle at all levels of government to give the minorities more power at the ballot box. Also, if the government financed all election campaigning, elected officials would not be indebted to small but affluent interest groups, and the power of the big manufacturing and professional lobbies to veto progressive legislation that benefits the consumer might be broken. At that point, the federal government might be able to bring the American welfare state closer to what has been achieved in the Scandinavian countries or in Cuba, and by increasing the number of free public services and improving their quality, to benefit the poor along with the rest of society.

But what is really needed is a more liberal interpretation of the Constitution, to make the glaring inequalities in American life unconstitutional, and to give the courts the power and the wherewithal to enforce policies and programs that will increase equality of race and income. The courts cannot change American society by themselves but, in a law-abiding society, law can initiate the process of social change.

In a democracy that is about 90 per cent white and about 60 per cent affluent, the elected officials of the executive and legislative branches of government will not be able to institute many programs that require reductions in power and privilege from the majority, however, and it seems unlikely that even the judicial branch could be freed from its political obligations to do what is needed. The prospect, then, is for more of the same, a slight and gradual improvement of the status quo. This offers little hope to the deprived minorities of America or the deprived majorities of the developing nations, but it explains why this country can expect further ghetto rebellions and more inexcusable wars in other Vietnams.

Still, the future is not easily predicted. If the present college student demand for more equality and democracy in American society spreads, and if enough students continue to voice this demand when they become breadwinners and parents, the pace of social change may speed up, and could even generate a more thorough transformation of the dominant economic and political institutions. Most likely, however, such a transformation can take place only if it is also sought by at least part of the lower-middle- and working-classes of America but their participation depends largely on what aspirations they develop after they have fully achieved and secured their own affluence.

Part VI ANOTHER APPROACH TO SOCIOLOGICAL ANALYSIS AND PLANNING

Introduction

The sociologist is sometimes discouraged from saying all that is on his mind by the need to have his conclusions fit his data; the planner is held back by his desire to make constructive policy suggestions. Partly because of these inhibitions, I started to write in a somewhat different vein on the topics about which I was also writing professionally.

All the pieces included here responded to a specific stimulus. The first was written when Vance Packard, the most popular of America's popularizers of sociology, joined John Keats and a long list of others in publishing a book attacking suburbia. The second came about after a heated discussion with a fellow sociologist about the extent of adultery in Levittown, in which he, certain that the suburbs were hotbeds of extramarital adventure, accused me of having failed to find the relevant data.

"The Poverty Tour" germinated after a meeting in New York to help Berman Gibson and his group of striking miners in the Appalachian coal country. The meeting was long and earnest, and eventually a committee was formed which aided Gibson. Still, I felt the frustration common to middle-class liberals and radicals who sit in a comfortable living room talking about someone else's problems, but are unable to do much about them and are unwilling to make the personal sacrifices necessary for any real effort. "The Princes and the Paupers" grew out of observing the War on Poverty become a minor skirmish in which, for almost inevitable political reasons, the main beneficiaries were a variety of middle-class professionals, including myself and other academics, who wrote and lectured about poverty to people who wanted to hear about the issues but did not want to do much about them.

The final piece was inspired by a friend's observation. When Leonard Duhl returned from a visit to Israel, he told me that European-born Israelis were greatly concerned about the "cultural deprivation" of the so-called Oriental newcomers, and he wondered what would happen once the latter became the majority in the country and were politically strong enough to denigrate the culture of the Westerners. From there, it was only a short step to applying the same idea to the American city, which may one day have a majority of Negro voters.

Most of these pieces are based on a recurring idea: that people's stereotypes about other people prevent their doing the right thing by their fellow man. I do not really subscribe to that idea; in fact, I am sure that stereotypes disappear only when threatening differences among people that generate stereotypes are removed. But pieces like these tend to write themselves and sometimes reach conclusions that the sociologist does not share.

Despite my strenuous attempts to have these pieces published, only one has ever appeared in a national magazine. I suspect they do not satisfy the literary standards of the journals of opinion, and I know they violate the decorum of professional and academic journals. But I enjoyed writing them and would like others to see them.

25

Suburbia Reclaimed

It is not often that an ordinary suburban family can affect the literary output of a nation, but this is just what happened after Shelley Nash stayed with us to gather material for his newest book, *Suburbia Reclaimed*. Shelley and I had been in college together, but I had not seen him again until last year, when he came to study the market-research agency in which I work. Even at school, he had been an excellent, albeit overly earnest journalist; he had a habit of jumping to conclusions so quickly that he perpetually discovered Crises in American Life where the rest of us saw only the blessed variability of the human species. As I read his earlier best sellers on yet other crises, it was clear that adulthood had not changed him a bit; his observations on my firm, which appeared in *The Business Seekers,* were so exaggerated that I shuddered to think what he would do with and to our suburban community.

I was thus somewhat relieved when he told me that the many books on the conformity and mediocrity of suburban life, including his own, *The Split-Level Prestige Pursuers,* were no longer accurate. His recent observations suggested that suburbanites were really just the opposite: individualistic, diverse, anticonformist, family-minded, and much less status-conscious than most other Americans. And since the suburbs themselves had not changed over the past decade, the great transformation could have come about only because suburbanites had read these books, altered their ways, and thus reclaimed Suburbia.

I tried to point out that most of my neighbors had never even heard of the books and that perhaps suburbanites were actually no different from anyone else, but he was already off on a second point. Whereas his first book had ended with a stirring appeal to suburbanites to move out to the rural towns where—and only where—salvation lay for our fast-crumbling society, he now proposed that it was Suburbia which had made America Great. Many of the Founding Fathers had been gentlemen-farmers—"the suburbanites of an agrarian society," he called them—and undoubtedly

Previously unpublished.

both the Declaration of Independence and the Constitution reflected the democratic perfection of their suburban towns. Moreover, his rereading of the Civil War literature had convinced him that since many of the Abolitionists had also lived in the suburbs, it could well have been the impossibility of housing slaves in these strictly zoned communities that first aroused their opposition to slavery.

Shelley came home with me one Tuesday night, and from the moment we met on the train, he began to point out evidence for his new theories. His earlier book had stressed the drinking that took place on the commuter run, arguing that this was a major cause of the increasing alcoholism among the middle class. Now our fellow commuters were talking soberly, playing cards, or sleeping, signifying to him the great change that had occurred.

As we talked further at dinner, I realized that Shelley was no longer interested in doing a study of our community. Having already reached his conclusions, he now only wanted evidence to support them and to collect such piquant anecdotes as filled his other books. My wife, a sociology major in college, had long felt Shelley's approach was giving that social science a bad name, and by the end of the evening she was muttering under her breath that something had to be done about the Nashian method of social research.

The next morning, Shelley had to come back to the city with me—an airline wanted to promote his recent exposé of Detroit, *The Crack in the Windshield*—but when we returned that night, a row of eight identical station wagons met us at the train, and as if on cue, eight similarly attired women stepped out to kiss their surprised husbands, of which I was one. In the clinch, my wife whispered in the best detective-heroine fashion that she had a plan and that I would be briefed the moment the two of us were alone.

We had been home only a few minutes when the front door opened and in burst my next-door neighbor. "Sorry, wrong house," he stuttered, but loudly enough for Shelley to hear that "dammit, someday I'll learn to tell my place from the others." I was taken aback, but there was more to come. That evening, we had planned a potluck dinner to give Shelley a chance to meet some of our neighbors. The dinner was, to put it mildly, unusual. Every women had brought exactly the same dish and then proceeded to rend the air with abject apologies that this was happening much too often and that they would just have to stop reading the same homemaker magazines. After dinner, these very women, whom my wife had so long tried to enroll in civic activities, talked at length about their hectic, overorganized lives, and then the men complained that it was impossible to live on $20,000 because they were always having to buy the new things for their house that the neighbors had just acquired. Even the children pitched in. My eldest talked straight-facedly about his favorite course at school, something he called Applied Status-Seeking, and later, when the discussion turned to poverty, he argued that as a result of everyone's now living in suburbia, the poor had all become middle-class. I was nonplussed, for only the week before he had nearly been expelled from school for organizing a petition drive urging the remaining farmers in the county to provide decent housing for their migrant labor force.

Meanwhile, Shelley tried valiantly to defend his thesis of suburbia reclaimed, but even he was left speechless when one of my neighbors told him that last month the president of her women's club had accidentally come to the meeting with mismatched shoes and that just at last night's gathering, almost a fifth of the members had appeared shod this way.

I had begun to glimpse some method in all this madness, and when I came to bed that night, my wife explained everything. To teach Shelley a sociological lesson he would never forget, we were performing for him the suburban life he had described in his first book, and handing me a marked copy, she pointed out all the descriptions that were to be staged during his stay.

Over the next few days, it became evident that she had done a superb job of organizing her latest project. Shelley circulated through our community and brought back reports of children who claimed never to have met their grandparents; men who described how the clean air and the lawns of what they called their junior estates, none of which exceeded a quarter-acre, had converted them to Republicanism; and women who proudly pointed to four Junior Leagues, six Art Seminars, and nine Country Clubs that had made our little community the most exclusive suburb of all. But some of the women, he noted, kept liquor bottles next to the detergents so that they would be up with their husbands when these came home filled with what they, quoting Nash, called the commuter cocktails. Several confessed that suburban life was ruining their marriages. On Saturday morning, that last point was amply illustrated when our breakfast was interrupted by a loud fight across the street, in which the wife said clearly and quite profanely to her husband that she would leave him this minute if he did not begin at once to do something about the crab grass.

That evening, some friends were giving a good-by party for Shelley— he was to leave the next day—which was announced as a Westport dance.

Quoting from Shelley's book, my host informed me, "Such parties are a mainstay of suburban social life and a widely used method of coping with its ever-present boredom. . . . The nature of these parties varies," he continued, "but in most Eastern suburbs, everyone is blindfolded and scrambled for the final dance of the evening, and each man then spends the night with whoever happens to be his last dance partner." Shelley is a bachelor, but the host knew a self-styled model who had recently retired to write her autobiography. She had consented to come to the party provided she had first publication rights (she intended to call that chapter "Sin on the Patios"), and it was arranged that she would be dancing with Nash when the blindfolds came off.

At about midnight, our hostess signaled for silence and announced the closing event, which was greeted by lascivious comments from all present that it had been much too long since the last one. Shelley was quite shocked, but the matter-of-fact way in which the newly paired couples went off—actually for nothing more than coffee—left him no choice but to go home with his fledgling authoress.

The next morning, Shelley reviewed his research for us. Admitting that there had been some unexpected findings, he nevertheless announced triumphantly that he had met three families who fitted his new theory perfectly. It seemed as if our sociological lesson had failed, and we had no choice but to reveal the entire scheme, not forgetting to mention that the three families he described were the core of an opposing faction in the local P.T.A. who had refused to go along with us.

Shelley was terribly angry and left without another word. Consequently, I was surprised to hear from him a few days later and to be thanked profusely for what he now considered the most important week in his life. It seems that when he unpacked, he came on a couple of my wife's sociology books which he thought must have accidentally slipped into his luggage. Highly excited by his first brush with this subject, he soon realized the shortcomings of his own approach. He had decided to shelve the new book on suburbia, as well as several others, and had that morning enrolled for graduate study in sociology at N—— University.

26

The Disenchanted Suburbanite

For the past several years, I have been doing a study of people who move to the suburbs, asking them to write case histories about their reasons for leaving the city. One of these case histories sheds light on a significant but almost totally ignored cause of the great suburban migration.

* * *

My wife and I had been living in one of the new downtown apartment buildings for about three years. Like most other young couples, we complained constantly about the disadvantages of raising children in the city and were waiting only for the arrival of our second child to make the move to the suburbs. But I would not be completely honest if I did not mention another reason for moving there which featured prominently in my thinking—so prominently, in fact, that I could hardly wait to leave the city.

For a long time I had been reading newspaper and magazine articles which reported that various forms of extramarital sex were rampant in the new settlements beyond the city limits. Journalists, psychologists, and even ex-suburbanites wrote ominously, but in deliciously voluminous detail, of beautiful young housewives alone all day, yearning for male companionship, and of week ends filled with adultery and wife-swapping. I was especially fascinated by the key clubs, informal parties which ended with the wives placing their house key in a hat, and taking home whatever man had drawn theirs. The opportunity of participating in these types of community activity was my real reason for wanting to move to the suburbs.

After many weeks of looking at houses, we purchased in a development I shall call Parkleigh. My wife had fallen in love with the house, and I had learned from acquaintances that Parkleigh boasted the kind of suburban living for which I lusted. But after we had moved in and I

Previously unpublished.

asked my acquaintances for specific leads, they suddenly became vague. Of course there were women who played extramarital games, they assured me, but unfortunately all the ones they knew had moved out a short time earlier. There were no key clubs on their own blocks, either, but they had heard of some a couple of streets over. When I tried to track this down, however, I was always sent yet a couple of blocks further, until I was finally directed to my own block. Yet all the men I talked with indicated that if life in Parkleigh was perhaps at present quite monogamous, it was not so in Springdale, a nearby suburb, which, many said enviously, should really have been called Dallying-on Springs.

As luck would have it, a substantial pay raise and a fearful run-in with our next-door neighbors made it possible for me to persuade my wife that we should move to Springdale. But once there, I found that my sources of information had erred again. Life in Springdale was no different than in Parkleigh, and eventually we moved again, this time to a newly opened and highly recommended development called Mountjoy.

Needless to say, Mountjoy turned out to be as proper as all the others, and I realized that I would have to try a different approach. For several weeks, I dutifully attended meetings of all the local organizations—the coed ones—until, after downing hundreds of doughnuts at innumerable postmeeting social hours, I met a fellow resident who responded to my overtures. I had finally made contact with suburban adultery.

Our first get-together took place soon afterwards, and we enjoyed a late afternoon of exploratory dalliance before her husband came home. But then complications set in. My new friend explained that coming together at her house was out of the question, for all comings and goings were visible from every picture window on the block. Elsewhere in Mountjoy was impossible because the development lacked meeting places, other than for civic activities. Nor would she dare meet me within a ten-mile radius of Mountjoy for fear of being spotted by a neighbor. She was even wary of seeing me in the city, for her neighbors were forever going on shopping trips. Of course, she could do the same, and then slip off to meet me in a nearby hotel, she suggested, if I could provide the money for her purchases. In addition, I would have to pay the cost of her baby-sitter, who, as every suburbanite knows, commands a healthy wage. When I added up all the expenses, I realized that I simply could not afford the affair.

Wife-swapping was out, since my wife is a firm believer in monogamy, and besides, the only man I met in Mountjoy who was willing to let me have his wife made the stipulation that I could not return her. I renewed my search for a key club, but I soon realized that the only solution was to organize one of my own. After my wife had conveniently gone off to visit her mother I initiated a word-of-mouth campaign among the more broad-minded people I had met in Mountjoy, announcing the initial meeting of my club a week hence.

My living room was quite full on the appointed evening, but before I even had a chance to open the meeting, I learned that I had brought together a set of people devoted to the collection of antique keys. All of them had been waiting for someone to start a collectors' club, and it was only by the skillful use of parliamentary procedure that I was able to pass the honor of becoming the club's first president to a collector of medieval church locks.

Once under way, my word-of-mouth campaign rolled on with disastrous effectiveness. During the days that followed, I was called on the phone constantly, and at all hours, by people who had locked themselves out of their homes or cars and had heard that I ran an organization to extricate them from their dilemma. But worse was yet to come. One evening I was invited to speak on the key club to a local women's group. I accepted only in the faint hope that I would perhaps find a member with my own extramarital hobby; but before the meeting was over, I had become the leader of a petition drive to persuade the builder to equip our Colonial-style homes with Colonial-style keys, one of a number of well-advertised promises he had failed to keep. I should mention that the young lady who finally persuaded me to accept the assignment intimated that I would get a copy of her key if I was successful, but for the next few weeks I was so busy organizing the petition drive that I did not even have the time, much less the energy, to carry out my marital obligations at home.

The petition drive was a complete success, and the builder made good on his promise. But the lady who had inveigled me into the campaign did not. When I came to collect, she said she had only been kidding, adding sternly that what I was asking her to do just was not done, at least not in the suburbs.

My enthusiasm for suburban living had been diminishing rapidly anyway, but her last remark convinced me beyond all doubt. By no coincidence, my wife felt the same way. In fact, she was ready to divorce me if I did not return to her bed at once, and this, she felt, could happen only if we returned to the city, where hobby clubs and petition drives were less fashionable.

And so we moved back to the city. As luck would have it, I found an apartment development which advertized "all the suburban satisfactions you never had in the suburbs," and I expect to discuss these with the rental agent next week. If I don't find what I am looking for there—well, I have been reading a series of newspaper articles entitled "The Swinging Slums.". . .

27

The Poverty Tour

A government bureau participating in the economic redevelopment of Appalachia recently received a letter from the owner of a New York travel agency which proposed a novel solution to a mutual problem.

"*My* problem," the writer began, "is that business is bad; the customers are getting bored with expensive foreign tours. Over the past year, they have become extremely interested in American poverty. They buy books about it, they talk about it, and they constantly attend meetings to find a way of eliminating it.

"*Your* problem is Appalachia's lagging economy. The area is not attracting new industry, and its scenery does not seem to interest the ordinary tourist. But it does have one commodity in great supply—genuine American Poverty—and that now being in demand, why not make it a tourist attraction? My proposition is the poverty tour: a fortnight's immersion in Appalachian poverty."

With patriotic generosity and a modest suggestion that his agency was well equipped to set up suitable packaged trips, the writer included copy and layout for a prospectus to be advertised in selected upper-middle-class publications. It read as follows:

"Are you one of the perceptive Americans who have recently discovered that the affluent society isn't? Have Lyndon Johnson and Michael Harrington made you feel that perhaps you are not doing your share in the War on Poverty? If your answer is Yes, you will want to take this opportunity to act. Be Our Guest In The Other America. Spend Two Weeks in Abject Appalachian Poverty." The rest of the ad described the tour itself:

"You drive to Appalachia in a 1933 Chevrolet, equipped with original tires, and accompanied by seven other travelers. Soon after you leave, a cleverly planned holdup relieves you of your money. (You will not be

Reprinted from the *Center Forum* (New York Center for Urban Education), I, No. 3 (November 15, 1966), 4.

harmed, and you'll get it all back at the end of the trip.) Now, genuinely poverty-stricken, you are on your way.

"Expertly prepared maps route you on little-known but absolutely free highways, with thrice daily stops at government surplus food stations. At your destination, you will be housed in two-room shacks, some over a hundred years old, and featuring historic outhouses. Four local children, two white and two Negro, will live with you and will act as your personal guides in the culture of poverty.

"At once you are immersed in that culture. You meet your new neighbors as you carry water from the neighborhood pump and try to get credit from the local supermarket. You join them in looking for work, stand in line with them for unemployment benefits, and participate in group efforts to decipher government application forms for antipoverty grants. Afterward, while the men hunt for rabbits, the women and children gather bits of coal and firewood for the home.

"Evenings and week ends you participate in indigenous leisure pursuits. One night you clean out your privy or patch the roof. Another, you go out on an after-dark poaching expedition. On week ends, there will be visits to the back country to savor the product of the local stills and informal concerts of country music, recorded between night-club engagements by young people who grew up here. On Sunday afternoons, you take a ride to the highway construction projects that will supposedly reduce the area's poverty.

"Among the high lights of your stay will be visits from welfare agents checking into the paternity of your children and interviews with noted television personalities on the real meaning of poverty. Then, as you suffer the first pangs of deprivation, you begin to feel a bond with the victims of automation, and before long, there wells up within you that primitive urge for violence to set things right. . . .

"The entire trip costs only $299.95, and you get absolutely free 50 color slides to provide you and your friends with a permanent record of your experience. But best of all, the tour will relieve you forever of that nagging sense of political apathy. Take the Poverty Tour, and Come Away with the Proud Feeling That You Have Been in the Front Line of the War on Poverty."

The government agency held hearings about the scheme among businessmen and civic leaders in the Appalachian region and also conducted market research among prospective tourists. Both revealed surprisingly negative reactions. The businessmen objected to the tour's emphasis on the area's backwardness and proposed instead a demonstration of the accomplishments of private initiative. One speaker suggested: "Take the tourists to our newly automated coal mines. Show them how we are replacing downtown slums with parking lots to revive the retail trade. Invite them to our luxury motels, and let them share the optimism that prevails at church services and Chamber of Commerce meetings."

The few civic leaders who favored the scheme disturbed the government agency even more, for they argued that it would do away with the need for federal redevelopment projects. "If the tour brings in enough money," one of them testified, "we could bid good-by to the government agents and the New York radicals who are now coming down here to stir up our people. In fact, if the tourists enjoy their taste of poverty, they will themselves oppose any changes in Appalachia."

The market research, conducted among subscribers to liberal news magazines and travel publications, revealed considerable curiosity about the tour, but also some resentment at the implication that the interviewees were laggards in the war against poverty. A typical respondent pointed out: "I'm terribly active. I've set up poverty seminars in all my organizations, even in my investment club. But it would be interesting to go down there and meet some poor people."

The various objections finally persuaded the government to reject the scheme, but the travel agent, convinced of its basic soundness, called in a motivation researcher to design a solution that would satisfy both the Appalachians and the prospective visitors. On the basis of intensive depth interviewing, he dropped the tour's stress on what he called original guilt and suggested it appeal instead to "middle-class reality needs." Advertisements will soon appear in a number of magazines announcing the Appalachian trip. Only, it will be called a study tour.

28

The Princes and the Paupers

Once upon a time, in a rich country far across the sea, there lived some minstrels, wandering and stationary, who told stories about the sad life of the poor. Since minstrels usually only told stories about the sad life of the rich, people flocked around them, and one day even the king came to listen. Surprised by what he heard, he called in his ministers and bade them abolish poverty.

Now the ministers, living as they did at the court, knew very little about poverty and called in the wise men, paying them well to tell how it could be abolished. But the wise men, who lived on campuses, did not know much either. When they had run out of wise observations about their servants, they urged the ministers to consult the guilds whose job it was to deal with the poor.

Guild members came to the court from far and wide and were paid handsomely to tell the ministers what ought to be done. The teachers explained that the poor did not learn well and needed more instruction, which the teachers would gladly provide for overtime pay. The counselors, who had long advised the poor to stop acting like paupers, reported that many were too stubborn to listen, but suggested that if the king hired more counselors, they would reach even the most obstinate. The healers also said the poor were stubborn, refusing to take their costliest potions, but if the king promised to pay whatever the healers charged, they would cure the stubbornness. The barristers asked for funds to defend the poor against the law, which brought on the constables, who pointed out that with more men they would defend the law against the poor. Finally, even the merchants and artisans arrived at the court, promising that if the king paid, they would show poor people how to work and afterward they might even hire some.

The ministers listened to all of them, and even to some wise men who insisted the poor needed only money. But then came the keepers of the

Reprinted from the *Center Forum* (New York Center for Urban Education), II No. 7 (January 8, 1968), 8.

sacred texts, who proclaimed that giving money to the poor violated the king's divine mandate. The royal way, they said, was to help the rich become richer, so that they could set a better example for the poor, who would then learn to be rich too. Even so, the ministers gave the guilds the money they asked for, but ruled that its expenditures had to be justified by sayings from the sacred texts and that the poor could earn some of the money by helping the guilds help them. The guilds agreed, provided the poor behaved respectfully in their presence, and the king told all his subjects poverty would soon be banished from the kingdom. Naturally, they were very excited by the good news, and the minstrels were kept busy making up new stories about the poor, all of which sold well. And when the king died, the new king announced at once that he would work even harder to defeat poverty.

About that time, some young people, apprentices to the wise men, decided to live with the poor and help them help the guilds. Before long, however, they began to say that the king's program was evil; it made the guilds richer, but the poor were just as poor as before. The king summoned the guilds to the court, but they told him that young people—and unpaid ones at that—could not possibly know what was going on among the poor. The young people replied that they were no longer children—several even had beards to prove it—and claimed that they were carrying on the work of the little boy who had seen the king's ancestor without his clothes on. A wise man was quickly hired to restudy the ancient scrolls, however, and he reported that the little boy had been wrong; the king was wearing flesh-colored tights all along.

Disgusted, the apprentices told their poor friends to come together to tell the kingdom the truth about how poor they still were and to march around the king's palace and the palaces of the local barons until everyone believed them. This upset the noblemen, who hurried to the king for money to persuade the poor not to tell the truth. Now even angrier, some poor people beat up the noblemen's constabulary and tried to become less poor by helping themselves to the merchants' goods. The minstrels reported it all and said such dastardly acts were surely the result of poverty, but the barons claimed magicians had come into their domains to bewitch the poor, and they hired more constables to make sure it would not happen again.

Then the apprentices and the poor people sat down together to figure out what to do next. One apprentice found an old elixir, called Poorpower, which he said paralyzed rich people and would persuade them to give money to the poor. He and his friends made new batches of the elixir, but this created a terrible hubbub in the kingdom. Now the ministers, the guilds, and the minstrels said the barons were right; the poor really were bewitched, for Poorpower was too weak, and only Richpower would help them. The king advised the poor people to come to court and ask politely for money, using Richpower just like the guilds, but every time they did so, the ministers said that their hands were tied; by law, Richpower could only be used to give money to the guilds. Some wise men then suggested that the poor could become apprentice members of the guilds, but the guilds admitted only a few. The king was nonplussed, for he really wanted to help the poor, but after all, the guilds were keeping the court in the style to which it had become accustomed, and what had the poor ever done for him?

While he was trying to decide what to do, an unexpected thing happened. People in another country became extremely unhappy about being poor and started a war against the king's friends. The king sent out warriors to help his friends, and now he could no longer afford to think about giving money to his own poor. Helping one's friends came first, or else he would not be respected by the other kings, and besides, the war would also be good for his poor subjects. Some would be paid for making guns, others for becoming warriors, and some would be killed, so that all in all, there would be fewer poor people afterward.

Now the poor decided to fight harder, and the king had to send some of his warriors to help the constables and the merchants. During the cooler months, while the poor were resting from the battle, the young people took over the fight, even attacking the big castle which housed the minister of war and his warlords. The king called in a new set of wise men to teach him why the poor were so warlike, but he did not want to know anything about the young people and put a curse on them instead.

Some of the young people had found a forbidden potion which blotted out all the fighting and in technicolor to boot. Then some of the king's subjects wanted to fight them; others wanted the king to fight everybody, and yet others wanted him to stop all the fighting. A few even called for a new king, and although several noblemen stepped forward to take his place, they immediately began to quarrel among themselves about whom they would fight once they were crowned.

The minstrels naturally made up many new stories about the fighting, and except for the people actually involved in the battles, everyone lived happily ever after.

29

The White Problem

As demographers have predicted ever since the 1960's, many American cities are now predominantly negro and have elected negro mayors and city councils. This has generated widespread unrest among the minority White population, and as a result, the worried mayor of a large eastern city recently called a conference of negro social scientists and White race leaders to discuss the White problem.

The conference was opened by a prominent educator, who diagnosed the White problem in three ways. First, he demonstrated that the minority population has traditionally suffered from "muscular deprivation," which he traced to the failure of the White family to teach physical fitness to its children, making them unable to learn once they entered school. Or, as a flippant delegate later put it, "Mr. Charley just doesn't have a natural sense of rhythm."

Second, the educator pointed to "cognitive deterioration," a speech defect that had developed in nineteenth-century universities and was being perpetuated by outmoded grammar texts used in minority public schools. This speech defect prevented children from talking in accepted twentieth-century ways and created problems when they applied for jobs. Nor could the White youngsters hold jobs, he went on, because of their cultural predisposition to "careerism," a type of occupational motivation that encouraged them to prepare for only one kind of work, making them unemployable in a rapidly changing economy.

The next speaker, a social worker, talked about the "independency pattern," the Whites' inability to depend on others, and their need to do everything by themselves. As a result, they could not be reached by public welfare and casework techniques, would not accept job retraining, muscular enrichment, or aspirational counseling, and ultimately regressed into a state of despair he called ragged individualism.

Both analyses of the White problem were questioned by the luncheon speaker, a psychiatrist, who pointed out that in our leisure society, the

Reprinted from *Dissent*, XIII, No. 5 (September–October 1966), 538–540.

emphasis on jobs and job training was misplaced. The real problem was the minority population's reluctance to relax and enjoy itself, which he traced to "deferred gratification," the tendency to put off having fun, and "reality obsession," the failure to escape which produced anxiety and even mental illness. As a result, Whites had become seriously addicted to nicotine, which was now leading to high rates of lung cancer, heart disease, and other forms of self-destruction.

These consequences were a natural outcome, he argued, of the centuries-long subjection to Puritanism, which forced men and women to spend all their time either at work or at church and denied them the normal human pleasures that were essential to mental health.

He was followed on the podium by a minister, who agreed that Puritanism had done considerable damage in the past, but felt recent White difficulties should be ascribed to "moral confusion," brought about by the illness and death of God. When the minority population was still a majority, it had committed immoral acts which it considered moral, among them waging war, cheating in school, and defending monogamy while taking lovers or subscribing to *Playboy*. He called for the resurrection of the deity and the introduction of moral education courses in schools for the racially disadvantaged.

The afternoon session was given over to the White race leaders, who argued that the minority problem was fundamentally economic and political. There was neither enough work nor leisure to go around, and until the federal government stepped in to provide both, the retraining, enrichment, and counseling schemes could only increase White despair. Moreover, they insisted, the Whites were suffering from powerlessness; being outvoted at the polls, they were subject to police brutality and to more subtle indignities from the very legal, educational, and welfare agencies that were set up to help them. The negro population, one speaker suggested, had in the past suffered from similar degradations, but had overcome them by protests, demonstrations, and riots, while the Whites, who valued order above all, could not use these methods. He argued for government programs to train the minority population in civil disobedience. A young radical who had tried to organize in minority neighborhoods supported this proposal, but added that the Whites' apathy also resulted from having too much money and proposed a revival of the positive income tax.

The conference received so much favorable publicity that other cities held similar meetings, and one mayor commissioned a well-known negro sociologist to write the now famous Patterson paper. Patterson located the problem in two characteristics of the White family. One he called "mate-fixation," the preference for living with one spouse, which he thought harmful because children growing up with a single set of parents could not cope with the diversity of modern life. The other he ascribed to patriarchy, and the mother's resulting inability to serve as a proper model for her daughters. Hung up on their fathers, many girls could not marry, others were driven to adultery with older men, and some even resorted to incest. While these difficulties stemmed initially from the male's position during Puritanism, they were currently exacerbated by suburban renewal, which was forcing White families, though untrained for urban life, to move back to the city.

The report was debated bitterly, the White race leadership arguing that Patterson's portrayal of White family difficulties was insulting, and negro social scientists charging that his findings had been old hat for a generation. Patterson fought back, upsetting the White leaders by backing their own proposals for government action and pointing out that city hall was not given to reading sociological texts.

This set off another round of arguments, and nothing has yet been done about the White problem, producing a loud sigh of relief among urban politicians, who are thus spared from taking action that could only lose them votes among the majority population.

INDEX

Abel, T., 152 n.
Abrams, C., 261
Addams, J., 232
adolescents, 116, 185, 195
advocate planning, 73
aesthetics, 91, 179–180, 268
age and social structure, 45
Aid for Families of Dependent Children (AFDC), 280, 283, 308, 314
Aldrich, N., 305
all-black city, 272–273, 381
Altshuler, A., 63 n.
American Institute of Planners, 73, 231 n.
American Jewish Committee, 260 n.
American Library Association, 98, 103
Anderson, M., 68 n., 206, 261–265
anthropology, 326–330
anti-poverty planning: citizen participation, 242; economic planning, 239; education, 233, 238; employment, 233–234, 238; family structure, 238; federal expenditures for, 298–299; goal-oriented planning, 239–244; heterogeneity, 177–178; housing problems in, 274; housing programs in, 289; income redistribution, 239; job training, 233; lower class, 238; neighborhood planning, 234–235; nonprofessionals, 284–286; origins of, 231–232; physical planning, 234–235; planning ideology, 232, 234–235, 241–242; politics, 239, 300; private enterprise, 291–292, 298–299; professionals in, 378–380; recommendations for, 283–294, 296–299; recommendations for federal administration of, 297–298; settlement house, 249, 254–258; social sciences, 295–296; social services, 233; types of research needed, 337–345; urban renewal, 232; working class, 235–236; see also social planning
anti-poverty research: the affluent, 337–345; biases of, 321–324; culture, 332; history of, 322; methodology of, 343–345; social mobility, 344–345; types of, needed, 337–345; types of policy studies needed, 341–345;
Architectural Forum, 25
Asheim, L., 98
Axelrod, M., 34 n.

Back, K., 19 n., 152 n., 153 n., 155
Back-of-the-Yards (Chicago), 27–31
balanced community, 127–128, 166, 167–168; see also heterogeneity
Balbo, L., 13 n.
Baldwin, J., 317
Banfield, E. C., 63 n., 67 n., 71 n.
Barth, N., 74 n.
Barton, P., 307
Bassett, E. M., 61 n.
Bauer, C., 64, 166 n.
Beacon Hill, 213
Beck, B., 323 n.
Becker, H. S., 128 n.
Beckman, N., 65 n.
Bell, W., 45 n.
Bendix, R., 322 n.
benefits and costs: all-black city, 272–273; ghetto rebellions, 362; planning and class, 244–247; public housing, 267–268; recreation planning, 124; relocation, 215–217, 224–225; rent subsidies, 272; social and physical planning, 244–247
Bennett, E. H., 59 n.
Bensman, J., 40 n.
Berelson, B., 98, 104
Berger, B., 14, 40 n., 41 n., 138
Berger, M., 152 n.
Black Power, 317, 318–319, 349
Blum, Z., 345 n.
Blumenfeld, H., 58 n.
Boston Redevelopment Authority, 204, 217
Bremner, R. H., 322 n.

for, 221–222, 275–276; return of middle class, 48, 287–288; settlement house, 253–254, 257–258; slum creation, 225; social costs of, 214–215, 261–265; social planning, 73; subsidy of high income population, 215, 220; urban rehousing, 266–267, 273–274; in West End criticized, 211–220; *see also* relocation; urban rehousing

Urban Renewal Administration, 261, 297

Urban Review, 305

urban sociology, 12, 34, 44–47, 133

urbanity, 50

user-orientation, 53, 94; governmental market research, 296; library planning, 97–107; park planning, 6–7; planning, ix, 20–24; recreation planning, 120–124; settlement house, 256–257

users, 96

Vidich, A. J., 40 *n.*
Vietnam, 320, 361, 363, 380
Vorhees, A. M., 66 *n.*

Wallace, A., 154 *n.*
War on Poverty, viii, 69; ghetto rebellions, 323–324, 348; history of, 378–380; planning, 69, 70–71, 73; urban renewal, 271, 277; *see also* anti-poverty planning
Wattel, H., 40 *n.*, 41 *n.*
Webber, M. M., 34 *n.*, 69 *n.*, 73 *n.*, 152 *n.*
Weinberg, R. C., 180 *n.*

West End (Boston), viii, 203, 204, 208–225, 262, 263; area and population described, 7, 209, 211–213; settlement house, 253

West Rittenhouse Square (Philadelphia), 31

Wheaton, W. L. C., 129, 152 *n.*, 298

Whyte, W. F., 34 *n.*, 249 *n.*, 254 *n.*, 322 *n.*

Whyte, W. H., Jr., viii, 25, 45 *n.*, 152 *n.*, 157 *n.*, 162 *n.*

Wilensky, H. L., 34 *n.*, 36 *n.*, 205 *n.*

Willmott, P., 34 *n.*, 159 *n.*, 322 *n.*

Wilson, A. B., 172 *n.*

Wilson, J. Q., 71 *n.*

Wirth, L., 34–48

Wood, E., 166 *n.*, 171, 173

Woods, R., 250 *n.*, 251

work, journey to; *see* journey to work

working class: anti-poverty planning, 235; described, 235; education, 135–136, 354–355; educational aspirations in, 145–146; family structure, 144–146; ghetto rebellions, 353–358; grievances, 353–355; housing preferences, 16, 211–213; master plan, 62; neighborhood, 28–30; not so affluent, 280; politics, 353–355; problems of, 280; social mobility, 172–173, 355; suburbs, 14, 138–139

Yancey, W. L., 304 *n.*, 307 *n.*
Yinger, J. M., 171 *n.*
Ylvisaker, P., 204
Young, M., 34 *n.*, 159 *n.*, 322 *n.*

zoning, 59–60, 267